Quest for the Gold Plates

Also by
Stan Larson

What E'er Thou Art, Act Well Thy Part:
The Missionary Diaries of David O. McKay

The Truth, The Way, The Life,
An Elementary Treatise on Theology:
The Masterwork of B. H. Roberts

Can Science Be Faith-Promoting?
By Sterling B. Talmage

A Ministry of Meetings:
The Apostolic Diaries of Rudger Clawson

My Continuing Quest:
Sociological Perspectives on Mormonism
By Ray R. Canning

Prisoner for Polygamy:
The Memoirs and Letters
of Rudger Clawson

Working the Divine Miracle:
The Life of Apostle Henry D. Moyle
By Richard D. Poll

The Notebooks and Letters of
William E. McLellin

Unitarianism in Utah:
A Gentile Religion in Salt Lake City
(with Lorille Miller)

QUEST
FOR THE
GOLD PLATES

Thomas Stuart Ferguson's Archaeological Search for The Book of Mormon

Stan Larson

Freethinker Press
in association with
Smith Research Associates

Salt Lake City

Photo of Thomas Stuart Ferguson reproduced from the Thomas Stuart Ferguson Collection, courtesy of the Marriott Library, University of Utah.

∞ *Quest for the Gold Plates* was printed on acid-free paper, and meets the permanence of paper requirements of the American National Standard for Information Sciences. This book was composed, printed, and bound in the United States.

07 06 05 04   7 6 5 4 3

Library of Congress Cataloging-in-Publication Data
Larson, Stan.
    Quest for the gold plates : Thomas Stuart Ferguson's archaeological search for the Book of Mormon / Stan Larson.
        p. cm.
    Includes bibliographical references and index.
    ISBN 0-9634732-6-3 (alk. paper)
    1. Ferguson, Thomas Stuart--Contributions in criticism of Mormon Scriptures. 2. Book of Mormon--Criticism, interpretation, etc. 3. Book of Mormon--Antiquities. 4. Book of Mormon --Geography. 5. Book of Abraham--Criticism, interpretation, etc. 6. Excavations (Archaeology)--Mexico. 7. Excavations (Archaeology)--Central America. 8. Mexico--Antiquities. 9. Central America--Antiquities.
    I. Title
    BX8627.L37 1996
    289.3'22--dc20   94-20959
                                                              CIP

Thomas Stuart Ferguson, 1952

Table of Contents

List of Illustrations

Preface

This book focuses on the efforts of Thomas Stuart Ferguson to verify the authenticity of the Book of Mormon through archaeology. Because of this limiting condition, almost nothing is related concerning his professional career as a lawyer, his various real estate investments, his talent as a singer, his activities as a tennis player, or his family life.

In August of 1993 I found that one of Ferguson's life-long friends living in Orinda, California, had in his possession a box of office files documenting Ferguson's research activities in the 1970s and early 1980s. Soon after Ferguson's death Ester Ferguson, his widow, gave these files to this individual, in whose home they lay undisturbed for ten years; he anonymously donated them to the Marriott Library. I extend to Martha Stewart of Salt Lake City my appreciation for her financing a trip to Orinda for the purpose of acquiring these newly found letters written by Ferguson. Without this valuable collection the present work would never have been written.

Acknowledgement is extended to Gregory C. Thompson in Special Collections at the Marriott Library for his encouragement during this project. Stephen E. Thompson, from his perspective as an Egyptologist, made valuable remarks concerning the chapter on "Book of Abraham Papyri Rediscovered." Marvin S. Hill, emeritus professor of history at Brigham Young University, gave proposed revisions to the chapter on "The Letter-Writing

Closet Doubter." Glenna Nielsen Grimm and Richard Paine, with their background in Mesoamerican archaeology and anthropology, critically reviewed the chapter on "Book of Mormon Archaeological Tests." Patricia Larson, Raymond T. Matheny, Sterling M. McMurrin, William Mulder, George D. Smith, and Nancy V. Young read a draft and recommended many further improvements. Margery W. Ward and Betty Dalgliesh edited the manuscript to improve its clarity. Martha Sonntag Bradley and Allen Dale Roberts, coeditors of *Dialogue*, granted permission to use material from the article, "The Odyssey of Thomas Stuart Ferguson," which was published in the Spring 1990 issue. Dennis D. Gardner painted the picture for the book jacket and drew the chapter illustrations, all of which are copied from inscriptions discovered at Quiriguá and Palenque--the two sites identified by Joseph Smith as probable Book of Mormon cities. James and Dan Larson provided invaluable technical support on all computer aspects of this project. I gratefully acknowledge the many insights and helpful suggestions offered by these individuals; their assistance has significantly improved this volume. However, I take final and full responsibility for both the text and notes.

The assistance of the staff, librarians, and curators at the following institutions is much appreciated: the J. Willard Marriott Library, University of Utah, Salt Lake City; the Harold B. Lee Library, Brigham Young University, Provo, Utah; the University Research Library, University of California, Los Angeles; the George C. Page Museum of La Brea Discoveries, Los Angeles; the Milton R. Merrill Library, Utah State University, Logan, Utah; the Orinda Public Library, Orinda, California; the Charles T. Hayden Library, Arizona State University, Tempe, Arizona; the M. D. Anderson Library, University of Houston; the Sterling C. Evans Library, Texas A&M University, College Station, Texas; the library of the Utah State Historical Society, Salt Lake City; and the Archives and Church Library, Historical Department, the Church of Jesus Christ of Latter-day Saints, Salt Lake City. Unfortunately, the current policy of the LDS Church Archives does not allow research in most collections of General

Authorities, many of whom had significant connections with Ferguson.

Capitalization, punctuation, and spelling have sometimes been corrected in the quotations in accordance with modern style. The Arabic numbers 1 to 99 have usually been written out as words. The ampersand (&) has been changed to "and," except in the scriptural abbreviation for the Doctrine and Covenants, i.e., D&C. The wording and grammar in the quotations have not been altered.

The names and time periods for Maya culture are as follows: the Archaic Period covers 7500 to 1800 B.C.; the Early Preclassic Period covers 1800 to 1000 B.C.; the Middle Preclassic Period covers 1000 to 300 B.C.; the Late Preclassic Period covers 300 B.C. to A.D. 250; the Early Classic Period covers A.D. 250 to 600; the Late Classic Period covers A.D. 600 to 800; the Terminal Classic Period covers A.D. 800 to 925; the Early Post-Classic Period covers A.D. 925 to 1200; the Late Post-Classic Period covers A.D. 1200 to 1530. Thus, the Book of Mormon chronology (including the Jaredites of the Book of Ether) corresponds to approximately the last ten to twelve centuries of the Archaic, all of the Preclassic, and almost the first two hundred years of the Early Classic.

At this point it seems appropriate to explain why I undertook to tell the story of Tom Ferguson's archaeological search for verification of the Book of Mormon. In the fall of 1977 I first heard from a fellow church employee in the LDS Translation Services Department in Salt Lake City that Ferguson no longer believed in the historicity of the Book of Mormon. To me this unfounded rumor--for so I considered it--seemed absolutely unbelievable, for I had over the years faithfully followed Ferguson's writings on the Book of Mormon. After repeated affirmations that this statement was indeed true, I decided to verify or falsify this assertion by contacting Ferguson himself. I remember trying to decide between either writing him a letter or calling him on the phone. Since he might not be fully open in response to a letter (or might not even answer it at all), I chose to make an unannounced telephone call. I used the then-available WATS line from my office on the twenty-first floor of the Church Office Building.

With no other introduction than giving my name and identifying myself as an employee of Church's Translation Services in Salt Lake City, Ferguson spoke freely to me. I first talked about my having read *Cumorah--Where?*, *Ancient America and the Book of Mormon*, and *One Fold and One Shepherd*--and then I hesitantly mentioned that I had heard that he had reached some very critical conclusions concerning the Book of Mormon. With no bitterness but with a touch of disappointment, Ferguson agreed with this statement and openly discussed with me his present skepticism about the historicity of the Book of Mormon, the lack of any Book of Mormon geography that relates to the real world, and the absence of the long-hoped-for archaeological confirmation of the Book of Mormon. This was just a few months before our family moved to Birmingham, England, for six and a half years. When we returned to Salt Lake City in 1984, I made inquiry concerning Ferguson, but unfortunately was told that he had died the previous year. Though our personal contact was thus minimal, I feel confident that Ferguson would want his intriguing story to be recounted as honestly and sympathetically as possible. The tortuous odyssey of Thomas Stuart Ferguson deserves to be told.

1

Early Book of Mormon Studies

Thomas Stuart Ferguson is best known among Mormons as a popular fireside lecturer on Book of Mormon archaeology, as well as the author of *One Fold and One Shepherd*, and coauthor of *Ancient America and the Book of Mormon*.[1] Like Heinrich Schliemann searching for the city of Troy described in Homer's "Iliad," Tom Ferguson devoted his life attempting to locate the actual cities mentioned in the Book of Mormon. His intense passion drove him to accomplish results only dreamed of by others. Ferguson was born in Pocatello, Idaho, on 21 May 1915, the son of Samuel Stuart Ferguson and Pearl Jenkins. When he was fifteen, he dutifully received his patriarchal blessing. The patriarch promised him that "he would do many mighty things to the wonderment of the world."[2] Belief in the Book of Mormon had been an axiom of his faith since childhood, and this

Fig. 1--The Prophet Joseph Smith (1805-1844), at the age of 36. Reproduced from painting by Sutcliffe Maudsley, courtesy of Buddy Youngreen.

blessing may have been a factor in the growing conviction of his personal role to demonstrate to the world the authenticity of the Book of Mormon and the prophetic role of its translator, Joseph Smith (fig. 1).

In 1933 Tom Ferguson was an eighteen-year-old freshman at the University of California at Berkeley. At a time when a university education was still the privilege of the few, Berkeley was a place where an earnest student could be exposed to the passionate political causes and lively intellectual currents of the 1930s. Due to the influence of M. Wells Jakeman, a fellow LDS student at Berkeley, Ferguson developed a keen interest in the history, culture, and archaeology of Mesoamerica.[3] Though he had a lifelong fascination with these fields, he did not pursue a degree in any of these subjects. His interest was focused on how these various studies related to the unique historical claims of the Book of Mormon (fig. 2). His years of study culminated in an A.B. degree in political science in 1937. While at the university he began dating Ester Israelsen and often spoke excitedly about the Book of Mormon --so much that Ester once remarked to her mother that she felt like she was going out with the Book of Mormon. In 1940 he married Ester, and they had five children--Thomas, Jennie,

Jon, Larry, and Sherilee.[4] Perhaps, considering the uncertainties of the times, Ferguson decided he could better finance his archaeological avocation as an attorney than if he had chosen to make it his vocation. He received his LL.B. degree in 1942 from the same institution. Ferguson remained an amateur in archaeology, with Book of Mormon studies being a thread woven through the fabric of his whole life.

The Enigma concerning Thomas Stuart Ferguson

A major enigma, however, revolves around the true identity of Thomas Stuart Ferguson. Proponents on both sides of this intense controversy present diametrically opposed portrayals of the man. The story of Ferguson's odyssey is intimately connected with the growing corpus of archaeological data on the early civilizations of ancient America and the question of whether this information tends to support or supplant the cultures described in the Book of Mormon. Emotions run high for both positions, so an attempt will be made to present a balanced perspective.

On one side of this issue and with a keen eye to the lucrative Latter-day Saint book market, various Utah radio stations aired in 1987 and 1988 the following dramatic radio commercial about Ferguson:

> In 1949 [1946] California lawyer, Tom Ferguson, rolled up his sleeves, threw a shovel over his shoulder, and marched into the remote jungles of southern Mexico. Armed with a quote by Joseph Smith that the Lord had "a hand in proving the Book of Mormon true in the eyes of all the people," Ferguson's goal was: Shut the mouths of the critics who said such evidence did not exist. Ferguson began an odyssey that included twenty-four trips to Central America, eventually resulting in a mountain of evidence supporting Book of Mormon claims.[5]

The book being advertised was *The Messiah in Ancient America*, and the coauthors were supposedly Bruce W. Warren, who received his Ph.D. in anthropology from the University of Arizona, and Thomas Stuart Ferguson.[6] The main point of the commercial--taking into consideration the potential hyperbole of paid advertising--was that Ferguson had amassed evidence so overwhelming that any fair-minded person would have no alternative but to accept the historical claims of the Book of Mormon. Warren's preface referred to Ferguson's "abiding testimony of the Book of Mormon."[7] Paul R. Cheesman, emeritus professor of religious instruction at Brigham Young University, stated in his foreword that this book "should reinstate Thomas Stuart Ferguson as a source of enrichment in the fields of study concerning Mesoamerica and the Book of Mormon."[8]

On the other side, Jerald and Sandra Tanner, anti-Mormon publishers in Salt Lake City, presented a completely different image of Ferguson. First of all, the Tanners reproduced Ferguson's study of problems in Book of Mormon geography and archaeology that he had prepared for a written symposium on the subject. The Tanners entitled this 1988 publication *Ferguson's Manuscript Unveiled*, alluding to the genre of exposé going back to E. D. Howe's 1834 *Mormonism Unvailed.*[9] At the same time the Tanners published an article, sensationally titled "Ferguson's Two Faces: Mormon Scholar's 'Spoof' Lives on after His Death," in the September 1988 issue of their *Salt Lake City Messenger*. The article briefly reviews Ferguson's early association with the New World Archaeological Foundation, but the principal interest of the Tanners is in documenting his purported disillusionment and loss of faith by recounting his visit to their home in December 1970 and by quoting from seven letters which Ferguson allegedly wrote from 1968 to 1979. These letters record his apparent disappointment at the failure to identify any Book of Mormon cities, his conviction that the Book of Mormon is a work of fiction by Joseph Smith, his loss of faith in Joseph Smith as a prophet, his conclusion that Joseph Smith could not translate Egyptian hieroglyphics, and his characterization of the Church

And now as I said concerning faith : Faith, is not to have a
perfect knowledge of things ; therefore if ye have faith, ye
hope for things which is not seen, which are true.   And now,
behold, I say unto you : and I would that ye should remember that God is merciful unto all who believe on his name ;
therefore he desireth, in the first place, that ye should believe,
yea, even on his word.   And now, he imparteth his word by
angels, unto men ; yea, not only men, but women also.   Now
this is not all : little children doth have words given unto them
many times, which doth confound the wise and the learned.

And now, my beloved brethren, as ye have desired to know
of me what ye shall do because ye are afflicted and cast out :
now I do not desire that ye should suppose that I mean to
judge you only according to that which is true ; for I do not
mean that ye all of you have been compelled to humble yourselves ; for I verily believe there are some among you which
would humble themselves, let them be in whatsoever circum-
stances they might.   Now as I said concerning faith—that it was
not a perfect knowledge, even so it is with my words.   Ye cannot
know of their surety at first, unto perfection, any more than
faith is a perfect knowledge.   But behold, if ye will awake
and arouse your faculties, even to an experiment upon my
words, and exercise a particle of faith ; yea, even if ye can no
more than desire to believe, let this desire work in you, even
until ye believe in a manner that ye can give place for a portion of my words.   Now we will compare the word unto a
seed.   Now if ye give place, that a seed may be planted in
your heart, behold, if it be a true seed, or a good seed, if ye
do not cast it out by your unbelief, that ye will resist the spirit
of the Lord, behold, it will begin to swell within your breasts ;
and when you feel these swelling motions, ye will begin to say
within yourselves, It must needs be that this is a good seed,
or that the word is good, for it beginneth to enlarge my soul ;
yea, it beginneth to enlighten my understanding ; yea, and it
beginneth to be delicious to me.   Now behold, would not this
increase your faith ?   I say unto you, yea ; nevertheless it hath
not grown up to a perfect knowledge.   But behold, as the
seed swelleth, and sprouteth, and beginneth to grow, and then
ye must needs say, That the seed is good ; for behold it swelleth, and sprouteth, and beginneth to grow.   And now behold,
are ye sure that this is a good seed ?   I say unto you, Yea ;
for every seed bringeth forth unto its own likeness ; therefore, if a seed groweth, it is good, but if it groweth not, be-

*Fig. 2--Original 1830 edition of the Book of Mormon,
showing a page in which the typesetter accidentally
skipped thirty-five words concerning strengthening
faith (Alma 32:30, fourth line from bottom).*
Courtesy of Marriott Library, University of Utah.

of Jesus Christ of Latter-day Saints[10] as a great myth-fraternity. In an oversimplification of the situation the Tanners concluded that "Ferguson believed that archaeology *disproved* the Book of Mormon."[11]

Thus, two radically different pictures of Ferguson are being promulgated. Warren's portrayal of Ferguson in *The Messiah in Ancient America* entertained only traditional beliefs about the Book of Mormon, while the Tanners presented a man who lost his faith and rejected his former convictions. Warren is no more interested in Ferguson's testimony possibly not surviving his scrutiny of the available evidence than the Tanners are interested in how Ferguson may have resolved his problems by finding positive values within the framework of Mormon culture. Where does the truth lie? As is frequently (but not always) the case, somewhere between the extremes. One needs to examine all the relevant evidence in order to have as well-rounded a picture of Ferguson as possible. Consequently, all of the surviving documents spanning 1937 to 1983 which came directly from Ferguson must be examined to determine if, when, and how his ideas developed through time. Then the reader can better judge which of these opposing views of Ferguson more closely approaches the truth.

Publication of First Article in "The Improvement Era"

Ferguson believed LDS Church members entertained certain misconceptions about the Book of Mormon. He asserted that it was vital to keep clear the distinction between what the Book of Mormon says and what people say about it. In 1941 Ferguson published his first article, which he had originally entitled "Some Controversial Book of Mormon Questions." M. Wells Jakeman felt that the adjective was too harsh and suggested that it be softened to "important," so Ferguson accordingly altered the title.[12] When submitting the article, he expressed pride concerning his convictions about the Book of Mormon:

> For many years I have been actively interested in the Book of Mormon, and I believe I have an unusually strong testimony of its divinity. I have found that many Latter-day Saints have misconceptions regarding some Book of Mormon questions. Should this article be published in the *Era* it might retard the spreading of a few of the more common misunderstandings.[15]

In the article Ferguson made clear that contrary to rumor professional archaeologists at the Smithsonian Institution and the Carnegie Institution do not use the Book of Mormon as a guide to discovering lost cities, and exhorted Latter-day Saints to read the book "more frequently and more carefully, especially in the light of its ancient historical background as gradually revealed by the discoveries of modern scientists."[14] Ferguson tackled the difficult problem of the geographic area encompassed by the events described in the Book of Mormon. Did Book of Mormon peoples occupy most of the Western Hemisphere or some limited area? Ferguson concluded that, since a group including women and children (mentioned in Mosiah 23-24) traveled from Nephi to Zarahemla in only twenty-one days, the distance was most likely only 200 to 300 miles. Consequently, the Book of Mormon lands comprised a comparatively small area in the New World.

Diverse Theories of Book of Mormon Geography

To illustrate his article, Ferguson used a map which had been prepared by Jakeman, showing the boundaries of the Middle American or Tehuántepec Theory and the South American or Panama Theory. Ferguson discussed the estimated boundaries of these two general geographies. The South American or Panama Theory, which is the traditional view held by most believers in the Book of Mormon, identified North America and South America as the land northward and the land southward, respectively, and the Isthmus of Panama as the "narrow neck" of land (Alma 22:31-33; 63:5). The earliest available map of this traditional, pan-American geographical understanding dates to 1880 and was made by Heber C. Comer.[15] This most popular interpretation even found its way into the margins of editions of the Book of Mormon from 1879 to 1920, embodied in Orson Pratt's notes.[16] The Middle American or Tehuántepec theory was based on the view that the peoples of the Book of Mormon occupied a limited area in Mesoamerica and that the "narrow neck of land" was accordingly the Isthmus of Tehuántepec. Ferguson supported the latter viewpoint. Today, most students of the problem, especially those who study the internal statements of Book of Mormon geography and who examine the archaeological evidence for early culture in the Americas, look for Book of Mormon lands in Mesoamerica.

However, the question of the implied geography of the Book of Mormon is far from settled; the wide diversity of opinions that attempt to correlate the internal geographical requirements with the external world extends to the present. There exists a bewildering array of variation in locating the lands, cities, and the one named river in the Book of Mormon. Just focusing on the location of the "narrow neck of land," the following twelve different identifications have been made:

1. The Isthmus of Panama.[17]
2. The Isthmus of Tehuántepec.[18]
3. A coastal corridor (not an isthmus) along the Pacific coast of Chiapas in southeastern Mexico.[19]
4. The southern part of the peninsula of Yucatán.[20]
5. The strip of land at Laguna de Términos in the southwest part of the Yucatán Peninsula.[21]
6. The isthmus from southeast Yucatán at Lago de Izabal southwest to the Pacific.[22]
7. The Bay of Honduras.[23]
8. Between Golfo Dulce and the Bay of Honduras.[24]
9. Costa Rica.[25]
10. The Golfo de Guayaquil in Ecuador.[26]
11. The peninsula of Florida.[27]
12. Between southwestern Lake Ontario and northeastern Lake Erie.[28]

Accordingly, students of the Book of Mormon have made widely divergent maps showing the proposed locations of Book of Mormon lands.[29] The only Book of Mormon geographies which avoid insurmountable difficulties are those which merely show relationships between lands and make no attempt to locate places on a map of the real world.[30]

First Trip to
Mexico and Guatemala

Filled with confidence and fired with enthusiasm, Ferguson embarked on a real-life odyssey in search of the origins of the high civilizations of Mesoamerica, firmly believing that such investigations would bring forth incontrovertible evidence supporting the historical claims of the Book of Mormon.[31] His mission of discovery began on 1 February 1946 with his first trip to Mexico, and he made many more trips in pursuit of this goal. Ferguson was not solely interested in the ancient Mesoamericans, for two of the goals of this trip were to determine "the receptibility of the Mayas to Mormonism, with the idea in mind that a mission would be established" among them, and to decide on ways to improve their economic conditions and standard of living.[32]

In Mexico City, Ferguson was joined by businessman J. Willard Marriott, his wife Alice, and their son Billy, who accompanied him on this two-week trip to Mexico and Guatemala.[33] They took fifty rolls of movie film during the trip, visiting or viewing from the air such places as Mexico City, Cholula, Puebla, Teotihuacán, Tula, Chichén Itzá, Mérida, and Uxmal in Mexico, and Guatemala City, Kaminaljuyú, Tikal, Uaxactún, and Chichicastenango in Guatemala. At this time Ferguson felt that "this great river [Usumacinta], which has been called 'the river of ruins,' was identical with the River Sidon of the Book of Mormon."[34] Ferguson was absolutely thrilled with this trip and told the Marriotts that he would never forget this marvelous experience.[35] Marriott said that during their trip they "studied Book of Mormon geography, placed a lot of Book of Mormon

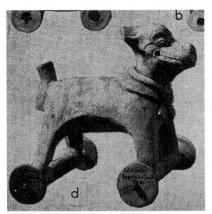

Fig. 3--Wheeled pottery figurine,
Tres Zapotes, Vera Cruz, Mexico.
Reproduced from Gordon F. Ekholm,
"Wheeled Toys in Mexico," *American*
Antiquity (1946), courtesy of Society for
American Archaeology.

cities, and saw a lot of interesting ruins."[36]

At the National Museum in Mexico City Ferguson saw a stone monument having a calendar date that corresponds to A.D. 9 and made an exciting discovery of a small wheeled dog made of pottery, which Ferguson referred to as a child's toy, but which might be a ritual figurine (fig. 3). Marriott reminisced about this sightseeing tour through Mexico, saying concerning Ferguson: "I have never known anyone who was more devoted to that kind of research [Book of Mormon archaeology] than was Tom."[37]

Based on the wheeled object found in the museum, Ferguson wrote another article for *The Improvement Era*, "The Wheel in Ancient America," which correlated the archaeological discovery of several wheeled figurines with the use of a chariot (and by implication, functional wheels) in the Book of Mormon. In the article Ferguson discussed the charge raised by critics of the Book of Mormon to the effect that, although the Book of Mormon mentioned the use of a chariot, the wheel was unknown in pre-Columbian America. Because of the existence of wheeled figurines, Ferguson proclaimed that "Joseph Smith has been vindicated on this technicality."[38] While it can now be stated that "the existence in this hemisphere of pre-Columbian wheeled figurines and of spindle whorls of pottery" show knowledge of the wheel principle, yet there is still no pre-Columbian evidence of carts, chariots, or utilitarian wheels.[39] Almost three decades later Ferguson conceded the existence of this problem.[40]

To Ferguson it seemed likely that part of highland Guatemala was the Book of Mormon land of Nephi. At this time Ferguson (doubtless influenced by Jakeman's viewpoint) felt that the Usumacinta River was probably the River Sidon. After Marriott told John A. Widtsoe of the Quorum of the Twelve Apostles about their expedition and showed him the movies they had taken, Widtsoe told Ferguson that he hoped a new age of interest in the Book of Mormon would come.[41] Often encouraging Ferguson in his investigations of the Book of Mormon, Widtsoe became his mentor. Ferguson told Ezra Taft Benson that the natives of southern Mexico and Guatemala do not wholeheartedly support Catholicism, but persistently cling to their ancient religious practices. To Ferguson there was "every reason for believing the Maya people are probably the nearest of any to being pure 'Lamanites.'"[42]

Publication of
"Cumorah--Where?"

Late in 1947 Ferguson published his first book, *Cumorah--Where?* In preparing this small book Ferguson carefully studied all geographical statements in the Book of Mormon and then analyzed the relationships of places, distances from each other, and stated travel times. These investigations led him again to the conclusion that the whole Book of Mormon geographical area covered only a few hundred miles and he became even more convinced that these conditions related only to the real world in Mesoamerica. In his first draft Ferguson only discussed his particular Mesoamerican reconstruction of the geographical location of Book of Mormon lands and places. Later he realized that the fairness and balance of his projected book would be much improved by stating the case for both major positions. Accordingly, he presented the evidence for what he called "The New York View" and "The Middle American View," and then followed with several points of criticism against each viewpoint. Although Ferguson showed the support for both positions, he still strongly favored the setting of a limited area in Mesoamerica.

A significant statement coming directly from Joseph Smith favors "The New York View." In January 1833 Smith told a newspaper editor that "the Book of Mormon is a record of the forefathers of our western Tribes of Indians."[43] Similarly, Joseph Smith related in November 1835 that the angel Moroni revealed to him that "the Indians were the literal descendants of Abraham."[44] Even more important information from Joseph Smith concerns the finding of a human skeleton and an arrowhead in an Indian burial mound near the Illinois River in Pike County, Illinois, in June 1834. After the discovery of this skeleton Joseph Smith received a vision and declared that it was a white Lamanite named Zelph, a warrior under Onandagus.[45] Joseph Smith wrote in a letter to his wife Emma that he and the men in Zion's Camp had been "wandering over the plains of the Nephites, recounting occasionally the history of the Book of Mormon, roving over the mounds of that once beloved people of the Lord, picking up their skulls and their bones, as a proof of its divine authenticity."[46] This indicates not only that Joseph Smith felt that this land consisted of plains and mounds belonging to the Nephites of the Book of Mormon, but more importantly, that to him simply finding Indian bones constituted proof of the truthfulness of the Book of Mormon. In his discussion of "The New York View" Ferguson quoted from the secondary account in the *History of the Church*.[47] Then he responded to the Zelph story--since the focus of his interest is the location of the Hill Cumorah--by saying that "surely this does not prove that the battle of Cumorah was fought in New York."[48]

In March 1947 Ferguson sent his completed manuscript to George Albert Smith, president of the Mormon Church, adding that he was convinced that "there are good reasons for believing that many of the natives of those countries [Mexico and Guatemala] are direct descendants of Book of Mormon people."[49] Smith turned the manuscript over to Widtsoe for his advice as to whether it should be published. Widtsoe wrote to Ferguson, saying that he was recommending that *Cumorah--Where?* be published.[50] However, the church-owned Deseret Book Company refused to "publish any material relative to Book of Mormon geography," so Ferguson had to turn to a lesser-known LDS press, Zion's Printing and Publishing Company of Independence, Missouri, for publication.[51] Widtsoe also contributed the foreword to the book, in which he stated that many have tried to "reconcile places and distances mentioned in the Book [of Mormon] with present-day mountains, rivers, and cities in ruins or yet used by man," but no unanimity had been achieved among LDS students.[52] In Widtsoe's review of the book in January 1948 he mentioned that readers want to know where the events related in the Book of Mormon actually took place and this desire has led to the various attempts to identify its geography.[53]

Ferguson felt convinced that the "narrow neck of land" was the Isthmus of Tehuántepec and that the Jaredite hill named Ramah (which is identical to the Nephite Cumorah) was near Mexico City in the Valley of Mexico. Rather than trying somehow to accommodate the traditional identification of the Hill Cumorah being in New York State into his hypothesis, Ferguson boldly proposed that the 17,887-foot Popocatépetl and the 16,883-foot Ixtaccíhuatl met all the internal requirements for being Ramah-Cumorah and Shim, respectively.[54] Though he owed much to Jakeman's earlier research, Ferguson prided himself that he had concluded quite independently of Jakeman that the Hill Cumorah must be in Mexico, and Ferguson reminded Jakeman that his original map had placed Cumorah in its traditional location in New York State (fig. 4).[55] Ferguson closed his book with an expression of his opinion favoring the Mesoamerican identification of Book of Mormon geography and a spirited appeal to keep one's mind open in the search for truth:

> The writer favors the Middle American view. . . .
> Mormon people have always taken pride in the fact that the Church is constantly in search of truth. If truth can be found in our day which was not readily obtainable in the first decade of Church history, surely our minds will be open to receive it. Let the reader exercise his free agency and formulate his own opinion on the question, "Cumorah --Where?" The writer only seeks the truth of the matter and has no thought of forcing his views.[56]

It perturbed Ferguson that the Deseret Book Company would not even sell *Cumorah--Where?* since his discussion of Book of Mormon geography was considered too controversial-- even though an apostle had favorably reviewed the book in the church-owned *Improvement Era.*[57]

Second Trip to Mexico

In January 1948 Ferguson, along with Jakeman and W. Glenn Harmon, president of the Berkeley Stake, departed on a BYU Archaeological Expedition to explore the Xicalango area of western Campeche in southeastern Mexico.[58] They found examples of Chicanel-type pottery, which date from the third century B.C. to the third century A.D.[59] At this time both Ferguson and Jakeman felt that the site of Aguacatal was the Book of Mormon Bountiful.[60] Lying in his jungle hammock at the site of Aguacatal during a heavy tropical rain, Ferguson wrote the following by the light of a small flashlight:

> We have discovered a very great city here in the heart of "Bountiful" land. Hundreds and possibly several thousand people must have lived here anciently. This site has never been explored before. Sixteen years ago an explorer arrived here in May and the mosquitoes drove him away after one day's work. We have explored four days and have found eight pyramids and many lesser structures and there are more at every turn. Our wonderful native guide knows the area well and leads us to important places. I'm the only white man to have seen one large pyramid here. It lies beyond a small swamp and north of the other ruins seen by our group. I was the only man with water-tight boots, so [I] went alone with the guide to see it. Quite an experience.[61]

After returning to the United States Ferguson made arrangements to travel to Salt Lake City to show films in April 1948 of both the 1946 trip and the 1948 expedition to Elder Ezra Taft Benson, then a member of the Quorum of the Twelve Apostles. Ferguson also showed the same films to the General

Fig. 4--Hill Cumorah, near Manchester, New York, 1923. Reproduced from Elton L. Taylor Collection, courtesy of Marriott Library, University of Utah.

Authorities and their wives at their annual party at the Lion House, explaining to them why investigations of Book of Mormon lands were concentrated in Mesoamerica and not the whole hemisphere.[62] Ferguson felt that the presentation was successful, but to add a little more weight to his arguments he left copies of *Cumorah--Where?* the next morning for each General Authority.[63] Having paved the way with pictures, Ferguson followed this presentation with a document requesting that the LDS Church intensify missionary work in and fund archaeological expeditions to Mesoamerica and Peru.[64]

Publication of
"Ancient America and the Book of Mormon"

After publishing *Cumorah--Where?* in 1947, Ferguson began work on a book which he intended to call simply "Book of Mormon Commentary." During 1948-1950 Milton R. Hunter, who had become a member of the First Council of Seventy in 1945, joined Ferguson in the project. Since Ferguson had worked so closely with Jakeman--in fact had received much of his material directly from Jakeman--during the 1930s and early 1940s, Ferguson expressed to Hunter his grave concern that if they delayed telling Jakeman about their project until the book was published, Jakeman would "think it a complete breach of faith on my part."[65] It is not known exactly what either Ferguson or Hunter told Jakeman, but after the book was published Jakeman told Hunter that some people who asked him about the new book were "somewhat puzzled by the sudden appearance of these findings [of Jakeman] in a publication not my own."[66] The resultant rift between Ferguson and Jakeman was never completely healed.[67]

John A. Widtsoe, Ezra Taft Benson, and Antoine R. Ivins read galley proofs of the book, and Ferguson hoped to get their endorsements to use in publicizing it. In mid-1950 the intended name for the book became "Other Sheep I Have" and Ferguson, feeling that it would be a powerful influence for world peace, offered this pre-publication assessment:

> We believe it is probably the first book containing concrete and factual evidence, archaeological and historical, establishing the actual and physical resurrection of Christ. The most important theme in the book is that the resurrected Christ visited the early Mayas in Chiapas-Tabasco, Mexico, shortly after his resurrection.[68]

The book *Ancient America and the Book of Mormon* was published in November 1950 and presented for the first time in English a translation of the early seventeenth-century historical account of Fernando de Alva Ixtlilxóchitl and how this material related to the claims of the Book of Mormon.[69] Ferguson felt that there were strong parallels between Ixtlilxóchitl's work and the Book of Mormon.[70] Ixtlilxóchitl referred to two or three groups of colonizers: (1) "The Tultecas," "the Ancient Ones," or "the Giants"--these Hunter and Ferguson identified with the Jaredites in the Book of Mormon; (2) the same term "Tultecas," also called "the artisans"--these Hunter and Ferguson distinguished as a separate group and identified with the Nephites; (3) "The Ulmecs" or the Olmecs, who are perhaps best known by the colossal heads (fig. 5)[71]--these are identified with the Mulekites.[72]

Hunter and Ferguson uncritically accepted anything in Ixtlilxóchitl that seemed to correlate with the Book of Mormon, and never distinguished between genuine native tradition and

Fig. 5--Colossal head, with an ornamental carved headband, La Venta, Mexico. Reproduced from Matthew W. Stirling, "Great Stone Faces of the Mexican Jungle," *National Geographic Magazine* (1940).

post-Columbian influence due to Spanish Catholicism. Ferguson felt that the account of Ixtlilxóchitl seemed "to sustain the existence of the Book of Mormon in rather direct fashion--a knowledge of the ancient fourth-century sacred compilation was known in sixteenth-century Mexico."[73] Others have not found the parallels between Ixtlilxóchitl and biblical chronology, events, and doctrines so impressive because Ixtlilxóchitl, though a grandson of the Aztec king of Texcoco, had been raised a Christian. One scholar cautioned that Ixtlilxóchitl was "doubt-less strongly influenced by Christian instruction, which would have tinged his stories of Indian creation, the flood, the ark, a

Babel-type tower, and a confusion of tongues with subsequent scattering of populations."[74] Each of these suspect items was used in their quotations from Ixtlilxóchitl: the creation of the world, the deluge and the ark, and building a very high tower, followed by changed languages and dispersed peoples.[75] In an unpublished review of *Ancient America and the Book of Mormon* Charles E. Dibble, professor of anthropology at the University of Utah, pointed out the problem of acculturation, which has special application to the various writings of Ixtlilxóchitl, in that "every native source dealing with native cultures subsequent to 1492 is potentially able to reflect Christian ideology."[76] J. Reuben Clark, Jr., second counselor in the LDS First Presidency, also warned that one must "be most careful to see that these traditions of the Indians are not the result of the early teachings of the Catholic priests."[77]

The name Quetzalcóatl is a compound formed from "the Nahuatl terms for the emerald plumed quetzal (*Pharomachrus mocinno*) and the serpent, or *coatl*."[78] The name can thus be translated as "quetzal-bird serpent." Hunter and Ferguson devoted an entire chapter comparing various legends about Quetzalcóatl with the account of the visit of the resurrected Jesus Christ to the Nephites in the Book of Mormon.[79] However, caution must be exercised in these comparisons and the radical differences between the two traditions should not be ignored.[80] Also, Basil C. Hedrick, director of the University of Alaska Museum, pointed out the chronological disparity, since "the earliest possible date at which Quetzalcóatl could have appeared--as a man--was at least 300+ years subsequent to the crucifixion."[81] The traditions about the god named Quetzalcóatl have been so mingled with the later, historical person, called Ce Acatl Topiltzin Quetzalcóatl, who was a high priest of Quetzalcóatl, that it is most difficult to separate the two.[82]

The editors of the *Mysteries of the Ancient Americas* commented on the various legends about Quetzalcóatl:

> There is, however, a serious flaw in the theories of the white-god-as-European. It is only after the Spanish Conquest that Quetzalcóatl is depicted as having a white skin,

and then only in accounts provided by the Spaniards themselves. In local Aztec art, he is usually depicted as a feathered serpent or as a human wearing a mask or shown to have a black face, sometimes with yellow stripes and a red mouth.[83]

In order to show a possible connection with the Near East, Hunter and Ferguson reproduced the bearded figure on La Venta Stela 3, known as "Uncle Sam,"[84] as well as the bearded face on the pottery jar at Quiriguá (fig. 6).[85] Such bearded figures appear to be non-Amerindian.[86] In their desire to identify more beards, Hunter and Ferguson saw a duck's bill as a human beard, on the Tuxtla Statuette (fig. 7), suggesting that "beneath his nose is what may be a well-groomed beard."[87]

In *Ancient America and the Book of Mormon* Hunter and Ferguson proposed several identifications of Book of Mormon places in various locations in Mesoamerica. For example, they tentatively advanced either the Usumacinta or the Grijalva rivers as the River Sidon and identified the southern Vera Cruz-Tabasco-Chiapas-Campeche area as the lands of Bountiful and Zarahemla.[88] Hunter feared ecclesiastical opposition to their geographical proposals and hoped to convert his fellow church leaders to their views. Their geographical correlations did not go unchallenged, for in 1954 Joseph Fielding Smith, then president of the Quorum of the Twelve, attacked in the

Fig. 6--Bearded man on vase, Quiriguá, Guatemala, which place Joseph Smith identified as a Book of Mormon city. Reproduced from Sylvanus G. Morley, "Excavations at Quiriguá," *National Geographic Magazine* (1913).

Church News the "modernist theory" that confined Book of Mormon activities to southern Mexico and Central America.[89] Nevertheless, the book proved to be very popular to its Mormon audience and 12,500 copies were sold.[90]

Palenque Identified as a Book of Mormon Place

In *Ancient America and the Book of Mormon* Hunter and Ferguson quoted Joseph Smith's editorial statement about the location of Book of Mormon places. It may very well be true that Joseph Smith did not have "specific knowledge of ancient

Fig. 7--Tuxtla Statuette, San Andrés Tuxtla, Veracruz, Mexico. Reproduced from Jacques Soustelle, *The Olmecs* (1984), courtesy of Smithsonian Institution.

Book of Mormon geography,"[91] but Joseph Smith's editorial opinions--if that is what they are--in three issues of the church's *Times and Seasons* deserve a detailed examination. In September 1841 John M. Bernhisel sent Smith two volumes of the recently published *Incidents of Travel in Central America*, which was written by John Lloyd Stephens, an American explorer, and illustrated by Frederick Catherwood, a British artist. After reading this account Joseph Smith wrote to Bernhisel that "it unfolds and develops many things that are of great importance to this generation and corresponds with and supports the testimony of the Book of Mormon; I . . . must say that of all histories that have been written pertaining to the antiquities of this country it is the most correct, luminous, and comprehensive."[92] In March 1842 Joseph Smith became editor of the *Times and Seasons* and expressed his responsibility for the issues published during his editorship.[93] In mid-July in a signed editorial Smith mentioned how Book of Mormon cities related to the ruins described in Stephens's books:

> Stephens's and Catherwood's researches in Central America abundantly testify of this thing [i.e., that a great civilization existed on the American continent]. The stupendous ruins, the elegant sculpture, and the magnificence of the ruins of Guatemala, and other cities, corroborate this statement, and show that a great and mighty people--men of great minds, clear intellect, bright genius, and comprehensive designs inhabited this continent. Their ruins speak of their greatness; the Book of Mormon unfolds their history.[94]

In the mid-September 1842 issue of the *Times and Seasons* the unnamed editor (either Joseph Smith or John Taylor)[95] quoted eight columns of an extract from John Lloyd Stephens's book concerning the ruins of Palenque.[96] At the end of this quotation he said:

> The foregoing extract has been made to assist the Latter-Day Saints, in establishing the Book of Mormon as a revelation from God. It affords great joy to have the world assist us to so much proof, that even the most credulous cannot doubt. . . . Let us turn our subject, however, to the Book of Mormon, where these wonderful ruins of *Palenque* are among the mighty works of the Nephites--and the mystery is solved.[97]

Inside the palace at Palenque appears a stone tablet depicting Lord Pacal, seated on a double-headed jaguar throne and receiving a royal drum-major headdress from his mother, Lady Zac-Kuk. In 1952 Alberto Ruz Lhuillier excavated the Temple of the Inscriptions (fig. 8) and discovered that this temple-pyramid was a royal funerary shrine, with Pacal's tomb being eighty feet below the floor of the temple.[98] The sepulcher was covered with a creamy white limestone slab weighing five tons, depicting Pacal at the moment of death descending into the earth monster (fig. 9).[99] Inside the sepulcher were the bones of Pacal, as well as necklaces, ear spools, rings, mother of pearl ornaments, and the remnants of a jade-mosaic mask which had covered his skull (fig. 10).[100] The buildings in Palenque were constructed in Otolum times, beginning about A.D. 600. The earliest dated buildings in Palenque are over two centuries after the final destruction recounted in the Book of Mormon.[101] Michael D. Coe, professor of anthropology at Yale University, commented on the difficulty of dating the ruins of Palenque to the Book of Mormon time period:

> How is one to reconcile this dating [Nephites from 600 B.C. to A.D. 385] with the flat statement of Joseph Smith himself that Palenque was a Nephite city? This Maya center was built *after* 600 A.D., according to all modern scholarship, some 215 years after the Nephites had been wiped from the surface of the earth. I can only sympathize with the Mormon scholar who has to work that one out![102]

Quiriguá Identified as
a Book of Mormon Place

In *Ancient America and the Book of Mormon* Hunter and Ferguson quoted Joseph Smith's tentative identification of the archaeological site of Quiriguá in Guatemala with the Book of Mormon location known as Zarahemla. Quiriguá is actually 250 miles southeast of the southern Vera Cruz-Tabasco-Chiapas-Campeche area, which Hunter and Ferguson proposed as the location of the lands of Bountiful and Zarahemla,[103] but to them the important fact was that Smith placed Book of Mormon events within Mesoamerica.

After the publication of the September 1842 extract from Stephens's book the unnamed editor located "another important fact relating to the truth of the Book of Mormon." First, he stated that the city known as Zarahemla was situated in "this land," meaning the area of Central America north of the Isthmus of Darien (Panama). Then he said:

Fig. 8--The Temple of the Inscriptions, Palenque, Mexico, which place Joseph Smith identified as a Book of Mormon city. Reproduced from George F. Andrews, *Maya Cities* (1975), courtesy of University of Oklahoma Press.

> It is certainly a good thing for the excellency and veracity, of the divine authenticity of the Book of Mormon, that the ruins of Zarahemla have been found where the Nephites left them: and that a large stone with engravings upon it, as Mosiah said; and a *'large round* stone, with the sides sculptured in hieroglyphics,' as Mr. Stephens has published, is also among the left remembrances of the (to him) *lost and unknown.*[104]

The argument is that Zarahemla can be identified with Quiriguá because each place is a location where a large stone with ancient engravings was found. In the Book of Mormon, Mosiah lived in the city of Zarahemla at the time when "there was a large stone brought unto him with engravings on it" (Omni 1:20). Through God's power Mosiah interpreted the inscriptions which "gave an account of one Coriantumr, and the slain of his people [the Jaredites]. . . . It also spake a few words concerning his fathers. And his first parents came out from the tower, at the time the Lord confounded the language of the people" (Omni

1:21-22). Thus, the engravings on this particular stone were translated and the content of that translation is clearly indicated in the Book of Mormon record.

The unnamed editor then drew the parallel to the "*large round* stone, with the sides sculptured in hieroglyphics," which was found in Quiriguá.[105] He cautiously qualified this identification--"We are not agoing [*sic*] to declare positively that the ruins of Quiriguá are those of Zarahemla." Notwithstanding this disclaimer, the editor then continued:

> But when the land and the stones and the books tell the story so plain, we are of [the] opinion, that it would require more proof than the Jews could bring to prove the disciples stole the body of Jesus from the tomb, to prove that the ruins of the city in question, are not one of those referred to in the Book of Mormon.[106]

Consequently, one should not insist on the specific identification of the Mayan site of Quiriguá with the Book of Mormon city of Zarahemla, but rather that Quiriguá is "one of those [cities] referred to in the Book of Mormon." The chronological difficulty is that the dated monuments in Quiriguá range from A.D. 478 to 805--all after the close of the Book of Mormon period.[107] Then the *Times and Seasons* editor issued the challenge that "it will not be a bad plan to compare Mr. Stephens's ruined cities with those in the Book of Mormon." Since the reason for identifying Zarahemla with Quiriguá was the "large round stone" found in both places, attention will be focused on this point.

In order to identify correctly this "large round stone," one must examine the original 1841 account. Stephens published a description of this stone in his account of the new site of Quiriguá, which his artist, Frederick Catherwood, discovered:

> One of them [the altars] is round, and situated on a small elevation within a circle formed by a wall of stones. In the centre of the circle, reached by descending very narrow steps, is a large round stone, with the sides sculptured in hieroglyphics, covered with vegetation, and supported on what seemed to be two colossal heads.[108]

Fig. 9--Pacal at the moment of death descending down the world tree into the grotesque head of the earth monster, The Temple of the Inscriptions, Palenque, Mexico. Reproduced from Merle G. Robertson, *The Sculpture of Palenque* (1983), courtesy of Princeton University Press.

Catherwood did not draw a representation of this "large round stone" at Quiriguá, but instead provided an illustration of a twenty-four-foot columnar stela (fig. 11). However, the stone in question is sufficiently well described and its location given in such detail as to enable a definite identification. Seventy years later Edgar L. Hewett, sponsored by the St. Louis Society of the Archaeological Institute of America, conducted an archaeological investigation of the various monuments at Quiriguá. When the vegetation and moss was removed from the stone described by Catherwood, a massive cream-colored sandstone boulder (measuring seven-feet high, nine-and-a-half feet long, and eleven-feet wide) was revealed with impressive carvings over its entire surface (fig. 12).[109] Concerning this sculpted stone Hewett commented that "in the beauty of its design, the richness of its execution, and the breadth of its conception, it is not approached by any other American example."[110]

The dedicatory date of this particular stone in Quiriguá marks the death of the ruler Sky Xul.[111] It is inscribed with the Mayan Long Count date of 9.18.5.0.0 4 *Ahau* 13 *Ceh*. This means nine elapsed *baktuns* of 144,000 days (i.e., 1,296,000 days), eighteen *katuns* of 7200 days (i.e., 129,600 days), and five *tuns* of 360 days (i.e., 1800 days), together with a Calendar Round position equal to the day 4 *Ahau* of the *tzolkin* and the thirteenth day of the month *Ceh* in the *haab* or vague year. Adding these days to the base date of 13 August 3114 B.C. gives a correlation to the European calendar of a day in the year A.D. 795--four centuries after the last battle in the Book of Mormon.[112]

Since most of the glyphs on this Quiriguá monument can now be understood, Andrea Joyce Stone described this massive animal-shaped boulder:

> The principal image of the north face is the head of the Cosmic Monster and portrait of the ruler seated in the giant maw. . . . The ruler's costume is standard Quiriguá attire: "Triad" pectoral, God C loincloth, God K manikin scepter, and shield. In the customary fashion, the headdress bears the qualifying visual information. A generic grotesque mask rests on the ruler's head and is flanked by vertical serpent heads and bordered by feathers.[113]

Fig. 10--Life-sized jade mosaic mask of Lord Pacal, made of 200 pieces of jade with shell and obsidian eyes, funerary crypt, The Temple of the Inscriptions, Palenque, Mexico. Reproduced from Time-Life Books, *The Magnificent Maya* (1993), courtesy of Werner Forman Archive/Art Resource.

Fig. 11--Stela F, Quiriguá, Guatemala. Reproduced from drawing by Frederick Catherwood, in John Lloyd Stephens, *Incidents of Travel in Central America, Chiapas, and Yucatán* (1841).

Robert J. Sharer, professor of anthropology at the University of Pennsylvania, provided an up-to-date interpretation of this monolithic animal:

> The front (north) side presents a central sculpted portrait of a youthful Quiriguá ruler, probably Sky Xul, successor to Cauac Sky, in full regalia seated in the cave-like gaping jaws of the reptilian cosmological monster. The human figure is wearing a multi-masked headdress and holds a manikin scepter in his right hand, along with a small shield in the left. The portrait's nose appears to have been battered quite some time ago, probably as part of rituals following the ruler's death (a common Maya custom). . . . The prevailing motifs appeared to be aquatic in theme. The sides depict the legs of the cosmological monster (nearly obscured) and seven animal figures interwoven into a series of Cauac Monster masks. The top is covered by a huge mask of this monster.[114]

Obviously, the translation of the Mayan hieroglyphs on this "large round stone" at Quiriguá reveals no information about Coriantumr and the Jaredites--nor any Book of Mormon story or its Christian theology. Also, this massive stone at Quiriguá weighs twenty tons, but the stone that was translated in the Book of Mormon was "brought" to Mosiah, and so cannot refer to this massive boulder. Consequently, the 1842 suggestion (either written or supported by Joseph Smith) that "the large round stone" had been located and that the site of Quiriguá might be "one of those referred to in the Book of Mormon" must be dropped.

Further Publicity
of Ferguson's Views

In February 1952 Ferguson published a soft-covered booklet entitled *Great Message of Peace and Happiness.*[115] Fifteen of its pages were illustrations of buildings in Yucatán, of ceramic and sculptured faces from Vera Cruz and Guatemala, of the gold tablets of Darius, and of Joseph Smith. Quotations were made from John 10:14-16, Ixtlilxóchitl, and the Mayan lords of Totonicapán. Ferguson wrote the booklet to interest non-members in the Book of Mormon, and asserted the following concerning its account of Jesus' ministry in 3 Nephi:

> That Christ appeared in the New World after being put to death in the Old World is important to you, to me, and to all people. We have positive evidence of life after death—positive evidence that Jesus is our Lord and Savior—and that all men are brothers and should live together in peace and happiness.[116]

Ferguson sent copies of this booklet to LDS General Authorities. Apostle Widtsoe wished God's blessings on Ferguson in his "work of defending the Book of Mormon and its translator [Joseph Smith],"[117] while LeGrand Richards, then the Presiding Bishop of the Church, replied that "you are laying away many treasures in heaven in the efforts you are putting forth to establish in the minds of men the divinity of the Book of Mormon."[118]

Essentially what Hunter and Ferguson had compiled in *Ancient America and the Book of Mormon* was a theoretical construct that offered documentary support for the Book of Mormon, mainly from the writings of Ixtlilxóchitl. Their book, based on an examination of the Book of Mormon text and the available literary sources of the sixteenth and seventeenth centu-

Fig. 12--Monument 16, Quiriguá, Guatemala, which Joseph Smith suggested might be the "large stone" Mosiah translated. Reproduced from Sylvanus G. Morley, "Excavations at Quiriguá, Guatemala," *National Geographic Magazine* (1913).

ries, was a necessary precedent to doing real archaeological work in Mesoamerica. Ferguson knew that the efforts would be difficult, but the possibility of scientific confirmation of the Book of Mormon constituted to him the beginning of a most exciting adventure.

Notes

1. Thomas Stuart Ferguson, *One Fold and One Shepherd* (San Francisco: Books of California, 1958; Salt Lake City: Olympus Publishing Co., 1962). Milton R. Hunter and Thomas Stuart Ferguson, *Ancient America and the Book of Mormon* (Oakland, CA: Kolob Book Co., 1950).

2. Norman B. Phillips, patriarchal blessing, in the Thomas Stuart Ferguson Collection, Accession 1350, Manuscripts Division, J. Willard Marriott Library, University of Utah, Salt Lake City; hereafter abbreviated to Ferguson Collection, UU.

3. Norman Hammond, "Preclassic Maya Civilization," in *New Theories on the Ancient Maya*, ed. Elin C. Danien and Robert J. Sharer, University Museum Monograph, no. 77 (Philadelphia: University Muse-

um, University of Pennsylvania, 1992), 137, defined the term "Meso-america" to indicate the high cultural area from central Mexico through to Honduras and El Salvador. In the 1930s this area was known as Middle America.

4. Fred W. Nelson, Jr., "In Honor of Thomas Stuart Ferguson, 1915-1983," *Newsletter and Proceedings of the S.E.H.A.* [Society for Early Historic Archaeology], no. 161 (May 1987): 1.

5. Steve Johnson, transcript of the advertisement for *The Messiah in Ancient America*, aired during 1987 and 1988 on KSFI radio, Salt Lake City, in the H. Michael Marquardt Collection, Accession 900, Box 77, Fd 13, Manuscripts Division, J. Willard Marriott Library, University of Utah, Salt Lake City.

6. Bruce W. Warren and Thomas Stuart Ferguson [*sic*], *The Messiah in Ancient America* (Provo, UT: Book of Mormon Research Foundation, 1987); hereafter abbreviated to Warren, *Messiah*. For an analysis of the reputed coauthorship between Warren and Ferguson, see the author's "The Odyssey of Thomas Stuart Ferguson," *Dialogue: A Journal of Mormon Thought* 23 (Spring 1990): 84*n*6, and Appendix B, "Examining the Authorship of *The Messiah in Ancient America*," below.

7. Warren, "Preface," *Messiah*, xiii. Joseph L. Allen, *Exploring the Lands of the Book of Mormon* (Orem, UT: S. A. Publishers, 1989), 187, 191, discussed only Ferguson's early position on Book of Mormon geography, perpetuating a one-sided view of his role.

8. Paul R. Cheesman, "Foreword," in Warren, *Messiah*, xi.

9. Jerald Tanner and Sandra Tanner, eds., *Ferguson's Manuscript Unveiled* (Salt Lake City: Utah Lighthouse Ministry, 1988). The entire text of Ferguson's study is reproduced in Appendix A, "Ferguson on Book of Mormon Archaeology," below.

10. The Church of Jesus Christ of Latter-day Saints will throughout this work be referred to as "the LDS Church," "the Mormon Church," and sometimes simply as "the Church" (with no further specification).

11. Jerald Tanner and Sandra Tanner, "Ferguson's Two Faces: Mormon Scholar's 'Spoof' Lives on after His Death," *Salt Lake City Messenger*, no. 69 (September 1988): 7, with emphasis in original.

12. M. Wells Jakeman, letter to Ferguson, 20 February 1941, in the Thomas Stuart Ferguson Collection, Manuscript 1549, Special Collections and Manuscripts, Harold B. Lee Library, Brigham Young University, Provo, Utah; hereafter abbreviated to Ferguson Collection, BYU.

13. Ferguson, letter to Richard L. Evans, [before 11 August 1941], in Ferguson Collection, BYU.

14. Ferguson, "Some Important Book of Mormon Questions," *The Improvement Era* 44 (September 1941): 571.

15. Heber C. Comer, map drawn in 1880, "under the personal direction of Dr. Karl G. Maeser," reproduced in J. A. Washburn and J. Nile Washburn, *An Approach to the Study of Book of Mormon Geography* (Provo, UT: New Era Publishing Co., 1939), 212.

16. For a listing of the seventy-five geographical comments and identifications by Orson Pratt in Book of Mormon editions from 1879

to 1920, see V. Mack Sumner, "An Exploration of the Footnotes in the 1911 Edition Used by the [James E.] Talmage Committee," 8-10, in the V. Mack Sumner Collection, Accession 1459, Manuscripts Division, J. Willard Marriott Library, University of Utah, Salt Lake City. For example, Pratt stated in his footnotes that Lehi landed on the coast of Chile in South America (1 Ne. 18:23), that the River Sidon was the River Magdalena in Colombia (Alma 2:15), and that the Waters of Ripliancum were Lake Ontario (Ether 15:8). In preparation for the 1920 edition of the Book of Mormon a church committee listened to the different geographical theories, but found none compelling and accordingly deleted all of Pratt's geographical footnotes.

17. Heber C. Comer, in Washburn and Washburn, *Geography*, 212.

18. John L. Sorenson, *An Ancient American Setting for the Book of Mormon* (Salt Lake City: Deseret Book Co., 1985; Provo, UT: Foundation for Ancient Research and Mormon Studies, 1985). Probably the most serious problem with the Isthmus of Tehuántepec model, proposed by both Ferguson and Sorenson, is the required reorientation of the cardinal directions 45° to 60°. According to David Freidel, Linda Schele, and Joy Parker, *Maya Cosmos: Three Thousand Years on the Shaman's Path* (New York: William Morrow and Co., 1993), 419, the Mayan east is oriented to the sun. John A. Tvedtnes, "Significant Contribution," review of *In Search of Cumorah*, by David A. Palmer, in *Newsletter and Proceedings of the S.E.H.A.*, no. 149 (June 1982): 9, criticized David A. Palmer (but the argument applies equally well to Sorenson, ibid., 38-39) that the Hebrew directional system was not based upon placing one's back to the sea, but rather both Hebraic systems of direction "were oriented toward the rising sun. . . . To me, it is not reasonable to believe that the Nephites living inland and no longer in view of the Pacific Ocean could have reoriented their directions according to the sea rather than the rising sun. From inland, the major phenomenon on which directions could be based was the daily sunrise." Also, Sorenson, ibid., 39, asserted that "it is interesting that in the Mayan languages of Mesoamerica, 'south' meant 'on the right' and north 'on the left,' in parallel to Hebrew." The latest information reverses that orientation, since Barbara Tedlock, *Time and the Highland Maya*, rev. ed. (Albuquerque, NM: University of New Mexico Press, 1992), 178, stated that Mayan speakers "describe the sun as a human or godlike figure . . . , who rises each day on the eastern horizon and faces his universe with north on his right hand and south on his left hand."

19. F. Richard Hauck, *Deciphering the Geography of the Book of Mormon: Settlements and Routes in Ancient America* (Salt Lake City: Deseret Book Co., 1988). Also see F. Richard Hauck, "Archaeology and the Setting of the Book of Mormon," *This People* 15 (Spring 1994): 70-72, 75-78, 80, 83; "Ancient Fortifications and the Land of Manti," *This People* 15 (Summer 1994): 46-47, 49-52, 54-55; and "In Search of the Land of Nephi," *This People* 15 (Fall 1994): 52-56, 58-60, 63. In reviewing Hauck's geography, John E. Clark, "A Key for Evaluating Nephite Geographies," review of F. Richard Hauck, *Deciphering the*

Geography of the Book of Mormon, in *Review of Books on the Book of Mormon* 1 (1989): 67-69, overwhelmingly favored Sorenson's geography. However, in comparing both Hauck's and Sorenson's geographies with three ideal Book of Mormon geographies (based solely on reading the text), T. Michael Smith, *Generic Book of Mormon Geographies: A Baseline Evaluation of Current Research,* S.E.H.A. paper no. 3 (Orem, UT: Society for Early Historic Archaeology, a division of the Ancient America Foundation, 1993), 9-11, favored Hauck's geography over Sorenson's.

20. Calvin D. Tolman, "Book of Mormon History and Geography," typescript, 1961, in Calvin D. Tolman Collection, Accession 1445, Manuscripts Division, J. Willard Marriott Library, University of Utah, Salt Lake City.

21. Eugene L. Peay, *The Lands of Zarahemla: A Book of Mormon Commentary* (Salt Lake City: Northwest Publishing, 1993), 275-76.

22. B. Keith Christensen, "Geology as a Basis in Identifying Book of Mormon Lands," typescript, ca. 1969, in the Calvin D. Tolman Collection, Accession 1445, Manuscripts Division, J. Willard Marriott Library, University of Utah, Salt Lake City; hereafter abbreviated to Tolman Collection. Cf. B. Keith Christensen, "The Unknown Witness: Jerusalem, Geology, and the Origin of the Book of Mormon," "Manuscript Edition," n.p., ca. 1992.

23. Jean R. Driggs, *The Palestine of America* (Salt Lake City, 1928).

24. Norman C. Pierce, *Another Cumorah, Another Joseph* (Salt Lake City, 1954).

25. Robert B. Ellsworth, *Lecture Notes on an Interpretation of a Map of Zarahemla and the Land Northward as Described in the Book of Mormon* (Ogden, UT: Rob-Ell, 1980).

26. Arthur J. Kocherhans, *Lehi's Isle of Promise: A Scriptural Account with Word Definitions and a Commentary* (Fullerton, CA: Et Cetera Et Cetera Graphics and Printing, 1989).

27. The originator of the Florida theory is not identified but the map is shown in Paul R. Cheesman, *These Early Americans: External Evidences of the Book of Mormon* (Salt Lake City: Deseret Book Co., 1974), 176-77, and Paul R. Cheesman, *The World of the Book of Mormon* (Bountiful, UT: Horizon Publishers, 1984), 78.

28. Delbert W. Curtis, *Christ in North America: Christ Visited the Nephites in the Land of Promise in North America* (Tigard, OR: Resource Communications, 1993), 122-37.

29. Clark, "Key," 20, referred to the various geographies as "a cacophony of plausible alternatives." Calvin D. Tolman, map, 1983, in Box 1, Fd 17, Tolman Collection, drew a tongue-in-cheek map, locating the "narrow neck of land" between the eastern-most extension of the Great Salt Lake and the mountains east of Centerville and Farmington in Utah, in order to show how the ambiguities of the Book of Mormon text can be made to fit many different geographical correlations.

30. Even those who examine the internal requirements of the Book of Mormon run into difficulty. For J. Nile Washburn, *Book of Mormon Lands and Times* (Bountiful, UT: Horizon Publishers, 1974), 152-53,

156, pointed out that there is a geographical inconsistency in the Book of Mormon at Alma 53:6; the mention of the city named Mulek (which is clearly in the land of Zarahemla) as being in "the land of Nephi," Washburn feels, must either be emended to "the land of the Nephites" or "the land of Zarahemla." For the contradiction concerning which year Helaman led his 2000 stripling warriors, see John L. Sorenson, *The Significance of the Chronological Discrepancy between Alma 53:22 and Alma 56:9* (Provo, UT: Foundation for Ancient Research and Mormon Studies, 1990). For the error concerning when the city of Nephihah was captured by Amalickiah, see J. Nile Washburn, *Book-of-Mormon Guidebook and Certain Problems in the Book of Mormon* ([Orem, UT: J. N. Washburn], 1968), 33-40.

31. Ferguson, "Mexico and Guatemala, February 1946," typescript, 25 April 1946, in the John Willard and Alice Sheets Marriott Collection, Manuscript 164, Box 70, Fd 9, Manuscripts Division, J. Willard Marriott Library, University of Utah, Salt Lake City; hereafter abbreviated to Marriott Collection.

32. Ferguson, letter to M. Wells Jakeman, 15 September 1945, in Ferguson Collection, BYU.

33. Robert O'Brien, *Marriott: The J. Willard Marriott Story* (Salt Lake City: Deseret Book Co., 1977), 201-203.

34. Ferguson, "Mexico and Guatemala," 5.

35. Ferguson, letter to Bill and Allie [Marriott], 9 July 1946, in Ferguson Collection, BYU.

36. J. Willard Marriott, letter to Ezra Taft Benson, 23 March 1946, in Box 12, Fd 14, Marriott Collection.

37. J. Willard Marriott, letter to Ester Ferguson, 17 March 1983, quoted in Warren, *Messiah*, 250.

38. Ferguson, "The Wheel in Ancient America," *The Improvement Era* 49 (December 1946): 785. Ferguson made use of Gordon F. Ekholm, "Wheeled Toys in Mexico," *American Antiquity* 11 (April 1946): 222-28. Cf. Hasso von Winning, "Further Examples of Figurines on Wheels from Mexico," *Ethnos* 25 (1960): 63-72.

39. Stanley H. Boggs, *Salvadoran Varieties of Wheeled Figurines*, Contributions to Mesoamerican Anthropology, no. 1 (Miami, FL: Institute of Maya Studies of the Museum of Science, 1973), 3. In explanation of the uncertainty of how these wheeled figurines were used, Boggs explained that "at first they were thought to have been children's toys, but more recent researchers have concluded that they were most probably ritual objects employed in ceremonial, adult contexts."

40. Ferguson, "Written Symposium on Book of Mormon Geography: Response of Thomas S. Ferguson to the Norman and Sorenson Papers," typescript, 12 March 1975, 28, in Ferguson Collection, UU.

41. John A. Widtsoe, letter to Ferguson, 15 March 1946, in Ferguson Collection, BYU.

42. Ferguson, letter to Ezra T. Benson, 4 September 1947, in Ferguson Collection, BYU.

43. Joseph Smith, letter to N. C. Saxton, 4 January 1833, in Dean

C. Jessee, comp. and ed., *The Personal Writings of Joseph Smith* (Salt Lake City: Deseret Book Co., 1984), 273. The next month Joseph Smith declared that this letter was written "by the commandment of God," quoted in Brent Lee Metcalfe, "Apologetic and Critical Assumptions about Book of Mormon Historicity," *Dialogue: A Journal of Mormon Thought* 26 (Fall 1993): 160-61.

44. Scott H. Faulring, ed., *An American Prophet's Record: The Diaries and Journals of Joseph Smith* (Salt Lake City: Signature Books, 1987), 51.

45. After analyzing the variations among the primary documents Kenneth W. Godfrey, *The Zelph Story* (Provo, UT: Foundation for Ancient Research and Mormon Studies, 1989), 23, concluded that "most sources agree that Zelph was a white Lamanite who fought under a leader named Onandagus."

46. Joseph Smith, letter to Emma Smith, 4 June 1834, in Jessee, *Personal Writings*, 324. The spelling has been corrected.

47. Ferguson, *Cumorah--Where?* (Independence, MO: Zion's Printing and Publishing Co., 1947), 7-8, quoting the amalgamated version of the Zelph episode in B. H. Roberts, ed., *History of the Church of Jesus Christ of Latter-day Saints, Period I: History of Joseph Smith, the Prophet by Himself* (Salt Lake City: Deseret News, 1902), 2:79.

48. Ferguson, *Cumorah*, 61.

49. Ferguson, letter to George Albert Smith, 3 March 1947, in Box 17, Fd 2, Marriott Collection.

50. Ferguson, letter to J. Willard Marriott, 14 April 1947, in Box 70, Fd 4, Marriott Collection.

51. Ferguson, letter to J. Willard Marriott, 19 September 1947, in Box 70, Fd 4, Marriott Collection.

52. Ferguson, *Cumorah*, v.

53. John A. Widtsoe, review of *Cumorah--Where?* by Thomas Stuart Ferguson, in *The Improvement Era* 51 (January 1948): 42.

54. Ferguson, *Cumorah*, 43, 46-48. David A. Palmer, *In Search of Cumorah: New Evidences for the Book of Mormon from Ancient Mexico* (Bountiful, UT: Horizon Publishers, 1981), 91, countered that the Valley of Mexico "appears to be too far from the sea."

55. Ferguson, letter to M. Wells Jakeman, 27 April 1947, in Ferguson Collection, BYU.

56. Ferguson, *Cumorah*, 68-70.

57. Ferguson, letter to Milton R. Hunter, 10 March 1948, in Ferguson Collection, BYU.

58. Ferguson, letter to M. Wells Jakeman, 10 October 1947, in Ferguson Collection, BYU, explained that the LDS First Presidency refused to allow Milton R. Hunter to accompany them on this trip, and Ferguson added: "This clearly indicates their attitude toward Book of Mormon archaeology. It is obviously secondary with them."

59. Hunter and Ferguson, *Ancient America*, 171.

60. Dee F. Green, "Book of Mormon Archaeology: The Myths and the Alternatives," *Dialogue: A Journal of Mormon Thought* 4 (Summer

1969): 73, pointed out that "after excavating at Aguacatal in 1961 and conducting the only study yet made of the artifacts and data recovered, Ray Matheny, then a graduate student at BYU, privately demonstrated that Aguacatal is not Bountiful."

61. Ferguson, letter to [addressee unknown], 21 January 1948, in Ferguson Collection, BYU.

62. Ferguson, letter to J. Willard Marriott, 12 March 1948, in Box 70 Fd 5, Marriott Collection; cf. Ezra Taft Benson, letter to Ferguson, 30 March 1948, in Ferguson Collection, BYU.

63. Ferguson, letter to Mr. and Mrs. J. Willard Marriott, 20 April 1948, in Box 70, Fd 5, Marriott Collection.

64. Ferguson, "Suggestions for Making Greater and More Effective Use of the Book of Mormon," typescript, 9 April 1948, in Box 70, Fd 5, Marriott Collection.

65. Ferguson, letter to Milton R. Hunter, 14 May 1949, in Ferguson Collection, BYU.

66. M. Wells Jakeman, letter to Milton R. Hunter, 6 February 1951, in Ferguson Collection, BYU.

67. John L. Sorenson, *The Geography of Book of Mormon Events: A Source Book*, rev. ed. (Provo, UT: Foundation for Ancient Research and Mormon Studies, 1992), 38.

68. Ferguson, letter to Ralph E. Henderson, 28 June 1950, in Box 17, Fd 5, Marriott Collection.

69. Hunter and Ferguson, *Ancient America*, passim; cf. Ferguson and Jakeman, "Ancient Mexico," in Ferguson Collection, BYU. Hunter and Ferguson did not refer to the earlier study of Louis E. Hills, *A Short Work on the Popol Vuh and the Traditional History of the Ancient Americans by Ixt-lil-xochitl* (Independence, MO, 1918), which draws extensive parallels from Ixtlilxóchitl, even though Ferguson received a complimentary copy in 1942 (Israel A. Smith, letter to Ferguson, 11 February 1942, in Ferguson Collection, BYU). Ixtlilxóchitl's text was first published in Spanish by Lord Kingsborough in 1848. The latest Spanish edition is Fernando de Alva Ixtlilxóchitl, *Obras Históricas*, ed. Edmundo O'Gorman, 2 vols., 4th ed. (Mexico City: Universidad Nacional Autónoma de México, 1985).

70. Ferguson, letter to David O. McKay, 11 December 1957, in Ferguson Collection, BYU, developed such a strong emotional attachment to Ixtlilxóchitl that in 1957 he asked President David O. McKay for permission to perform a baptism for the dead in his behalf.

71. Matthew W. Stirling, "Great Stone Faces of the Mexican Jungle," *The National Geographic Magazine* 78 (September 1940): 310.

72. Hunter and Ferguson, *Ancient America*, 19-20, 33, 57. Eight years later Ferguson, *One Fold*, 314, changed the identification of the Olmecs from the Mulekites (who date after 600 B.C.) to the Jaredites (who date many years after 3000 B.C.). Most modern writers on Book of Mormon geography identify the Jaredites with the Olmecs. The difficulty with both of these identifications is the chronology of the Olmec, which, according to Richard E. W. Adams, *Prehistoric Meso-*

america, rev. ed. (Norman, OK: University of Oklahoma Press, 1991), 51, spanned from 1750 to 100 B.C., with the period of high culture being 1150 to 400 B.C. Deanne G. Matheny, "Does the Shoe Fit? A Critique of the Limited Tehuántepec Geography," in *New Approaches to the Book of Mormon: Explorations in Critical Methodology*, ed. Brent Lee Metcalfe (Salt Lake City: Signature Books, 1993), 320, commented that the "Olmec civilization still seems very different from the Jaredite civilization described in the Book of Mormon. As discussed above [in her article], the metallurgy, plants, and animals ascribed to the Jaredites have not been found in connection with the Olmecs."

73. Ferguson, Note to Omer C. Stewart, 23 May 1952, in Ferguson Collection, UU.

74. Robert Wauchope, *Lost Tribes and Sunken Continents: Myth and Method in the Study of American Indians* (Chicago: University of Chicago Press, 1962), 63.

75. Hunter and Ferguson, *Ancient America*, 20, 22, 24, 89, 234.

76. The Charles E. Dibble Collection, Accession 1371, Manuscripts Division, J. Willard Marriott Library, University of Utah, Salt Lake City.

77. J. Reuben Clark, Jr., letter to Ferguson, 16 May 1957, in Ferguson Collection, BYU.

78. Mary Ellen Miller and Karl Taube, *The Gods and Symbols of Ancient Mexico and the Maya: An Illustrated Dictionary of Mesoamerican Religion* (London: Thames and Hudson, 1993), 141.

79. Hunter and Ferguson, *Ancient America*, 195-222. According to Brant Gardner, "The Christianization of Quetzalcóatl: A History of the Metamorphosis," *Sunstone* 10, no. 11 (1986): 7, other proposed identifications of Quetzalcóatl include the Apostle Thomas, a Viking, a Chinese explorer, an extraterrestrial, and Moses.

80. William J. Hamblin, review of *Archaeology and the Book of Mormon*, by Jerald Tanner and Sandra Tanner, in *Review of Books on the Book of Mormon* 5 (1993): 267, suggested such constraint, though he is speaking generally of "some Latter-day Saint writers" and not Hunter and Ferguson specifically.

81. Basil C. Hedrick, letter to Dan Vogel, 23 January 1981, in the Dan Vogel Collection, Accession 1444, Box 1, Fd 4, Manuscripts Division, J. Willard Marriott Library, University of Utah, Salt Lake City. Hedrick continued: "In fact, adjusted calendars would suggest a time sometime about 900+ years subsequent to the crucifixion. It frankly appears to me to be poppycock that the Mormons attempt to tout. They take advantage of similarities and seemingly logical comparisons to support a stand which they wish to take but choose to ignore all types of other information which would lead them to quite the opposite conclusion, if they were totally objective in their approach." Similarly, Dee F. Green, "Recent Scholarship on New World Archaeology," *Dialogue: A Journal of Mormon Thought* 7 (Spring 1972): 117, said that "the equating of Christ with Quetzalcóatl by many Mormons is another example of our naive myth building using trait comparisons."

82. Burr Cartwright Brundage, *The Phoenix of the Western World: Quetzalcóatl and the Sky Religion* (Norman, OK: University of Oklahoma Press, 1982), 253-71. Davíd Carrasco, *Quetzalcóatl and the Irony of Empire: Myths and Prophecies in the Aztec Tradition* (Chicago and London: University of Chicago Press, 1982), 40, 48, discussed how Quetzalcóatl was early identified with King Charles I of Spain and decades later with Hernán Cortés.

83. Reader's Digest, *Mysteries of the Ancient Americas: The New World before Columbus* (Pleasantville, NY: Reader's Digest Association, 1986), 38.

84. Stirling, "Stone Faces," 327.

85. Sylvanus G. Morley, "Excavations at Quiriguá, Guatemala," *The National Geographic Magazine* 24 (March 1913): 359.

86. Stephen C. Jett, "Before Columbus: The Question of Early Transoceanic Interinfluences," *Brigham Young University Studies* 33, no. 2 (1993): 258-59. Cf. Kirk A. Magleby, *A Survey of Mesoamerican Bearded Figures* (Provo, UT: Foundation for Ancient Research and Mormon Studies, 1983).

87. Hunter and Ferguson, *Ancient America*, 170, fig. 21. Román Piña Chan, *The Olmec: Mother Culture of Mesoamerica*, ed. Laura Laurencich Minelli, trans. from the Italian by Warren McManus (New York: Rizzoli International Publications, 1989), 186, said that this jade artifact displays a man "wearing a duck-beak mask."

88. Hunter and Ferguson, *Ancient America*, 168, 171, 174.

89. Joseph Fielding Smith, "Where Is the Hill Cumorah? Book of Mormon Establishes Location of Historic Region," *Deseret News*, Church News, 27 February 1954, 2. Brent Lee Metcalfe, "Apologetic and Critical Assumptions about Book of Mormon Historicity," *Dialogue: A Journal of Mormon Thought* 26 (Fall 1993): 158-61, discussed how many modern Mormon writers place the hill Cumorah in Mexico while Joseph Smith and most nineteenth century Mormon writers place it in New York state.

90. Ferguson, letter to J. Willard Marriott, 5 September 1958, in Box 70, Fd 7, Marriott Collection. Richard O. Cowan, "Aztec History and the Book of Mormon," *The Instructor* 102 (March 1967): 131-32, is based upon Hunter and Ferguson, *Ancient America*.

91. William J. Hamblin, "An Apologist for the Critics: Brent Lee Metcalfe's Assumptions and Methodologies," review of "Apologetic and Critical Assumptions about Book of Mormon Historicity," by Brent Lee Metcalfe, in *Review of Books on the Book of Mormon* 6, no. 1 (1994): 471.

92. Joseph Smith, letter to John M. Bernhisel, 16 November 1841, in Jessee, *Personal Writings*, 502.

93. Joseph Smith, "To Subscribers," *Times and Seasons* 3 (1 March 1842): 710.

94. Joseph Smith, "American Antiquities," *Times and Seasons* 3 (15 July 1842): 860.

95. According to William J. Hamblin, "Basic Methodological

Problems with the Anti-Mormon Approach to the Geography and Archaeology of the Book of Mormon," *Journal of Book of Mormon Studies* 2 (Spring 1993): 176n53, John Taylor was the managing editor of the *Times and Seasons* during this period. However, it is immaterial whether Joseph Smith wrote these two following editorials or just approved of them as the senior editor.

96. For recent books on Palenque, see Merle Greene Robertson, *The Sculpture of Palenque*, 4 vols. (Princeton, NJ: Princeton University Press, 1983-1991) and Mercedes de la Garza, *Palenque*, Chiapas Eterno (Tuxtla Gutiérrez, Chiapas: Gobierno del Estado de Chiapas, 1992).

97. [Joseph Smith], "Extract from Stephens's *Incidents of Travel in Central America*," *Times and Seasons* 3 (15 September 1842): 914, with emphasis in original.

98. Patricia A. McAnany, *Living with the Ancestors: Kinship and Kingship in Ancient Maya Society* (Austin, TX: University of Texas Press, 1995), 51.

99. William M. Ferguson and Arthur H. Rohn, *Mesoamerica's Ancient Cities: Aerial Views of Precolumbian Ruins in Mexico, Guatemala, Belize, and Honduras* (Niwot, CO: University Press of Colorado, 1990), 126.

100. Davíd Carrasco, *Religions of Mesoamerica: Cosmovision and Ceremonial Centers*, Religious Traditions of the World (San Francisco: Harper and Row, 1990), 92; reprinted in Davíd Carrasco, "Religions of Mesoamerica: Cosmovision and Ceremonial Centers," in H. Byron Earhart, ed., *Religious Traditions of the World: A Journey through Africa, Mesoamerica, North America, Judaism, Christianity, Islam, Hinduism, Buddhism, China, and Japan* (San Francisco: HarperSanFrancisco, 1993), 190.

101. Robertson, *Palenque*, 2:3.

102. Michael D. Coe, "Mormons and Archaeology: An Outside View," *Dialogue: A Journal of Mormon Thought* 8, no. 2 (1973): 45, with emphasis in original.

103. Hunter and Ferguson, *Ancient America*, 143, 160-61. Three years earlier Ferguson, *Cumorah*, 60, quoted Joseph Smith's editorial statement to show that even the prophet was not sure of the location of Zarahemla, since he "readily admitted not knowing exact Book of Mormon locations."

104. [Joseph Smith], "Zarahemla," *Times and Seasons* 3 (1 October 1842): 927, with emphasis in original.

105. John L. Sorenson, "The Book of Mormon as a Mesoamerican Codex," *Newsletter and Proceedings of the S.E.H.A.*, no. 139 (December 1976): 5, 7, interpreted the "large stone" of Omni 1:20-22 as a "memorial stela."

106. [Smith], "Zarahemla," 927.

107. Robert J. Sharer, *Quiriguá: A Classic Maya Center and Its Sculptures*, Centers of Civilization Series (Durham, NC: Carolina Academic Press, 1990), 103.

108. John Lloyd Stephens, *Incidents of Travel in Central America*,

Chiapas, and Yucatán (New York: Harper and Brothers, 1841), 2:122-23, quoted in [Smith], "Zarahemla," 928.

109. For photographs before and after the removal of the moss from the stone monument, see Edgar L. Hewett, "Two Seasons' Work in Guatemala," *Bulletin of the Archaeological Institute of America* 2 (1911): pl. xxxi. For a beautiful color photograph of this monument, see Wendy Ashmore and Robert J. Sharer, "Excavations at Quiriguá, Guatemala: The Ascent of an Elite Maya Center," *Archaeology* 31 (November-December 1978): 10.

110. Hewett, "Work," 132. In another assessment of its worth, Sylvanus G. Morley, *Guide Book to the Ruins of Quiriguá*, supplementary publication, no. 16 (Washington, D.C.: Carnegie Institution of Washington, 1935), 109, said that "W. H. Holmes, former director of the National Art Gallery, held it to be the finest example of ancient American sculpture extant." Also, C. Bruce Hunter, *A Guide to Ancient Maya Ruins*, 2d ed., rev. and enl. (Norman, OK: University of Oklahoma Press, 1986), 118, said that this monument is "one of the most magnificent stones ever carved by the Maya."

111. Norman Hammond, *Ancient Maya Civilization*, updated ed. (New Brunswick, NJ: Rutgers University Press, 1994), 206-207, pointed out that this monument was set up in A.D. 795 to mark the death of Sky Xul. According to Andrea Joyce Stone, "The Zoomorphs of Quiriguá, Guatemala" (Ph.D. dissertation, University of Texas at Austin, 1983), 124, Sky Xul's name is depicted "as a T122 smokescroll in front of a large head."

112. For an explanation of the Mayan calendar system, see Muriel Porter Weaver, *The Aztecs, Maya, and Their Predecessors: Archaeology of Mesoamerica*, 3d ed., Studies in Archaeology (San Diego: Academic Press, 1993), 145-52.

113. Stone, "Zoomorphs," 108, 111. Stone devoted twenty-eight pages of analysis and interpretation to this monument.

114. Sharer, *Quiriguá*, 60-61. William M. Ferguson and John Q. Royce, *Maya Ruins in Central America in Color: Tikal, Copán, and Quiriguá* (Albuquerque, NM: University of New Mexico Press, 1984), 336, described this monument as follows: "Zoomorph P, 'The Great Turtle,' is Quiriguá's most famous monument. It is almost unbelievable that this great boulder could be so intricately and delicately carved by hand with stone tools."

115. John A. Widtsoe, review of *Great Message of Peace and Happiness*, by Ferguson, in *The Improvement Era* 55 (May 1952): 334.

116. Ferguson, *Great Message of Peace and Happiness* (Orinda, CA: [Sun Lithographing, 1952]), [15].

117. John A. Widtsoe, letter to Ferguson, 5 March 1952, in Ferguson Collection, BYU.

118. LeGrand Richards, letter to Ferguson, 14 March 1952, in Ferguson Collection, BYU.

2

The
New
World
Archaeological
Foundation

Having a strong belief in the Book of Mormon all his life, Tom Ferguson tackled the project of archaeologically verifying it with unbounded enthusiasm. Because he was aware that the documentary support for the Book of Mormon from post-Conquest chronicles was insufficient without independent confirmation, he wanted to carry out--or be the instrument to carry out--professional archaeological investigations in Meso-america.

A number of Latter-day Saint scholars hold the "conviction that proof of the Book of Mormon *does* lie in Central America,"[1] but the clear realization of the need to substantiate this convic-tion spurred Ferguson on to develop an archaeological plan to excavate in Mesoamerica and to raise the funds necessary to get it started. What was desperately needed was an organization to do professional archaeological work in this area. Impartiality would be necessary if the claims of the Book of Mormon were to be vindicated.

Archaeological Proposal
to the LDS Church

The idea of active archaeological digging in Mesoamerica to produce evidence for the claims of the Book of Mormon began to solidify for Ferguson in 1951. Ferguson suggested to LeGrand Richards the formation of a Book of Mormon committee, one function of which would be to sponsor expeditions to investigate archaeological sites in Book of Mormon lands. He expressed his firm conviction that sufficient archaeological digging in Mesoamerica would bring forth translatable scripts on artifacts or monuments, which "will virtually clinch the position of Joseph Smith."[2] Ferguson then sent a complimentary copy of *Ancient America and the Book of Mormon* to one of the leading American archaeologists, Alfred V. Kidder, who had recently retired from his position as director of the Carnegie Institution of Washington, D.C. It happened that Kidder was coming to the University of California at Berkeley, so they were able to meet to discuss Ferguson's book, but more especially Ferguson's ideas about doing archaeological work relating to the origin of Mesoamerican civilization.[3] Kidder encouraged Ferguson, but emphasized the strict separation between an archaeologist's reporting of his findings and a Mormon's interpretation of the same data. Ferguson agreed with this important distinction, remarking to Kidder: "Let the evidence from the ground speak for itself and let the chips fall where they may."[4] Investigating the origins of Mesoamerican civilization in an effort to correlate with Book of Mormon peoples meant focusing on approximately the last eleven or twelve centuries of the Archaic, all of the Preclassic,[5] and almost the first two hundred years of the Early Classic cultural periods in Mesoamerica.[6]

In April 1951 Kidder and Ferguson presented a twelve-page

plan to the General Authorities of the LDS Church concerning explorations and excavations of Preclassic sites in Mesoamerica. They explained:

> The portion of southern Mexico adjacent to the Isthmus of Tehuántepec bears every sign of being the most important archaeological zone in the New World. Work has been done on all sides of it. Scarcely any work has been undertaken in the area in question. This Tehuántepec locale may well hold the conclusive answers to the paramount problem of origins of the great civilizations of Middle America. The opportunity is now at hand to do the necessary archaeological fact-finding in that area.[7]

The plan outlined an ambitious project of archaeological investigation in Mesoamerica, for which Kidder and Ferguson asked the Church provide financial support in the amount of $150,000 over a five-year period. Shortly thereafter Ferguson wrote a letter to Apostle John A. Widtsoe, saying that he was "hoping and praying" that the plan would be approved by the LDS leaders at their upcoming meeting in the Salt Lake Temple.[8] Ferguson could not conceive of the LDS Church rejecting the plan.

Several months later, having still not received an official response from the church leaders, Ferguson asked Widtsoe for advice on writing a letter to David O. McKay concerning the earlier proposal, and said confidently that "the publicity which will accrue to the Church from the important discoveries which will be made confirming the Book of Mormon will reach millions of people and will have infinite value."[9] The next month Ferguson inquired of President McKay concerning the status of their April proposal and mentioned the willingness of Gordon R. Willey, professor of Mexican and Central American Archaeology at Harvard University, and Pedro Armillas, a leading Mexican archaeologist, to join the group. Ferguson affirmed that the forthcoming "artifacts will speak eloquently from the dust" in support of the Book of Mormon and bring worldwide publicity.[10] Less than one week later the Church politely rejected the archaeological proposal and offered no financial assistance.

In spite of this crushing negative response, Ferguson refused to be discouraged and began immediately to raise funds on his own from private individuals. At this point Ferguson thought of naming the organization either the Middle American Archaeological Foundation or the American Archaeological Foundation. By June of the next year he thought the proposed non-profit corporation should be the New World Archaeological Foundation, which was the name finally adopted. Ferguson traveled widely in California, Utah, and Idaho to raise funds for the organization and in one six-day period obtained pledges for $30,000: only $22,000 was actually received.[11] Ferguson was much encouraged by Widtsoe, who remarked that "should specific and factual evidences be discovered [through Ferguson's archaeological program] sustaining the Book of Mormon, archaeology will have struck a mighty blow for the cause of God and freedom."[12] Ferguson's deep faith in the Book of Mormon gave him the necessary drive to continue on his own, without LDS institutional support. Single-handedly he would see to it that a professional archaeological organization was established.

Organization of the New World Archaeological Foundation

In October 1952 Ferguson organized the New World Archaeological Foundation in California. The officers were himself as president; Alfred V. Kidder, as first vice-president;[13] Milton R. Hunter, of the First Council of Seventy of the LDS Church as another vice-president; and Scott H. Dunham, a C.P.A. in San Francisco, as secretary-treasurer. The board of directors included these officers, as well as John A. Widtsoe of the Quorum of the Twelve Apostles;[14] Charles S. Hatch, a doctor in Idaho Falls; J. Poulson Hunter, a doctor in Salt Lake City; R. Verne McCullough, an attorney in Salt Lake City; and Nicholas G. Morgan, Sr., an attorney and philanthropist in Salt Lake City.[15] The committee of archaeologists, which performed an advisory role to the foundation, consisted of: Alfred V. Kidder; Pedro Armillas, professor of Mexican Archaeology of the Mexico City College, Mexico; Gordon F. Ekholm, archaeologist of the American Museum of Natural History, New York; Gordon R. Willey, professor of Mexican Archaeology, Harvard University, Cambridge, Massachusetts;[16] and M. Wells Jakeman, chairman of the Department of Archaeology, Brigham Young University, Provo, Utah.

During the years from 1952 to 1961 in which Ferguson served as president of NWAF he received no salary or remuneration.[17] In 1952 Kidder mapped the objectives of the NWAF by delineating the three main views of the origin of the high civilization of Mesoamerica that were to be tested by archaeological investigations:

> The purpose of the Foundation is to carry on explorations and excavations to add to knowledge of Mesoamerican archaeology and to test the several theories as to the origin of the high civilizations of the Americas: (1) That they were autochthonous [indigenous]; (2) That, as set forth in the Book of Mormon, they were derived from ancient Israel; (3) That their rise was due to stimuli from some Asiatic source.
>
> Mr. [Thomas Stuart] Ferguson is an advocate of the second of these theories; Dr. [Gordon F.] Ekholm . . . views with some favor the third;[18] I feel that, although the problem is *still unsolved*, these civilizations were essentially the product of native American Indian creativeness. So all shades of opinion are represented![19]

This important NWAF project would acquire archaeological evidence using scientifically controlled procedures and would, they hoped, provide a positive answer to one of the three main theories about the origin of Mesoamerican civilization. While preparing to go to southern Mexico to begin work, Ferguson expressed his own opinion concerning these three theories: "I feel the Mormon theory is the strongest of the three propounded explanations of the origin of the great cultures of Middle America--finding more support from the early sixteenth century histories."[20] The NWAF would now set out to explore, excavate, and analyze the archaeological material in the ground in

Mesoamerica to determine which of the theories would be supported by concrete evidence. From its inception NWAF had a firm policy of objectivity. J. Alden Mason, editor of numerous NWAF publications, made clear that "the stated purpose of this Foundation is *not* to seek corroboration of the Book of Mormon account, but to help to resolve the problem of whether civilization in Middle America developed autochthonously or as a result of diffused or migrated influence from some area of the Old World."[21] While that was the official position of NWAF and while all field directors and working archaeologists were explicitly instructed to do their work in a professional manner and make no reference to the Book of Mormon, Ferguson placed the following statement in the very first news release issued by NWAF: "It is the opinion of the organizers of the Foundation who are Mormons that the excavations being undertaken will sustain the truth of the Book of Mormon."[22]

In December 1952 the first NWAF exploratory team cleared pristine jungle and looked for ruins in Huimanguillo, Tabasco, Mexico, an area Ferguson felt was the Book of Mormon land of Zarahemla. Although Ferguson did not expect to "dig up a dead Nephite with a Book of Mormon name carved on a bone," he hoped to discover a striking artifact during this initial archaeological season.[23] Ferguson was convinced that the Nephite leaders had left behind inscriptions, monuments, and artworks. When these were discovered, people would be convinced that Jesus Christ really appeared anciently to the Book of Mormon people. Also, the practically-minded Ferguson was aware that noteworthy finds would certainly make it much easier to raise funds for the project the next year.

Ferguson's Fund-Raising Efforts

Having received only $22,000 for NWAF for the 1952-1953 season, Ferguson felt disappointed with the amount of money raised. It was a difficult task to get the necessary funds to keep the fieldwork in the field going, and Ferguson compared his efforts with those of Christopher Columbus: "I feel like Columbus --trying to get help for a great cause and with a strong conviction on the matter."[24] Then on 9 April 1953, through the influence of J. Willard Marriott, he met for over an hour with David O. McKay and J. Reuben Clark, Jr., of the First Presidency; Apostles Harold B. Lee, Henry D. Moyle, Marion G. Romney, LeGrand Richards, Spencer W. Kimball; and other invited General Authorities.[25] He appealed to them for church funds to continue the work of NWAF--$15,000 to finish out the current year and $120,000 to cover the next four years.[26] Near the end of the presentation Ferguson told the assembled church leaders that he "had prayed to [the] Lord and asked him to stop me if it weren't his will that we go forward."[27] At this point President David O. McKay replied with a smile, "Brother Ferguson, you are a hard man to stop."[28] Ten months later during a visit to Guatemala President McKay wrote in his diary--possibly as a result of Ferguson's repeated references to the importance of Meso-america--that the "legends, stories, 'many waters' etc., and general atmosphere awaken the impression that we are in B[ook] of M[ormon] land."[29]

On 10 April 1953 Ferguson wrote a letter to the First Presidency, covering points he had not had time to mention in his meeting with them. He reminded them:

> The Church cannot afford to pass up title to Nephite works of art and handcraft; the Church cannot afford to let all of the priceless artifacts of Book of Mormon people fall into other hands. We can make wonderful use of them in missionary work and in letting all the world know of the Book of Mormon. We cannot afford to let this work go undone now that we are so well prepared to undertake it.[30]

A week later J. Reuben Clark, Jr., second counselor in the First Presidency, replied with a partially favorable decision: the church would contribute $15,000 to Ferguson for the present year only, with the strict condition that "no publicity whatever in any way or at any time" be given to this private donation.[31] As far as Ferguson could tell the First Presidency had "not even told the other General Authorities" about these funds.[32] When

Ferguson received this money, the agreement (as he understood it) was that all possible financial support for the 1954 excavation work would come from Nicholas G. Morgan, Sr., whom Ferguson described as his chief patron[33]--and only when Morgan's funds were exhausted would Ferguson call on the Church for additional help.

In May 1953 Ferguson went to Mexico for the third time to join the NWAF exploratory group in Tabasco. Unfortunately, most of the effort and money so far had been spent on Ferguson's hunch that Tabasco was the area of Zarahemla, but this had produced nothing substantive.[34] Then, when John L. Sorenson, a graduate student working for NWAF, suggested that Zarahemla was likely in Chiapas, Ferguson took him there on a jeep reconnaissance of the upper Grijalva River area. At Acala (about fifty miles south of Tuxtla Gutiérrez) they found thousands of potsherds and several figurines dating to the B.C. time period in the Preclassic era. Ferguson now enthusiastically accepted Sorenson's notion for the location of Zarahemla. Ferguson wrote to the LDS First Presidency that "now that we have studied the area [at Acala] on the ground and from the air, and have obtained a sampling of ancient artifacts from it, Sorenson and I are of the personal opinion that it is highly probable that it is the land of Zarahemla."[35] Ferguson was confident that within a few years positive identification of Nephite cities would be made, for he was convinced that the artifacts discovered in 1953 were made by Book of Mormon peoples. Because his foremost desire was to produce evidence for the Book of Mormon, Ferguson seemed more interested in trying to determine "if local people had found any figurines of 'horses'" than in documenting new archaeological sites.[36]

In August 1953 Ferguson told the First Presidency that "earth-shaking Book of Mormon discoveries may very well take place in the next field season, or two, as extensive excavations go forward."[37] The next month Ferguson expressed his sentiments that the work of NWAF was providing archaeological support for "some of the amazing and fascinating claims" of the Book of

Mormon.[38] Ferguson was confident that the sites they discovered in May "were occupied by Nephite people during Book of Mormon times" and that, therefore, the first season of NWAF work had been extremely successful.[39]

As it turned out Morgan agreed to only a $1,000 donation, so in September 1953 Ferguson asked the LDS Church for the remaining $29,000 needed, emphasizing that "we have now located what are surely important Book of Mormon cities and towns."[40] Ferguson sent the First Presidency a formal report of the first year's work at Acala. The First Presidency replied through their secretary, Joseph Anderson, their surprise at the request for $29,000; he stated that Ferguson's reference to an agreement of further financial commitment was "a serious misapprehension" and politely declined any further help at all.[41] Ferguson promptly apologized for having overstated the case, explaining that he felt he was not debarred from asking for more help from the church, even though they had made it clear that there was no future commitment, stated or implied.[42]

During this period Ferguson was pleased that Milton R. Hunter made numerous references in his general conference sermons to their joint work on the sixteenth-century accounts and how they relate to the Book of Mormon.[43] Though Ferguson looked forward to getting back to Mexico at the beginning of 1954 to begin excavating the area found the previous May, lack of money meant that no archaeological work could be done that season. The First Presidency again told him that no church financial assistance would be forthcoming.[44] Since he could not get any more money directly from the church, he hoped to get from the First Presidency a strong endorsement of the archaeological project and use it as a lever to influence prospective donors to NWAF. Ferguson prepared a brochure concerning the work of NWAF and his latest scheme was to solicit $200 each from 200 wealthy Mormon families (hoping to get a positive response from 150 of them) to finance the 1955 season.[45] He asked J. Willard Marriott to write to the First Presidency for "a list of 200 of the biggest tithe payers" from the records of the Presiding Bishopric.[46]

At the beginning of 1955 Ferguson's convictions seemed to grow even stronger, and in an emotion-packed letter to the First Presidency he again plead the case for the church's financial support:

> The exploring which was carried out in 1953 with the help of your confidential contribution was highly successful. I know beyond a shadow of doubt that certain of the locations discovered were occupied by Nephites during Book of Mormon times. The importance of the work cannot be overestimated.
>
> After many years of careful study, the real importance of Book of Mormon archaeology has dawned on me. It will take but a moment to explain. The Book of Mormon is the only revelation from God in the history of the world that can possibly be tested by scientific physical evidence. ... To find the city of Jericho is merely to confirm a point of history. To find the city of Zarahemla is to confirm a point of history but it is also to confirm, through tangible physical evidence, divine revelation to the modern world through Joseph Smith, Moroni, and the Urim and Thummim. Thus, Book of Mormon history is revelation that can be tested by archaeology. To confirm Book of Mormon history through archaeological discoveries is to confirm revelation to the modern world. ... I know, and I know it without doubt and without wavering, that we are standing at the doorway of a great Book of Mormon era.[47]

Apparently this argument was persuasive, for he was permitted to make another presentation to the LDS First Presidency on 9 March 1955. At this time Ferguson pointed out that the scholarly world would accept the archaeological discoveries of NWAF, since non-Mormon archaeologists would be used and NWAF was not an official church organization.[48] As a result of this plea, Ferguson received a commitment for $200,000 from the Church, which would be enough money to carry out four seasons of archaeological excavations in Mesoamerica.[49] Ferguson was ecstatic. It had not been an easy task, but his dogged persistence had finally paid off. Ross T. Christensen of the Department of Archaeology at BYU explained his own feeling of jealousy about Ferguson's success:

The New World Archaeological Foundation, headed by
Thomas Stuart Ferguson, has been granted a vast sum to
carry out his archaeological plans. The source of the
money is none other than the First Presidency itself.
. . . Sometimes, I confess, the un-Christian sentiment of
envy arises within me when I see the means with which
some have been blessed, and then contemplate the pinch-
penny conservatism with which we have been treated
here in this department.[50]

Ferguson, knowing that this substantial support from the
LDS Church was now assured, arranged with Edwin M. Shook,
archaeologist of the Carnegie Institution's excavation in Yucatán,
to make a reconnaissance along the Grijalva River near Acala and
Comitán in late April and early May 1955 to determine good sites
for excavation the next year.[51] The test pit by Shook brought
forth many examples of Preclassic pottery and a carbon-14 date
of A.D. 255.[52] This provided further evidence of the value of this
area in gaining increased knowledge of the Preclassic era.[53]

The Anthon Transcript of
Book of Mormon Characters

Ferguson had often wondered about the so-called Anthon
Transcript. This is a copy of the characters (possibly made in
February 1828 by Joseph Smith himself) from the Book of
Mormon plates for Martin Harris to take to Professor Charles
Anthon of New York. In July 1835 Joseph Smith still had a copy
of the inscriptions on the Book of Mormon plates, for at that
time he showed Michael H. Chandler a copy of the "reformed
Egyptian" characters on them.[54] There are two main versions of
the Anthon Transcript: (1) the copy consisting of seven horizontal lines of text (fig. 13),[55] and (2) the 1844 black broadside
with gold letters containing the first three lines of text of the
RLDS copy with some additional characters.[56] However, Anthon describes the characters as being in vertical columns.[57]

In March 1955 Paul M. Hanson, president of the Council of
Twelve Apostles of the Reorganized Church of Jesus Christ of
Latter Day Saints, asked Ferguson if the Anthon Transcript had

ever been given to Egyptologists to be analyzed.[58] Ferguson responded that he knew of no such analysis and then suggested that Hanson write to his friend, William F. Albright of Johns Hopkins University, for the name of the most qualified Egyptologist.[59] Albright suggested Sir Alan H. Gardiner of Oxford, England, and in June 1956 Hanson sent Gardiner a copy of the Anthon Transcript for his comment on the similarity between the Book of Mormon characters and Egyptian writing. Gardiner replied to Hanson: "I see no resemblance between the characters of which you sent me a photograph [the Anthon Transcript] and any form of Egyptian writing."[60] Accordingly, the characters on the Anthon Transcript can not be successfully identified with various forms of Egyptian.

Carl Hugh Jones, curator of anthropology at the Nebraska State Historical Society, compared the Anthon Transcript with two Mesoamerican scripts and found some similarities.[61] Deanne G. Matheny, who formerly taught anthropology at BYU, summarized the current situation by saying that "no one has convincingly demonstrated a link between any of them [the writing systems of Mesoamerica] and any Near Eastern derived system or to anything resembling the Anthon Transcript."[62] Asael C. Lambert, former dean of the graduate school of BYU, compared the Anthon characters with astrological signs and magical talismans.[63] Some suggested a connection between various Masonic symbols and the Anthon Transcript.[64] One scholar pointed out that some of the characters closely resemble hieroglyphics of the Micmac Indians of New England.[65]

Four Mayan codices have survived from pre-Columbian times to the present:[66] the Dresden Codex (fig. 14), the Paris Codex (fig. 15), and the Madrid Codex (fig. 16) of the fourteenth century[67] and the Grolier Codex (fig. 17) of the thirteenth century.[68] These native American screen-fold codices--essentially illustrated storybooks--were made of strips of bark paper and painted with brushes.[69] These Mayan codices are astronomical almanacs providing lists of days for either good or bad luck and the particular gods associated with parts of the calendar.[70] The

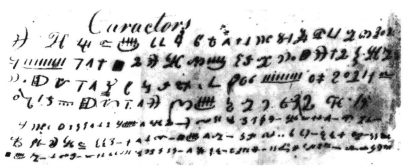

Fig. 13--Anthon transcript, showing characters inscribed on the Book of Mormon plates. Courtesy of Reorganized Church of Jesus Christ of Latter Day Saints Library-Archives.

pages of the Mayan codices "were divided into horizontal sections by red lines, and the order of reading was usually from left to right, top to bottom, remaining in the same horizontal section through one to as many as eight folds, then descending to the next section."[71] The familiar hieroglyphic inscriptions on Classic Mayan stone monuments usually "appear in vertical columns, and these are so lined up that the reading is from left to right and top to bottom, in pairs of glyphs."[72]

In contrast Joseph Smith explained the origin of the title page of the Book of Mormon and specifically states that the text was read like Hebrew, that is, from right to left:

> The Title Page of the Book of Mormon is a literal translation, taken from the very last leaf, on the left hand side of the collection or book of plates, which contained the record which has been translated; the language of the whole running same as all Hebrew writing in general.[73]

The horizontal characters of the Book of Mormon text were inscribed on golden plates. To date no known examples of metal plates with an inscribed text have been found anywhere in the Americas.[74]

John L. Sorenson, professor of anthropology at BYU, claimed that "several examples of possible bar-and-dot numerals (such as the Maya and their neighbors used) can be picked out of the Anthon material."[75] Examination of the transcript shows that there is indeed one instance of a horizontal line with four spaced-dots underneath, and there are five instances which may be a more elaborate form of the same symbol with four short vertical marks above the dots and intersecting the horizontal line, as well as a curving line at the bottom enclosing the dots.[76] Since the Mayan bar-and-dot notation involves a vigesimal number system with up to four dots (each representing one) and up to three bars (each representing five),[77] there is only one Anthon character readable in Mayan notation, but there are two instances in the Anthon Transcript of a horizontal line with nine short vertical marks above it, which cannot fit the bar-and-dot notation.

Expected Confirmation of the Book of Mormon

Early the next year Ferguson excitedly reported to the First Presidency that an NWAF reconnaissance party had discovered ancient potsherds extending for ten miles along the west bank of the Grijalva River. Pleased about how rapidly things were developing, Ferguson felt that soon they would have "vital news for the world concerning the Book of Mormon and the divine calling of Joseph Smith."[78] He was "thrilled beyond measure at the wonderful Nephite sites" found on the Grijalva and now thought that Santa Rosa was "a wonderful candidate for Zarahemla."[79]

Ferguson was aware that Mesoamerica is the only place in the New World where written language was an established tradition. He wanted to discover a decipherable inscription that would identify a Book of Mormon person, place, or event. If one could be found, competent scholars and professional archaeologists might be convinced of the book's historicity. Even the discovery of a script fitting the writing system described in 1 Nephi would be very persuasive, since a writing system is the most complex aspect of culture. In an article published in the LDS publication, *The Millennial Star*, Ferguson reminded his readers of what he believed would constitute the ultimate confirmation of the Book of Mormon:

Fig. 14--Dresden Codex, showing a woman facing a dog (top) and three women facing three deities in amorous poses (bottom). Reproduced from William E. Gates, The Dresden Codex (1932).

The discovery in Mexico or Central America of an ancient writing in one of the early scripts of the Near East and actually mentioning a people, city, person, or event of the Book of Mormon, would of course constitute final and complete vindication of the American prophet, Joseph Smith. . . . Such a discovery must now be considered well within the bounds of possibility.[80]

Similarly, Hugh Nibley, professor of history and religion at BYU, emphasized the value of documentary confirmation of the Book of Mormon: "Nothing short of an inscription which could be read and roughly dated could bridge the gap between what might be called a pre-actualistic archaeology and contact with the realities of Nephite civilization."[81]

Since the preliminary exploratory work had successfully located several Preclassic sites, NWAF was ready to start serious excavations. Explaining why the special executive committee of non-LDS experts should direct the field work and publish the results (just as had been carefully planned when NWAF was organized in 1952), Ferguson said:

We anticipate important discoveries bearing upon the Book of Mormon and deem it wise to have non-L.D.S. personnel in charge of the field operations. Up to this point I have personally played a very active role in directing the explorations and test-excavations, relying largely on the Book of Mormon and the Lord as guides. The results have been excellent. It would seem that now is the time to turn the digging over to the experts. All agree that the sites are [of] major proportions and offer great promise.[82]

Since the carbon-14 measurement on material from Santa Rosa gave the date of 94 B.C. ± 150 years, Ferguson felt that "there is no question but what we have a great Nephite center at the finca [Santa Rosa] area."[83] Once again noting the need to find translatable inscriptions, Ferguson notified the First Presidency in December 1956 that "we are earnestly praying for the discovery of Nephite script--but it may be necessary to work a long time before we are blessed with such good fortune."[84]

Ferguson felt that his work in life was to be an instrument in verifying the historical claims of the Book of Mormon through archaeological excavations in Mesoamerica. Since Milton R.

Fig. 15--Paris Codex, *showing a scorpion, a sea turtle, and a rattlesnake hanging from the constellation band.* Reproduced from Bruce Love, *The Paris Codex* (1994), courtesy of Bibliothèque Nationale de France.

Hunter and a friend were going to do some aerial reconnaissance in Mexico, Ferguson suggested in all seriousness that they circle the mountains in the Tuxtla area "looking for any large rock formations that might contain Ether's cave."[85] Expressing an expectation of important archaeological discoveries in the next three or four years, Ferguson excitedly wrote to Hunter that this work would "shake the entire world to its foundations."[86] Ferguson felt compelled to drive forward with this work and offered his assessment of the Book of Mormon: "The Book of Mormon is like a sleeping volcano, ready to burst forth with knowledge of greatest import for the whole world."[87]

Ferguson knew that it was impossible to verify the existence of miracles and the reality of spiritual experiences, but he was convinced that confirmation of the physical reality of the Book of Mormon civilization would be forthcoming through archaeological discovery. Similarly, Luke P. Wilson, executive director of the Institute for Religious Research, explained the role of archaeology to the Book of Mormon:

> Of course there are limits to what archaeology can investigate. It is not suited to proving or disproving the supernatural claims or spiritual truths of the Book of Mormon. However, by searching for evidence of the civilization described in the Book of Mormon, archaeology can help us evaluate the underlying historical credibility of this scriptural record. Evidence regarding the *historical* claims of the Book of Mormon may well have a bearing on our confidence in its *spiritual* message.[88]

In March 1958 Ferguson expressed to the First Presidency his fervent beliefs and the unique position of the Book of Mormon as a historical document subject to scientific verification:

> For the first time in history, a true prophet of the Lord can be--and is being--vindicated by tangible, physical evidence of an enduring and unimpeachable nature. Joseph Smith was the first prophet, and the only prophet, to reveal the lost and forgotten history of ancient cities of stone--and the Lord saw to it that he was unaided by learned men (for had the Lord included men of learning in the bringing forth of the Book of Mormon, the world would credit the Book to those men)--and now those cities are being found and are beginning to testify that Joseph Smith knew the truth concerning the very ancient cities of Middle America 128 years before the most learned men of the world. . . . The Book of Mormon is either fake or fact. If fake, the cities described in it are nonexistent. If fact--as we know it to be --the cities will be there. If the cities exist, and they do, they constitute tangible, physical, enduring, unimpeachable evidence that Joseph Smith was a true prophet of God and that Jesus Christ lives.[89]

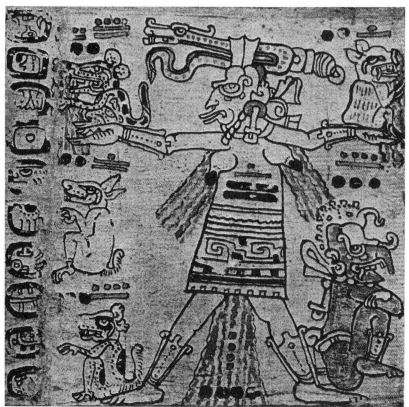

Fig. 16--Madrid Codex, showing a goddess pouring rain water from her armpits and from between her legs. Reproduced from Ferdinand Anders, *Codex Tro-Cortesianus (Codex Madrid)*, (1967), courtesy of Museo de América.

Publication of
"One Fold and One Shepherd"

Utilizing the evidence that had been uncovered by NWAF, in late 1958 Ferguson published *One Fold and One Shepherd* to make known evidence supporting the antiquity of the Book of Mormon. This book gave a legalistic presentation of evidence from post-Conquest chronicles and the available archaeological data to support the Book of Mormon. Ferguson did not always use his evidence in a critical fashion. For example, he quoted without comment a passage from the sixteenth-century Spanish missionary and historian in the Americas, Bartolomé de las Casas, which shows obvious signs of direct influence from Roman Catholic Christianity, even its Trinitarianism.[90] Ferguson now favored the Grijalva as the Book of Mormon River Sidon and completely dropped Jakeman's Usumacinta.[91] In the book Ferguson reported his 1958 trip to Totonicapán, Guatemala, and his futile attempt to locate the original 1554 manuscript of the *Title of the Lords of Totonicapán.*[92]

The evidence that Ferguson presented was not convincing to a non-Mormon audience. As an example, the editors of the *Mysteries of the Ancient Americas* said the following:

> No other document, inscription, or legend now known shows a close correspondence with this [the Book of Mormon] account of the peopling of America, but there are tempting inferences that can be drawn from the evidence that does exist. . . . These suggestive items, however, are not found convincing by traditional scholars of ancient America. They feel that each can be explained as coincidence, as *ex post facto* European influence, or as muddling of the evidence.[93]

An important report in the book was the discovery in October 1957 of cylinder seals at Chiapa de Corzo. Ferguson felt that some of the designs on one of the seals might be Egyptian. In May 1958 he submitted a photograph of the impression made by this cylinder seal to William F. Albright, professor of Semitic languages at Johns Hopkins University, and Albright reported that the seal contained "several clearly recognizable Egyptian hieroglyphs."[94] After the publication of this find in *One Fold and One Shepherd* Bishop Duane G. Hunt, the Roman Catholic Bishop of Salt Lake City, asked Albright for "something with which to refute or destroy the information" about the seal in Ferguson's book, but Albright refused the bishop's request, saying "they are Egyptian hieroglyphs and I cannot deny it."[95] Other scholars, however, have not agreed with Albright's identi-

Fig. 17--Grolier Codex, showing a skeletal Venus, as the evening star, beheading a bound victim. Reproduced from Michael D. Coe, *The Maya Scribe and His World* (1973), courtesy of Grolier Club of New York.

fication. Matthew W. Stirling of the Bureau of American Ethnology in Washington, D.C., stated that Ferguson had made too much of the fact that "a simple design on a Chiapas stamp" resembled a hieroglyph.[96] J. Alden Mason, field advisor of

NWAF, cautioned that "an Egyptologist's decision that an element in the seal--or several elements--*might* be debased or corrupted Egyptian glyphs will not be enough; there must be elements that couldn't be anything else, or better, a series of elements that would make sense."[97] Since consideration of the entire seal as Egyptian does not produce any plausible translation, David H. Kelley of the University of Nebraska concluded that the simple elements do not constitute "presumptive evidence of Egyptian influences by themselves."[98]

A major argument in *One Fold and One Shepherd* was that New World cultural development was significantly influenced by transoceanic transfer of ideas from the Old World, rather than by independent invention.[99] Ferguson listed 298 cultural parallels between the Near East and Mesoamerica.[100] He included some very general traits or objects, which are found in many diverse cultures, such as: aqueducts, bows, bronze objects, chickens, childless women considered shameful, coconuts, eagles, gods in the image of man, helmets for warriors, historical annals, human sacrifices, idols, irrigation canals, kilts, knitting, maces, metallurgy, nose rings, oil lamps, pearls, phallic symbols, ropes, sandals, slaves, slings, spears, textiles, thrones, tunics, turbans, and umbrellas.[101] It is not the number of parallels but the significance of them that must be carefully assessed.[102] Also, the cultural parallels being compared should be from two specific geographical areas and from nearly the same time period.[103] The general traits used by Ferguson could be used to support the thesis that Book of Mormon peoples migrated to Southeast Asia or almost any other selected area.[104] Sometimes the parallels provided by Ferguson are improperly compared.[105]

Merely listing parallels has been called the "shopping list fallacy," since the parallels are not significant *unless* they are either very complex or uniquely found in the two cultures being compared.[106] One needs to exercise caution in drawing parallels between two cultures, especially in reaching any conclusions from the comparisons. Basil C. Hedrick, director of the University of Alaska Museum, pointed out that "simply because a given motif may have a similar appearance or connotation in two widely spread locales does not necessarily infer [imply], let alone prove, that that motif was directly disseminated from one place to another."[107] Ferguson's argument would certainly have been more forceful if he had discussed only the most specific and detailed parallels between the two cultures. Michael D. Coe, professor of anthropology at Yale University, said that Ferguson relied "on a vast quantity of archaeological and documentary data, some sound, some poor, and some really unreliable."[108]

In *One Fold and One Shepherd* Ferguson affirmed that:

The Book of Mormon, purporting to contain the very ancient history of a given area during a given period of time, must fall into one of the following ratings:

I	II	III
FICTION	HISTORY preserved and translated by man.	HISTORY preserved and translated by Jehovah-Christ.

Number II is eliminated at once--by the admissions of the scholastic experts of the world, which have disclaimed the Book of Mormon. This leaves the two extreme positions for consideration:

I	II
FAKE--FRAUD the named towns, cities, people, nations, civilizations, and events, being fictitious under this choice, should never be found.	REVEALED HISTORY-- A TRULY DIVINE BOOK the named towns, cities, people, nations, civilizations, and events, being truly historical, can be and will be found-- NOW if we look.[109]

Izapa Stela 5
and Lehi's Dream

In *One Fold and One Shepherd* Ferguson also cited the recent study on Stela 5 at Izapa, which M. Wells Jakeman, in a controversial identification, interpreted as a representation of Lehi's dream of the Tree of Life in 1 Nephi 8.[110] A miniature model of the Lehi Tree-of-Life Stone has "taken on the function of a kind of cult object" in the LDS community, since many homes have a replica in the living room serving as a conversation piece about the Book of Mormon.[111] Jakeman claimed to have deciphered the personal names Lehi and Nephi from name-glyphs on the stela:

> For the meaning of the name Lehi is the jaws--especially the upper jaw--in side view, i.e., "cheek." And we have already noted that Feature 9, the *cipactli* glyph held above the old bearded man, mainly depicts a pair of huge jaws (those of the crocodile)--especially the upper jaw--in side view, i.e., a great cheek! That is, this glyph is essentially a portrayal of what the name Lehi means. It therefore constitutes--*whether intended or not*--a symbolic recording of that name. . . .
> There is, however, a defensible Egyptian derivation [of Nephi] that has not previously been noted. This is that the name Nephi . . . is Lehi's rendering of the Egyptian name of the personification or "god" of grain in Egyptian belief, N(e)pri (from *n[é]prî*, the Egyptian word for grain). . . .[112]

The interpretation offered by Jakeman impressed many LDS General Authorities. For example, on a trip to Izapa in June 1960 Marion G. Romney, a member of the Quorum of the Twelve Apostles, wrote in his diary: "It could well be what he [Jakeman] says it is--a representation of that dream which Lehi had."[113]

However, Mormon archaeologist V. Garth Norman said that "the inaccuracies in the Jakeman reproduction of Stela 5" make his interpretations invalid.[114] Jakeman has been charged with altering the latex mold of the stela to fit his interpretation.[115] Norman supported Jakeman's use of the *cipactli* glyph (a bared jawbone) being correlated with the Hebrew word *lᵉchî* "jawbone" or "cheek,"[116] but doubted Jakeman's "interpretation of 'Nephi' for the other name glyph."[117] Gareth W. Lowe, archaeologist for NWAF, in summation of his analysis of this monument, said: "I cannot escape the impression that Stela 5 presents an original creation myth, closely similar to those recorded very much later in the Popol Vuh."[118] Coe, representing non-Mormon archaeologists, said that Jakeman's parallels are "a matter of mere chance based upon only superficial similarities."[119] Jakeman's interpretation of Izapa Stela 5 which connects it with the Book of Mormon remains unproven speculation, while the interpretation which understands this monument as a Mesoamerican creation account, like the Popol Vuh, gains more support.[120]

Reorganization of the New World Archaeological Foundation

Jack Dunford, president of the BYU chapter of the University Archaeological Society, extended an invitation to Ferguson to speak in January 1959 to the campus chapter, because NWAF was excavating year after year in proposed Book of Mormon lands.[121] Both M. Wells Jakeman and Ross T. Christensen advised Dunford against inviting Ferguson.[122] Ferguson agreed to come to Provo, feeling that it would be good to give publicity to the work of NWAF, as well as to discuss his recent book, *One Fold and One Shepherd*. Ferguson told the group that NWAF had found along the Grijalva River fifty sites which by radiocarbon dating fit into the Book of Mormon period, but the most important discovery was a cylinder seal with Egyptian hieroglyphics. Ferguson also predicted to the archaeology enthusiasts that "history books will be rewritten very soon, and will have to take into consideration Book of Mormon accounts."[123]

When the first four years of LDS Church funding was scheduled to run out by the fall of 1959, Ferguson was assured that NWAF would continue to receive funds through BYU, so that NWAF could merge with the sporadic archaeological investigations performed by the Archaeology Department. In August 1959 Ernest L. Wilkinson, president of BYU, along with Earl C. Crockett and John Bernhard, deliberated "whether we should propose to the First Presidency a large excavation program in Central America to verify the Book of Mormon."[124] Since there was still no definite word about the future of NWAF by October 1959, Ferguson filed a petition with the National Science Foundation for a $432,000 grant covering a five-year period.[125] He did this in order to carry on the NWAF work just in case the LDS Church "deserts the ship."[126]

In January 1960 Ferguson traveled to Salt Lake City and was allowed an hour with the First Presidency to plead the cause of NWAF. President David O. McKay described Ferguson as being "very enthusi-astic regarding the accomplishments of his organization."[127] The next month Ferguson came up with a novel idea to carry on Book of Mormon archaeological research. He suggested that a two or three year test be conducted in which Jakeman and Christensen of BYU be given $50,000 per year and NWAF be given $50,000 per year since the former would work in sites on the Usumacinta and the latter would continue work in sites on the Grijalva. Ferguson justified this proposal by saying that "one or the other of those rivers is doubtless the Sidon."[128] Later Ferguson also petitioned the Ford Foundation for support for NWAF, and two of his main points were the discovery of Egyptian hieroglyphs and Izapa Stela 5.[129]

In June 1960 a delegation of two church leaders (apostles Mark E. Petersen and Marion G. Romney) and two BYU officials (Ernest L. Wilkinson, president, and Joseph T. Bentley, comptroller) went to Mexico to observe NWAF operations in Chiapas and make a recommendation whether the LDS Church should continue the NWAF. In Mexico City the group was joined by Daniel Taylor Pierce, superintendent of Church Schools in Mexico.[130] They inspected the NWAF exhibit in the state museum at Tuxtla Gutiérrez and the sites of Chiapa de Corzo, Vista del Rio, El Mirador, and Izapa.[131] Wilkinson reminisced that "this committee was not only impressed with what they saw, but found that the Mexican government was strongly supportive of what the Foundation was doing."[132] During the return plane flight both Petersen and Romney sounded enthusiastic about the project. Ferguson knew they were impressed with what they had seen, but he was uncertain about NWAF's future and waited anxiously for a final decision from BYU. The ninety-page report which was submitted to the First Presidency was positive, and led to the announcement that NWAF would be reorganized as part of a new and continued support by the LDS Church through BYU.[133] Becoming part of the university structure would give NWAF more professional prestige, and it also allowed employees to receive BYU benefits. In December 1960 Ferguson still did not know how he would fit into the new organization of NWAF. He wrote to Elder LeGrand Richards of the Quorum of the Twelve: "I burn with a desire to see the work expanded and pushed forward with zeal."[134] Ferguson was still confident that the future would bring archaeological discoveries in Mesoamerica confirming the Book of Mormon.

Before the official announcement was made, the recommended leaders of the new Archaeological Committee (which would supervise the work of NWAF) had been decided. Apostle Marion G. Romney was named chairman with Tom Ferguson as his assistant.[135] However, President David O. McKay changed this arrangement and appointed Howard W. Hunter, the youngest member of the Quorum of the Twelve Apostles, as chairman in January 1961.[136] At the same time Ferguson was demoted to the position of secretary. Despite the severe blow to his pride, Ferguson kept a brave face and wrote to Apostle Hunter, asking what his duties would be.[137] Ferguson had spent an extraordinary amount of money, energy, and time on NWAF during the previous thirteen years. Yet in a phone conversation the next week Ferguson told Hunter that he would be "content to eat whatever piece of pie is thrown my way, however small or humble."[138] From this time until his death, Ferguson served in this comparatively minor role of secretary to the reorganized BYU-NWAF.

Expected Verification
of the Book of Mormon

Ferguson was still expecting to discover some inscriptions which would date to the time of Christ. Heavy digging would be done at Chiapa de Corzo and he anticipated that evidence would be discovered of an ancient script of "those people whose identity is still unknown through scientific endeavors."[139]

Ferguson sent a letter to the editor of *Christianity Today*, in which he affirmed, by quoting *One Fold and One Shepherd*, that the Book of Mormon is "the only revelation ever given to man concerning tangible things--in it the Lord revealed names of cities and nations. . . . The cities are now being found."[140] Ferguson's letter brought a response from Harold H. Hougey, a Church of Christ minister, in which he challenged the statement that "the discovery of ancient cities in Central America is proving the truth of the Book of Mormon."[141] Ferguson clarified his position directly to Hougey, by saying that "when money, time, and effort have been spent on the Book of Mormon in proportion to what has been spent on the Bible, it is my opinion that we will have an equal number of Book-of-Mormon cities identified."[142] In reply Hougey promised Ferguson that "if and when Book of Mormon cities are positively identified," he would readily accept its authenticity.[143] Then Ferguson set a timetable for his expected positive identification of Book of Mormon cities: ". . . I sincerely anticipate this happening within the next ten years."[144]

In June 1963 after receiving a telegram that Alfred V. Kidder had passed away, Ferguson wrote to his widow:

> The balance of my lifetime will be spent in direct and indirect effort to seek out the facts from the earth in Ted's great land--Middle America--relating to the alleged appearance there of Jesus Christ eleven months after His crucifixion in Jerusalem. I firmly believe that this claim of the Book of Mormon is true, and if it is, all of us, including you and my wonderful friend, Ted, shall one day experience life beyond this one.[145]

Scattered comments surface in Ferguson's letters indicating that he wondered why the evidence for the antiquity of the Book of Mormon was not coming forth as expected. He was genuinely disappointed that the archaeological support for the Book of Mormon was not being discovered at the rate he had anticipated. By the mid-1960s hope of finding translatable inscriptions still persisted, but it had become more distant. His major goal in life-- proving that Jesus Christ really appeared in ancient Mexico after his crucifixion and resurrection--would never "be achieved," he wrote, "until significant ancient manuscript discoveries are made. I hope it happens during our lifetime. It could."[146]

Though the efforts of NWAF accumulated a phenomenal amount of information about the important Preclassic era and gained the respect of Mesoamerican scholars, after years of excavation there was still no specific archaeological or inscriptional verification of any of the Book of Mormon peoples or places. After summarizing various aspects of New World prehistory John A. Price, professor of anthropology at York University, pointed out that "there are simply no gaps in the record of archaeological surveys and excavations large enough to admit of the possible existence of Near Eastern style societies anywhere in the New World."[147]

In a similar manner Michael D. Coe asserted the following about the state of the archaeological evidence:

> Let me now state uncategorically that as far as I know there is not one professionally trained archaeologist, who is *not* a Mormon, who sees any scientific justification for believing the foregoing to be true [i.e., that the Book of Mormon is an authentic document describing a New World civilization],[148] and I would like to state that there are quite a few Mormon archaeologists who join this group. . . .
>   The bare facts of the matter are that nothing, absolutely nothing, has ever shown up in any New World excavation which would suggest to a dispassionate observer that the Book of Mormon, as claimed by Joseph Smith, is a historical document relating to the history of early migrants to our hemisphere. The archaeological data would strongly suggest that the Liahonas[149] are right about the Book of Mormon.[150]

In 1993 Coe reaffirmed his opinion:

> I have seen no archaeological evidence before or since that [1973] date which would convince me that it [the Book of Mormon] is anything but a fanciful creation by an unusually gifted individual living in upstate New York in the early nineteenth century.[151]

All the available evidence indicates that at least through the mid-1960s Ferguson had a strong, unwavering belief in the authenticity of the Book of Mormon; he continued to hope for evidence to demonstrate its historicity. However, with many others during the Civil Rights Movement he questioned the rightness of the Mormon Church's ban on priesthood for the blacks, and due to that position he developed a quiet skepticism concerning the Book of Abraham, which speaks of someone being cursed "as pertaining to the Priesthood" (Abr. 1:26). The stage was set for a radical change in his understanding of that Mormon scripture.

Notes

1. Hugh Nibley, *An Approach to the Book of Mormon*, 3d ed., The Collected Works of Hugh Nibley, ed. John W. Welch (Salt Lake City: Deseret Book Co., 1988; Provo, Utah: Foundation for Ancient Research and Mormon Studies, 1988), 6:442, with emphasis in original.

2. Thomas Stuart Ferguson, letter to LeGrand Richards, [after 2 February 1951], in the Thomas Stuart Ferguson Collection, Manuscript 1549, Special Collections and Manuscripts, Harold B. Lee Library, Brigham Young University, Provo, Utah; hereafter abbreviated to Ferguson Collection, BYU.

3. Alfred V. Kidder, letter to Thomas Stuart Ferguson, 9 January 1951, in Ferguson Collection, BYU.

4. Ferguson, letter to Alfred V. Kidder, 23 July 1951, in Ferguson Collection, BYU.

5. Raymond T. Matheny, "El Mirador: An Early Maya Metropolis Uncovered," *National Geographic Magazine* 172 (September 1987): 321, 329, indicated that an excellent Preclassic site is the city-state of El Mirador, which flourished from about 100 B.C. to A.D. 150. See Raymond T. Matheny, "Investigations at El Mirador, Petén, Guatemala," *National Geographic Research* 2 (1986): 332-53.

6. Michael D. Coe, *The Maya*, 5th ed, fully rev. and exp., Ancient Peoples and Places (London: Thames and Hudson, 1993), 9, 23-24, dated the time periods for Mayan culture as follows: the Archaic Period covers 7500 to 1800 B.C.; the Early Preclassic Period covers 1800 to

1000 B.C.; the Middle Preclassic Period covers 1000 to 300 B.C.; the Late Preclassic Period covers 300 B.C. to A.D. 250; the Early Classic Period covers A.D. 250 to 600; the Late Classic Period covers A.D. 600 to 800; the Terminal Classic Period covers A.D. 800 to 925; the Early Post-Classic Period covers A.D. 925 to 1200; the Late Post-Classic Period covers A.D. 1200 to 1530.

7. Alfred V. Kidder and Ferguson, "Plan for Archaeological Work in an Important Zone in Middle America," typescript, 1951, in the John Willard and Alice Sheets Marriott Collection, Manuscript 164, Box 70, Fd 6, Manuscripts Division, J. Willard Marriott Library, University of Utah, Salt Lake City; hereafter abbreviated to Marriott Collection.

8. Ferguson, letter to John A. Widtsoe, 17 April 1951, in Ferguson Collection, BYU.

9. Ferguson, letter to John A. Widtsoe, 14 November 1951, in Ferguson Collection, BYU.

10. Ferguson, letter to David O. McKay, 14 December 1951, in Ferguson Collection, BYU.

11. Ferguson, letter to Mr. and Mrs. Alfred V. Kidder, 16 November 1953, in Ferguson Collection, BYU. In Bruce W. Warren and Thomas Stuart Ferguson [sic], *The Messiah in Ancient America* (Provo, UT: Book of Mormon Research Foundation, 1987), 260, Warren shortchanged the money, saying that Ferguson "scraped together $3,000, a painfully small sum but sufficient to fund the year's short field expedition."

12. John A. Widtsoe, letter to Ferguson, 20 June 1952, in the Nicholas Groesbeck Morgan Collection, Accession 1500, Box 1, Fd 5, Manuscripts Division, J. Willard Marriott Library, University of Utah, Salt Lake City; hereafter abbreviated to Morgan Collection.

13. For an account of Kidder's involvement with Ferguson in the beginnings of the NWAF, see Richard B. Woodbury, *Alfred V. Kidder* (New York and London: Columbia University Press, 1973), 83-84.

14. For an autobiography of Widtsoe, see John A. Widtsoe, *In a Sunlit Land* (Salt Lake City: Deseret News Press, 1952).

15. For a biography of Morgan, see Jean R. Paulson, *Nicholas Groesbeck Morgan: The Man Who Moved City Hall* (Provo, UT: Press Publishing Limited, 1979).

16. For a short autobiography of Willey, see Glyn Daniel and Christopher Chippindale, eds., *The Pastmasters: Eleven Modern Pioneers of Archaeology* (New York: Thames and Hudson, 1989), 100-13.

17. Ferguson, letter to Earl C. Crockett, 23 February 1960, in Joseph T. Bentley Collection, Box 52, Fd 4, Administrative Council, Locked Case, Special Collections and Manuscripts, Harold B. Lee Library, Brigham Young University, Provo, UT; hereafter abbreviated to Bentley Collection.

18. After being sent a complimentary copy of *Ancient America and the Book of Mormon*, Gordon F. Ekholm, letter to Ferguson, 26 April 1951, in Ferguson Collection, BYU, responded: "I am inclined to believe at the present time that there may have been some historical

connection between the peoples of Middle America and those of southern Asia, and thus indirectly with early peoples in the Near East."

19. Alfred V. Kidder, letter to don Ignacio Marquina, 21 July 1952, quoted in Ferguson, "Introduction concerning the New World Archaeological Foundation," *New World Archaeological Foundation*, publication no. 1 (Orinda, CA: New World Archaeological Foundation, 1956), 4, with emphasis in original.

20. Ferguson, letter to L. Bryce Boyer, 7 November 1952, in Ferguson Collection, BYU.

21. J. Alden Mason, "Foreword," *Research in Chiapas, Mexico*, Papers of the New World Archaeological Foundation, nos. 1-4 (Orinda, CA: New World Archaeological Foundation, 1959), iii, with emphasis in original. Likewise, Ernest L. Wilkinson and Leonard J. Arrington, eds., *Brigham Young University: The First One Hundred Years* (Provo, UT: Brigham Young University Press, 1976), 3:123, explained that "while an underlying Mormon hope for illuminating results in relation to the Book of Mormon was clear enough, the operational rule was impeccably down-the-line scientific archaeology."

22. "Great Archaeologists Explore Book of Mormon Lands," news release, 18 December 1952, New World Archaeological Foundation, in Box 1, Fd 2, Morgan Collection.

23. Ferguson, letter to Alfred V. Kidder, 16 February 1953, in Ferguson Collection, BYU.

24. Ferguson, letter to Mr. and Mrs. J. Willard Marriott, 17 December 1952, in Box 70, Fd 6, Marriott Collection.

25. Ferguson, letter to Milton R. Hunter, 11 April 1953, in Thomas Stuart Ferguson Collection, Accession 1350, Manuscripts Division, J. Willard Marriott Library, University of Utah; hereafter abbreviated to Ferguson Collection, UU.

26. Ferguson, letter to Mr. and Mrs. J. Willard Marriott, 20 May 1953, in Box 17, Fd 8, Marriott Collection. Warren, *Messiah*, 262, reported that Ferguson "asked for $30,000 for the 1954 field season," but the request was for $15,000 for the rest of 1953.

27. Ferguson, diary, 9 April 1953, in Ferguson Collection, BYU.

28. Ferguson, letter to Mr. and Mrs. J. Willard Marriott, 10 April 1953, in Box 9, Fd 17, Marriott Collection.

29. David O. McKay, diary, 13 February 1954, in the David O. McKay Collection, Manuscript 668, Manuscripts Division, J. Willard Marriott Library, University of Utah, Salt Lake City. That same day President McKay spoke to the local members on "Book of Mormon Evidence," and having heard a rumor about a River Lamoni and a River Moroni, asked Gordon Romney to authenticate it.

30. Ferguson, letter to the First Presidency, 10 April 1953, in Ferguson Collection, BYU.

31. J. Reuben Clark, Jr., letter to Ferguson, 17 April 1953, in Ferguson Collection, BYU.

32. Ferguson, letter to J. Willard Marriott, 1 July 1953, in Box 17, 8, Marriott Collection.

33. Ferguson, letter to Alfred V. Kidder, 25 November 1952, in Box 1, Fd 5, Morgan Collection.

34. John L. Sorenson, *The Geography of Book of Mormon Events: A Source Book*, rev. ed. (Provo, UT: Foundation for Ancient Research and Mormon Studies, 1992), 89.

35. Ferguson, letter to the First Presidency, 4 June 1953, in Box 70, Fd 7, Marriott Collection.

36. John L. Sorenson, "Addendum," to John Gee's review of *By His Own Hand upon Papyrus: A New Look at the Joseph Smith Papyri*, by Charles M. Larson, in *Review of Books on the Book of Mormon* 4 (1992): 118.

37. Ferguson, letter to the First Presidency, 14 August 1953, in Ferguson Collection, BYU.

38. Ferguson, letter to John T. Williamson, 10 September 1953, in Ferguson Collection, BYU.

39. Ferguson, letter to the First Presidency, 10 September 1953, in Ferguson Collection, BYU.

40. Ferguson, letter to the First Presidency, 21 September 1953, in Ferguson Collection, BYU.

41. Joseph Anderson, letter to Ferguson, 9 October 1953, in Ferguson Collection, BYU.

42. Ferguson, letter to the First Presidency, 16 October 1953, in Ferguson Collection, BYU.

43. Milton R. Hunter, Conference Talks, in *One Hundred Twenty-fifth Semi-annual Conference of the Church of Jesus Christ of Latter-day Saints*, October 1954, 106-14, and in *One Hundred Twenty-fifth Annual Conference of the Church of Jesus Christ of Latter-day Saints*, April 1955, 102-107.

44. David O. McKay, Stephen L. Richards, and J. Reuben Clark, Jr., letter to Ferguson, 2 June 1954, in Ferguson Collection, BYU.

45. Ferguson, letter to the First Presidency, 28 September 1954, in Ferguson Collection, BYU.

46. Ferguson, letter to Bill [J. Willard Marriott], 11 October 1954, in Box 70, Fd 7, Marriott Collection.

47. Ferguson, letter to the First Presidency, 27 January 1955, in Ferguson Collection, BYU.

48. Ferguson, notes of presentation to First Presidency, 9 March 1955, in Ferguson Collection, BYU.

49. Ferguson, letter to the First Presidency, 18 March 1955, and Stephen L. Richards and J. Reuben Clark, Jr., letter to Ferguson, 15 September 1955, in Ferguson Collection, BYU. Warren, *Messiah*, 265, incorrectly reported the amount granted as $250,000 and the time period as five years.

50. Ross T. Christensen, letter to Clark S. Knowlton, 1 November 1955, in the Clark S. Knowlton Collection, Accession 153, Manuscripts Division, J. Willard Marriott Library, University of Utah, Salt Lake City; hereafter abbreviated to Knowlton Collection.

51. Ferguson, *One Fold and One Shepherd* (San Francisco: Books of

California, 1958; Salt Lake City: Olympus Publishing Co., 1962), 260. Edwin M. Shook, "An Archaeological Reconnaissance in Chiapas, Mexico," in *New World Archaeological Foundation*, publication no. 1 (Orinda, CA: New World Archaeological Foundation, 1956), 20-33.

52. Warren, *Messiah*, 264, pointed out that more recent carbon-14 dating methods lowered this date to the early first century A.D.

53. Warren, ibid., 264-65, reversed the historical order of events, suggesting that Ferguson's being "armed with this persuasive analysis" of Shook was a significant factor in receiving the long-awaited approval of LDS funding. The documents show that the announcement of LDS financial support preceded Shook's reconnaissance.

54. Oliver Cowdery, letter to William Frye, 22 December 1835, partially printed in "Egyptian Mummies--Ancient Records," *Latter Day Saints' Messenger and Advocate* 2 (December 1835): 235, said that Joseph Smith showed Chandler "a number of characters like those upon the writings of Mr. C. [i.e., the Egyptian papyri owned by Chandler] which were previously copied from the plates, containing the history of the Nephites, or book of Mormon."

55. The seven-lined sheet entitled "Caractors" is located in the archives of the Reorganized Church of Jesus Christ of Latter Day Saints, Independence, MO. The exact provenance of this Anthon Transcript is not known, but it corresponds closely with the broadside published in Nauvoo in 1844 and the 21 December 1844 issue of the LDS newspaper in New York, *The Prophet*.

56. Copies of "The Stick of Joseph" broadside are located in Special Collections and Manuscripts, Harold B. Lee Library, Brigham Young University, Provo, UT, and Archives, Historical Department, The Church of Jesus Christ of Latter-day Saints, Salt Lake City.

57. Renewed interest in the Anthon Transcript developed when Mark Hofmann brought forth in 1980 a new manuscript with columns of Book of Mormon characters. After the murders of Steven F. Christensen and Kathleen W. Sheets, Hofmann was imprisoned for their deaths and it was shown that he had forged this transcript of characters by using the Anthon accounts. See Linda Sillitoe and Allen D. Roberts, *Salamander: The Story of the Mormon Forgery Murders* (Salt Lake City: Signature Books, 1988), 235-41, 488-92, 538-39, and Richard E. Turley, Jr., *Victims: The LDS Church and the Mark Hofmann Case* (Urbana and Chicago: University of Illinois Press, 1992), 24-39, 296-97, 314-17, 348.

58. Paul M. Hanson, letter to Ferguson, 22 March 1955, in Ferguson Collection, BYU.

59. Ferguson, letter to Paul M. Hanson, 29 March 1955, in Ferguson Collection, BYU. At the end of this letter Ferguson told Hanson that "it is our earnest prayer, of course, that we will find significant Book of Mormon evidences."

60. Paul M. Hanson, "The Transcript from the Plates of the Book of Mormon," *The Saints' Herald* 103 (12 November 1956): 1098. Hanson solicited and received the opinions of two other Egyptian experts. William C. Hayes said: "The inscription of which you enclosed a photo-

stat in your letter of June 4 could conceivably have been an inaccurate copy of an Egyptian account or something of the sort written in hieratic script"; and John A. Wilson said: "This is not Egyptian writing, as known to the Egyptologist. It obviously is not hieroglyphic, nor the 'cursive hieroglyphic' as used in the Book of the Dead." John A. Wilson, letter to Ferguson, 5 February 1957, in Ferguson Collection, BYU, said that the Anthon Transcript "cannot be recognized or read as any form of ancient Egyptian from the beginning of writing in Egypt about 3000 B.C. to the terminal stage of Coptic about 1000 A.D."

61. Carl Hugh Jones, "The 'Anthon Transcript' and Two Meso-american Cylinder Seals," *Newsletter and Proceedings of the S.E.H.A.* [Society for Early Historic Archaeology], no. 122 (September 1970): 1-8.

62. Deanne G. Matheny, "Does the Shoe Fit? A Critique of the Limited Tehuántepec Geography," in *New Approaches to the Book of Mormon: Explorations in Critical Methodology*, ed. Brent Lee Metcalfe (Salt Lake City: Signature Books, 1993), 321.

63. Asael Carlyle Lambert Collection, Manuscript 35, Boxes 5 and 52, Manuscripts Division, J. Willard Marriott Library, University of Utah, Salt Lake City.

64. David J. Buerger, "A Preliminary Approach to Linguistic Aspects of the Anthon Transcript," typescript, 1978, 7-8, in the H. Michael Marquardt Collection, Accession 900, Box 47, Fd 6, Manuscripts Division, J. Willard Marriott Library, University of Utah, Salt Lake City.

65. Edward H. Ashment, "The Book of Mormon and the Anthon Transcript: An Interim Report," *Sunstone* 5 (May-June 1980): 30.

66. All four Mayan codices are reproduced in color in Thomas A. Lee, Jr., *Los Códices Mayas: Introducción y Bibliografía* (Tuxtla Gutiérrez, Chiapas: Universidad Autónoma de Chiapas, 1985). Paul R. Cheesman, "External Evidences of the Book of Mormon," in *By Study and Also by Faith*, ed. John M. Lundquist and Stephen D. Ricks (Salt Lake City: Deseret Book Co., 1990; Provo, UT: Foundation for Ancient Research and Mormon Studies, 1990), 2:81, referred to two additional Mayan codices located in the Vatican Library, but he meant Mixtec codices. Paul R. Cheesman, *Ancient Writing on Metal Plates: Archaeological Findings Support Mormon Claims* (Bountiful, UT: Horizon Publishers, 1985), 43-45, earlier gave the correct identifications.

67. Ferdinand Anders, ed., *Codex Dresdensis, Sächsische Landes-bibliothek Dresden* (Graz, Austria: Akademische Druck- und Verlags-anstalt, 1975). Ferdinand Anders, ed., *Codex Tro-Cortesianus (Codex Madrid), Museo de América, Madrid: Einleitung und Summary* (Graz, Austria: Akademische Druck- und Verlagsanstalt, 1967). Bruce Love, *The Paris Codex: Handbook for a Maya Priest* (Austin: University of Texas Press, 1994).

68. Robert J. Sharer, *The Ancient Maya*, 5th ed. (Stanford, CA: Stanford University Press, 1994), 603, indicated that some scholars consider the Grolier Codex to be a forgery since "the style of the pictures is incorrect" and it portrays the Venus almanac "in a simplistic

fashion." However, John B. Carlson, "America's Ancient Skywatchers," *National Geographic* 177 (March 1990): 99, indicated that the Venus cycle is accurate and the bark paper dates to the thirteenth century.

69. Coe, *Maya*, 173, indicated that "pictorial representations on Classic Maya funerary pottery show that in Classic times the codices had jaguar-skin covers, and were painted by scribes using brush or feather pens dipped in black or red paint."

70. George E. Stuart, "The Calendar," in Gene S. Stuart and George E. Stuart, *Lost Kingdoms of the Maya* (Washington, D.C.: National Geographic Society, 1993), 187.

71. Sharer, *Maya*, 599. The reverse order of reading is known, but when the texts are to be read from right to left, then the glyphs with recognizable faces are oriented to the right.

72. Michael D. Coe, "Early Steps in the Evolution of Maya Writing," in *Origins of Religious Art and Iconography in Preclassic Mesoamerica*, ed. Henry B. Nicholson, UCLA Latin American Studies, no. 31 ([Los Angeles:] UCLA Latin American Center Publications and Ethnic Arts Council of Los Angeles, 1976), 110.

73. Dean C. Jessee, ed., *The Papers of Joseph Smith* (Salt Lake City: Deseret Book Co., 1989), 1:300. The five words "and not by any means" appeared in the original but were struck out only to reappear in the subsequent clause, probably indicating that this passage was written down at dictation. This statement about the Book of Mormon title page was published in Joseph Smith, "History of Joseph Smith," *Times and Seasons* 3 (15 October 1842): 943.

74. John L. Sorenson, *An Ancient American Setting for the Book of Mormon* (Salt Lake City: Deseret Book Co., 1985; Provo, UT: Foundation for Ancient Research and Mormon Studies, 1985), 283. Paul R. Cheesman and Millie F. Cheesman, *Ancient American Indians: Their Origins, Civilizations and Old World Connections* (Bountiful, UT: Horizon Publishers, 1991), 185, showed a pre-Columbian gold plate from Peru with various designs, but it does not qualify as writing. Michael T. Griffith, *Refuting the Critics: Evidences of the Book of Mormon's Authenticity* (Bountiful, UT: Horizon Publishers, 1993), 46, reported the native Indians of Chiapas, "claimed their people possessed a record written by their ancestors which was engraved on gold leaves," but this oral tradition is derived from the unreliable Harold T. Wilkins, *Mysteries of Ancient South America* (New York: Citadel Press, 1956), 180.

75. John L. Sorenson, "The Book of Mormon as a Mesoamerican Codex," *Newsletter and Proceedings of the S.E.H.A.*, no. 139 (December 1976): 3. Immediately previous to this assertion, Sorenson rightly cautioned about comparing the Anthon Transcript with Mayan hieroglyphs: "An active imagination could see some parallels between the Anthon Transcript characters and certain Maya glyphs, but of course such random, perhaps strained, comparisons are of little value."

76. One of these five instances does not have the four dots.

77. John S. Justeson, "The Origin of Writing Systems: Preclassic Mesoamerica," *World Archaeology* 17 (February 1986): 440-41.

78. Ferguson, letter to the First Presidency, 31 January 1956, in Ferguson Collection, BYU.

79. Ferguson, letter to Milton R. Hunter, 5 June 1956, in Ferguson Collection, BYU. Though Ferguson changed his suggested identification of Zarahemla several times, the difficulty of understanding its location has been increased by a textual error in earlier editions of the Book of Mormon. For the explanation of the loss of ten words about the land between Zarahemla and Bountiful from all editions of the Book of Mormon from 1837 to 1976, see the author's "Changes in Early Texts of the Book of Mormon," *The Ensign* 6 (September 1976): 81.

80. Ferguson, "The World's Strangest Book: The Book of Mormon," *The Millennial Star* 118 (February 1956): 42-46.

81. Hugh Nibley, *Since Cumorah: The Book of Mormon in the Modern World*, 2d ed., The Collected Works of Hugh Nibley, ed. John W. Welch (Salt Lake City: Deseret Book Co., 1988; Provo, UT: Foundation for Ancient Research and Mormon Studies, 1988), 7:213. William J. Hamblin, review of *Archaeology and the Book of Mormon*, by Jerald Tanner and Sandra Tanner, in *Review of Books on the Book of Mormon* 5 (1993): 271, suggested the same requirement to confirm the Book of Mormon: "What, then, would provide conclusive proof of the historicity of the Book of Mormon? Perhaps the only type of discovery which would be conclusive would be a dated inscription, discovered and interpreted by a non-Mormon archaeologist in an undisturbed archaeological context, which makes explicit mention of people, places, or events unique to the Book of Mormon. Unless such an inscription should be discovered, the best we will be able to establish is plausibility."

82. Ferguson, letter to the First Presidency, 20 September 1956, in Ferguson Collection, BYU.

83. Ferguson, letter to the First Presidency, 27 November 1956, in Ferguson Collection, BYU.

84. Ferguson, letter to the First Presidency, 12 December 1956, in Ferguson Collection, BYU.

85. Ferguson, letter to Milton R. Hunter, 11 April 1957, in Ferguson Collection, BYU.

86. Ferguson, letter to Milton R. Hunter, 10 May 1957, in Ferguson Collection, BYU.

87. Ferguson, letter to the First Presidency, 22 November 1957, in Box 1, Fd 5, Morgan Collection.

88. Luke P. Wilson, "The Scientific Search for Nephite Remains," *Heart and Mind: The Newsletter of Gospel Truths Ministries* (Fall 1992): 2, with emphasis in original.

89. Ferguson, letter to the First Presidency, 15 March 1958, in Ferguson Collection, BYU.

90. Ferguson, *One Fold*, 140, quoted from Bartolomé de las Casas, that Francisco Hernandez "had met a principal lord or chief, and that on inquiring of him concerning his faith and the ancient belief all over his realm, he answered him that they knew and believed in God who

was in Heaven; that God was the Father, the Son, and the Holy Ghost. . . . The Son's name was *Bacab*, who was born from a maiden who had ever remained a virgin, whose name was *Chiribirias*, and who is in heaven with God. . . . About *Bacab*, who is the Son, they say that he was killed and lashed and a crown of thorns put on him, and that he was placed on a timber with his arms stretched out. . . . And he was dead for three days, and on the third day he came to life and went up to heaven, and that he is there with his Father," with emphasis in original.

91. Ferguson, *One Fold*, 259.

92. Robert M. Carmack, professor of anthropology at the State University of New York at Albany, discovered the large, leather-bound manuscript of the *Title of the Lords of Totonicapán*. Ferguson, letter to Robert M. Carmack, 7 January 1982, in Ferguson Collection, UU, asked Carmack if the Quiché Maya might have said certain things just to please the Catholic Spaniards and wondered why, if they really were descended from the house of Israel, there is no evidence of the Hebrew language in the New World. Robert M. Carmack, "New Quichean Chronicles from Highland Guatemala," *Estudios de Cultura Maya* 13 (1981): 87, described the manuscript as follows: "Of special interest, of course, is the first section of the text which was not translated by [Dionisio José] Chonay. He correctly stated that this part contains an account which is similar to that of the Old Testament, from the creation to the Babilonian [*sic*] captivity. While it is true that this part of the narration follows the Bible much more closely than does the *Popol Vuh*, it nevertheless diverges in subtle and interesting ways. I recommend it highly as one of the first attempts by native Guatemalans to syncretize their historical tradition with the Christian one."

93. Reader's Digest, *Mysteries of the Ancient Americas: The New World before Columbus* (Pleasantville, NY: The Reader's Digest Association, 1986), 41.

94. Ferguson, *One Fold*, 22, 25. George F. Carter, "Before Columbus," in *The Book of Mormon: The Keystone Scripture*, ed. Paul R. Cheesman, Book of Mormon Symposium Series, no. 1 (Provo, UT: Religious Studies Center, Brigham Young University, 1988), 164, also a faculty member at Johns Hopkins University, related that Albright asked him to Albright's office to examine the seals and Albright "recognized a letter or two and concluded that these were degenerate cartouches of Mediterranean inspiration."

95. Ferguson, letter to Ernest L. Wilkinson, 29 February 1960, in the Joseph T. Bentley Collection, Box 52, Fd 4, Administrative Council, Locked Case, Special Collections and Manuscripts, Harold B. Lee Library, Brigham Young University, Provo, UT; hereafter abbreviated to Bentley Collection.

96. Matthew W. Stirling, review of *One Fold and One Shepherd*, by Ferguson, in *Archaeology* 13 (September 1960): 229.

97. J. Alden Mason, letter to Ferguson, 8 June 1958, in Ferguson Collection, BYU, with emphasis in original. In 1960 J. Alden Mason, letter to Ferguson, 22 January 1960, in Ferguson Collection, BYU,

added: "I'm sure you realize that the professional [NWAF] staff does not believe that that cylinder seal--or better called a stamp--is a true hieroglyphic inscription or that the people who made it were literate, though we are willing to be convinced and eager to find further data pro or con. But one symbol that resembles one Egyptian hieroglyph doesn't constitute proof of literacy."

98. David H. Kelley, "A Cylinder Seal from Tlatilco," *American Antiquity* 31 (July 1966): 745.

99. Stephen C. Jett, "Precolumbian Transoceanic Contacts," in *Ancient South Americans*, ed. Jesse D. Jennings (San Francisco: W. H. Freeman and Co., 1983), 342, cautioned that "even if all of the Old World artifacts, inscriptions, and cultivated plants that are claimed to be Precolumbian in the New World were proved to be absolutely genuine and of preconquest date, they would not, in themselves, demonstrate anything more than casual contacts and occasional plant transfers." For a comprehensive bibliography on this subject, see John L. Sorenson and Martin H. Raish, *Pre-Columbian Contact with the Americas across the Oceans: An Annotated Bibliography*, 2 vols. (Provo, UT: Research Press, 1990).

100. Cheesman and Cheesman, *American Indians*, 245-49, listed 229 "Cultural Similarities" in the same manner as Ferguson.

101. Fifteen years after the publication of Ferguson's *One Fold*, John L. Sorenson delivered a paper at the Twenty-third Annual Symposium on the Archaeology of the Scriptures and Allied Fields, 20 October 1973, held on the campus of Brigham Young University, Provo, UT. Sorenson, "Mesoamerican Codex," 7-9, listed seventy-seven cultural parallels between Mesoamerican codices (or broadened to Mesoamerican archaeology), the Book of Mormon, and the Near Eastern background of the Book of Mormon. Actually, since nine of the cultural traits have no Book of Mormon component the list is reduced to sixty-eight. The most astonishing aspect of these comparisons is how Sorenson sometimes distorted and de-Christianized the Book of Mormon theology in order to make his parallels fit. For example, Sorenson asserted that "the cosmos was considered to be formed in layered fashion with multiple realms above, the earth's surface between, and one or more under-worlds," and his support for a concept of multiple heavens is the Book of Mormon use of the plural "heavens" at 1 Ne. 1:8; Alma 1:15; 18:30, but in the Book of Mormon "heaven" and "heavens" are used synonymously and in one of the passages Sorenson cites it is specifically stated that "the heavens [pl.] is a place [sing.] where God dwells" (Alma 18:30). Also, Sorenson maintained that "water holes, lakes, moist caves, and similar spots were sacred because of their presumed connection with the waters beneath the earth," which is quite different from the simple Christian baptism by immersion performed by Alma at the waters of Mormon and Zarahemla (Mosiah 18:5-16; 25:18; Alma 5:3) and Nephi at Bountiful (3 Ne. 19:10-13, 36). Finally, Sorenson claimed that "a fenced haven on or in a mountain was provided for blessed spirits," though his Book of

Mormon passages refer six times to a sheep's "fold" (1 Ne. 15:15; 22:25; 2 Ne. 9:2; Mosiah 18:8; Alma 5:39; 3 Ne. 15:7) and once to a "gate" (Hel. 3:28), though the wording and imagery is much closer to John 10:16. To avoid straining the interpretation of Book of Mormon passages, Dan Vogel, "The New Theory of Book of Mormon Geography: A Preliminary Examination," typescript, 1985, 32, in the Dan Vogel Collection, Accession 1444, Box 1, Fd 22, Manuscripts Division, J. Willard Marriott Library, University of Utah, Salt Lake City, suggested that "the Book of Mormon is better understood in the context of early American Protestant theology rather than Mayan religion"; this collection is hereafter abbreviated to Vogel Collection.

102. Eugene R. Fingerhut, *Explorers of Pre-Columbian America? The Diffusionist-Inventionist Controversy*, Guides to Historical Issues, no. 5 (Claremont, CA: Regina Books, 1994), 5, was impressed by Sorenson's earlier list of 250 cultural traits, though Fingerhut did say that "an independent development advocate might respond by claiming that the common intellectual and psychological qualities found in all humans would produce similar responses in similar environments." See John L. Sorenson, "The Significance of an Apparent Relationship between the Ancient Near East and Mesoamerica," in *Man across the Sea: Problems of Pre-Columbian Contacts*, ed. Carroll L. Riley et alia (Austin, TX: University of Texas Press, 1971), 219-41.

103. Stephen C. Jett, "Before Columbus: The Question of Early Transoceanic Interinfluences," *Brigham Young University Studies* 33, no. 2 (1993): 260, explained that "similarities are less convincing indicators of contact if they are thousands of years apart than if they are from about the same time period. Geographical clustering is another factor, because the greater the number of co-occurring commonalities, the greater the probability that there was historical contact and exchange between the specific locations involved."

104. Dee F. Green, "Book of Mormon Archaeology: The Myths and the Alternatives," *Dialogue: A Journal of Mormon Thought* 4 (Summer 1969): 74.

105. For example, Nigel Davies, *Voyagers to the New World* (Albuquerque, NM: University of New Mexico Press, 1986), 143, criticized Ferguson's comparing the crucifixion with "the gruesome sacrifice peculiar to the Mexican god of hunting, in which the human victim was tied to a cross-shaped bracket and slain with arrows."

106. Martin Raish, "All That Glitters: Uncovering Fool's Gold in Book of Mormon Archaeology," *Sunstone* 6 (January-February 1981): 13.

107. Basil C. Hedrick, letter to Dan Vogel, 31 December 1980, in Box 1, Fd 4, Vogel Collection. The next month Basil C. Hedrick, letter to Dan Vogel, 23 January 1981, expressed his opinion about Sorenson's article, "The Book of Mormon as a Mesoamerican Codex," as follows: ". . . I am quite disappointed to see him [John L. Sorenson] using basically good research data, then attempting to plug it in to a preordained hypothesis. I have no patience with this approach."

108. Michael D. Coe, review of *One Fold and One Shepherd*, by Ferguson, in *American Antiquity* 25 (October 1959): 290.

109. Ferguson, *One Fold*, 350-51, with emphasis in original.

110. Ibid., 227-29.

111. Michael D. Coe, "Mormons and Archaeology: An Outside View," *Dialogue: A Journal of Mormon Thought* 8, no. 2 (1973): 44.

112. M. Wells Jakeman, *Stela 5, Izapa, Chiapas, Mexico: A Major Archaeological Discovery of the New World, Detailed Commentary on the Carving*, The University Archaeological Society Special Publications, no. 2 (Provo, UT: The University Archaeological Society, 1958), 32-33, 40-42. Cf. Hugh Nibley, "Hamlet Left Out," review of *Stela 5, Izapa, Chiapas, Mexico*, by M. Wells Jakeman, typescript, ca. 1958, Box 33, Fd 16, in Buerger Collection. M. Wells Jakeman, *The Complex 'Tree-of-Life' Carving on Izapa Stela 5: A Reanalysis and Partial Interpretation*, Brigham Young University Publications in Archaeology and Early History, Mesoamerican Series, no. 4. (Provo, UT: Brigham Young University, 1958), 12-23, never mentioned the Book of Mormon.

113. Marion G. Romney, "Excerpts from Diary of Marion G. Romney pertaining to Trip to Mexico," attached to Marion G. Romney, letter to Ernest L. Wilkinson, 12 July 1960, in Box 53, Fd 3, Bentley Collection.

114. V. Garth Norman, *Izapa Sculpture, Part 2: Text*, Papers of the New World Archaeological Foundation, no. 30 (Provo, UT: New World Archaeological Foundation, Brigham Young University, 1976), 167. Hildegard Delgado Pang, *Pre-Columbian Art: Investigations and Insights* (Norman, OK: University of Oklahoma, 1992), 70-72, followed Norman's, not Jakeman's, interpretation of Izapa Stela 5.

115. Green, "Book of Mormon Archaeology," 75. Green also claimed that "plate 5 in Jakeman's Stela 5 publication was drawn from a photograph of the monument and not from the monument itself." This is supported by Ross T. Christensen, historical note no. 20, 24 November 1958, in College of Family, Home, and Social Science Records, UA 661, Box 9, Fd 8, Special Collections and Manuscripts, Harold B. Lee Library, Brigham Young University, Provo, UT, who said that Jakeman "made a change in a detail of the cast"; hereafter abbreviated to BYU Family, Home, and Social Science Records. For a light-hearted parody of Jakeman's methodology, see Hugh Nibley, "Bird Island," *Dialogue: A Journal of Mormon Thought* 10 (Autumn 1977): 122.

116. Ludwig Koehler and Walter Baumgartner, *Hebräisches und aramäisches Lexikon zum Alten Testament*, ed. Johann J. Stamm, 3d ed. (Leiden: E. J. Brill, 1974), 2:499, s.v. *lᵉchî*.

117. V. Garth Norman, "What is the current status of research concerning the 'Tree of Life' carving from Chiapas, Mexico?" *The Ensign* 15 (June 1985): 54. Cf. V. Garth Norman, *Izapa Stela 5 and the Lehi Tree-of-Life Vision Hypothesis: A Reanalysis*, Mesoamerican Research Papers (American Fork, UT: Archaeological Research Consultants, 1985).

118. Gareth W. Lowe, "Izapa Religion, Cosmology, and Ritual,"

in *Izapa: An Introduction to the Ruins and Monuments,* ed. Gareth W. Lowe, Thomas A. Lee, Jr., and Eduardo Martinez Espinosa, Papers of the New World Archaeological Foundation, no. 31 (Provo, UT: New World Archaeological Foundation, Brigham Young University, 1982), 305. In line with Lowe's view Linda Schele and Mary Ellen Miller, *The Blood of Kings: Dynasty and Ritual in Maya Art* (New York: George Braziller, in association with the Kimbell Art Museum of Fort Worth, 1986), 140, provided the following interpretation of Izapa Stela 5: "The main face of the stela depicts the emergence of man at the dawn of time. A central figure drills a hole in a cosmic tree from which barely-formed humans flow. An old couple, possibly ancestors, conduct a divination over an incensario at the lower left; behind them, another seated figure holds out a spiny bloodletter. At the lower right, a small figure wearing a spangled turban, the characteristic attire of the scribes, shapes a human body, shown at a stage when it still lacks arms and legs."

119. Coe, "Archaeology," 44. For an anti-Mormon treatment of Izapa Stela 5, see Harold H. Hougey, *The Truth about the "Lehi Tree-of-Life" Stone* (Concord, CA: Pacific Publishing Co., 1963).

120. Mary Ellen Miller and Karl Taube, *The Gods and Symbols of Ancient Mexico and the Maya: An Illustrated Dictionary of Mesoamerican Religion* (London: Thames and Hudson, 1993), s.v. "creation accounts," 68-71, and s.v. "Popol Vuh," 134-36. For a modern translation of the Popol Vuh, see Dennis Tedlock, trans., *Popol Vuh: The Definitive Edition of the Mayan Book of the Dawn of Life and the Glories of Gods and Kings* (New York: Simon and Schuster, 1985). Roberta H. Markman and Peter T. Markman, *The Flayed God, The Mesoamerican Mythological Tradition: Sacred Texts and Images from Pre-Columbian Mexico and Central America* (San Francisco: HarperSanFrancisco, 1992), 155, labelled Izapa Stela 5 as "an Izapan Creation Myth."

121. Jeddy LeVar, "Archaeology Author to Speak," *Daily Universe* 11 (9 January 1959): 1.

122. Ross T. Christensen, letter to Clark S. Knowlton, 13 January 1959, in Knowlton Collection. Because of the long-standing jealousy between NWAF and the University Archaeological Society, Christensen told Knowlton that "it will be a very strange--and in fact strained --situation, since both Wells [Jakeman] and I have strong feelings with reference to this gentleman [Ferguson] and his undercutting of our efforts."

123. [Jeddy LeVar], "Author Says Book of Mormon Defense Sure," *Daily Universe* 11 (16 January 1959): 1.

124. Ernest L. Wilkinson, diary, 22 August 1959, in the Ernest L. Wilkinson Collection, Manuscript 629, Manuscripts Division, J. Willard Marriott Library, University of Utah, Salt Lake City.

125. Ferguson, "Application to the National Science Foundation for a Grant for Archaeological Excavations of Pre-classic Sites in the State of Chiapas, Mexico," typescript, 13 October 1959, in Box 9, Fd 8, Ferguson Collection, BYU.

126. Ferguson, letter to Alfred V. Kidder, 22 January 1960, in

Ferguson Collection, BYU.

127. David O. McKay, diary, 27 January 1960, in the David J. Buerger Collection, Manuscript 622, Box 8, Fd 16, Manuscripts Division, J. Willard Marriott Library, University of Utah, Salt Lake City.

128. Ferguson, letter to Ernest L. Wilkinson, 29 February 1960, in Box 52, Fd 4, Bentley Collection. Ferguson felt strongly that the LDS Church should continue funding the archaeological project. Ferguson, letter to Eugene Vincent, 15 July 1960, in Ferguson Collection, BYU, stated the following in response to Vincent's Mesoamerican map with specific Book of Mormon locations identified: "Several of the powerful leaders of the Church still insist that Cumorah is in New York, and right now we don't want to offend them. We are trying desperately to get the Church to put cash into the work and nothing should interfere with such a program."

129. Ferguson, letter to J. M. McDaniel, Jr., 15 April 1960, in Ferguson Collection, BYU.

130. Part of their tour of NWAF operations consisted of a visit to Izapa Stela 5. A photograph of the inspection of this monument by five members of the group is printed by Martin Raish, "Tree of Life," in *Encyclopedia of Mormonism*, ed. Daniel H. Ludlow (New York: Macmillan Publishing Co., 1992), 4:1486, with Tom Ferguson identified as the second from the left. This photo is the only mention of Ferguson in the entire four-volume encyclopedia, but it is incorrect since the person in question is Daniel Taylor Pierce, with Ferguson himself taking the picture. See the LDS newspaper for southern California, *California Intermountain News*, 20 October 1960, where the photograph is first printed with correct identifications.

131. [Mark E. Petersen, Marion G. Romney, and Ernest L. Wilkinson], "Report respecting Archaeological Work in Mexico, Presented to the First Presidency and Board of Education," typescript, September 1960, 6-7, in Box 15, Fd 3, BYU Family, Home, and Social Science Records.

132. Ernest L. Wilkinson and W. Cleon Skousen, *Brigham Young University: A School of Destiny* (Provo, UT: Brigham Young University Press, 1976), 740.

133. Earl C. Crockett, "Welcome to Brigham Young University," in *Papers of the Thirteenth Annual Symposium on the Archaeology of the Scriptures*, ed. by Dee F. Green (Provo, UT: Department of Extension Publications, Brigham Young University, 1962), 2.

134. Ferguson, letter to LeGrand Richards, 23 January 1961, in Ferguson Collection, BYU.

135. "Recommended Advisory Committee on Archaeological Work," undated typed sheet with penciled corrections, and Joseph T. Bentley, memorandum to Ernest L. Wilkinson, 4 October 1960, in Box 52, Fd 4, Bentley Collection.

136. Eleanor Knowles, *Howard W. Hunter* (Salt Lake City: Deseret Book Co., 1994), 198.

137. Ferguson, letter to Howard W. Hunter, 10 February 1961, in Box 52, Fd 5, Bentley Collection.

138. Ferguson, note of telephone conversation with Howard W. Hunter, 16 February 1961, in Ferguson Collection, BYU.

139. Ferguson, letter to William F. Albright, 6 March 1961, in Ferguson Collection, BYU.

140. Ferguson, letter to the editor, *Christianity Today* 5 (27 March 1961): 551.

141. Harold H. Hougey, letter to the editor, *Christianity Today* 5 (22 May 1961): 727.

142. Ferguson, letter to Harold H. Hougey, 14 September 1961, in Ferguson Collection, UU.

143. Harold H. Hougey, letter to Ferguson, 19 September 1961, in Ferguson Collection, UU.

144. Ferguson, letter to Harold H. Hougey, 4 October 1961, in Ferguson Collection, UU.

145. Ferguson, letter to Mrs. Alfred V. Kidder, 17 July 1963, in Ferguson Collection, BYU.

146. Ferguson, letter to Paul Bush Romero, 25 August 1966, in Ferguson Collection, BYU.

147. John A. Price, "The Book of Mormon vs. Anthropological Prehistory," *The Indian Historian* 7 (Summer 1974): 38-39. Price, ibid., 35, said that "this story [about the Book of Mormon] was important to me as a child because I was raised as a Mormon in Salt Lake City."

148. William J. Hamblin, "Basic Methodological Problems with the Anti-Mormon Approach to the Geography and Archaeology of the Book of Mormon," *Journal of Book of Mormon Studies* 2 (Spring 1993): 196, asserted that when Coe makes this statement "he is belaboring the obvious, not stating an important truth. It is rather like claiming that 'there is not one professionally trained archaeologist, who is not a (Christian), who sees any scientific justification for believing (the New Testament accounts of the resurrection of Jesus)." However, Hamblin constructed an improper analogy here, for the point of comparison with the historicity of the Book of Mormon ought to be the historical reality of the New Testament--not faith in the miracle of Jesus's resurrection.

149. Coe's use of the term "Liahonas" refers to Richard D. Poll's metaphor which contrasts an "Iron Rod" (1 Ne. 8:19) approach which leads one step by step on the journey of life with a "Liahona" (Alma 37:38) approach which merely points one in the right direction. See Richard D. Poll, "What the Church Means to People like Me," *Dialogue: A Journal of Mormon Thought* 2 (Winter 1967): 107-17 and "Liahona and Iron Rod Revisited," *Dialogue: A Journal of Mormon Thought* 16 (Summer 1983): 69-78.

150. Coe, "Archaeology," 42, 46.

151. Michael D. Coe, letter to William McKeever, 17 August 1993, printed in William McKeever, "Yale anthropologist's views remain unchanged," *Mormonism Researched: An Outreach Publication of Mormonism Research Ministry*, no. 15 (Winter 1993): 6.

3

Book
of
Abraham
Papyri
Rediscovered

Ironically, Thomas Stuart Ferguson spent the greater part of his life studying Book of Mormon geography and the material culture of the ancient peoples of Mesoamerica, but the catalyst to the abrupt change in his theological views occurred in the late 1960s because of the rediscovery and translation of some of Joseph Smith's original papyri of the Book of Abraham.

The Joseph Smith
Egyptian Papyri

The front page of the 27 November 1967 *Deseret News* announced that a portion of the Egyptian papyri once owned and studied by Joseph Smith had been discovered. The article mentioned eleven papyrus pieces and an 1856 certificate of sale signed by Emma Smith Bidamon, Joseph Smith's widow.[1] They had been brought to the attention of Aziz S. Atiya, professor of Middle Eastern studies at the University of Utah, while he was researching at the Egyptian section of the Metropolitan Museum of Art in New York City in May 1966; he arranged for them to be donated to the LDS Church.[2] These eleven pages of the Joseph Smith Egyptian Papyri were numbered and named as follows:[3] Joseph Smith Papyrus I--Facsimile No. 1, Joseph Smith Papyrus II--Plowing Scene, Joseph Smith Papyrus IIIA--Court of Osiris (on throne), Joseph Smith Papyrus IIIB--Court of Osiris (Thoth recording), Joseph Smith Papyrus IV--Framed ("Trinity") Papyrus, Joseph Smith Papyrus V--The Serpent with Legs, Joseph Smith Papyrus VI--The Swallow, Joseph Smith Papyrus VII--Man with Staff (entering into glory), Joseph Smith Papyrus VIII--Inverted Triangle, Joseph Smith Papyrus IX--Church Historian's Fragment,[4] Joseph Smith Papyrus X--the "Sensen" Papyrus, and Joseph Smith Papyrus XI--Small "Sensen" Papyrus.

By far the most significant item was the original papyrus of what is generally known as Facsimile No. 1 (fig. 18), an "explanation" of which, along with a translation of the Egyptian text, Joseph Smith gave in the Book of Abraham, now part of the LDS scriptural book, the Pearl of Great Price. Hugh Nibley, professor of history and religion at Brigham Young University, placed the importance of this discovery into perspective:

> This [announcement] was a far more momentous transaction than might appear on the surface, for it brought back into play for the first time since the angel Moroni took back the golden plates a tangible link between the worlds. What we have here is more than a few routine scribblings of ill-trained scribes of long ago; at least one of these very documents was presented to the world by Joseph Smith as offering a brief and privileged insight into the strange world of the Patriarchs.[5]

That "tangible link" is the original Egyptian papyrus of Facsimile No. 1. In order to appreciate what was announced in 1967 it is necessary to understand clearly what materials were originally in the possession of Joseph Smith. In the mid-1820s

Antonio Lebolo, an Italian excavator and adventurer, discovered a number of mummies with associated papyri in catacombs near Thebes.[6] These were later acquired by Michael H. Chandler, an antiquities dealer, who in 1835 brought the four remaining mummies to Kirtland, Ohio, and showed them to Joseph Smith and the Mormon leaders. Joseph Coe, Simeon Andrews, and some other individuals provided $2,400 to enable Joseph Smith to purchase the mummies and papyri from Chandler.[7]

W. W. Phelps, who served as scribe to Joseph Smith during this period, provided a contemporary account of this episode:

> The last of June [1835] four Egyptian mummies were brought here: there were two papyrus rolls, besides some other ancient Egyptian writings with them. As no one could translate these writings, they were presented to President [Joseph] Smith. He soon knew what they were and said they, the "rolls of papyrus," contained the sacred record kept of Joseph in Pharaoh's Court in Egypt, and the teachings of Father Abraham.[8]

The *History of the Church*, this part of which was dictated by Joseph Smith in 1843, presented the following as his account concerning the Egyptian papyri in July 1835:

> There were four human figures [mummies], together with some two or more rolls of papyrus covered with hieroglyphic figures and devices.
> . . . with W. W. Phelps and Oliver Cowdery as scribes, I commenced the translation of some of the characters or hieroglyphics, and much to our joy found that one of the rolls contained the writings of Abraham, another the writings of Joseph of Egypt, etc.--a more full account of which will appear in its place, as I proceed to examine or unfold them. Truly we can say, the Lord is beginning to reveal the abundance of peace and truth.[9]

Joseph Smith here clearly stated that it was his translation of the hieroglyphic characters--not just looking at the illustrations--that led to the surprising discovery that one scroll was the writing of Abraham and the other scroll contained the writing of his great-grandson, Joseph, both of whom lived sometime in the period from 2000 to 1500 B.C.[10] In January 1836 Joseph Smith showed his Hebrew teacher, Joshua Seixas, the Egyptian scroll of the

Book of Abraham and he "pronounced them [Abraham's records] to be original beyond all doubt."[11] Present day scholars agree that these documents are genuine Egyptian papyri.

When the four Egyptian mummies were being exhibited a few months earlier in Cleveland, a Mr. Farmer described the mummies and the associated documents in a contemporary newspaper, the Painesville *Telegraph*.

> No. 1--[a human figure] 4 feet 11 inches [long], female-- supposed age 60; arms extended, hands side by side in front; the head indicating motherly goodness. There was found with this person a roll or book, having a little resemblance to birch bark; language unknown. Some linguists, however, say they can decipher 13-36, in what they term an epitaph; ink black and red; many female figures.
> No. 2--Height 5 ft. 1½ inch; female; supposed age 40. Arms suspended by the side; hands brought in contact; head damaged by accident; found with a roll as No. 1, filled with hieroglyphics, rudely executed.
> No. 3--4 ft. 4½ [inches]; male, very old, say 80; arms crossing on the breast, each hand on its opposite shoulder; had a roll of writing as No. 1 and 2; superior head, it will compare in the region of the sentiments with any in our land; passions mild.
> No. 4--Height 4 ft. 9 [inches]; female. I am inclined to put her age at about 20 or 25, others call her an old woman; arms extended, hands by her side; auburn hair, short as girls at present in their new fashion. Found with her a braid of hair, three stran[d]s of the color of that on her head and 18 inches long.[12]

Commenting on this 1835 list, Klaus Baer, professor of Egyptology at the Oriental Institute of the University of Chicago, suggested that the first mummy (whose scroll Joseph Smith identified as being the Book of Joseph) is "almost certainly Tshenmîn" and proposed that the male mummy (whose scroll Smith identified as the Book of Abraham) is perhaps Hôr.[13] The Painesville *Telegraph* account, with its indication of three scrolls, helps to clarify the statement in the *History of the Church* that with the four mummies were "some two or more rolls of papyrus." Oliver Cowdery also mentions that when Chandler opened the coffins in New York he found not only the two scrolls already mentioned but also "two or three other small pieces of papyrus, with astronomical calculations, epitaphs, etc."[14] The most likely resolution of the differing numbers is that there were two fairly complete scrolls, damaged parts of a third scroll with the third mummy, and perhaps fragments from other mummies.

After careful examination of the new papyri Baer concluded that they are from three separate documents: (1) the Breathing Permit of the priest Hôr, the son of Osorwêr and Tikhebyt; (2) the *Book of the Dead* of the lady Tshenmîn, daughter of Skhons; and (3) the *Book of the Dead* of the female musician of Amon-Re Neferirnûb.[15] There is evidence of at least two other Egyptian documents. Facsimile No. 2, the original of which has not survived, belonged to Sheshonq. In the "Valuable Discovery" booklet, which has Joseph Smith's signature on the title page, there are transcribed characters from the Egyptian papyrus which belonged to Amenhotep, the son of Hôr, but again the original is not available.[16] Certainly the Egyptian papyri that Joseph Smith possessed from 1835 to 1844 were more numerous than the papyri fragments that have survived.

Joseph Smith's Ability to Translate Egyptian

Orthodox Mormons believe that Joseph Smith's acquisition of Egyptian mummies with scrolls containing the Book of Abraham and the Book of Joseph demonstrate conclusively the hand of God in their preservation. Non-Mormons, on the other hand, skeptically question the likelihood of the story. For example, a Gentile observer in 1837 expressed his opinion:

> Is it possible that a record written by Abraham, and another by Joseph, containing the most important revelation that God ever gave to man, should be entirely lost by the tenacious Israelites, and preserved by the unbelieving Egyptians, and by them embalmed and deposited in the catacombs with an Egyptian priest. . . . I venture to say no, it is not possible. It is more likely that the records are those of the Egyptians.[17]

It is, however, not the theoretical probability or improbability of the account about the mummies and papyri that is important, but rather whether the translation of the Joseph Smith Egyptian papyri by Egyptologists provides dramatic confirmation of Joseph Smith's translations and explanations, or whether the translation of Egyptologists reveals texts with no connection to either Abraham or Joseph. To Ferguson this was the key issue. One needs to examine the actual Egyptian papyri (both text and illustration), not just printed woodcuts of the three facsimiles published in 1842, before being warranted to draw conclusions about the accuracy of Joseph Smith's translation. Consequently, the discovery of any of the original Egyptian papyri once in Smith's possession would be immensely significant to the LDS people and provide a chance to vindicate his claim.

This unexpected discovery allowed an independent test of the accuracy of Joseph Smith's interpretation of the papyri. Ferguson, the seeker after truth, considered this to be the acid test of Smith's ability to translate ancient documents, and he seized the opportunity to verify the prophet's translation of the Book of Abraham. The announcement issued in November 1967 and the developments which ensued not only required a radical change in Ferguson's thinking, but also affected how Mormons viewed the Book of Abraham. Its impact on the study of Mormon scriptures continues to the present. Richard D. Poll, emeritus professor of history at Western Illinois University, explained the effect of this discovery:

> I turn now to a case of more traumatic dissonance--a case in which the discovery of documents has had substantial impact upon an important faith-related historical myth. . . . It is "The Case of the Book of Abraham." The rediscovery of some of the Egyptian papyri associated with the Pearl of Great Price certainly challenged the LDS tradition--the historical myth--that the Book of Abraham is a literal translation of an ancient document.[18]

Ferguson did not wait for further information to filter down through official church channels. As soon as the announcement came out he wrote letters to various LDS leaders in Salt

Lake City. Ferguson asked Milton R. Hunter, a member of the LDS Church's First Council of the Seventy, to tell him anything he could and inquired whether the Church would release information about the papyri. He also specifically asked Hunter whether any non-Mormon scholar had translated the papyri, and if so, whether such a translation resembled the Book of Abraham.[19] Hunter answered that Hugh Nibley had told him that "the scholars wouldn't touch them [the papyri] with a ten-foot pole."[20] As to whether the Church would release information about the papyri, Hunter responded that President N. Eldon Tanner said that they would when the documents were translated.

Ferguson immediately set out to put these new discoveries to the test. Since Aziz S. Atiya was mentioned in the newspaper announcements, Ferguson decided to write directly to him about the discovery:

> I am a Mormon and recognize immediately that your discovery has a strong bearing upon the validity of the foundations of the Mormon Church. Since today Egyptologists can read and translate the documents on which the "Book of Abraham" is based, we can readily determine whether, as of July 3, 1835 (the date when Joseph Smith claimed the manuscripts included writings of Abraham and Joseph) Joseph Smith was fabricating, lying, and conjuring up "scripture" for the Church. If the manuscript material which you found is nothing more nor less than a bit of one of the *Book of the Dead*, such would be the required deduction as to Joseph Smith as of 1835. . . . The Book of Abraham has been "suspect" to me for some time. On the other hand, 99.99% of the Book of Mormon has held up wonderfully well--in my opinion. This now presents a strange quandary to me. And it is interesting that the foundation for the policy of the church toward the Negro [i.e., barring black males from priesthood ordination] is predicated upon the validity of the Book of Abraham and it appears to be in direct conflict with the Book of Mormon.[21]

This letter provides insight into Ferguson's thinking about the Book of Abraham and reveals that in early December 1967 Ferguson already had some doubt about its authenticity, due mainly to the denial of priesthood authority to blacks, who were believed to have inherited the curse of Ham (Abr. 1:25-27). Ferguson was still 99.99 percent in favor of the historicity of the Book of Mormon, and even considered seriously the possibility that Joseph Smith was a true prophet of God in 1829 when he translated the Book of Mormon, but had become a fallen prophet by 1835.

Scholars Translate
the Egyptian Papyri

Because no Egyptologist had yet studied the papyri, Ferguson made his own arrangements to have them examined and translated by Egyptologists who were available to him in the San Francisco Bay area. The day after Christmas in 1967, Ferguson tried to contact Leonard H. Lesko, an instructor in Egyptology at the University of California at Berkeley. Not reaching him, he left a note, saying that he wanted him to translate some Egyptian hieroglyphs.[22] The next day Ferguson tried again and this time met Henry L. F. Lutz, emeritus professor of Egyptology at the University of California at Berkeley. Ferguson asked him to examine some Egyptian hieroglyphs he had clipped from the "Church Section" of the *Deseret News* for 2 December 1967.[23] They spent one and a half hours together, and Ferguson--being careful not to influence his opinion in any way--did not indicate where the hieroglyphs "came from or that they had any significance to the LDS people. He [Lutz] gave me a perfectly candid and honest opinion, that all are from the Book of the Dead."[24] This identification of the papyri caused Ferguson to become "very upset specifically--not at the Church, of course, but at Joseph Smith especially."[25]

Not content with just one Egyptologist's opinion, Ferguson again approached Lesko to translate the Egyptian hieroglyphs. Newspaper reproductions were unsatisfactory, so Ferguson contacted Hugh B. Brown, first counselor in the LDS First Presidency, and received from him enlarged photographs of the papyri.[26] Ferguson sent these photos to Lesko with a request that he translate them.[27] After having the material for a month, Lesko gave his opinion that "all of these are spells [magical incantations] from the Egyptian *Book of the Dead*."[28]

In November 1968 Ferguson ordered a copy of the controversial publication *The Joseph Smith Papyri* from Modern Microfilm Company of Salt Lake City, complimenting the "gentlemen" there for "doing a great thing--getting out some truth on the Book of Abraham."[29] At this point Ferguson was not aware that this company was run by a husband and wife team of former Mormons, Jerald and Sandra Tanner--only distantly related to N. Eldon Tanner. Other than the two Egyptologists whom Ferguson contacted directly, he studied the published translations of two others who worked on the Joseph Smith Egyptian papyri: Klaus Baer, an Egyptologist at the University of Chicago,[30] and Dee Jay Nelson of Billings, Montana, a member of the LDS Church and a self-taught translator of Egyptian.[31] This procedure provided Ferguson with four independent assessments of the Joseph Smith Egyptian papyri, particularly Facsimile No. 1 with Abraham shown on a lion couch. In the 1970s Ferguson distributed photocopies of Baer's article to people with whom he discussed the Book of Abraham. Summarizing the disparity between Joseph Smith and the Egyptologists, Ferguson discussed the problem from the standpoint of a lawyer examining the credibility of evidence and witnesses:

> Joseph Smith announced, in print (*History of the Church*, Vol. II, page 236) that "one of the rolls contained the writings of Abraham, another the writings of Joseph of Egypt. . . ." Since four scholars, who have established that they can read Egyptian, say that the manuscripts deal with neither Abraham nor Joseph--and since the four reputable men tell us exactly what the manuscripts do say--I must conclude that Joseph Smith had not the remotest skill in things Egyptian-hieroglyphics.[32]

The contact that amateur Dee Jay Nelson had with the papyri cost him his membership in the LDS Church. In January 1968 at BYU Hugh Nibley showed Nelson new color photographs of the Joseph Smith Egyptian papyri and they compared them with the original papyri.[33] Then Nibley wrote a note of introduction, which Nelson was to take to N. Eldon Tanner.[34] That same day Nelson traveled to Salt Lake City and talked to Tanner, who had some 8 by 10 photographs made for Nelson to use to make his translation. Even though he was not a professional Egyptologist, the amateur Dee Jay Nelson was able to finish his translation about two months later. Since his translation did not support the Book of Abraham, Tanner suggested to Nelson that it was his duty as an Elder in the Church to handle the matter in a way that would be sympathetic to LDS doctrine, but Nelson refused to make any alterations to his translation. Because N. Eldon Tanner would not publish his translation, Nelson had it published by Jerald and Sandra Tanner through their Modern Microfilm Company as a booklet entitled *The Joseph Smith Papyri*. Nibley hailed Nelson's translation as "a conscientious and courageous piece of work . . . supplying students with a usable and reliable translation." Nibley had become aware that translations of the papyri were not confirming the Book of Abraham, and commented that "it is doubtful whether any translation [of the Joseph Smith Egyptian papyri] could do as much good as harm."[35] In December 1975 Nelson resigned from the LDS Church. Nelson earned his place in Mormon history as the first to translate any of the Joseph Smith Egyptian papyri discovered at the Metropolitan Museum of Art.[36]

Facsimile No. 1
of the Book of Abraham

Of all the newly discovered Egyptian papyri, Ferguson's main interest focused on Facsimile No. 1. Joseph Smith had been proud of the illustration of Abraham on the lion couch, displaying it and its associated text to many Nauvoo visitors--both members of the Church and nonmembers--in the early 1840s. In April 1840 Smith showed the Egyptian papyri to a newspaper correspondent, and then, pointing at a particular hieroglyph, he said, "That is the signature of the patriarch Abraham."[37] In May

1844 Smith showed the papyri to two distinguished visitors, Charles Francis Adams, a member of the Massachusetts legislature and a son of John Quincy Adams, and Josiah Quincy, who the following year would become the mayor of Boston. Adams quoted Smith as saying: "This . . . was written by the hand of Abraham and means so and so. If anyone denies it, let him prove the contrary. *I* say it."[38] Quincy reported Smith's words as: "That is the handwriting of Abraham, the Father of the Faithful."[39]

In the March 1842 issue of the *Times and Seasons* Joseph Smith gave the following twelve "explanations" concerning Facsimile No. 1 (fig. 19):

Fig. 1. The Angel of the Lord.
  2. Abraham, fastened upon an Altar.
  3. The Idolatrous Priest of Elkenah attempting to offer up Abraham as a sacrifice.
  4. The Altar for sacrifice, by the Idolatrous Priests, standing before the gods of Elkenah, Libnah, Mahmachrah, Korash, and Pharaoh.
  5. The Idolatrous God of Elkenah.
  6. The   "   "   " Libnah.
  7. The   "   "   " Mahmachrah.
  8. The   "   "   " Korash.
  9. The   "   "   " Pharaoh.
  10. Abraham in Egypt.
  11. Designed to represent the pillars of Heaven, as understood by the Egyptians.
  12. Raukeeyang, signifying expanse, or the firmament, over our heads; but in this case, in relation to this subject, the Egyptians meant it to signify Shaumau, to be high, or the heavens: answering to the Hebrew word, Shaumahyeem.[40]

In order to make a comparison with Joseph Smith's explanations, Ferguson asked Leonard H. Lesko particularly concerning the papyrus original of Facsimile No. 1, without indicating "any relationship of the manuscript material to the Mormon Church, Joseph Smith, Book of Abraham--or whatever."[41] In response to this, Lesko gave the following explanation concerning the lion-couch scene, or Facsimile No. 1:

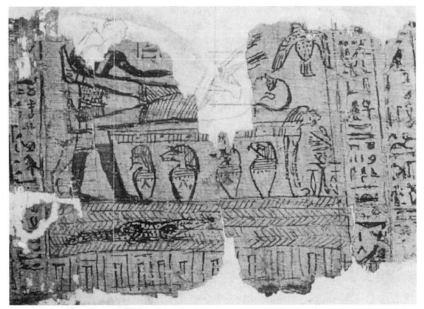

Fig. 18--Book of Abraham papyrus, lion couch illustration, Joseph Smith Papyrus I, discovery announced in 1967. Courtesy of Deseret News.

Fig. 19--Facsimile No. 1, Book of Abraham. Reproduced from "The Book of Abraham," *Times and Seasons* (1842).

The scene in which you are most interested is darker and being surrounded by often poor hieroglyphic rather than hieratic signs should be the only piece in this group of a very late copy of the *Book of the Dead*. The owner of this was a man whereas the owner of the others was a woman. The vignette [illustration] should be related to spell 151--the deceased [2] on a bier [4] on whom Anubis [3] lays hands. The restoration is incorrect as the god should be the jackal-headed Anubis (god of embalming). I have not been able to find the deceased depicted so elsewhere though it is not too unexpected; usually the figure is a mummified human or fish. The Ba (soul) bird [1] can be more easily explained from spells 85 and 89, also cf. L. V. Žabkar's book[42] to appear this year in the series: Studies in Ancient Oriental Civilization. Canopic jars beneath the bier contained the deceased's internal organs and represent the four sons of the god Horus, i.e., Imesti [i.e., Imseti] [8], Hapi [7], Duamutef [6], and Khebeksenuef [5].[43]

No statement has been located which was written by Henry L. F. Lutz, who was the first Egyptologist that Ferguson met. However, the following is the explanation given by Richard A. Parker, professor of Egyptology at Brown University--which undoubtedly was read by Ferguson since it was published in *Dialogue*:

This is a well-known scene from the Osiris mysteries, with Anubis [3], the jackal-headed god, on the left ministering to the dead Osiris [2] on the bier [4]. The penciled (?) restoration is incorrect. Anubis should be jackal-headed. The left arm of Osiris is in reality lying at his side under him. The apparent upper hand is part of the wing of a second bird which is hovering over the erect phallus of Osiris (now broken away). The second bird is Isis and she is magically impregnated by the dead Osiris and then later gives birth to Horus who avenges his father and takes over his inheritance. The complete bird represents Nephthys [1], sister of Osiris and Isis. Beneath the bier are the four canopic jars with heads representative of the four sons of Horus, human-headed Imseti [8], baboon-headed Hapy [7], jackal-headed Duamutef [6], and falcon-headed Kebehsenuf [5]. The hieroglyphs refer to burial, etc., but I have found no exact parallel in the time at my disposal and the poor photography precludes easy reading of the whole. I see no obvious personal name.[44]

Dee Jay Nelson, who published the first translation of these documents, said the following concerning the original papyrus of Facsimile No. 1, which he incorrectly referred to as Ter Papyrus, Fragment No. 3:[45]

> It shows Osiris [2], lying upon a funeral bier [4], being embalmed by Anubis [3]. The ba or soul of Osiris flies above his head in the form of a hawk [1]. Below the bier are four canopic jars [5-8] which will receive the viscera of Osiris. In the waters below the bier Set, the brother and murderer of Osiris, waits in the form of a crocodile [9].[46]

Klaus Baer said the following concerning the original papyrus of Facsimile No. 1:

> The vignette shows the resurrection of Osiris (who is also the deceased owner of the papyrus) and the conception of Horus. Osiris (2) is represented as a man on a lion-couch (4) attended by Anubis (3), the jackal-headed god who embalmed the dead and thereby assured their resurrection and existence in the hereafter. Below the couch are the canopic jars for the embalmed internal organs. The lids are the four sons of Horus, from left to right Imset (8), Hapi (7), Qebeh-senuwef (6), and Duwa-mutef (5),[47] who protect the liver, lungs, intestines, and stomach, respectively. At the head of the couch is a small offering stand (10) with a jug and some flowers on it. The ba of Osiris (1) is hovering above his head.[48]

John A. Wilson, professor of Egyptology at the Oriental Institute of the University of Chicago, wrote the following about Facsimile No. 1: "About the embalming scene . . . I am comforted to see that the standing figure has no head. I am sure that it never had a human head, as all of these illustrations show an animal head. In Ryerson, Pl. xlviii, the vignette for B.D. [*Book of the Dead*] 151 shows the jackal-god Anubis bending over a couch, with his hands on a recumbent human figure."[49] Four years later Wilson summarized the situation: "What Egyptologists see as the god Anubis embalming a corpse, he [Joseph Smith] declared to be 'the idolatrous priest of Elkenah attempting to offer up Abraham as a sacrifice.'"[50] More recently Stephen E. Thompson, an LDS Egyptologist at Brown University, confirmed the opinions of the earlier Egyptologists:

Papyrus Joseph Smith 1 . . . depicts the god Anubis [3] . . . officiating in the embalming rites for the deceased individual, Horus [2] . . . , shown lying on the bier. This scene does not portray a sacrifice of any sort. To note just a few instances in which Joseph Smith's interpretations of these figures differ from the way they are to be understood in their original context, consider the fact that Figure 11 . . . which Joseph Smith interprets as "designed to represent the pillars of heaven, as understood by the Egyptians," is actually a palace façade, called a *serekh*, which was a frequent decoration on funerary objects. The *serekh* originally depicted "the front of a fortified palace . . . with its narrow gateway, floral tracery above the gates, clerestories, and recessed buttresses." . . . In fact, these strokes [of Fig. 12] represent water in which the crocodile [9], symbolizing the god Horus . . . , swims.[51]

Improper Restorations to the Book of Abraham Papyrus

The original of Joseph Smith Papyrus I has missing material along the top edge of the papyrus and a controversy rages over the restorations of two heads in Facsimile No. 1. It involves the head of the bird known as Figure 1 and the head of the standing person known as Figure 3. Ordinary logic would suggest that a bird's body has a bird's head and a human body has a human head, but conventional canons of Egyptian art require a human head for the *ba*-bird and a jackal head or mask for the god Anubis.

BYU professor Hugh Nibley argued that in the background of an old painting of Lucy Mack Smith, Joseph Smith's mother, is her "most prized possession--the original of Facsimile 1. . . . It [the painting] matches our printed reproductions, and not the proposed restoration."[52] Countering Nibley's view James Boyack of Marblehead, Massachusetts, pointed out that "the standing figure is behind the couch in the painting and the facsimile but [it is] between the couch and the legs of the reclining figure in the original." Boyack noticed several other details, all of which align the painting and facsimile together against the original papyrus.[53]

Joseph Smith identified Figure 3 in Facsimile No. 1 as "the

idolatrous priest of Elkenah," but Egyptologists identified that individual as the jackal-headed god Anubis. Nibley admitted: "Well, you do go so far as to assume without question that the priest in Facsimile No. 1 should have a jackal's mask. And you are quite right--he *should* have, and the human head is an error."[54] Nibley later argued that the human head on Figure 3 was "not missing when the Mormons still had the thing in their possession."[55] Egyptologists identified Figure 3 as Anubis, and Baer, Lesko, Parker, and Wilson specifically indicated that Anubis should be jackal-headed, not human-headed. Edward H. Ashment, a doctoral candidate in Egyptology at the University of Chicago, found clues that the standing person is the god Anubis: "The narrow stripes clearly are the bottom edge of Anubis's headdress."[56] Some clues still survive to help discern a bearded human head on the bird identified as Figure 1 of Facsimile No. 1.[57]

Commenting on the opposing viewpoints of Nibley and Ashment, Richard D. Poll said:

> So let me say that I find Ed [Ashment]'s arguments per-
> suasive, both as to the relationship between the Prophet's
> work with the *sn-sn* text [Joseph Smith Papyrus XI] and the
> Book of Abraham and the limitations of Dr. Hugh Nibley's
> effort to handle the dissonances involved.[58]

Klaus Baer concluded that the papyri "neither say nor depict what Joseph Smith claimed they did, and . . . they were damaged and Joseph Smith supplied restorations, apparently from his imagination in some cases."[59] Thus, Facsimile No. 1 shows Horus (the owner of the papyrus) in the form of Osiris with his human-headed *ba*-bird above his head being embalmed for the next life on a funerary lion-couch by a jackal-headed Anubis, and not Abraham with an attending angel of the Lord being sacrificed on an altar by the idolatrous priest of Elkenah. In spite of these discrepancies one Mormon writer inexplicably affirmed that "the Prophet's explanations of each of the facsimiles accord with present understanding of Egyptian religious prac-tices,"[60] but such an assertion does not survive scrutiny.[61]

The Importance of the
Book of Breathings Papyrus

Joseph Smith Papyrus XI is the second most significant piece among the recovered papyri. The Joseph Smith Papyri X and XI are two parts of the Sensen Papyrus. The Egyptian word "sensen," which is more properly transliterated without vowels as "sn-sn," means "breathing," and this text is known as the *Book of Breathings*, or the Breathing Permit of Hôr.[62] The *Book of Breathings*, which is a later and shortened version of the *Book of the Dead*, was composed about the third or fourth century B.C., but this manuscript dates to the two-hundred-year period covering the first century B.C. through the first century A.D.[63]

In 1968 Hugh Nibley conceded that "Joseph Smith had them [the papyri], that he studied them, and that the smallest and most insignificant-looking of them [Joseph Smith Papyrus XI] is connected in some mysterious way to the Pearl of Great Price."[64] It is helpful to understand how these pieces of Egyptian papyri were originally connected. Klaus Baer's study demonstrated how the original of Facsimile No. 1 and the papyrus of the *Book of Breathings* (Joseph Smith Papyrus XI) fit together as the beginning sections of a single scroll.[65] The fragile papyrus roll had first been glued to the backing paper and then later cut into individual pieces. The cut edges match perfectly when they are placed next to each other. Just before Baer's article was published he had the opportunity to examine the actual papyri, permitting him to state: "The fiber patterns show that the papyri were adjoining parts of the same scroll and not simply mounted on adjoining pieces of paper."[66] Utilizing the published findings of Baer, Charles M. Larson in his book, *By His Own Hand upon Papyrus*, provided a visual demonstration of how the available papyri of the Book of Abraham scroll fit together. The long foldout sheet, entitled "The Book of Abraham Papyrus Scroll," shows how (from right to left) three papyri were connected: Joseph Smith Papyrus I, then Joseph Smith Papyrus XI, then a small section missing, then Joseph Smith Papyrus X (fig. 20).[67]

Hôr or Horus, the son of Osorwêr and Tikhebyt, was the priest-owner of this papyrus roll, and his name occurs six times in the hieratic text of Joseph Smith Papyri X and XI. The identity of the owner is important to determine. Facsimile No. 3 is the only place in the Book of Abraham in which Joseph Smith identified and translated specific Egyptian hieroglyphs. In the explanation to that facsimile Joseph Smith asserted that Figure 5 is "Shulem, one of the king's principal waiters, as represented by the characters above his hand."[68] The first professional Egyptologist to interpret the illustrations in Facsimiles No. 1-3 and translate their hieroglyphs and hieratic characters was Théodule Devéria, a young French scholar, who in the late 1850s translated the indicated hieroglyphs as Horus--not Shulem.[69] Likewise, over a century later Klaus Baer, professor of Egyptology at the Oriental Institute of the University of Chicago, translated these particular hieroglyphs as identifying and describing the owner of the papyrus as "Osiris Hôr, justified forever."[70] This identification supports the conclusion that Facsimile No. 3 was located at the end of the same *Book of Breathings* scroll of which Facsimile No. 1 was the beginning.

Consequently, we now know that the original of Facsimile No. 1 was at the beginning of the scroll and adjoined to it was the *Book of Breathings* papyrus (Joseph Smith Papyrus XI). Thus, when this lion-couch scene is described in 1842 as "A Facsimile *from* the Book of Abraham," it implies a connection between the illustration and the text of the Book of Abraham.[71] This implied connection is supported by the text of the Book of Abraham, for in the first chapter Abraham makes the following statement:

> And . . . that you may have a knowledge of this altar, I [Abraham] will refer you to the representation at the commencement of this record. It was made after the form of a bedstead, . . . and it stood before the gods of Elkenah, Libnah, Mahmackrah, Korash, and also a god like unto that of Pharaoh, king of Egypt. That you may have an understanding of these gods, I have given you the fashion of them in the figures at the beginning (Abr. 1:12-14).

Fig. 20--The Reconstructed Scroll of the Book of Abraham. Reproduced from Charles M. Larson, *By His Own Hand upon Papyrus* (1992), courtesy of Institute for Religious Research.

Only Facsimile No. 1 contains a representation of the altar and the gods Elkenah, Libnah, Mahmackrah, and Korash, so this statement strikingly confirms that that particular illustration was located at the beginning of the scroll before the hieratic text of Joseph Smith Papyrus XI.[72]

Joseph Smith's Egyptian Alphabet and Grammar

The available documents associated with Joseph Smith's work on the Egyptian papyri in Kirtland were published in 1966 as *Joseph Smith's Egyptian Alphabet and Grammar.*[73] This publication contains two manuscript copies of most of the first chapter and the beginning of the second chapter of the Book of Abraham, one in the handwriting of W. W. Phelps and the other in the handwriting of Warren Parrish. In 1937 Wilford C. Wood gave the LDS Church another Book of Abraham manuscript, containing the text of Abr. 1:1--2:18 in the handwritings of W. W. Phelps and Warren Parrish.[74] All three of these manuscripts have associated Egyptian hieratic characters in the left column.[75] The first to publish the fact that these characters, in exactly the same order, were also located in the first two rows of the first column of the papyrus of the *Book of Breathings* (Joseph Smith Papyrus XI) were two non-Egyptologists, Grant S. Heward and Jerald Tanner.[76] Hugh Nibley admitted that the arrangement of hieratic characters on the left and paragraphs of the English text of the Book of Abraham on the right indicated "a definite connection" between the two, but he was unsure exactly what was intended.[77] Nibley later clarified his position that, though the exact connection was unknown, he was sure that "the relationship between the two texts was never meant to be that of a direct translation."[78]

To avoid problematic evidence of which there exists genuine differences of interpretation, one can examine an instance in Book of Abraham Manuscript #1 which identifies precisely the Egyptian character and the corresponding English translation.[79] It so happens that it is an appropriate example for the study of the Book of Abraham, since it is Abraham's own name. W. W. Phelps, Joseph Smith's scribe, attached a number 2 to the Egyptian *w*-loop character and likewise to the word "Abraham" in the associated English text.[80] However, the *w*-loop character does not refer to Abraham and has no meaning on its own, since it is simply a consonantal letter functioning as part of thousands of Egyptian words. Now that all the Joseph Smith Egyptian papyri have been translated, it can be stated that neither the story found in the Book of Abraham nor even the name of Abraham is found anywhere among the papyri.[81]

Ferguson suggested to James Boyack that he read the *Egyptian Alphabet and Grammar*,[82] which was made by Joseph Smith "during his struggle with the Egyptian papyrus."[83] Smith's diary for 1 October 1835 indicated that he "labored on the Egyptian alphabet in company with Brs O[liver] Cowdery and W[illiam] W. Phelps."[84] The beginning of Egyptian Manuscript #1 illustrates a grammatical explanation in the *Egyptian Alphabet and Grammar*:

> This [character] is called Za ki-on hish, < or > chalsidon hish. This character is in the fifth degree, independent and arbitrary. It may be preseved [perceived] in the fifth degree while it stands independent and arbitrary: That is, without a straight mark inserted above or below it. By inserting a straight mark over it thus (2), it increases its signification five degrees: by inserting two straight lines thus: (3), its signification is increased five times more. By inserting three straight lines thus (4), its signification is again increased five times more than the last. By counting the number of straight lines, or considering them as qualifying adjectives, we have the degrees of comparison. There are five connecting parts of speech in the above character, called Zaki on hish. These five connecting parts of speech [are] for verbs, participles, prepositions, conjunctions, and adverbs. In Translating this character, the subject must be continued until there are as many of these connecting parts of speech used as there are connections or connecting points found in the character.[85]

Reading distinctions of meaning into mere horizontal lines either above or below a character is not true for the Egyptian language, nor has it ever been encountered in any known human language. The pure speculation in this document is in no sense a grammar of the Egyptian language.[86] Hugh Nibley asked a rhetorical question about the relation of the Book of Abraham to the hieratic characters of the Sensen Papyrus: "How on earth could Joseph Smith or anybody else have derived a condensed and detailed account of fifty [rather, eleven] pages from less than twenty hieratic signs?"[87] If the rule which states "in Translating this character, the subject must be continued until there are as many of these connecting parts of speech used as there are connections or connecting points found in the character" were followed, then it is certainly conceivable that a very expanded translation would be the result. Also, Oliver Cowdery, one of Smith's scribes during this period, expressed his opinion that the Egyptian language "in which this record is written is very comprehensive."[88]

While most of the pages in the *Egyptian Alphabet and Grammar* are in the handwriting of Joseph Smith's scribes, some parts are written by Smith himself. His handwriting occurs throughout the "Egyptian Alphabet" known as Egyptian Manuscript #4 (fig. 21).[89] Joseph Smith used the names "Kolob," "Jah-oh-eh," "Flo-ees," and "Kli-flos-isis" from this manuscript in an 1843 display of erudition in which he quoted phrases from six foreign languages, and as a seventh instance of his learning quoted what purport to be Egyptian words describing a solar eclipse followed by his translation: "Were I an Egyptian, I would exclaim Jah-oh-eh, Enish-go-on-dosh, Flo-ees-Flos-is-is; [O the earth! the power of attraction, and the moon passing between her and the sun]."[90] Some of these words also appear in the explanation to Facsimile No. 2.[91] Joseph Smith's signature appears on the title page to a little booklet entitled "Valuable Discovery of hid[d]en records that have been obtained from the ancient bur[y]-ing place of the Egyptians."[92]

I. E. S. Edwards, keeper of the Egyptian Antiquities at the British Museum, said that the *Egyptian Alphabet and Grammar* "is largely a piece of imagination and lacking in any kind of scientific

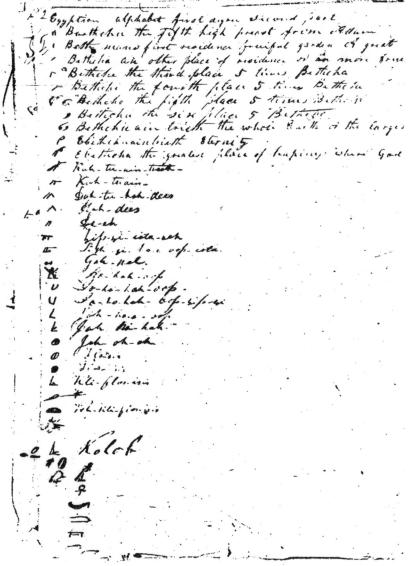

Fig. 21--Egyptian Alphabet, Egyptian Manuscript #4, in the hand-
writing of Joseph Smith, with the names "Kolob," "Jah-oh-eh,"
"Flo-ees," and "Kli-flos-isis" appearing in Facsimile No. 2.
Reproduced from Jerald Tanner and Sandra Tanner, *Joseph Smith's Egyptian
Alphabet and Grammar* (1966), courtesy of Utah Lighthouse Ministry.

value."[93]   In a similar way Egyptologist Richard A. Parker expressed the opinion that "the interpretation of signs purported to be Egyptian have no resemblance to the meanings ascribed to them by Egyptologists."[94] Tom Ferguson claimed that by study of the *Egyptian Alphabet and Grammar* and the recently discovered papyri "it is perfectly obvious that we now have the original manuscript material used by Jos. Smith in working up the Book of Abraham."[95]

The Book of Joseph
among the Egyptian Papyri

In 1835 W. W. Phelps stated that Joseph Smith identified one of the scrolls as being "the sacred record kept of Joseph in Pharaoh's Court in Egypt."[96] Some of the Metropolitan Museum of Art's donation of papyri appear to be from this long-lost Book of Joseph. Milton R. Hunter told N. Eldon Tanner, second counselor in the First Presidency, how some of the newly discovered papyri seemed to be from the Book of Joseph, and then reported that conversation back to Ferguson:

> One plate [i.e., illustration on the papyrus] was very interesting to me. Look at it in the *Deseret News*. It has the serpent walking on two tall legs. I told President Tanner that Oliver Cowdery wrote to William Fry[e] and told him that the Book of Joseph told the best story of the creation that he had ever seen and that it depicted the serpent walking on its legs before it had to crawl on its belly. I suggested [to Tanner] that that page might be from the Book of Joseph. He [Tanner] didn't want that suggestion made and that information to get out, so I wouldn't say that (if I were you) to anybody, but just for your own curiosity look at it.[97]

Consequently, as early as December 1967 both Tanner and Hunter were aware of the relationship between the Book of Joseph and some of these Egyptian papyri that were once in the possession of Joseph Smith. However, the advice of a member of the First Presidency was that he did not want it even suggested that some of the papyri may be from the Book of Joseph.

Fig. 22--Illustration of the Serpent with Legs (top) and illustration of Enoch's Pillar (bottom), Joseph Smith Papyrus V, from the document Joseph Smith identified as the Book of Joseph. Reproduced from Thomas Stuart Ferguson Collection, courtesy of Marriott Library, University of Utah.

Oliver Cowdery said that with the Egyptian mummies were two papyrus scrolls, which he identified as "the writings of Abraham and Joseph."[98] From Cowdery's description at least three illustrations in the newly discovered papyri can be identified as part of the Book of Joseph. Cowdery said concerning the Serpent on Legs (fig. 22, top) that "the serpent, represented as walking, or formed in a manner to be able to walk, standing in front of and near a female figure, is to me one of the substance."[99] In May 1844 when Josiah Quincy asked Joseph Smith about a serpent having legs, Smith is reported to have made the following comment: "Before the Fall snakes always went about on legs, just like chickens. They were deprived of them, in punishment for their agency in the ruin of man."[100]

The representation of the serpent walking on legs is located in chapter or spell 74 of the *Book of the Dead*. John A. Wilson explained that in the illustration "the dead woman stands beside a two-legged serpent, a symbol of earth, since snakes live underground."[101] Wilson translated the associated text as:

> The speech for stretching the legs [and going forth from earth. Words to be spoken] by the Osiris T-N:[102] "You will do what you should do [against him], O Sokar, Sokar, who is in his cave, who is the obstructor in the necropolis. I shine as the one who is over this district of heaven. I climb upon the sun's rays, being weary, weary. I have gone, being weary, weary in the necropolis, upon the banks of taking away their speech in the necropolis. My soul is triumphant in the house of Atum, lord of Heliopolis."[103]

Wilson also commented concerning "The Serpent with Legs":

> One of the illustrations . . . shows a walking snake. It is just above three other illustrations all of which occur in regular order in late Books of the Dead. Papyrus Ryerson (about 500-200 B.C.) and Papyrus Milbank (about 350-100 B.C.), both in the Oriental Institute, published by T. George Allen, *The Egyptian Book of the Dead* (Chicago, 1960),[104] with the texts here noted on plates xxiv-xxv and lxviii. In each papyrus, vignette of a man with a stick, along with a snake walking on two legs--vignette for Book of the Dead, chapter 72 [74].[105]

Richard A. Parker said concerning this same illustration:

> The fragment with the snake walking on two legs is surely from some chapter of the Egyptian Book of the Dead. I doubt that the name Joseph occurs anywhere in it. It could, of course, be claimed that it was written by someone named Joseph.[106]

Parker's comments were made in January 1968, and now that all the hieratic characters have been read it can be stated that the name Joseph was never located in the papyri.

Cowdery said concerning Enoch's Pillar (fig. 22, bottom) that "Enoch's Pillar, as mentioned by Josephus, is upon the same scroll. . . . Josephus says . . . that, in consequence of the prophecy of Adam that the world should be destroyed once by water and again by fire, Enoch wrote a history or an account of the same, and put [it] into two pillars one of brick and the other of stone."[107] Wilson explained that the text adjacent to this illustration is the *Book of the Dead*, spell 75, which "shows the dead person standing beside a column, which is the hieroglyph for Heliopolis." Wilson translated the associated text as follows:

> The speech for going forth to Heliopolis and taking a place there. Words to be spoken by the Osiris T-N: "I have gone forth from the underworld. I have come from the limits of the earth. I shine upon the water. I understand about the entrails of a baboon. I have taken the ways to the holy gates. I occupy the places [of the pure ones] who are in [shrouds]. I break into the houses of Remrem. I have reached the seat of Ikhsesfi. I have penetrated the sacred areas upon which Thoth stepped in pacifying the two warriors. I go, I go to Pe; I come to Dep."[108]

Concerning the illustration of the Trinity (fig. 23) Cowdery said that "the representation of the god-head--three, yet in one--is curiously drawn to give simply, though impressively, the writer's views of that exalted personage."[109] This fragment was described

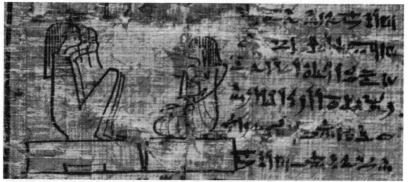

Fig. 23--Illustration of the Trinity, Joseph Smith Papyrus IV, from the document Joseph Smith identified as the Book of Joseph. Reproduced from Thomas Stuart Ferguson Collection, courtesy of Marriott Library, University of Utah.

as the "Framed ('Trinity') Papyrus," because at the time of the donation by the Metropolitan Museum of Art this papyrus was in a frame, which possibly had been done during Joseph Smith's lifetime.[110] Wilson explained that this illustration, which is a part of spell 104 in the *Book of the Dead*, "shows a normal vignette of the deceased sitting with the gods." The associated Egyptian text refers to "the great gods," as shown by Wilson's translation:

> [The speech for sitting among] the great gods. Words to be spoken [by the Osiris] T-[N: "I sit among] the great gods. [I] have passed [by] the house of the evening-barque. It is a butler, the porter of Horus, son of Isis, who comes to me on business of Re. Food and sustenance are at the proper place, to provision the offering-bread for the great gods. It is a fowler whom he has brought." As for the one who knows this speech, he sits among the [great] gods.[111]

Jay M. Todd, editor of *The Improvement Era*, after quoting from these descriptions of parts of the Book of Joseph by Oliver Cowdery, admitted that "scenes somewhat similar to these verbal descriptions [of Cowdery] seem to be on the papyri rediscovered by Dr. Atiya."[112] Though Joseph Smith identified one of the two main scrolls as being the Book of Joseph, he never produced a translation of the Book of Joseph, as he did for the Book of Abraham. On the back of his photograph of Joseph Smith Papyrus V, Ferguson expressed his opinion that this illustration is "clearly . . . part of the hieroglyphic manuscript described by Joseph Smith as the *Book of Joseph*. . . . It is part of the *Book of the Dead* and has nothing to do with 'Joseph.'"[113] Egyptologists have read all these papyri and find nothing about the life or writings of Joseph.

Denial That the Book of Abraham
Papyrus Has Been Found

Ferguson insisted strongly that the original papyri used by Joseph Smith had been found and competent translations were available, but he predicted that "of course the dodge as to the Book of Abraham must be: '*We don't have the original manuscript from which the Book of Abraham was translated.'*"[114] Interestingly Nibley used precisely this argument, claiming that the *Book of Breathings* papyri discovered at the Metropolitan Museum of Art were not used by Joseph Smith in translating the Book of Abraham:

> Whatever exercises, discreet or indiscreet, the brethren in Kirtland may have engaged in, the Prophet Joseph himself has supplied us with the most conclusive evidence that the manuscript today identified as the Book of Breathings, J.S. Papyri X and XI, was *not* in his opinion the source of the Book of Abraham. For he has furnished a clear and specific description of the latter: "The record of Abraham and Joseph, found with the mummies, is (1) beautifully written on papyrus, with black, and (2) a small part red, ink or paint, (3) in perfect preservation."[115]

Nibley's source for this purported quotation from Joseph Smith is the *History of the Church*, which at this point is actually derived from Oliver Cowdery's 1835 account.[116] Cowdery's *Messenger and Advocate* account contains an important sentence previous to the one quoted by Nibley, showing that Cowdery was speaking about the works of both Abraham and Joseph: "Upon the subject of the Egyptian records, or rather the writings of Abraham and Joseph, I may say a few words."[117] One must examine Nibley's three points. The first can be disposed of quickly, since how beautiful the Egyptian hieratic characters are was based upon the personal opinion of Cowdery. Likewise, the third point represented Cowdery's estimation of the papyrus's physical condition, which was reworded from an earlier certificate written by five medical doctors in Philadelphia. In this case Cowdery added the adjective "beautiful" and upgraded the condition of the papyrus from their description of "excellent" to "perfect."[118]

The hieroglyphs and hieratic characters in Egyptian papyri are written in black or red ink, with the black ink being made from soot and the red ink from finely ground burnet ochre, both mixed with papyrus juice.[119] Nibley expanded on his second point about the red ink by saying:

> In the second place, the text which Joseph Smith [actually, Oliver Cowdery] relates, directly or indirectly, to Abraham contained the rubrics or brief notations in red ink common to Egyptian manuscripts. He is plainly describing a real manuscript and a rather typical one; and since no one could read it, there is no reason why he should not have described it correctly. Hence, the fact that there is not the slightest indication of rubrics in the J. S. Papyri X and XI--not so much as a speck of red ink, though such rubrics are common in the other Joseph Smith manuscripts--is alone enough to disqualify it as a candidate for the Abraham source.[120]

Nibley misinterpreted the Cowdery quotation since the discussion is about both scrolls--the Book of Abraham and the Book of Joseph. Cowdery indicated that these documents as a group contain both black and red ink, not that each page of both scrolls contain both colors. At this point it is appropriate to reexamine the 1835 description in the Painesville *Telegraph,* which stated that the first mummy, a female, had a scroll with "ink black and red" and with "many female figures."[121] This matches the two colors and many illustrations found in Joseph Smith Papyri II and IV-VIII, which have been titled "The Untranslated Book of Joseph Papyrus Scroll."[122] The third mummy, a male, had a scroll, but the Painesville *Telegraph* mentioned no special ink color. This was the only male mummy and Klaus Baer translated his name as Hôr as it is found in Joseph Smith Papyri I, X, and XI, and concluded that "Joseph Smith thought that this papyrus contained the Book of Abraham."[123]

John Gee claimed that the first color photographs of the newly discovered papyri were published in the February 1968 issue of *The Improvement Era.*[124] It is, indeed, to the credit of the LDS Church that good reproductions were soon published of all the papyri. However, for some reason they were not color but two-toned sepia reproductions. Accordingly, there is no way for a reader to see where the distinctive red ink occurred in the originals. Twenty-five years after the announcement about the papyri Charles M. Larson published color photographs of the Joseph Smith Egyptian papyri. This book, *By His Own Hand upon Papyrus,* is unique for the beautiful full-color foldout, providing reproductions of the papyri measuring 9 by 22 inches.[125] Examination of this publication shows the Book of Joseph with sets of red-ink characters scattered throughout the black text and the surviving parts of the Book of Abraham solely in black ink. Thus, the evidence does not support Nibley's theory that the Book of Abraham papyrus had red ink.[126]

Another tactic is to claim that Joseph Smith's Book of Abraham was not a translation of Egyptian papyri but rather is an inspired document produced by revelation from God. Nibley admitted that the Joseph Smith Egyptian papyri contain hieroglyphs, hieratic characters, and pictorial illustrations that have symbolic meanings, but asserted that Joseph Smith in the Book of Abraham "dealt only with the third type," that is, with the symbolic pictures.[127] This strategy effectively denies a connection between any of the hieratic texts and the Book of Abraham. Nibley ignored Joseph Smith's assertions about translating the Egyptian characters on the papyri and claimed that the Book of Abraham was produced "by direct revelation."[128] Ferguson was not impressed with Nibley's arguments.

Ferguson's Opinion
of Nibley's Interpretations

Hugh Nibley, though not an Egyptologist, is a wide-ranging polyglot who took upon himself the role of defender of the faith with respect to the Book of Abraham. From 1968 to 1970 Nibley published in *The Improvement Era* a series of twenty-seven erudite articles on the Book of Abraham.[129] In March 1971 Ferguson expressed his opinion to James Boyack about these articles written by Nibley:

> Nibley's *Era* articles on the Book of Abraham aren't worth a tinker--first, because he is not impartial, being the commissioned and paid defender of the faith. Second, because he could not, he dared not, he did not, face the true issue: "Could Joseph Smith translate Egyptian?" I clipped every one of his articles and have them in a single file--and I have reviewed them--looking in vain for that issue.[130]

Ferguson charged that Nibley unfailingly reached the pre-established conclusion about Joseph Smith. Ferguson was convinced that Nibley deliberately avoided the central question and his articles in *The Improvement Era* were simply a smoke screen to divert attention from the real issues. This perception was not in Ferguson's imagination, for Nibley admitted that in his articles written during the late 1960s he "frankly skirmished and sparred for time."[131] Ferguson is not the only one to criticize Nibley's methodology. Stephen E. Thompson said:

> The approach taken in attempting to support Joseph's interpretations of these figures is to compare them with figures found in other historical and textual contexts. It is simply not valid, however, to search through 3,000 years of Egyptian religious iconography to find parallels which can be pushed, prodded, squeezed, or linked in an attempt to justify Joseph's interpretations.[132]

Ferguson felt that Nibley's attempt "to explain away and dodge the trap into which Joseph Smith fell" was absurd.[133] Samuel W. Taylor, a free-lance writer on Mormon topics, remembered what Ferguson told him concerning Nibley's effort:

> Nibley's articles in the *Era* were beautifully written, making an impressive display of literary erudition, bolstered by voluminous footnotes. Yet as Ferguson studied the pyrotechnics of Nibley's articles, he was puzzled. Amid the rocket's red glare and the bombs bursting in air, Tom Ferguson failed to find authentic facts to support the splendid literary fireworks, and his faith wasn't still there. In fact, Ferguson suspected it was all stonewalling.[134]

Nibley has espoused conflicting explanations about the Book of Abraham. It is surely significant that previous to the discovery of the Joseph Smith Egyptian papyri at the Metropolitan Museum of Art there was a consistent explanation in Mormonism that Joseph Smith--through the gift and power of God--translated Egyptian characters into the English language resulting in a modern-day restoration of Abraham's record. Only after the 1967 announcement of the discovery of the papyri and their subsequent translation has the traditional explanation been replaced by a variety of contradictory theories.[135]

Ferguson's Conclusions
on the Book of Abraham

In December 1967 before the papyri had been translated, N. Eldon Tanner of the LDS First Presidency was cautious about not overstating exactly what the Joseph Smith Egyptian Papyri were. However, he told Milton R. Hunter that "the important thing was that we have part of the manuscript of the Book of Abraham which certainly sustains the fact that Joseph Smith wrote the Book of Abraham from ancient papyri manuscripts."[136] Now that all the papyri have been translated and not a single trace of Abraham has been found, even Tanner's minimal position has been abandoned. In 1970 Ferguson told some friends that he "entirely repudiated the Book of Abraham."[137]

Michael D. Rhodes, a researcher in ancient scriptures at BYU, offered two different explanations as to why the translation of these Egyptian papyri does not coincide with the text of the Book of Abraham: either the Book of Abraham "may have been taken from a *different* portion of the papyrus rolls in Joseph Smith's possession" or "instead of making a literal *translation*, as scholars would use the term, he used the Urim and Thummim as a means of receiving revelation."[138] Rhodes's first suggested explanation ignored three facts: (1) Baer's reconstruction of how the original of Facsimile No. 1 and the Small Sensen Papyrus of the *Book of Breathings* (Joseph Smith Papyri I and XI, respectively) are now known to have fitted together, (2) the hieratic characters from the first two lines of the *Book of Breathings* papyrus being discovered in the left column of the three earliest manuscripts of the Book of Abraham (Book of Abraham Manuscripts #1, #2, and #3), and (3) the hieroglyphics surrounding the original of Facsimile No. 1 being found in Joseph Smith's *Egyptian Alphabet and Grammar.* Rhodes's second explanation reversed the consistent claim of Joseph Smith that he was, with the inspiration of God, translating the characters on the ancient scroll, not just receiving inspired revelation in response to looking at the Egyptian characters or illustrations. Joseph Smith dictated that "with W. W. Phelps and Oliver Cowdery as scribes, I commenced the translation of some of the characters or hiero-glyphics, and much to our joy found that one of the rolls contained the writings of Abraham, another the writings of Joseph of Egypt."[139] Rhodes's proposed explanation presents a seemingly faith-promoting alternative, but it does so at the expense of Joseph Smith's clear statement that he was in fact translating Egyptian characters.

A third possibility exists--though unstated by Rhodes--which is that the first two parts (i.e., Joseph Smith Papyri I and XI) of the actual papyrus utilized by Joseph Smith have been found, but that his interpretation concerning Abraham has no relationship to the now-translatable Egyptian text. As a result of investigations using four independent witnesses, Ferguson, the lawyer, decided that the third option was correct, since these Egyptian authorities "all agree that the original manuscript Egyptian text translates into the *Breathing Permit of Hôr*."[140]

In the summer of 1970 an LDS scholar felt that the Joseph Smith Egyptian papyri "may well represent the potentially most damaging case against Mormonism since its foundation."[141] According to one of Ferguson's friends, the discovery and translation of these Egyptian documents was absolutely devastating to his faith.[142] Ferguson concluded that there was no real connection between these Egyptian papyri and the Book of Abraham. He was "very upset by the discovery that it was only a [copy of the] *Book of the Dead*."[143] Ferguson wrote to a non-Mormon friend that "the Egyptian papyri showed that Joseph Smith could not read Egyptian and simply faked it when he was presented with a MS."[144]

In March 1976 John W. Fitzgerald, a retired elementary school principal, wrote Ferguson a letter concerning Dee Jay Nelson, who first translated the Joseph Smith Egyptian Papyri. Fitzgerald claimed that N. Eldon Tanner, second counselor in the First Presidency, first requested Nelson to translate these papyri with the commitment that the Church would publish his translation, and then reputedly, when the LDS church leader learned that Nelson's translation "was not supportive of Joseph Smith's rendition of the Egyptian, they refused to publish it."[145] The developments concerning the translation of these papyri were close to Ferguson's heart and he promptly replied: "I wonder what really goes on in the minds of church leadership who know of the data concerning the Book of Abraham, the new data on the First Vision, etc. I guess we'll never know. It would tend to devastate the church if a top leader were to announce the facts."[146] A forthright attitude by the LDS Church leaders about the Book of Abraham and the First Vision would radically alter the perceptions of most members, but Ferguson probably overestimated the reaction when he suggested that such admissions "would tend to devastate" the LDS Church. When Ferguson was asked if it was true that most Egyptologists "agree that a correct translation of the ancient papyri owned by Joseph Smith has absolutely no connection or similarity" to the Book of Abraham, he answered succinctly, "Yes."[147]

Wesley P. Walters, a Presbyterian minister in Illinois, obtained Ferguson's permission to relate the story of his disillusionment concerning Joseph Smith and the Book of Abraham,[148] but Ferguson did not allow Walters to divulge his name:

> One life-long defender of Joseph Smith made his own independent investigation of Joseph's ability as a translator of Egyptian records, utilizing recognized Egyptologists without telling them a word about the issues that were at stake. Their verdict agreed with the findings of Mr. [Dee Jay] Nelson and Dr. [Klaus] Baer. Consequently, he came to reject the Book of Abraham and the claims put forth by Joseph Smith as a translator of ancient languages.[149]

Ferguson concluded that Facsimile No. 1 did not depict the biblical Abraham being sacrificed on an altar by the idolatrous priest of Elkenah but rather the Egyptian god Osiris being embalmed by jackal-headed Anubis for the next life of Egyptian mythology. In January 1983--just two months before he passed away--Ferguson told an LDS Church employee that the Joseph Smith papyri were nothing more than various kinds of Egyptian "funeral texts."[150] Thus, Ferguson's original excitement in 1967 about the opportunity of authenticating the Book of Abraham turned into a nightmare. Ferguson's former belief system-- nurtured and sustained from childhood--could not withstand the shock of this disillusionment. Everything in his theological world came crashing down. This forced Ferguson to reexamine his assumptions not only about the Book of Abraham, but also concerning Joseph Smith and the Book of Mormon. This process thrust Ferguson into a completely new approach to religious questions in his life.

Notes

1. Jack E. Jarrard, "Rare Papyri Presented to Church," *Deseret News*, 27 November 1967, A-1, A-3.

2. Glen Wade, "A Conversation with Professor Atiya," *Dialogue: A Journal of Mormon Thought* 2 (Winter 1967): 51-53. Keith Terry and Walter L. Whipple, *From the Dust of Decades: A Saga of the Papyri and Mummies* (Salt Lake City: Bookcraft, 1968), 104, pointed out that in 1962 Whipple received photos of the Joseph Smith Egyptian papyri from the Metropolitan Museum of Art, but "he did little with his discovery and is now at a loss as to why."

3. Hugh Nibley provided the names and numbering to the papyri illustrations associated with Jay M. Todd, "Background of the Church Historian's Fragment," *The Improvement Era* 71 (February 1968): 40a- 40i, 41.

4. By the time Hugh Nibley assigned the numbering for the papyri the two pages of the Court of Osiris were given the same number (J.S. Pap. IIIA and IIIB) and the Church Historian's Fragment (which was not part of the donation from the Metropolitan Museum of Art) was designated as J.S. Pap. IX. See Hugh Nibley, "Fragment Found in Salt Lake City," *Brigham Young University Studies* 8 (Winter 1968): 191-94.

5. Hugh Nibley, "Prolegomena to Any Study of the Book of Abraham," *Brigham Young University Studies* 8 (Winter 1968): 171.

6. H. Donl Peterson, *The Story of the Book of Abraham: Mummies, Manuscripts, and Mormonism* (Salt Lake City: Deseret Book Co., 1995), 36-75. Cf. Warren R. Dawson and Eric P. Uphill, *Who Was Who in Egyptology*, 2d ed. (London: The Egypt Exploration Society, 1972), 166.

7. Milton V. Backman, Jr., *The Heavens Resound: A History of the Latter-day Saints in Ohio, 1830-1838* (Salt Lake City: Deseret Book Co., 1983), 218.

8. William W. Phelps, letter to Sally Phelps, 19-20 July 1835, partially printed in Leah Y. Phelps, "Letters of Faith from Kirtland," *The Improvement Era* 45 (August 1942): 529. Oliver Cowdery, writing in the *Latter Day Saints' Messenger and Advocate*, described the materials

as follows: "Upon the subject of the Egyptian records, or rather the writings of Abraham and Joseph, I may say a few words. This record is beautifully written on papyrus with black, and a small part, red ink or paint, in perfect preservation. The characters are such as you find upon the coffins of mummies, hieroglyphics, etc. with many characters or letters exactly like the present (though probably not quite so square) form of the Hebrew without points," 2 (December 1835): 234.

9. B. H. Roberts, ed., *History of the Church of Jesus Christ of Latter-day Saints, Period I: History of Joseph Smith, the Prophet by Himself* (Salt Lake City: Deseret News, 1904), 2:235-36.

10. Stephen E. Thompson, "Egyptology and the Book of Abraham," *Dialogue: A Journal of Mormon Thought* 28 (Spring 1995): 153-54, said: "The answer to this [i.e., when Abraham lived] is by no means simple, and scholarly estimates for the age of the patriarchs range from 2200 to 1200 B.C. . . . Others would argue that while it is not possible to assign a date to the lifetime of Abraham, it is possible to situate chronologically the so-called 'Patriarchal Age.' Many scholars would place this sometime during the first half of the second millennium, i.e., 2000-1500 B.C., while others would narrow the time frame within this period." Thompson's suggested five-hundred-year period encompasses the dates given in the LDS Bible Dictionary, where Abraham's birth is 1996 B.C. and Joseph's death is 1635 B.C. Some scholars consider Abraham to be a mythical character. See Henry J. Flanders, Jr., Robert W. Crapps, and David A. Smith, *People of the Covenant: An Introduction to the Old Testament*, 3d ed. (New York: Oxford University Press, 1988), 116-28.

11. Scott H. Faulring, ed., *An American Prophet's Record: The Diaries and Journals of Joseph Smith* (Salt Lake City: Signature Books, 1987), 127.

12. The Painesville, Ohio, *Telegraph*, 27 March 1835, quoted in John A. Larson, "Joseph Smith and Egyptology: An Early Episode in the History of American Speculation about Ancient Egypt, 1835-1844," in *For His Ka: Essays Offered in Memory of Klaus Baer*, ed. David P. Silverman, Studies in Ancient Oriental Civilization, no. 55 (Chicago: The Oriental Institute of the University of Chicago, 1994), 162. James R. Harris, *The Facsimiles of the Book of Abraham: A Study of the Joseph Smith Egyptian Papyri* (Payson, UT: Harris House Publication, 1990), 19, incorrectly gave the date as July 1835.

13. Klaus Baer, letter to [Jay M.] Todd, 20 December 1968, in the H. Michael Marquardt Collection, Accession 900, Box 78, Fd 1, Manuscripts Division, J. Willard Marriott Library, University of Utah, Salt Lake City; hereafter abbreviated to Marquardt Collection.

14. Cowdery, in *Messenger and Advocate* 2 (Dec. 1835): 234.

15. Klaus Baer, "The Breathing Permit of Hôr: A Translation of the Apparent Source of the Book of Abraham," *Dialogue: A Journal of Mormon Thought* 3 (Autumn 1968): 111, with the Breathing Permit of Hôr being found in J.S. Pap. I, X, and XI, the *Book of the Dead* of the Tshenmîn being found in J.S. Pap. II, IV-IX, and most of IV, and the

Book of the Dead of Neferirnûb being found in J.S. Pap. IIIA and IIIB. See Raymond O. Faulkner, trans., *The Ancient Egyptian Book of the Dead*, ed. Carol Andrews, rev. ed. (London: Trustees of the British Museum, 1985).

16. John Gee, "A Tragedy of Errors," review of *By His Own Hand upon Papyrus: A New Look at the Joseph Smith Papyri*, by Charles M. Larson, in *Review of Books on the Book of Mormon* 4 (1992): 94.

17. William S. West, *A Few Interesting Facts respecting the Rise, Progress, and Pretensions of the Mormons* ([Warren, OH], 1837), 6.

18. Richard D. Poll, "Dealing with Dissonance: Myths, Documents, and Faith," *Sunstone* 12 (May 1988): 20.

19. Thomas Stuart Ferguson, letter to Milton [R. Hunter], 30 November 1967, in the Thomas Stuart Ferguson Collection, Accession 1350, Manuscripts Division, J. Willard Marriott Library, University of Utah, Salt Lake City; hereafter abbreviated to Ferguson Collection, UU.

20. Milton R. Hunter, letter to Ferguson, 4 December 1967, in Ferguson Collection, UU.

21. Ferguson, letter to Aziz S. Atiya, 4 December 1967, in the Aziz S. Atiya Collection, Accession 480, Manuscripts Division, J. Willard Marriott Library, University of Utah, Salt Lake City.

22. Ferguson, note to Leonard H. Lesko, 26 December 1967, in Ferguson Collection, UU.

23. Jack E. Jarrard, "Church Receives Joseph Smith Papyri," *Deseret News*, Church News, 2 December 1967, 7-10.

24. Ferguson, letter to [addressee unknown], 28 December 1967, partially printed in *Newsletter and Proceedings of the Society for Early Historic Archaeology*, no. 105 (1 March 1968): 9.

25. Pierre Agrinier Bach, interview with author, 25 May 1993, transcript in Everett L. Cooley Oral History Project, Accession 814, Manuscripts Division, J. Willard Marriott Library, University of Utah, Salt Lake City; hereafter abbreviated to Bach Interview in Cooley Oral History Project. Bach remembered this as being "maybe a week" after the announcement, but it is more likely about a month.

26. Ferguson, letter to James Boyack, 13 March 1971, in Ferguson Collection, UU.

27. Ferguson, letter to Leonard H. Lesko, 31 January 1968, in Ferguson Collection, UU.

28. Leonard H. Lesko, memorandum to Ferguson, 4 March 1968, in Ferguson Collection, UU.

29. Ferguson, letter to Modern Microfilm Co., 12 November 1968, in Ferguson Collection, UU.

30. Baer, "Breathing Permit," 109-34.

31. Dee Jay Nelson, *The Joseph Smith Papyri: A Translation and Preliminary Survey of the Ta-shert-Min and Ter Papyri* (Salt Lake City: Modern Microfilm Co., 1968); *The Joseph Smith Papyri, Part 2: Additional Translations and a Supplemental Survey of the Ta-shert-Min, Hor and Amen-Terp Papyri* (Salt Lake City: Modern Microfilm Co., 1968);

Joseph Smith's "Eye of Ra": A Preliminary Survey and First Translation of Facsimile No. 2 in the Book of Abraham (Salt Lake City: Modern Microfilm Co., 1968); and *A Translation and Study of Facsimile No. 3 in the Book of Abraham* (Salt Lake City: Modern Microfilm Co., 1969).

32. Ferguson, letter to Boyack, 13 March 1971.

33. Dee Jay Nelson, letter to Mr. [Jerald] Tanner, 17 April 1968, in Box 72, Fd 2, Marquardt Collection.

34. Hugh Nibley, note [to N. Eldon Tanner], 4 January 1968, in Box 72, Fd 2, Marquardt Collection.

35. Hugh Nibley, "Getting Ready to Begin: An Editorial," *Brigham Young University Studies* 8 (Spring 1968): 247, 251. Nibley, ibid., 254, concluded his article with the comment that "to Mr. Dee Jay Nelson goes the credit of being the first to make the plunge."

36. In May 1978 Nelson purchased for $195 a spurious Philosophiae Doctor degree from a Seattle diploma mill known as Pacific North-Western University, and for his false claim of having a Ph.D. degree Nelson has been justifiably condemned. See Robert L. Brown and Rosemary Brown, *They Lie in Wait to Deceive: "A Study of Anti-Mormon Deception"* (Mesa, AZ: Brownsworth Publishing Co., 1981), 1:1-44, and Jerald Tanner and Sandra Tanner, *Mormonism: Shadow or Reality*, 5th ed. (Salt Lake City: Utah Lighthouse Ministry, 1987), 309-11. The Browns are orthodox defenders of Mormonism, while the Tanners are anti-Mormon publishers.

37. "A Glance at the Mormons," *The Quincy Whig* 3 (17 October 1840): 1, quoted in Jay M. Todd, *The Saga of the Book of Abraham* (Salt Lake City: Deseret Book Co., 1969), 211.

38. Henry Adams, "Charles Francis Adams Visits the Mormons in 1844," *Proceedings of the Massachusetts Historical Society* 68 (1952): 285, transcribing Charles Francis Adams's diary entries, with emphasis in original. By ignoring all contemporary evidence of those who were shown the papyri by Joseph Smith, Hugh Nibley, "A New Look at the Pearl of Great Price," *The Improvement Era* 71 (February 1968): 20, can assert that "Joseph Smith never claimed that they [the Facsimiles] were autographic manuscripts or that they dated from the time of Abraham."

39. Josiah Quincy, *Figures of the Past from the Leaves of Old Journals* (Boston: Roberts Brothers, 1883), 386.

40. "A Fac-Simile from the Book of Abraham, No. 1," *Times and Seasons* 3 (1 March 1842): 703. According to Louis C. Zucker, "Joseph Smith as a Student of Hebrew," *Dialogue: A Journal of Mormon Thought* 3 (Summer 1968): 51, Joseph Smith's formal Hebrew classes from 26 January to 31 March 1836 affected the text of the Book of Abraham, where one finds the following Hebrew words (usually according to the transliteration of Seixas) and the correct English meanings: *Kokob* "star," *Kokaubeam* "stars," *Hah-ko-kau-beam* "the stars," *Raukeeyang* "firmament" or "expanse," *Shaumahyeem* "heavens," and *gnolaum* "eternal." These four different Hebrew words and numerous other Hebrew-like names which Zucker cited to show the influence of Smith's instruction in Hebrew are located in the first three chapters of the Book of Abra-

ham and Facsimiles No. 1 and 2. Zucker, ibid., 52, indicated that this contrasts with the polytheism found numerous times in the Book of Abraham, chapters four and five, which probably date to the Nauvoo period. Zucker's essay in *Dialogue* is reprinted as the introduction to J[oshua] Seixas, *A Manual Hebrew Grammar for the Use of Beginners,* 2d ed. enl. and improved (Andover, MA: Gould and Newman, 1834; reprint, Salt Lake City: Sunstone Foundation, 1981).

41. Ferguson, letter to Boyack, 13 March 1971.

42. Louis V. Žabkar, *A Study of the Ba Concept in Ancient Egyptian Texts,* Studies in Ancient Oriental Civilization Series, no. 34 (Chicago: University of Chicago Press, 1968).

43. Lesko, memorandum, 1968, in Ferguson Collection, UU. Bracketed numbers are added in this and the following quotations in order to more easily compare with Facsimile No. 1 of the Book of Abraham.

44. Richard A. Parker, "The Joseph Smith Papyri: A Preliminary Report," *Dialogue: A Journal of Mormon Thought* 3 (Summer 1968): 86.

45. Nelson, *Smith Papyri, Part 2,* 2, following the translation of Richard A. Parker, corrected his mistaken "Ter" to the name "Hor."

46. Nelson, *Smith Papyri,* 24; cf. 42-45.

47. Baer here reversed the identifications of Qebeh-senuwef and Duwa-mutef, but John Gee, *Notes on the Sons of Horus* (Provo, UT: Foundation for Ancient Research and Mormon Studies, 1991), 43-44, pointed out that such variation is known.

48. Baer, "Breathing Permit," 118. Baer added the numbers in parentheses in order to allow comparison with Joseph Smith's explanation, but Baer did not explain number 9.

49. John A. Wilson, letter to Marvin Cowan, 5 January 1968, in Box 78, Fd 7, Marquardt Collection.

50. John A. Wilson, *Thousands of Years: An Archaeologist's Search for Ancient Egypt* (New York: Charles Scribner's Sons, 1972), 174. In a noncommittal statement John A. Wilson, "A Summary Report," *Dialogue: A Journal of Mormon Thought* 3 (Summer 1968): 68, said only that J.S. Pap. I "shows a scene of a man lying upon a bed, while another figure leans over him."

51. Thompson, "Egyptology," 144-45. Cf. Daniel C. Peterson, "News from Antiquity," *The Ensign* 24 (January 1994): 18.

52. Nibley, "New Look," 71 (September 1968): 78. Nibley felt that the artist provided "a rapid, fairly accurate, and unbiased sketch of what the papyrus looked like before it was damaged."

53. James Boyack, letter, quoted in Todd, *Saga,* 214. Boyack also indicated that the artist copied the numbers designating the different figures in the published Facsimile No. 1, none of which appear on the original papyrus.

54. Hugh Nibley, "As Things Stand at the Moment," *Brigham Young University Studies* 9 (Autumn 1968): 98, with emphasis in original. Nibley attributed the lack of a jackal's mask to the original

Egyptian artist of J.S. Pap. I, not to Joseph Smith or anyone else in the early nineteenth century.

55. Nibley, "New Look," 71 (September 1968): 72. Nibley, ibid., 80n32, suggested that the "pencilled restoration" of Figure 3 was done sometime during the 111 years of the "post-Mormon" period--that is, from 1856 to 1967.

56. Edward H. Ashment, "The Facsimiles of the Book of Abraham: A Reappraisal," *Sunstone* 4 (December 1979): 36. For a response to Ashment's analysis, see Hugh Nibley, "The Facsimiles of the Book of Abraham: A Response [to Edward H. Ashment]," *Sunstone* 4 (December 1979): 49-51.

57. Ashment, "Facsimiles," 38; also, cf. his illustrations 20, 21, and 22 on p. 43. In a last-minute addition between footnotes 34 and 35, Baer, "Breathing Permit," 118n34*, explained: "One tends to see what one expects to see. So far as I know, Nelson, *The Joseph Smith Papyri*, p. 42, was the first to point out that the bird above the head of Osiris clearly has a human head and therefore must be his *ba*. In 'Facsimile No. 1,' it is drawn with a falcon's head, and I must confess with some embarrassment that I also 'saw' the falcon's head before reading Nelson's study."

58. Richard D. Poll, "Dealing with Dissonance: The Book of Abraham as a Case Study," typescript, 1984, 1, in the Richard D. Poll Collection, Accession 1472, Manuscripts Division, J. Willard Marriott Library, University of Utah, Salt Lake City.

59. Klaus Baer, letter to Mr. [Jerald] Tanner, 8 August 1968, in Box 78, Fd 1, Marquardt Collection.

60. Michael D. Rhodes, "Facsimiles from the Book of Abraham," in *Encyclopedia of Mormonism*, ed. Daniel H. Ludlow (New York: Macmillan Publishing Co., 1992), 1:136-37. Cf. Michael D. Rhodes, "The Book of Abraham: Divinely Inspired Scripture," review of *By His Own Hand upon Papyrus: A New Look at the Joseph Smith Papyri*, by Charles M. Larson, in *Review of Books on the Book of Mormon* 4 (1992): 126.

61. Thompson, "Egyptology," 160, responded to Rhodes's assertion by saying: "I see no evidence that Joseph Smith had a correct conception of 'Egyptian religious practices' or that a knowledge of such was essential to the production of the Book of Abraham."

62. Baer, "Breathing Permit," 109-34. Cf. Hugh Nibley, *The Message of the Joseph Smith Papyri: an Egyptian Endowment* (Salt Lake City: Deseret Book Co., 1975), 75.

63. Baer, "Breathing Permit," 111, gave a date of about 100 B.C.

64. Hugh Nibley, "Phase One," *Dialogue: A Journal of Mormon Thought* 3 (Summer 1968): 102.

65. Baer, "Breathing Permit," 112-13.

66. Ibid., 134.

67. Charles M. Larson, *By His Own Hand upon Papyrus: A New Look at the Joseph Smith Papyri*, rev. ed. (Grand Rapids, MI: Institute for Religious Research, 1992), 33.

68. That Joseph Smith is indicating the characters he is translating is further supported by his wording for fig. 2 "whose name is given in the characters above his head" and fig. 4 "as written above the hand."

69. Théodule Devéria, "Fragments of Egyptian Funerary Mss. Considered by the Mormons to be Autograph Memoirs of Abraham," in Jules Remy and Julius Brenchley, *A Journey to Great-Salt-Lake City* (London: W. Jeffs, 1861), 2:546.

70. Baer, "Breathing Permit," 127. Baer is understandably a little tentative, since the original to Facsimile No. 3 is not available. Baer continued that this facsimile "shows a man (5), his hand raised in adoration and a cone of perfumed grease and a lotus flower on his head (ancient Egyptian festival attire), being introduced by Maat (4), the goddess of justice, and Anubis (6), the guide of the dead, into the presence of Osiris (1), enthroned as king of the Netherworld. Behind Osiris stands Isis (2), and in front of him is an offering-stand (3) with a jug and some flowers on it." Baer's identifications should be compared with the six explanations offered by Joseph Smith for Facsimile No. 3.

71. "A Fac-Simile from the Book of Abraham, No. 1," *Times and Seasons* 3 (1 March 1842): 703, with emphasis added.

72. In an attempt to overcome the problem of the illustration of J.S. Pap. I being at least fifteen hundred years later than Abraham, Nibley, "As Things Stand," 78, suggested that "in fact, the remark [at Abr. 1:14] may well be the insertion of a later scribe." Concerning Nibley's explanation of this difficulty, Wesley P. Walters, "Joseph Smith among the Egyptians: An Examination of the Source of Joseph Smith's Book of Abraham," *The Journal of the Evangelical Theological Society* 16 (Winter 1973): 39, responded that "this leaves the reader wondering how a scribe could insert a remark into the Egyptian manuscripts of the Book of Abraham when Dr. Nibley has already concluded that the papyri 'did not contain any of the text of the Book of Abraham as we have it.'"

73. Jerald Tanner and Sandra Tanner, eds., *Joseph Smith's Egyptian Alphabet and Grammar* (Salt Lake City: Modern Microfilm Co., 1966).

74. Richard L. Evans, "Illinois Yields Church Documents," *The Improvement Era* 40 (September 1937): 543, 565, 573, though the handwriting is incorrectly identified as Joseph Smith's.

75. Harris, *Facsimiles*, 31, incorrectly stated that the fourth Book of Abraham manuscript, in the handwriting of Willard Richards and dated to 1841, also has hieratic signs in the left column.

76. Grant S. Heward and Jerald Tanner, "The Source of the Book of Abraham Identified," *Dialogue: A Journal of Mormon Thought* 3 (Summer 1968): 92-98. Nibley, "Getting Ready," 246-47, rightly criticized the inadequacies of Heward's translation of Egyptian, as published in the March 1968 issue of *The Salt Lake City Messenger*.

77. Nibley, "Phase One," 100.

78. Nibley, "As Things Stand," 102.

79. This page is reproduced in Evans, "Church Documents," 543.

80. The correlation of this *w*-loop character with the name "Abraham" is further supported by Egyptian Manuscripts #1, #3, #4,

and #5, where the character is identified as "Ah-brah-oam" (with slightly varying spelling and hyphenation). Confirming this connection to Abraham, Hugh Nibley, "The Meaning of the Kirtland Egyptian Papers," *Brigham Young University Studies* 11 (Summer 1971): 384, said: "Throughout all the 'Grammar and Alphabet' papers . . . the loop or 'w' symbol is always said in some way or other to refer to Abraham."

81. Bruce A. Van Orden, "The Book of Abraham and the Joseph Smith Papyri," typescript, 1983, 1, in the Max H. Parkin Collection, Accession 1539, Manuscripts Division, J. Willard Marriott Library, University of Utah, Salt Lake City, admitted that "the Book of Abraham is not a direct translation from any of the existing twelve papyri. In fact there appears to be very little, if anything, that relates in a direct textual way to the Book of Abraham. The name Abraham does not appear on any of the papyri." John Gee, "References to Abraham Found in Two Egyptian Texts," *Insights: An Ancient Window*, no. 5 (September 1991): 1, a doctoral student in Egyptology, proclaimed the discovery of Abraham's name in Egyptian documents and put forth an example which hints at Abraham on a lion couch, for "immediately below the scene are written the Greek words, 'Let Abraham who . . . upon . . . wonder marvelously." Gee also stated that "much of this compares closely with Joseph Smith's indication that Facsimile 1 from the Book of Abraham is an illustration of 'Abraham fastened upon an altar' to be sacrificed by idolatrous priests." In his next publication on this pagan text Gee, *Horus*, 28*n*168, repeated the same translation of the Greek words, adding his wonderment in a footnote: "Oddly enough, this is considered a love charm!" In his third publication John Gee, "Abraham in Ancient Egyptian Texts," *The Ensign* 22 (July 1992): 60, explained that this reference occurs in a love spell and it is a woman lying on the lion couch and translated the same passage as: "Let Abraham who . . . I adjure you by . . . and incinerate so-and-so daughter of so-and-so." In contrast to Gee's view, Edward H. Ashment, *The Use of Egyptian Magical Papyri to Authenticate the Book of Abraham: A Critical Review* (Salt Lake City: Resource Communications, 1993), 14), another doctoral candidate in Egyptology, argued that this lion-couch scene does not illustrate a sacrifice--either of Abraham or of the woman--since "its real purpose was intended to inflame a woman with passion." This magical incantation, among its abracadabra words, does indeed contain the name of Abraham, but there is no connection with the Book of Abraham, and the love charm intends that the woman will burn with passion, not literally be incinerated.

82. Ferguson was referring to the 1966 edition of Tanner and Tanner, *Egyptian Alphabet*. For a more up-to-date edition of these documents, see H. Michael Marquardt, comp., *The Joseph Smith Egyptian Papers* (Cullman, AL: Printing Service, 1981). For a transcription of the English texts, see William S. Harwell, ed., *Joseph Smith's Grammar and Alphabet of the Egyptian Language*, Doctrine of the Priesthood, vol. 5, no. 10 (Salt Lake City: Collier's Publishing Co., 1992). For an effort to make sense of the Egyptian Alphabet and Grammar, see Joe Sampson,

Written by the Finger of God: Decoding Ancient Languages, A Testimony of Joseph Smith's Translations (Sandy, UT: Wellspring Publishing, 1993).

83. Ferguson, letter to Boyack, 13 March 1971. Dean C. Jessee, comp. and ed., *The Personal Writings of Joseph Smith* (Salt Lake City: Deseret Book Co., 1984), 650n16, described the "Grammar and A[l]phabet of the Egyptian Language" as "the product of early study of these ancient materials."

84. Faulring, *Prophet's Record*, 35. Joseph Smith also mentioned the alphabet and grammar of the Egyptian language at 17 November 1835 and 13 November 1843 (Faulring, ibid., 65, 427).

85. "Grammar and A[l]phabet of the Egyptian Language," 1, in the handwriting of W. W. Phelps, reproduced in Tanner and Tanner, *Egyptian Alphabet* and Marquardt, *Egyptian Papers*. The word "or" enclosed in angle brackets was added above the line in the manuscript. The words "and preseving [perceiving] them" were written and then deleted from the sixth sentence of the manuscript.

86. Walters, "Egyptians," 42-43, presented an example of interpretation from pages 5 and 21 of the "Grammar and A[l]phabet of the Egyptian Language" to its developed form on p. 5 of Book of Abraham Manuscript #1: "The EAG [Egyptian Alphabet and Grammar] says that a straight horizontal line is pronounced 'Zip Zi' and means 'a woman married or unmarried, or daughter; signifies all or any woman.' A curved line like a smiling mouth signifies 'beneath' and is pronounced 'tou es,' while a dot is 'iota' and means either 'the eye, or I see.' When the three are joined together it is pronounced 'Iota tou es Zip Zi' and comes to mean 'the land of Egypt which was first discovered by a woman while under water, and afterwards settled by her sons, she being a daughter of Ham.' Consequently when this sign combination is found in the margin of the Book of Abraham manuscripts, the following translation occurs: 'The land of Egypt being first discovered by a woman, who was the daughter of Ham, and the daughter of Zeptah which in the Chaldea signifies Egypt, which signifies that which is forbidden. When this woman discovered the land it was under water, who after settled her sons in it, and thus from Ham sprang that race, which preserved the curse in the land' [cf. Abr. 1:23]. With the Prophet utilizing such an erroneous method of Egyptian translating, it is quite pointless to try to show that he actually understood the Egyptian text and derived the correct meaning from it."

87. Nibley, *Smith Papyri*, 1. Cf. H. Michael Marquardt, *The Book of Abraham Papyrus Found: An Answer to Dr. Hugh Nibley's Book "The Message of the Joseph Smith Papyri: An Egyptian Endowment" As It Relates to the Source of the Book of Abraham*, 2d ed., rev. and enl. (Salt Lake City: Modern Microfilm Co., 1981).

88. Cowdery, letter to Frye, 236. Cowdery explained: "Neither can I give you a probable idea how large volumes they [the translation of the Book of Abraham and the Book of Joseph] will make; but judging from their size, and the comprehensiveness of the language, one might reasonably expect to see a sufficient [volume] to develop much upon the

mighty acts of the ancient men of God."

89. Nibley, "As Things Stand," 70, and Nibley, "New Look," 73 (May 1970): 83, denied that any of the Kirtland Egyptian Papers included Joseph Smith's handwriting. Nibley, "Egyptian Papers," 351, corrected these earlier statements.

90. Joseph Smith, "Reply" [to James Arlington Bennett], 13 November 1843, in *Times and Seasons* 4 (1 November 1843): 373, with Smith placing his translation in square brackets.

91. Walter L. Whipple, *A Concordance and Dictionary to the Egyptian Alphabet and Grammar in Parallel with the Book of Abraham* (Glendale, CA, 1972), 167, said that "there is more than a passing relationship between the Book of Abraham and the Egyptian Alphabet, especially for Abraham chapters 1 and 3 and Facsimile number 2."

92. Nibley, "Egyptian Papers," 351, indicated that the entire title is in the handwriting of Joseph Smith, but probably only the signature is by Joseph Smith.

93. I. E. S. Edwards, letter to Grant S. Heward, 9 June 1966, in Box 78, Fd 2, Marquardt Collection. Edwards added that "the whole document [the Egyptian Alphabet and Grammar] reminds me of the writings of psychic practitioners which are sometimes sent to me."

94. Richard A. Parker, letter to Marvin Cowan, 9 January 1968, in Box 78, Fd 7, Marquardt Collection. Nibley, "Egyptian Papers," 367, stated that Smith's efforts in Egyptian Manuscript #4 were "a perfectly sane and rational approach to a problem."

95. Ferguson, letter to Boyack, 13 March 1971.

96. W. W. Phelps, letter to S. Phelps, 529.

97. Milton R. Hunter, letter to Ferguson, 4 December 1967, in Ferguson Collection, UU.

98. Cowdery, letter to Frye, 234.

99. Ibid., 236.

100. Quincy, *Figures*, 387.

101. Wilson, "Summary Report," 77.

102. Wilson's abbreviation "T-N" used the initials in the constantly recurring formula "*T*a-shere-Min, triumphant, born to *N*es-Khonsu, triumphant."

103. Wilson, "Summary Report," 77.

104. T. George Allen, ed., *The Egyptian Book of the Dead: Documents in the Oriental Institute Museum at the University of Chicago*, Oriental Institute Publications, vol. 82 (Chicago: University of Chicago Press, 1960).

105. Wilson, letter to Cowan, 5 January 1968. The top part of the page is from the *Book of the Dead*, spell 72, but the section next to the serpent illustration is spell 74, as corrected in brackets in the quotation.

106. Parker, letter to Cowan, 9 January 1968.

107. Cowdery, letter to Frye, 236.

108. Wilson, "Summary Report," 77-78. The biblical '*ōn*, On, which is the Hebrew name for Heliopolis, is mentioned in Gen. 41:45, 50; 46:20.

109. Cowdery, letter to Frye, 236. Cowdery also said that the hieroglyphics "were written by persons acquainted with the history of the creation, the fall of man, and more or less of the correct ideas of notions of the Deity."

110. D[oyle] L. G[reen], "New Light on Joseph Smith's Egyptian Papyri: Additional Fragment Disclosed," *The Improvement Era* 71 (February 1968): 40.

111. Wilson, "Summary Report," 82.

112. Todd, *Saga*, 194.

113. Ferguson, statement, located on back of his photograph of J.S. Pap. V, in Ferguson Collection, UU.

114. Ferguson, letter to Boyack, 13 March 1971, with emphasis in original.

115. Nibley, *Smith Papyri*, 2, with emphasis in original. Michael D. Rhodes, "Why doesn't the translation of the Egyptian papyri found in 1967 match the text of the Book of Abraham in the Pearl of Great Price?" *The Ensign* 18 (July 1988): 51, followed Nibley's argument that the Book of Abraham scroll had red ink.

116. Roberts, *History of the Church*, 2:348. Roberts, ibid., 2:350n, explained that this account was "adapted" from Oliver Cowdery letter as printed in the *Messenger and Advocate*.

117. Cowdery, letter to Frye, 234.

118. Cowdery, ibid., 235, quoted that certificate later in his letter: "The papyrus, covered with black or red ink, or paint, in excellent preservation, are very interesting"; reprinted in Roberts, *History of the Church*, 2:350n.

119. Eugen Strouhal, *Life of the Ancient Egyptians* (Norman, OK: University of Oklahoma Press, 1992), 219.

120. Nibley, *Smith Papyri*, 2. Three pages later Nibley referred to Roberts's note in the *History of the Church*, so Nibley knew that Cowdery really wrote this description he attributed to Joseph Smith.

121. The Painesville, Ohio, *Telegraph*, 27 March 1835, quoted in J. A. Larson, "Egyptology," 162-63.

122. C. M. Larson, *By His Own Hand*, 34.

123. Baer, "Breathing Permit," 111.

124. Gee, "Tragedy of Errors," 108-109.

125. C. M. Larson, *By His Own Hand*, 33-34.

126. Gee, "Tragedy of Errors," 106, criticizing C. M. Larson's "Missing Black and Red Scroll" Theory, asserted: "The most recent non-LDS Egyptologist to write on the subject, to my knowledge, said that 'the Pap. Joseph Smith XI and X containing the Book of Breathings were wrongly identified by others with Joseph Smith's Book of Abraham.'" However, this is not an Egyptologist's opinion about the source of the Book of Abraham, for Gee failed to quote the first four words of the sentence. What L. M. J. Zonhoven, bibliographic entry no. 77562, in *Annual Egyptological Bibliography / Bibliographie égyptologique annuelle, 1977*, comp. Jac. J. Janssen (Warminster, England: Aris and Phillips, 1981), 180, said is: "He [Nibley] makes clear that the Pap.

Joseph Smith XI and X containing the Book of Breathings were wrongly identified by others with Joseph Smith's Book of Abraham." Accordingly, Zonhoven's annotation merely summarized Nibley's own argument in *The Message of the Joseph Smith Papyri.*

127. Nibley, "Fragment Found," 192.

128. Hugh Nibley, *Abraham in Egypt* (Salt Lake City: Deseret Book Co., 1981), 2.

129. Nibley, "New Look," 71-73 (January 1968--May 1970). Concerning Nibley's articles Egyptologist John A. Wilson, *Thousands of Years*, said: "Mormon theologians have mounted a counterattack against our [John A. Wilson's and Klaus Baer's] translations. In a series of articles published in 1968-69 in the magazine *Improvement Era*, Dr. Hugh Nibley pointed out at some length that Egyptologists differed in their interpretations of the material upon which they worked. He therefore suggested that we were unreliable. . . . In this case Egyptologists may disagree as to whether the trace left at the edge of a break shows fingers of a man's hand or feathers of a flying bird's wing, but they will all agree that we have here normal ancient Egyptian Books of the Dead and a normal 'Breathing Permit.'"

130. Ferguson, letter to Boyack, 13 March 1971.

131. Hugh Nibley, "An Intellectual Autobiography," in *Nibley on the Timely and the Timeless: Classic Essays of Hugh W. Nibley*, ed. Truman G. Madsen, Religious Studies Monograph Series, vol. 1 (Provo, UT: Religious Studies Center, Brigham Young University, 1978), xxvi.

132. Thompson, "Egyptology," 146. Technically, Thompson did not attribute this flawed methodology to Nibley, since the quoted statement is a general principle that could apply to anyone. However, in the immediately following paragraph Thompson began to cite specific examples from Nibley.

133. Ferguson, letter to Boyack, 13 March 1971.

134. Samuel W. Taylor, "The Case for Carping Criticism: Report from the Dog House," typescript, Sunstone Symposium, 12 August 1993, 15, in the John Taylor Family Collection, Manuscript 50, Box 73, Fd 1, Manuscripts Division, J. Willard Marriott Library, University of Utah, Salt Lake City.

135. C. M. Larson, *By His Own Hand*, 114-40, surveyed eight different explanations: (1) The "Hidden Meaning" Theory, (2) The "Mnemonic Device" Theory, (3) The "Any Egyptian Connection" Theory, (4) The "Scribes Did It" Theory, (5) The "Missing Black and Red Scroll" Theory, (6) The "Mistaken Identity" Theory, (7) The "Catalyst" Theory, and (8) The "Nobody Really Understands Egyptian Anyway" Theory.

136. Milton R. Hunter, letter to Ferguson, 4 December 1967, in Ferguson Collection, UU. Hunter added his own comment--"This part is very important"--after quoting N. Eldon Tanner's words to him.

137. Jerald Tanner, letter to Dee Jay Nelson, 18 December 1970, in Ferguson Collection, UU.

138. Rhodes, "Why doesn't the translation," 51-52, with emphasis

in original. Concerning Rhodes's suggestion that the Book of Abraham was not a literal translation but an inspired revelation, Parker, letter to Cowan, 9 January 1968, said: "It is possible to claim that the Egyptological text has an obvious and a hidden meaning but I know of no Egyptologist who would support such a claim."

139. Roberts, *History of the Church*, 2:236.

140. Ferguson, letter to Boyack, 13 March 1971. Ferguson identified this Hôr as an "Egyptian god." Technically, Hôr is the name of the Egyptian priest, though according to Baer, "Breathing Permit," 111*n*8, the name itself means "[the god] Horus."

141. Klaus J. Hansen, "Reflections on *The Lion of the Lord*," review of *The Lion of the Lord: A Biography of Brigham Young*, by Stanley P. Hirshon, in *Dialogue: A Journal of Mormon Thought* 5 (Summer 1970): 104.

142. Claude Heater, letter to author, 13 June 1994, in author's possession.

143. Bach Interview, 25 May 1993.

144. George F. Carter, letter to author, 3 July 1989, in author's possession. Ferguson, letter to George F. Carter, 24 May 1977, in Ferguson Collection, UU, stated concerning the Joseph Smith Egyptian Papyri: "The leaders and aides to the Prophet [Joseph Smith] were told by the Prophet that he could read it and that it was 'The Book of Abraham,' written by Abraham. . . . At the insistence of the top aides he was pressured into coming up with his 'translation,' published and canonized by the Church--and still scripture in the Church. . . . Joseph made the mistake of not destroying the Egyptian after producing his 'translation.' . . . [Egyptologists] identified the original MS of the Book of Abraham as 'The Breathing Permit of Hôr.' Nothing whatever to do with Abraham or anything relating to Joseph Smith's fraudulent version and 'translation.' . . . Joseph Smith didn't know one glyph from another--a complete sham on his part. That the Breathing Permit MS is the one Joseph Smith had is beyond all questions. For in his English 'translation' he 'blew it' by copying into and publishing vignettes from the original--and there they are on the MS from N.Y.C."

145. John W. Fitzgerald, letter to Ferguson, 4 March 1976, in the John W. Fitzgerald Collection, Manuscript 102, Box 1, Special Collections, Milton R. Merrill Library, Utah State University, Logan, UT; hereafter abbreviated to Fitzgerald Collection.

146. Ferguson, letter to John W. Fitzgerald, 6 March 1976, in Fitzgerald Collection; photocopy in Ferguson Collection, UU.

147. J. Don Cerchione, letter to Ferguson, with handwritten response by Ferguson, 21 July 1976, in Ferguson Collection, UU.

148. Wesley P. Walters, letter to Ferguson, 23 June 1971, in Ferguson Collection, UU.

149. Walters, "Egyptians," 45.

150. Ronald O. Barney, interview with Thomas Stuart Ferguson, 4 January 1983, typed on 19 April 1984, in Box 77, Fd 13, Marquardt Collection.

4

Letter-Writing Closet Doubter

Not only did Thomas Stuart Ferguson's estimation of the Book of Abraham radically change as a result of the translations of the Joseph Smith Egyptian papyri, but he was forced to reexamine the religious beliefs of his lifetime. Such a process affected different people in varying ways. Klaus J. Hansen, professor of history at Queen's University, assessed the effect of translating the newly found Book of Abraham papyri:

> The recent translation of the Joseph Smith papyri may well represent the potentially most damaging case against Mormonism since its foundation. Yet the . . . [Church leaders] should take comfort in the fact that the almost total lack of response to this translation is an uncanny proof . . . that even the most devastating act of disconfirmation will have no effect whatever on true believers.[1]

Ferguson admitted that the problem that first made him "seriously question the Church was the papyri purported to be the source of the Book of Abraham."[2] Like falling dominoes, his belief in the prophetic status of Joseph Smith and the historicity of the Book of Mormon also collapsed. At first Ferguson still believed that Joseph Smith had been a true prophet of God in 1829 when he translated the Book of Mormon, but he decided that Joseph Smith had become a fallen prophet by 1835 when the Egyptian scrolls and mummies arrived in Kirtland. However, Ferguson, the logical lawyer, continued thinking: since the English text of the Book of Abraham cannot be considered a translation of the Egyptian papyri, maybe the Book of Mormon is not a real translation of an ancient document. Ferguson's conviction concerning the Book of Mormon was devastated as the chain reaction continued.

Ferguson Becomes a Closet Doubter

Ferguson's entire religious outlook changed as a direct result of the discovery and translation of the Book of Abraham papyri. Disenchanted, he became a Mormon "closet doubter," which is defined as:

> An active Latter-day Saint who has secretly rejected (or disbelieves) one or more of the fundamental tenets upon which the Church is based, such as Joseph Smith's first vision, his divine calling as a prophet of God, the Book of Mormon as an angel-delivered history of early Americans, or the divine origin of Joseph's later revelations as published in the Doctrine and Covenants and [the] Pearl of Great Price.[3]

Thus, a closet doubter privately disbelieves some of the basic teachings of the Church but keeps that disbelief hidden from his/her public image. Typically this state of skepticism is preceded by an extended period of strong belief in those same tenets.

Ferguson's doubts during the last years of his life have been difficult to document. When the Thomas Stuart Ferguson papers arrived at the Harold B. Lee Library of Brigham Young University soon after his death, the collection contained absolutely no letters after 1967 that indicate his views on the Book of Mormon, the Book of Abraham, or Joseph Smith.[4] As far as the Ferguson collection at BYU is concerned, the fifteen-year period before his death did not exist. This glaring gap in the record is inexplicable since Ferguson continued to write many letters, and as a lawyer had the long-established habit of keeping carbon copies of outgoing correspondence. However, he published no new articles or books after 1967, nor did he reprint any of his previous books. This absence of publications stands in stark contrast with his consistent record in the 1940s, 1950s, and early 1960s. If it were not for his conversations and letters, Ferguson's beliefs during the last years of his life would remain unknown. Ferguson's letters are important in any period, but those written after the discovery of the Joseph Smith Egyptian papyri are especially crucial to show the development of his thinking.

Samuel W. Taylor, a free-lance Hollywood script writer, described what Ferguson went through during this period:

> Subsequently, after the discovery of the lost papyri, Tom Ferguson stumbled over the Book of Abraham. At this time his son-in-law was my home teaching companion, and I got a blow-by-blow account of Tom's travail as he tried to cling to the faith despite the shattering evidence that the Book of Abraham was not a literal translation of the papyri. What Ferguson did was to get a copy of the papyri from Salt Lake, and take it to Egyptologists at U of Cal at Berkeley. They told him the text was an ordinary funeral document consigning the soul to the hereafter. . . . Subsequently, Grant Wade invited a group of free-thinking LDS to a meeting at my place (at which, I discovered subsequently, one person was a spy for the stake president, David B. Barlow), and Tom Ferguson said, "Joseph Smith, how I hate that phony bastard."[5]

Ferguson used this strong language to express his anger and disillusionment. In this period of severe disappointment, he also called Joseph Smith "a fake."[6]

His known letters during the twelve-month period from late November 1967 through mid-November 1968 deal with Ferguson's investigation concerning the correct translation of the Joseph Smith Egyptian papyri. The following years--1969 and 1970--are a documentary blank with no known letters. These two years appear to have been a period of soul-searching and reflection, because the original papyrus of Facsimile No. 1 and its associated papyri, all of which were translated by competent Egyptologists, failed to provide any support for the Book of Abraham. His childlike faith having been shaken, Ferguson agonized to find a spiritual meaning to his beliefs. He reexamined his assumptions about the Book of Abraham and even began to question the historicity of the Book of Mormon. The agony of his crisis of faith was intense, for what emerged at the end of this two-year struggle was a very different Tom Ferguson. His available letters from 1971 to 1983 have been gathered and can be examined in the Thomas Stuart Ferguson Collection at the University of Utah's Marriott Library. Every firsthand expression from Ferguson should be utilized to understand the radical change in his thinking during the last thirteen years of his life. Numerous letters and a 1975 study indicate Ferguson's real feelings about Joseph Smith, the Book of Mormon, and the Book of Abraham.[7]

Continual Shrinking of Book of Mormon Geography

In the 1940s Tom Ferguson had been instrumental in reducing the LDS conception of the geography of the Book of Mormon from North and South America to the small area limited to southern Mexico and Central America. During the 1950s and 1960s his New World Archaeological Foundation carried out professional archaeological reconnaissance and fieldwork in the Preclassic era in Mesoamerica, and Ferguson had hoped to thus discover scientific confirmation of the historicity of the Book of Mormon.

After many years of archaeological investigations, disappointed by not finding the long-hoped-for confirmation of the

Book of Mormon, Ferguson finally concluded that the book was "fictional" and that "what is in the ground will never conform to what is in the book."[8] But from 1970 to 1983 he reduced (as far as he was concerned) the geography of the book to nothing at all in the real world and no longer believed that archaeological evidence would ever substantiate the Book of Mormon.[9] He told O. Allen Israelsen, his brother-in-law, that "everything he had set out to prove in Central America/Mexico had proven to be wrong."[10] Ferguson decided that he could not suspend judgment and remain forever tentative just because the evidence was not all in. When would it ever be all in? During the last thirteen years of his life Ferguson's conviction was a skeptical view that placed the source of all Book of Mormon activities in the creative mind of Joseph Smith (and perhaps also the minds of Oliver Cowdery and Sidney Rigdon). His skepticism, however, was not a cold cynicism, since he sincerely wished that the situation were otherwise than what he perceived it to be.

Alfred L. Bush, curator of the Western Americana Collections at Princeton University, pointed out that "Ferguson did *not* seek to use archaeological evidence to prove theological dogma: he more properly sought to use archaeological evidence to test historical claims, certainly one of the clear functions of archaeology, as the mountainous literature on biblical archaeology attests."[11] Ferguson carefully made the distinction that archaeological findings in Mesoamerica should bring forth support for the historically verifiable parts of the Book of Mormon, and then when that was successfully accomplished, one would have greater justification for believing in the spiritual claims of the book. However, in the end he found only frustration and futility in attempting to confirm the authenticity of the Book of Mormon with archaeological evidence. Although Ferguson rejected the historicity of the Book of Mormon and the Book of Abraham, he still advocated most Mormon values. Surprisingly, there is no evidence that ecclesiastical action was taken to either disfellowship or excommunicate him for his resultant unorthodox beliefs, statements, and/or writings.

Pivotal Trip to
Salt Lake City

Early in December 1970 Ferguson visited Salt Lake City for a very important purpose. As if to dramatize his torn feelings, he bared his soul to people at opposing ends of the theological spectrum--on the one hand, the liberal LDS apostle, Hugh B. Brown, and on the other hand, the anti-Mormons, Jerald and Sandra Tanner. Ferguson first paid a visit to Brown in his office at LDS Church headquarters and reviewed with him the translations the Egyptologists had made of the Joseph Smith Egyptian papyri. During this conversation Ferguson emotionally exclaimed to Brown that Joseph Smith did not possess "the remotest skill" in translating Egyptian hieroglyphs. Ferguson reported an unexpected response from Brown: "To my surprise, one of the highest officials [Hugh B. Brown] in the Mormon Church agreed with that conclusion when I made that very statement to him."[12]

The following is another account of Ferguson's conversation with Hugh B. Brown:

> Ferguson said that the thing that first led him to seriously question the church was the papyri purported to be the source of the Book of Abraham. He said he took a photograph of the papyri to a couple of friends of his that were scholars at Cal., Berkeley. They described the documents as funeral texts. This bothered Ferguson in a serious way! Later he said that he took the evidence to Hugh B. Brown. ... After reviewing the evidence with Brother Brown he [Ferguson] said that Brother Brown agreed with him that it was not scripture. He did not say or infer [imply] that it was his evidence that convinced Brother Brown of this conclusion. But nevertheless, he did say that Hugh B. Brown did not believe the Book of Abraham was what the church said it was.[13]

Brown's harsh indictment of the official position of the LDS Church--that the Book of Abraham is not "what the church said it was"--cannot be either confirmed or disproved by the Hugh B.

Brown papers in the LDS Church archives, because they are closed to researchers.[14] During this meeting Ferguson "seemed to be absolutely convinced that [Hugh B.] Brown did not believe the Book of Abraham,"[15] that is to say, did not believe that the Book of Abraham was a translation from Egyptian. Since it is assumed that Brown believed that it was inspired scripture, this seems to indicate that Brown then held a non-historical, "mythic interpretation" of the Book of Abraham.[16]

Later that same December day Ferguson went to the home of Jerald and Sandra Tanner in Salt Lake City. According to their report, he discussed with them his repudiation of the Book of Abraham and his rejection of the authenticity of the Book of Mormon and stated that he had "spent twenty-five years trying to prove Mormonism, but now finds his work to have been in vain."[17] The twenty-five years mentioned would encompass the period from his first trip to Mexico in 1946 through 1970. Ferguson told a number of people about this quarter-century period, and his consistent reference to twenty-five years seems to indicate that he continued to struggle to prove the truth of Mormonism right up to the end of 1970. The Tanners told Dee Jay Nelson of Ferguson's visit and Nelson replied that "when Ferguson's stand becomes known it will have a great impact upon the thinking segment of the Church membership--the non-thinkers can't be reached under any conditions, I am afraid."[18]

Ferguson's skepticism first became public a year and eight months later when the Tanners published an account of his visit with them in a revised edition of their *Mormonism: Shadow or Reality*:

> At that time, Thomas Stuart Ferguson told us frankly that he had not only given up the Book of Abraham, but that he had come to the conclusion that Joseph Smith was not a prophet and the [sic] Mormonism was not true. He told us that he had spent 25 years trying to prove Mormonism, but had finally come to the conclusion that his work had been in vain. He said that his training in law had taught him how to weigh evidence and that the case against Joseph Smith was absolutely devastating and could not be explained away.[19]

Though this passage by the Tanners was pointed out to Ferguson many times, he never denied their account of his loss of faith. However, he did not actively promulgate his new ideas, and he told some people that he wanted to keep his views confidential. The tolerant apostle, Howard W. Hunter, who served as chairman of the Archaeology Committee supervising BYU-NWAF, was well aware of Ferguson's questioning attitude and liberal ideas, but still chose not to have him released as secretary of that organization.

The First Vision
of Joseph Smith

On 13 March 1971 Ferguson wrote to James Boyack of Lexington, Massachusetts, about what he felt was another critical issue in the history of the LDS Church--the First Vision of Joseph Smith, especially the recent studies by Paul R. Cheesman and Dean C. Jessee.[20] He recommended to Boyack that "if you haven't done so, I suggest you read, analyze, and even chart the very important data" published in Jessee's article on Joseph Smith's First Vision.[21] The earliest account in 1832 (fig. 24)--this part of which was written by Joseph Smith himself--contained no mention of religious revivals and more importantly only referred to the Lord Jesus, with no indication that both God the Father and his Son appeared:

> I cried unto the Lord for mercy for there was none else to whom I could go and obtain mercy and the Lord heard my cry in the wilderness and while in < the > attitude of calling upon the Lord < in the 16th year of my age > a pillar of light above the brightness of the sun at noon day come down from above and rested upon me and I was filled with the spirit of god and the < Lord > opened the heavens upon me and I saw the Lord and he spake unto me saying, Joseph < my son > thy sins are forgiven thee. ... Behold I am the Lord of glory, I was crucified for the world.[22]

The different accounts of the First Vision have stimulated research into this experience and as a result "considerable contro-

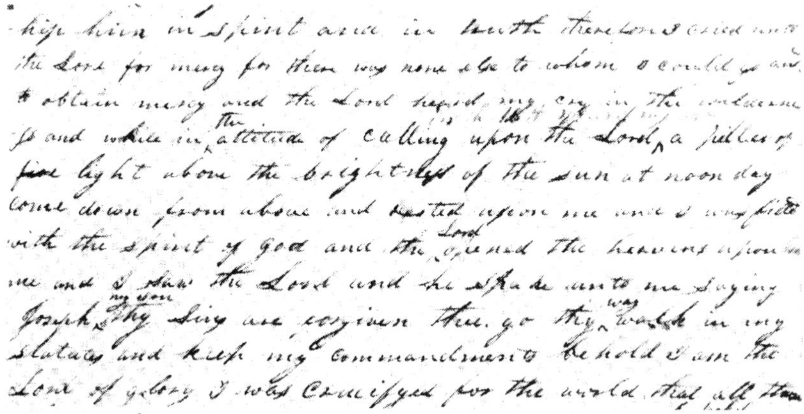

Fig. 24--Earliest manuscript account of the First Vision of Joseph Smith.
Reproduced from Dean C. Jessee, *The Personal Writings of Joseph Smith* (1984), courtesy of Deseret Book Co.

versy has been generated."[23] Joseph Smith's own family remember a different version of his early visions. His mother, Lucy Mack Smith, related his first vision as follows:

> One evening [at harvest time] we were sitting till quite late conversing upon the subject of the diversity of churches that had risen up in the world and the many thousand opinions in existence as to the truth contained in scripture. ... After we ceased conversation he [Joseph] went to bed < and was pondering in his mind which of the churches were the true way > but he had not laid there long till < he saw > a bright < light > enter the room where he lay. He looked up and saw an angel of the Lord standing by him. The angel spoke, I perceive that you are enquiring in your mind which is the true church. There is not a true church on Earth.[24]

Lucy then described the angel's instructions to locate the gold plates of the Book of Mormon. In a similar way Joseph's brother William stated that this angel was Joseph Smith's first encounter with a heavenly messenger.[25] Many Mormons consider the traditional account of Joseph Smith's First Vision as canonized in the Pearl of Great Price to be one of the cornerstones of the LDS Church. In December 1970 Ferguson admitted that his faith was devastated when "the strange accounts" of the First Vision were published by Jessee and Cheesman, for "they had plucked all the feathers out of the bird and shot it, and there it lies 'dead and naked on the ground.'"[26]

The 1826 Trial
of Joseph Smith

Ferguson wrote to Jerald and Sandra Tanner on 13 March 1971, telling them that he enjoyed his previous visit with them and intended to be in Salt Lake City in June, and if so, he would visit them again. After expressing his admiration to the Tanners, he continued:

> In writing to [James] Boyack, I want to send him a photocopy of the newspaper article (1830--I think) which was published in the Palmyra area, giving a detailed report on the Josiah Stoal [Stowell] charges and trial of JS [Joseph Smith] in connection with those charges. You provided me with a copy of that news article--which is one of the most damning things turned up yet. I can't find it--someone probably ran off with it. Please send me another.[27]

The article, written by Abram W. Benton, was actually published in 1831, not 1830, in the *Evangelical Magazine and Gospel Advocate*,[28] and Ferguson's source is the photomechanical reproduction made by the Tanners in 1970.[29] Ferguson had tried unsuccessfully to locate his copy of this article, which provided contemporary details of Joseph Smith's March 1826 pre-trial examination before a justice of the peace. Ferguson explained:

> In 1826 Joseph Smith was 21 [20] and at this point was midway between the *First Vision* and 1830. What a strange time to be convicted of fraud--fraudulently getting money after convincing the victim that he could detect the whereabouts of hidden treasure on the victim's land. Wow. . . .
> It is as genuine and sound as can be--published right in Joseph Smith's own camp.[30]

Benton asserted that Joseph Smith was linked to money-diggers and used a seer stone to locate lost goods and buried treasure. Ferguson's reaction to the Benton article was that this

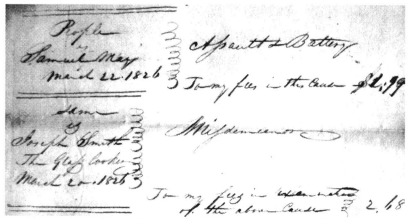

Fig. 25--Justice Albert Neely's 1826 bill concerning "Joseph Smith, The Glass Looker." Reproduced from H. Michael Marquardt and Wesley P. Walters, *Inventing Mormonism* (1994), courtesy of Chenango County Board of Supervisors, Norwich, New York

was "one of the most damning things turned up yet." Recognizing the grave consequences of Joseph Smith appearing before a court in 1826, Hugh Nibley, professor of history and religion at BYU, rhetorically addressed the discoverer of the court record, Daniel S. Tuttle, Episcopal Bishop of Salt Lake City, as if he were alive in 1961:

> You knew its immense value as a weapon against Joseph Smith *if* its authenticity could be established. . . . Now, Bishop Tuttle, *if* this court record is authentic, it is the most damning evidence in existence against Joseph Smith.[31]

In 1971 Wesley P. Walters, pastor of the Presbyterian Church in Marissa, Illinois, discovered the original of Justice Albert Neely's bill concerning this episode. The bill reads: "same [i.e., the people] vs Joseph Smith The Glass Looker, March 20, 1826, Misdemeanor, To my fees in examination of the above cause 2.68" (fig. 25, bottom). Walters also found constable Philip M. De Zeng's bill concerning the arrest of young Joseph Smith. These documents together establish the existence of the examination before Neely and the essentials of the published court record.[32] Though there exists variation concerning the charges, the witnesses, their testimony, and the final verdict, Marvin S. Hill, professor of history at BYU, concluded that "it is clear that a trial did take place and that at issue was Joseph Jr.'s money digging."[33]

Ferguson told Boyack that he "offered the data available [concerning the First Vision and the 1826 trial of Joseph Smith] to my stake pres. [Joseph R. Hilton] recently and he walked away without it--saying he didn't want to read it."[34] The official chronology of events in Joseph Smith's early life are his First Vision in the spring of 1820 and then annual visits from the angel Moroni in September of 1823, 1824, 1825, 1826, and receiving the plates of the Book of Mormon into his custody in September 1827. Ferguson's point is that in the midst of these annual instructions from the angel Moroni Joseph Smith is brought to trial as a magical glass-looker.[35]

Ethan Smith's Possible Influence on the Book of Mormon

Ethan Smith (no relation of Joseph Smith), a popular Congregational minister in Poultney, Vermont, wrote *View of the Hebrews* in 1823,[36] with an enlarged, second edition just two years later (fig. 26).[37] This book presented the then-known information about the antiquities of the American Indians and how this data related to his interpretation of the lost ten tribes of Israel in the Bible.[38] During this same period Ethan Smith wrote a series of articles on "The History of the Jews" in the local newspaper.[39] He also published at Poultney *The Blessing of Abraham Come on the Gentiles* and *View of the Trinity*.[40] Many of his Sunday sermons were also separately published. Several individuals have suggested that *View of the Hebrews* might have influenced Joseph Smith in the production of the Book of Mormon. In his later years Ferguson decided that Joseph Smith somehow had acquired a copy of Ethan Smith's *View of the Hebrews* in order to write the Book of Mormon.[41]

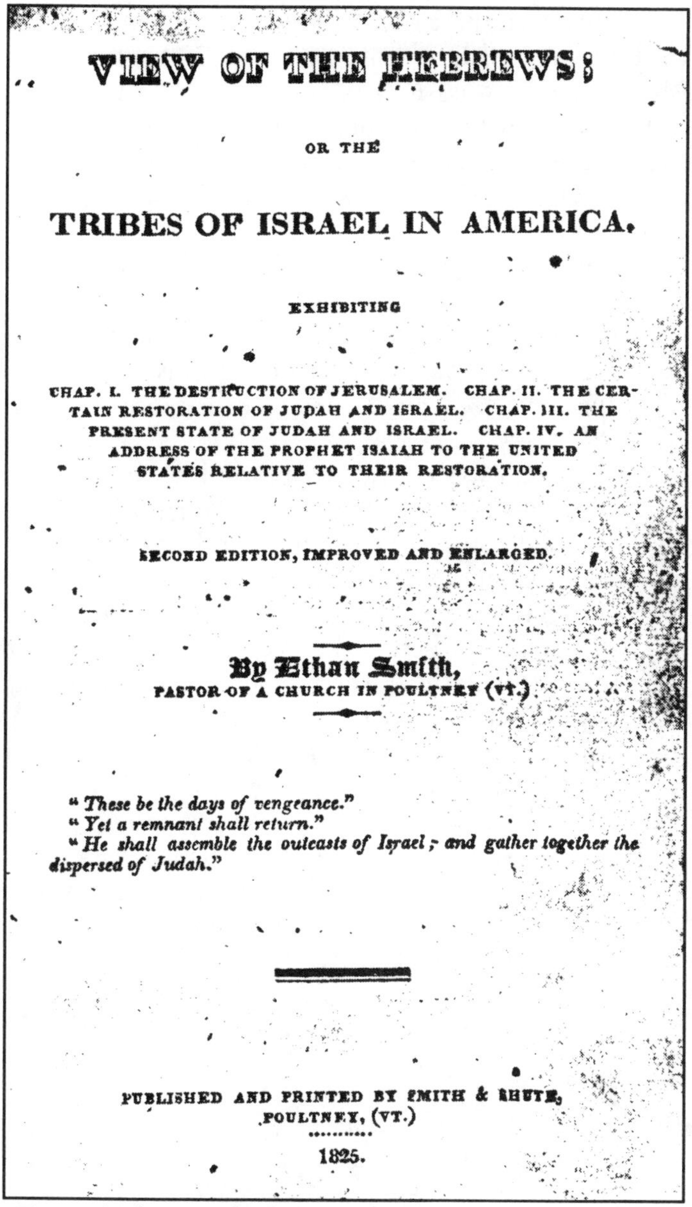

VIEW OF THE HEBREWS;

OR THE

TRIBES OF ISRAEL IN AMERICA.

EXHIBITING

CHAP. I. THE DESTRUCTION OF JERUSALEM. CHAP. II. THE CER-
TAIN RESTORATION OF JUDAH AND ISRAEL. CHAP. III. THE
PRESENT STATE OF JUDAH AND ISRAEL. CHAP. IV. AN
ADDRESS OF THE PROPHET ISAIAH TO THE UNITED
STATES RELATIVE TO THEIR RESTORATION.

SECOND EDITION, IMPROVED AND ENLARGED.

By Ethan Smith,
PASTOR OF A CHURCH IN POULTNEY (VT.)

" *These be the days of vengeance.*"
" *Yet a remnant shall return.*"
" *He shall assemble the outcasts of Israel ; and gather together the
dispersed of Judah.*"

PUBLISHED AND PRINTED BY SMITH & SHUTE,
POULTNEY, (VT.)
1825.

*Fig. 26--Title page of Ethan Smith, "View of the Hebrews,"
1825.* Reproduced from copy owned and annotated by B. H. Roberts,
courtesy of Marriott Library, University of Utah.

However, there is no direct evidence that Joseph Smith ever read Ethan Smith's book in the 1820s--before the Book of Mormon text was dictated in 1829.[42] Dale L. Morgan, an historian of nineteenth-century Mormonism, suggested that even though the parallels between the Book of Mormon and the *View of the Hebrews* are impressive, "it is more important that the ideas common to the two books should have been the common property of their generation."[43] The only definite indication of Joseph Smith's awareness of this book appeared in 1842, when an article was published in the church-owned *Times and Seasons* during his editorship. This article quoted from Josiah Priest, who in turn had quoted from Ethan Smith's *View of the Hebrews*.[44]

Oliver Cowdery was Joseph Smith's scribe for the major part of the dictation of the Book of Mormon.[45] Actually, they were distant cousins: "Oliver's mother, Rebecca Fuller Cowdery, was the great-grand-daughter of John Fuller and Mehitabel Rowley, who were also the second great-grandparents of Lucy Mack, Joseph's mother."[46] Ferguson wrote in 1979 that he had been able (through the research of a close friend) to establish that "Oliver Cowdery was in Ethan Smith's congregation" in Poultney, Vermont, before meeting Joseph Smith.[47] If he meant by this that Cowdery was a member of Ethan's church, then he went beyond the evidence, since it is only known that Cowdery's stepmother, Mrs. Keziah Pearce Austin, had enrolled as a member of that congregation.[48] However, if Ferguson meant that Cowdery attended Sunday meetings in that church, then he was probably right. Writing to Ronald Barney early in 1983, Ferguson provided the details of his historical investigations into possible connections between Oliver Cowdery and Ethan Smith:

> Since Oliver Cowdery was born in 1806 and was in Poultney from 1809 to 1825, he was resident in Poultney from 3 years of age until he was 19 years of age--16 years in all. And these years encompassed the publication of *View of the Hebrews*, in 1822 [1823] and 1825. His three little half sisters, born in Poultney, were all baptized in Ethan Smith's church. Thus, the family had a close tie with Ethan Smith.[49]

Cowdery's half sisters (Rebecca Marie, Lucy, and Phoebe) were baptized on 2 August 1818 at the Congregational Church in Poultney, though Ethan Smith himself did not serve as minister there until three years later--from November 1821 through December 1826.[50]

Ferguson continued to investigate the influence that Ethan Smith's *View of the Hebrews* may have had on Joseph Smith. He recommended that a friend purchase a reprint copy of *View of the Hebrews* as a significant document in understanding the origin of the Book of Mormon.[51] Because Ferguson learned about the Cowdery family's connection to Ethan Smith's congregation, he concluded that Oliver Cowdery had "influenced the text of the Book of Mormon by adding material ideas from Ethan Smith's *View of the Hebrews*."[52] His idea that Cowdery was a conscious conspirator with Joseph Smith in the production of the Book of Mormon goes against indications in the original manuscript that it was a dictated text with no signs of collusion.[53]

B. H. Roberts, an LDS General Authority, spent a considerable amount of time investigating the possible influence of Ethan Smith's *View of the Hebrews* on the Book of Mormon. Roberts wrote a 280-page manuscript entitled "A Book of Mormon Study" (fig. 27) as a result of this investigation.[54] Near the end of his lengthy comparisons Roberts asked the following question:

> But now to return . . . to the main theme of this writing-- viz., did Ethan Smith's *View of the Hebrews* furnish structural material for Joseph Smith's Book of Mormon? It has been pointed out in these pages that there are many things in the former book that might well have suggested many major things in the other. Not a few things merely, one or two, or a half dozen, but many; and it is this fact of many things of similarity and the cumulative force of them that makes them so serious a menace to Joseph Smith's story of the Book of Mormon's origin.[55]

Ferguson had decided to revise completely his earlier *One Fold and One Shepherd*. One of the small post-it notes he attached

-13-

they were all converted again unto the Lord."

But in addition to the striking parallelism in these incidents of Anti-Christs of the Book of Mormon, with the strong implication that they have their origin in one mind, I call attention again to the fact of "rawness" in dealing with this question of unbelief, the evidence of "amateurishness" increasingly evident in this story of Korihor. Does it not carry with it the proof that it is the work of a pious youth dealing with the very common place stock arguments clumsily put together for the belief in the existence of God, with an awkward turning from the request for a special miracle, in proof of God's existence, to the standing miracle of the creation and an orderly universe for that truth, rather than an adult appeal and argument on the great questions involved? And is not the vindication of God and his truth by a vindictive miracle on the person of the ranting blasphemer, rather the dream of a pious boy of what might very well have happened, rather than a matter of actual experience?

There were other anti-Christs among the Nephites, but they were more military leaders than religious innovators, yet much of the same kidney in spirit with these dissenters here passed in review; but I shall hold that what is here presented illustrates sufficiently the matter taken in hand by refering to them, namely that they are all of one breed and brand; so nearly alike that one mind is the author of them, and that a young and undeveloped, but piously inclined mind. The evidence I sorrowfully submit, points to Joseph Smith as their creator. It is difficult to believe that they are the product of history,

Fig. 27--B. H. Roberts, "Internal Evidence That the Book of Mormon Is of Human Origin--Considered," part II, chap. iii, 13, in "A Book of Mormon Study," 1922. Reproduced from B. H. Roberts Collection, courtesy of Marriott Library, University of Utah.

to his copy of the book is extremely significant, for Ferguson intended to discuss the influence of Ethan Smith's *View of the Hebrews* on the text of the Book of Mormon. Acknowledging such influence implies that the Book of Mormon was produced by Joseph Smith in the early nineteenth century, rather than being a translation from an ancient record.[56] The possibility of Ethan Smith's *View of the Hebrews* having influenced the Book of Mormon is still a question being seriously considered today.[57]

Sidney Rigdon's Suggested Influence on the Book of Mormon

Ferguson was also working on the much less likely connection between Joseph Smith and Sidney Rigdon in the late 1820s. He spent an incredible amount of energy in the late 1970s and early 1980s making photocopies of books, theses, and articles --pro-Mormon, anti-Mormon, and non-Mormon--on Sidney Rigdon. These Ferguson read, reread, underlined, made marginal notations, and attached numerous post-it notes.

This speculative theory has not been accepted by most modern investigators into Mormonism's early history, because the available evidence indicates that Rigdon did not know about the new church until the fall of 1830 and did not meet Smith until mid-December 1830. Ferguson ran across a statement that Rigdon late in life had spoken about having a "big secret,"[58] and he leaped to the conclusion that this secret related to Rigdon's being the real author of Mormonism. The theory was that Rigdon had written a 1500-page manuscript on the subject. For this reason Ferguson diligently tried "to find material on Rigdon to prove his theory that Rigdon was the genius behind the church and the actual author of the Book of Mormon."[59] One document that Ferguson found was the reminiscences of John W. Rigdon, a son of Sidney Rigdon. However, the rebaptized son took the strong position that his father had nothing to do with Joseph Smith or the Book of Mormon until late in 1830.[60] If the 1500-page manuscript ever existed, it appears to have been destroyed after Rigdon's death. According to Josephine Rigdon Secord, a granddaughter of Sidney Rigdon, after his death Rigdon's widow "burned all the records, and the brilliant sermons and orations lay in a heap of ashes."[61] Because F. Mark McKiernan had written a biography of Sidney Rigdon,[62] Ferguson wrote to him in January 1982, explaining his view that Rigdon worked with Joseph Smith before the publication of the Book of Mormon and asking McKiernan for advice. McKiernan gave Ferguson no encouragement concerning this theory.[63]

By means of Ferguson's research requests to the LDS Genealogical Society in Salt Lake City he tracked down a reference to letters about the Rigdon family in genealogy sheets submitted by Lloyd J. Neuffer of Ogden, Utah. With this clue in hand on 4 January 1983 Ferguson went to Ogden and told Neuffer that he was interested in tracking down writings by Sidney Rigdon.[64] Neuffer explained that as a counselor in the presidency of the LDS branch in Pittsburgh he had befriended the elderly Samuel M. Ellis, a son of Nancy Rigdon, who herself was a daughter of Sidney Rigdon. Also, Ellis had written Neuffer several letters in the 1930s.[65] However, Neuffer would not allow Ferguson to have these letters--or even to look at them--saying that he intended to donate them to the LDS Church. Ferguson's inability to examine these documents made him feel certain that they contained the information he was seeking.

Disappointed and frustrated, Ferguson returned to Salt Lake City and went to the LDS Church headquarters, where he met Ronald O. Barney in the archives. They had a "candid discussion about the origins of the Book of Mormon and the Book of Abraham."[66] Ferguson told Barney of the whereabouts of the letters by Ellis which Neuffer would not let him see.[67] Writing to Barney the next month Ferguson first thanked him for bringing to his attention two recent articles in *Dialogue* and *Sunstone*;[68] then he reminded Barney of his interest in the Ellis letters about Rigdon and requested copies if the Historical Department should receive them.[69]

The day after Ferguson's visit Neuffer gave the Ellis letters to his friend, Bruce R. McConkie, a member of the Quorum of the Twelve Apostles.[70] It was, however, a year before McConkie transferred them to the LDS Church archives, and by that time Ferguson had passed away. The Ellis letters did not contain what Ferguson was hunting for, since they say nothing about Rigdon's "big secret" and provide no hint of a pre-Book of Mormon connection with Joseph Smith. As it turns out, the most interesting items in the letters reveal more about Nancy Rigdon than her father, as Ellis's following comments illustrate:

> Some years after the Church was started, and before the doctrine of Polygamy was promulgated, Joseph Smith approached my grandfather [Sidney Rigdon], and suggested a second marriage with my beloved Mother [Nancy Rigdon]. Mr. Smith at this time was already married; the suggestion so incensed my grandfather that they came to an open break.[71]

The hearsay evidence possibly connecting Rigdon with Smith in the 1820s is very slim and Rigdon's most recent biographer concluded it had no validity.[72] There is still no solid evidence to support the theory that Sidney Rigdon knew Joseph Smith before December 1830.

The Value of Religious Myths

Ferguson became very sympathetic with the role of religious myth in people's lives. In February 1976 he referred Mr. and Mrs. Harold W. Lawrence of Providence, Utah, to a recent article by Gerald Clarke, in which emphasis was laid on the importance of human dependence on myths.[73] Ferguson told them the following:

> People must believe in something. (Otherwise we face the abyss of death and extinction.) Mormonism is probably the best conceived myth-fraternity to which one can belong. . . . Joseph Smith tried so hard he put himself out on a limb with the Book of Abraham, and also with the Book of Mormon. He can be refuted--but why bother when all religion is based on myth, and when man must have them, and his is one of the very best.[74]

Ferguson compared the refuting of religious myths to abolishing medical placebos. He granted that sometimes both placebos and religious myths can do harm, but he was convinced that overall both do much more good than harm. Ferguson pointed out that throughout recorded history political leaders used religion for the good results that it produced--personal peace and orderliness in family and national affairs. He attributed one of the main factors for the high crime rate in modern society to the breakdown of religious mythologies. Ferguson saw no value in combating religious myths and since he felt he had been deceived by Joseph Smith, he advocated a sort of counter-deception:

> So why try to be heroic and fight the myths--the Mormon one or any other that does more good than ill? Perhaps you and I have been spoofed by Joseph Smith. Now that we have the inside dope--why not spoof a little back and stay aboard?[75]

Ferguson explained that he wished to stay in Mormonism for the sake of some members of his family as well for the fact that he greatly valued his social participation in the LDS Church. The broad-minded Ferguson then offered some advice to the Lawrences:

> Belonging with my eyes wide open, is actually fun, less expensive than formerly, and no strain at all. I am now very selective in the meetings I attend, the functions I attend, the amounts I contribute, etc., etc., and I have a perfectly happy time. I never get up and bear testimony-- but I don't mind listening to others who do. I am much more tolerant of other religions and other thinking and feel fine about things in general. You might give my sugges- tions a trial run--and if you find you have to burn all the bridges between yourselves and the Church, then go ahead and ask for excommunication. The day will probably come--but it is far off--when the leadership of the Church will change the excommunication rules and delete as grounds non-belief in the 2 books mentioned [the Book of Abraham and the Book of Mormon] and in Joseph Smith as a prophet, etc.--but if you wait for that day, you probably will have died. It is a long way off--tithing would drop too much for one thing.[76]

Ferguson told the Lawrences not to worry about the tithing being paid by the members, since the LDS Church was as free from monetary corruption as any human organization. He then recommended to them a short reading list: an article about "Joseph Smith's First Vision," *Mormonism: Shadow or Reality*, *The True Believer*, and *No Man Knows My History*.[77] Since these works significantly affected Ferguson, he evidently felt that they would be valuable for them to read.

Mormonism in Comparison with Other Religions

In answer to an earlier letter from Rev. Wesley P. Walters of Marissa, Illinois, Ferguson replied in July 1971 that he had not decided whether the bad in the Church outweighed the good and, consequently, he was not prepared to engage in "open warfare." He explained to Walters his current view about prophets:

> Right now I am inclined to think that all of those who claim to be "prophets," including Moses, were without a means of communicating with deity--I'm inclined to think that when Moses was on top of the mount, he was talking to himself and decided that the only way he could get the motley crowd at the bottom of the slope to come to order and to listen to him and to heed him was to tell them that he had talked to God on the mount. If this view is correct, then prophets are nothing more than mortal men like the rest of us, except they saw a great need for change and had the courage to say they had communicated with God and had received a message for man, and were believed (though false in the basic claim that the message came from God and not from man). . . . Right now I am inclined to think that all who believe in "prophets" as true agents of God are being spoofed--but perhaps for their own good and welfare. When Joseph Smith crash-landed, a lot came down with him, as I see it.[78]

Ferguson told Harold H. Hougey, an anti-Mormon writer, that he admired his search for the truth but admonished him to work just as hard in searching for problems in Protestantism as he was in looking for difficulties in Mormonism. He felt that if

Hougey would do this, he would either reject them both or "come to the point of view to which I have come--even though untrue, they [Protestant Christianity and Mormonism] do more good than harm."[79] Ferguson did not want to be associated with an attack on anyone's religious beliefs. Attacking Mormonism, in his opinion, would likely produce more harm than good. He explained his views about different religions:

> All elements of religion that are supernatural (including the endless string of miracles in the New Testament) are fabrications of men like Joseph Smith. . . . Further, I presently believe that Mormonism is as good a brand of supernatural religion (which sells well) as any other-- including Protestantism. At the present time I am inclined to believe that supernatural religion, selling as it does, does more good than it does harm (although this is highly debatable). . . . In my opinion the average Protestant and the average Catholic is as blind to basic truths as is the average Mormon. If I were going to attack Joseph Smith, I would want to attack your beliefs, involving the super-natural, as well as the Mormon beliefs.[80]

In December 1979 Ferguson wrote a letter to James D. Still of Salem, Oregon, in which he said that he had "lost faith in Joseph Smith as having a pipeline to deity" and had concluded that no one ever had such a pipeline (fig. 28).[81] He held a broad-minded philosophy about world religions, though he felt that some were better than others:

> I believe that Judaism was an improvement on polytheism; Christianity was an improvement on Judaism (to some degree and in some departments only); that Protestantism is an improvement on Catholicism; that Mormonism is an improvement on Protestantism. So I give Joseph Smith credit as an innovator and as a smart fellow.[82]

Ferguson's assessment is similar to the opinion of Harold Bloom, professor of humanities at Yale University, who said that Joseph Smith was an "authentic religious genius."[83]

In July 1976 J. Don Cerchione of Idaho Falls, Idaho, asked Ferguson if he had lost faith in Mormonism, Ferguson answered: "I think [the] LDS Church [is] better than any other brand of organized religion and I have not lost faith in very large segments

Law Office of

Thomas Stuart Ferguson

[3 December 1979]

12-3-79

23 Orinda Way
Orinda, California 94563
254-3930

James Still:
4602 Sunnyview Road NE
Salem, Oregon

Dear Jim:

Milton Hunter died a few years ago.

I lost faith in Joseph Smith as one having a pipeline to deity --
and have decided that there has never been a pipeline to diety--
with any man. However, I believe that judaism was an improvement
on polytheism; Christianity was an improvement on Judaism (to
some degree and in some departments only); that protestantism is
an improvement on Catholicism; that Mormonism is an improvement
on protestantism. So I give Joseph Smith credit as an innovator
and as a smart fellow. I attend, sing in the choir and enjoy my
friendships in the Church. In my opinion it is the best fraternity
that has come to my attention -- too good to try to shoot it down --
and it is too big and prosperous to shoot down anyway (as Tanner's
ought to figure out).

I think that Joseph Smith may have had Ixtlilxochitl and View of the
Hebrews from which to work. I don't agree with Mrs. Tanner
at all (your quote)... Hunter and I did not play around with the
translation to make it fit the Book of Mormon. The translation
from Spanish to English was done by a non-Mormon Mexican who
knew nothing whatsoever about the Book of Mormon when he did the
job. And we never changed a word of his translation. How Joseph Smith
got his hands on Ixtlil I don't know--Kingsborough had him in England
and Ireland -- but how Joseph Smith got hold of him I don't know.
I have tried to find out.   Oliver Cowdery was in Ethan Smith's congregation
before he went from Vermont to New York to join Joseph Smith.
I have no copies of my books for sale. Sorry. You can borrow one
from anyone who has a copy, and have it xeroxed.

Best wishes.   Sincerely,

Fig. 28--Thomas Stuart Ferguson, letter to James D. Still, 1979.
Reproduced from Thomas Stuart Ferguson Collection, courtesy of Marriott
Library, University of Utah.

of it."[84] Another letter illuminates Ferguson's point of view in
the early 1980s. In September 1981 he wrote to Burt Stride of
San Jose, California, agreeing with him in loving the Church
while not accepting many of its doctrines. Ferguson had conclud-

ed that "Mormonism, although from the mind of a twenty-five-year-old frontiersman, is probably the best brand of religion on the market today."[85]

The Social Values
of the LDS Church

In October 1980 Ferguson wrote a short, noncommittal letter to Rosemary Brown of Mesa, Arizona, stating that he could not remember either meeting with or writing to Dee Jay Nelson, though he had read some of his Book of Abraham publications. Without commenting on his personal beliefs, Ferguson provided information about his activity and membership in the Church: "I am an active member of the Mormon Church and always have been. My relationship and membership with the Church has never been terminated."[86] The next month he wrote again and corrected some statements made by Jerald and Sandra Tanner. Avoiding any mention of the Book of Mormon or the Book of Abraham, Ferguson carefully stated:

> I have never left the Church and I have never proclaimed that the Church is not true. I consider it the most correct and true Church on earth and I think the Tanners and Dee Jay Nelson make a mistake in spending their time and energy attacking it. . . . And it [Mormonism] is sweeping along like a prairie fire in a heavy wind--the little air-rifles and BB shot of the likes of Tanners and Nelson certainly won't slow down the Church.[87]

Ferguson explained his relationship to and activity in the LDS Church: he attended meetings, sang in the ward choir, enjoyed his church friends, and found activity in the LDS community to be rewarding. In fact, he told James D. Still that Mormonism was "the best fraternity" he was aware of--"too good to try to shoot it down--and it is too big and prosperous to shoot down anyway (as [the] Tanners ought to figure out)."[88] Still asked Ferguson whether there was any possibility of getting back the tithing he had paid to the LDS Church. Ferguson gave him some free legal advice and told him that under the law a delivered gift could not be recalled: "Pay your money to a church and take your chances that the church is true or on the right track."[89]

Ferguson listed for Burt Stride some of the things that he liked about Mormonism:

> It is a bargain--free of fraud (monetary fraud, that is) in that money put in comes back to the people in the form of chapels, temples (modern-day awe-inspiring architecture and furnishings like the castles and cathedrals of old), welfare, great choirs, a great university, etc., etc. . . . The money is not going into the pockets of an elite. The people probably get a greater return for their money than in any other major organization in the world! Further--the program of the LDS Relief Society is one of the most advanced, most benevolent, most serving, most educational and worthwhile programs in the history of mankind. The LDS priesthood program is excellent, though somewhat dull--lots of room for improvement, but it beats anything found in any other religion. The youth programs of the LDS Church are little short of fantastic. The missionary program puts tens of thousands of young LDS in close and intimate touch with cultures and people all over the world. They return home as citizens of the world. The health program of the church is one of the modern wonders.[90]

Ferguson said the LDS Church had "the best available brand of man-made religion," and that he did not ever plan to leave it. With all these positive aspects of Mormonism, Ferguson still felt that "the evidence against the validity of certain of the basic supernaturals in the Church" had grown to such a degree that it would be unwise for the leaders of the Church to risk a public debate on these issues.[91]

Projected Magnum Opus
on the Book of Mormon

After going through all this internal turmoil, Ferguson decided to publish his new ideas concerning the origin of the Book of Mormon in a final book. A tantalizing string of evidence exists, showing that Ferguson had indeed researched and written another book-length manuscript and had decided to move ahead with publishing it. He had told Jerald and Sandra

Tanner in December 1970 that "he had been thinking of writing a book about the matter and that it would be a real 'bombshell.'"[92] Throughout the 1970s and the early 1980s Ferguson spent an immense amount of his spare time working on this new project. His basic assumption during this period was that the Book of Mormon was not an ancient document, but a product of the nineteenth century. By the early 1980s he had concluded that Joseph Smith, Sidney Rigdon, and Oliver Cowdery had made a covenant together to start the Mormon Church. In January 1983 Ferguson told Neuffer that "he considered Sidney [Rigdon] a neglected man in church history and was writing a book about him."[93] At the same time he told Barney about this "project."[94]

In February 1983 Ferguson, along with Howard W. Hunter and other board members of NWAF, went on what would turn out to be Ferguson's final trip to Mexico.[95] While there he told Pierre Agrinier Bach, a longtime friend and archaeologist, that "he was working on a project, a manuscript which would (according to him) expose Joseph Smith as a fraud" and that his manuscript was almost completed.[96] It would be a bombshell on the Book of Mormon, showing both positive and negative evidence from Mesoamerican archaeology, but concluding that the Book of Mormon was produced through Joseph Smith's own creative genius and through his use of contemporary sources, including Ethan Smith's *View of the Hebrews* and Sidney Rigdon. Ferguson's position would be very similar (except for the supposed role of Sidney Rigdon) to B. H. Roberts's concluding remarks in his detailed comparison of *View of the Hebrews*:

> In the light of this evidence, there can be no doubt as to the possession of a vividly strong, creative imagination by Joseph Smith, the Prophet, an imagination, it could with reason be urged, which, given the suggestions that are to be found in the "common knowledge" of accepted American antiquities of the times, supplemented by such a work as Ethan Smith's *View of the Hebrews*, would make it possible for him to create a book such as the Book of Mormon is.[97]

Ferguson's unexpected death in 1983 stopped his efforts, and, inexplicably, his final manuscript has to date never surfaced.

Ferguson Born Again?

Some have suggested that Tom Ferguson merely went through a temporary season of doubt and, after a deeply-troubled period, returned to his former convictions of faith. Terrence L. Szink, a doctoral student in Ancient Near Eastern Civilizations at the University of California at Los Angeles, in a book review of Bruce W. Warren's *Messiah in Ancient America* related the following about Ferguson, though Szink knew of no direct evidence that Ferguson regained his former testimony:

> Apparently in his latter years, although he remained active in the Church, Ferguson lost his testimony regarding both the Book of Abraham and the Book of Mormon. His family and friends claim that before his death he returned to a belief in the truthfulness of the Book of Mormon.[98]

In a similar tone, David S. King, president of the Washington, D.C., Temple, wrote an article for *Dialogue* in which he described Ferguson as going through a typical "faith-doubt-faith cycle." The problem with this scenario is that no evidence exists to support such a change in Ferguson's feelings or a reversion to his earlier beliefs. King also asserted (without offering any specific examples) the existence of "the overwhelming amount of virtually uncontested historical and archaeological evidence establishing the book's authenticity."[99] However, others have stated the direct opposite. For example, Dee F. Green, assistant professor of anthropology at Weber State College, cautioned Mormons to "rest assured that we are not accumulating a great flood of 'proof' or 'evidence' which will in a few years burst the dam of secular resistance to the Book of Mormon and flood Zion with hordes of people demanding baptism."[100] King's simplistic explanation does not do justice to the evidence about Ferguson.

The relevant Ferguson letters to various individuals after his crisis of faith fall into the following distribution: four letters in 1971, two in 1972,[101] five in 1976, three in 1977, three in 1979, two in 1980, two in 1981, eleven in 1982, and two in 1983. These letters all tell a consistent story of questioning the historicity of the Book of Mormon and the Book of Abraham, denying the prophetic status of Joseph Smith, and reevaluating the origin of the Book of Mormon, including the possible influence of Sidney Rigdon, Oliver Cowdery, and Ethan Smith. Wishful thinking and fond memories do not change the way things had changed in Ferguson's thinking. The anecdotal theory of Ferguson's having faith, losing it, and regaining it is just not supported by any available evidence from Ferguson himself.

His hundreds of letters, scores of articles, and three books written from 1937 to 1967 demonstrate his deep love for the Book of Mormon and his efforts to corroborate it.[102] During the 1950s and 1960s he was a very popular speaker at firesides, institute gatherings, sacrament meetings, and education weeks. After his crisis of faith precipitated by the translation of the Joseph Smith Egyptian papyri, Ferguson still continued to speak at some LDS gatherings, during which he would discuss the findings of NWAF and the archaeology of the Book of Mormon in a positive, faith-promoting manner. One of his best friends-- who knew his real feelings during the last thirteen years of his life--asked him how he could continue speaking in such a manner to these groups. Ferguson replied that it made them feel good about the Book of Mormon.

Larry S. Ferguson, a son of Thomas Stuart Ferguson, wrote a letter to *Dialogue* in which he related the following about his father:

> About one month before his death [i.e., February 1983], I was with him at our home in California when, for no apparent reason, he said, "Larry, the Book of Mormon is exactly what Joseph Smith said it was." Then he bore one of the strongest testimonies of the Book of Mormon I have ever heard. It was a statement of fact as the sun shines.[103]

It may well be true that this son never heard his father say anything negative about the Book of Mormon. Ferguson had a habit of, on the one hand, saying faith-promoting things to sincere members of the Church and, on the other, divulging critical views to those seeking answers about questions.

John L. Sorenson, emeritus professor of anthropology at BYU, asked a hard question about Ferguson:

> Ought we to respect the hard-driving younger man whose faith-filled efforts led to a valuable major [archaeological] research program, or should we admire the double-acting cynic of later years, embittered because he never hit the jackpot on, as he seems to have considered it, the slot-machine of archaeological research?[104]

Sorenson's "double-acting cynic" seems too strong. The two options presented by Sorenson are not mutually exclusive propositions. For one can appreciate the value of the younger Ferguson's establishment of NWAF, which conducted important archaeological investigations in Mesoamerica, and still respect Ferguson's resolution of the dilemma by retaining Mormon values and yet rejecting the antiquity of the Book of Mormon. Sorenson inappropriately compared Ferguson's long, dedicated search for archaeological confirmation to a gambler's disillusionment in not getting the million-to-one jackpot.

This awkward, two-sided stance earned Ferguson the unenviable epithet of "hypocrite" from both a faithful employee of the LDS Historical Department[105] and anti-Mormon critics.[106] In 1976 Ferguson suggested to Harold W. Lawrence and his wife a practice that might be considered "hypocritical":

> Why not say the right things and keep your membership in the great fraternity [the LDS Church], enjoying the good things you like and discarding the ones you can't swallow (and keeping your mouths shut)? Hypocritical? Maybe. But perhaps a realistic way of dealing with a very difficult problem. There is lots left in the Church to enjoy --and thousands of members have done, and are doing, what I suggest you consider doing.[107]

Labeling Ferguson a hypocrite seems unnecessarily harsh, for we all share this attitude to some degree in our daily lives. Ferguson tried to be all things to all people. He approached people at the point of their needs and concerns. For example, he never once worried his older sister about these new ideas he had acquired. To faithful Church members he couched his answers in a way to appear orthodox. However, to Mormons who raised questions he forthrightly revealed his doubts. It was a tightrope between sometimes speaking the party line and sometimes expressing his private thoughts.

Ferguson's Final Insights

On 4 January 1983 Ferguson met Ronald O. Barney at the LDS Historical Department in Salt Lake City. During the visit Barney asked Ferguson if he knew how Jerald and Sandra Tanner were using his 1971 letter to James Boyack, with its repudiation of the Book of Abraham. Barney recorded in his journal that Ferguson "began to shift in his chair, got pale, and acted as if I was a General Authority that had caught him committing adultery. He apologized all over the place, said the Tanners were creeps, etc." After Barney extolled the value of open discussion of problems, Ferguson disclosed his current beliefs: "After having once been a defender of the faith he now totally rejects the divine intervention of God in the workings of the affairs of men."[108] Also at this time Ferguson said that he "liked the [LDS] church very much" and saw no reason to leave as others do, since he "didn't see God in any of the churches."[109] The next week he sent Barney a letter, pointing out some connections between Oliver Cowdery's family and Ethan Smith, the author of *View of the Hebrews*.[110] Two short sentences in Ferguson's last known letter illustrate his persisting inquisitiveness: "I am continuing my research. It is fun and stimulating."[111]

These final two letters, together with Barney's two journal entries, confirm Ferguson's critical views just two months before his death in 1983. This crucial testimony functions like a kingpin to tie the last thirteen years together and it is comparable in value to the Wesley P. Lloyd diary, which discloses the non-historical view of the Book of Mormon still held by B. H. Roberts just two months before he died in 1933.[112]

In the 1970s and early 1980s Ferguson went back to the drawing board and reconsidered Mormon origins--especially the Book of Mormon and the role of its prophet-translator, Joseph

Smith. Ferguson had already invested so much time, money, and energy into authenticating the Book of Mormon that he could not simply leave this question alone. He felt compelled to search and research into the nineteenth-century origin of the Book of Mormon. More careful study revealed numerous writers from the sixteenth to the early nineteenth centuries who had advocated a connection between the American Indians and the Israelites.[113] Ferguson's desire was to formulate a plausible alternative explanation to the official version, that he had grown up with, of the origin of the Book of Mormon. He had devoted a lifetime to his public stand in favor of the historicity of the Book of Mormon and found it difficult to publish a reversal during the last years of his life. In fact, several of his friends--who were aware of his change of attitude--counseled him not to publish his "bombshell" manuscript which was strongly critical of the Book of Mormon. His disappointment was acute and the resulting changes in his attitude were monumental. However, he continued to speak on both sides of the issue. That approach may appear contradictory, but to Ferguson it was viable solution to a difficult problem. While the various letters he wrote provide insight into his views on a variety of topics, the best indication of his position concerning the archaeological setting of the Book of Mormon was a controversial paper he wrote in 1975 entitled "Written Symposium on Book of Mormon Geography."

Notes

1. Klaus J. Hansen, "Reflections on *The Lion of the Lord*," review of *The Lion of the Lord: A Biography of Brigham Young*, by Stanley P. Hirshon, in *Dialogue: A Journal of Mormon Thought* 5 (Summer 1970): 110. Hansen continued, with emphasis in original: "Perhaps an even more telling response is that of the 'liberals,' or cultural Mormons. After the Joseph Smith papyri affair, one might well have expected a mass exodus of these people from the Church. Yet none has occurred. Why? Because cultural Mormons, of course, do not believe in the historical authenticity of the Mormon scriptures in the first place. So there is nothing to disconfirm. Therefore, the Church Historian's Office could relax completely and allow unlimited access to its holdings without fear of potential repercussions from either orthodox or cultural Mormons. If as a historian I would applaud such a policy I deplore the *reasons* that make it possible, for I believe that it merely highlights the

melancholy fact that too many Mormons, whether 'orthodox' or 'liberal,' regard their history as irrelevant. It is perhaps a supreme irony, then, that the implications of the old restrictive policy of the Church Historian's Office reveal the members of that organization--much maligned by certain professional historians--as upholders of a waning belief in the power of history, although, admittedly, it was they who, in the late fifties and early sixties, presented obstacles rather more formidable than those faced by [Stanley P.] Hirshon to those very scholars who inaugurated the 'new' Mormon history."

2. Ronald O. Barney, interview with Thomas Stuart Ferguson, 4 January 1983, typed on 19 April 1984, in the H. Michael Marquardt Collection, Accession 900, Box 77, Fd 13, Manuscripts Division, J. Willard Marriott Library, University of Utah, Salt Lake City; hereafter abbreviated to Marquardt Collection.

3. D. Jeff Burton, *For Those Who Wonder: Managing Religious Questions and Doubts*, 3d ed. rev. (Bountiful, UT: IVE, 1994), 69-70. Cf. D. Jeff Burton, "The Phenomenon of the Closet Doubter: A Description and Analysis of One Approach to Activity in the Church," *Sunstone* 7 (September-October 1982): 35. Burton suggested four seemingly self-contradictory synonyms for "closet doubters": faithful doubters, faithful disbelievers, active disbelievers, or hopeful doubters.

4. See the author's *Register of the Thomas Stuart Ferguson Papers* (Provo, UT: Division of Archives and Manuscripts, Harold B. Lee Library, Brigham Young University, 1988). Eight innocuous letters written by Ferguson after November 1967 slipped through the screening process, because they were located in folders about the New World Archaeological Foundation.

5. Samuel W. Taylor, statement, ca. 1970, pasted inside the front cover of Taylor's copy of *One Fold and One Shepherd*, a photocopy of which was enclosed with his letter to author, 18 December 1987, in author's possession. Taylor, "The Case for Carping Criticism: Report from the Dog House," typescript, Sunstone Symposium, 12 August 1993, 16, in the John Taylor Family Collection, Manuscript 50, Box 73, Fd 1, Manuscripts Division, J. Willard Marriott Library, University of Utah, Salt Lake City, said: "It was during this period that I last saw Tom Ferguson. He called around, and I won't forget him, sitting in my living room, his face ashen, his voice thin with venom, as he said 'Joseph Smith! How I hate that phony bastard!'" Ferguson's use of the word "phony" in describing Joseph Smith is confirmed by Richard D. Baer, letter to author, 13 January 1995, in author's possession.

6. Pierre Agrinier Bach, interview with author, 25 May 1993, Everett L. Cooley Oral History Project, Accession 814, Manuscripts Division, J. Willard Marriott Library, University of Utah, Salt Lake City. In the pre-Joseph-Smith-Papyri period Ferguson had often referred to the theoretical possibility that the Book of Mormon may be fraudulent. For example, see Ferguson, *One Fold and One Shepherd*, 2d ed. rev. (Salt Lake City: Olympus Publishing Co., 1962), 351, for the juxtaposition of the two positions: either (a) the Book of Mormon is a

"Fake--Fraud" or (b) a "Revealed History--A Truly Divine Book."

7. The text of Ferguson's "Written Symposium on Book of Mormon Geography" is reproduced in Jerald Tanner and Sandra Tanner, eds., *Ferguson's Manuscript Unveiled* (Salt Lake City: Utah Lighthouse Ministry, 1988), and in Appendix A, "Thomas Stuart Ferguson on Book of Mormon Archaeology," below.

8. Ferguson, letter to Mr. and Mrs. Harold W. Lawrence, 20 February 1976, in the Thomas Stuart Ferguson Collection, Accession 1350, Manuscripts Division, J. Willard Marriott Library, University of Utah, Salt Lake City; hereafter abbreviated to Ferguson Collection, UU.

9. To understand how Book of Mormon geography shrank for Ferguson, compare the following three interpretations: the traditional nineteenth-century LDS concept of the North and South American continents as the lands of the Book of Mormon, which Ferguson learned and believed from his childhood until he went to the University of California at Berkeley in 1933, then the Tehuántepec theory of Mesoamerica, which he learned from his friend, M. Wells Jakeman, in 1933 and continued to believe (with some minor modifications) until about 1970, and finally Ferguson's view that Book of Mormon geography does not exist in the real world, which he believed from about 1970 until his death in 1983.

10. O. Allen Israelsen, letter to author, 2 April 1993, in author's possession.

11. Alfred L. Bush, "A Historical Witness," letter to the editor, *Dialogue: A Journal of Mormon Thought* 23 (Fall 1990): 10, with emphasis in original.

12. Ferguson, letter to James Boyack, 13 March 1971, in Ferguson Collection, UU. For a reproduction of this letter, see Charles M. Larson, *By His Own Hand upon Papyrus: A New Look at the Joseph Smith Papyri* (Grand Rapids, MI: Institute for Religious Research, 1992), 182-83.

13. Barney, interview with Ferguson, typed on 19 April 1984. Barney then recorded his own reaction to Ferguson's recounting of this episode with Brown: "I felt as Ferguson was telling me this that he was not making up the story. It appeared that he really believed what he was telling me."

14. The following is the only available paragraph of a photocopy of a letter purportedly dictated by Brown and sent to Robert Hancock: "I do not recall ever having said anything to Mr. Ferguson which would have led him to think I do not believe the Book of Abraham to be true. This is certainly not the case, for I know, even as I live that Christ is directing this Church and that Joseph Smith was His prophet chosen to restore His Church in its fullness" ([Hugh B. Brown], letter to [Robert Hancock], [partial photocopy], 26 September 1974, in Box 77, Fd 13, Marquardt Collection). It should be noted that Brown did not address the central question of whether he and Ferguson discussed Joseph Smith's inability to translate Egyptian hieroglyphics.

15. Tanner and Tanner, *Ferguson's Manuscript Unveiled*, 5.

16. Edgar C. Snow, Jr., "One Face of the Hero: In Search of the Mythological Joseph Smith," *Dialogue: A Journal of Mormon Thought* 27 (Fall 1994): 247n39.

17. Jerald Tanner, letter to Dee Jay Nelson, 18 December 1970, in Ferguson Collection, UU.

18. Dee Jay Nelson, letter to Most Beloved Friends [Jerald Tanner and Sandra Tanner], 31 December 1970, in Box 72, Fd 7, Marquardt Collection.

19. Jerald Tanner and Sandra Tanner, *Mormonism: Shadow or Reality*, 2d ed. (Salt Lake City: Modern Microfilm Co., 1972), 103.

20. Ferguson is referring to Paul R. Cheesman, "An Analysis of the Accounts Relating Joseph Smith's Early Visions" (M.R.E. thesis, Brigham Young University, 1965), and Dean C. Jessee, "The Early Accounts of Joseph Smith's First Vision," *Brigham Young University Studies* 9 (Spring 1969): 275-94. A more accessible transcript of the 1832 account is found in Milton V. Backman, Jr., *Joseph Smith's First Vision: Confirming Evidences and Contemporary Accounts*, 2d ed., rev. and enl. (Salt Lake City: Bookcraft, 1980), 155-57.

21. Ferguson, letter to Boyack, 13 March 1971.

22. Dean C. Jessee, ed., *The Papers of Joseph Smith* (Salt Lake City: Deseret Book Co., 1989), 1:6. Cf. Dean C. Jessee, comp. and ed., *The Personal Writings of Joseph Smith* (Salt Lake City: Deseret Book Co., 1984), 6. The words enclosed in angle brackets were added above the line in the manuscript. Also, the words "a pillar of fire" were first written in the manuscript, then "fire" was deleted and replaced by "light."

23. Marvin S. Hill, *Quest for Refuge: The Mormon Flight from American Pluralism* (Salt Lake City: Signature Books, 1989), 10. For studies of how the 1832 account relates to the other versions of the First Vision, see Richard P. Howard, "An Analysis of Six Contemporary Accounts Touching Joseph Smith's First Vision," in *Restoration Studies I: Sesquicentennial Edition*, ed. Maurice L. Draper (Independence, MO: Herald Publishing House, 1980), 95-117, and Paul R. Cheesman, *The Keystone of Mormonism: Early Visions of the Prophet Joseph Smith* (Provo, UT: Eagle Systems International, 1988).

24. Lucy Mack Smith Collection, preliminary manuscript, 46, transcribed by Martha Jane Coray in 1845, Accession 989, Manuscripts Division, J. Willard Marriott Library, University of Utah, Salt Lake City. This quotation is not printed in Lucy Mack Smith, *Biographical Sketches of Joseph Smith the Prophet and his Progenitors for Many Generations* (Liverpool, England: S. W. Richards, 1853).

25. William Smith, in *New York Observer*, July 1841, quoted in Hill, *Quest*, 193n49.

26. J. Tanner, letter to Nelson, 18 December 1970.

27. Ferguson, letter to Jerald and Sandra [Tanner], 13 March 1971, in Ferguson Collection, UU.

28. A[bram] W. B[enton], "Mormonites," *Evangelical Magazine and*

Gospel Advocate 2 (9 April 1831): 120.

29. Jerald Tanner and Sandra Tanner, *Joseph Smith and Money Digging* (Salt Lake City: Modern Microfilm Co., 1970), 33.

30. Ferguson, letter to Boyack, 13 March 1971, with emphasis in original.

31. Hugh Nibley, *Myth Makers* (Salt Lake City: Bookcraft, 1961), 141-42, with emphasis in original; reprinted in Hugh Nibley, *Tinkling Cymbals and Sounding Brass: The Art of Telling Tales about Joseph Smith and Brigham Young*, The Collected Works of Hugh Nibley, ed. David J. Whittaker (Salt Lake City: Deseret Book Co., 1991; Provo, UT: Foundation for Ancient Research and Mormon Studies, 1991), 11:246.

32. H. Michael Marquardt and Wesley P. Walters, *Inventing Mormonism: Tradition and the Historical Record* ([San Francisco]: Smith Research Associates, 1994), 70-75, 222-30. Cf. Wesley P. Walters, "Joseph Smith's Bainbridge, N.Y., Court Trials," *The Westminster Theological Journal* 36 (Winter 1974): 124, 129-30, and Paul Hedengren, *In Defense of Faith: Assessing Arguments against Latter-day Saint Belief* (Provo, UT: Bradford and Wilson, Ltd., 1985), 195-234.

33. Hill, *Quest*, 11. Cf. Gordon A. Madsen, "Joseph Smith's 1826 Trial: The Legal Setting," *Brigham Young University Studies* 30 (Spring 1990): 91-108.

34. Ferguson, letter to Boyack, 13 March 1971.

35. D. Michael Quinn, *Early Mormonism and the Magic World View* (Salt Lake City: Signature Books, 1987), 39-46, examined Joseph Smith's 1826 trial in the context of folk religion involving seer stones and treasure digging.

36. Ethan Smith, *View of the Hebrews: Exhibiting the Destruction of Jerusalem, the Certain Restoration of Judah and Israel, the Present State of Judah and Israel, and an Address of the Prophet Isaiah Relative to Their Restoration* (Poultney, VT: Smith and Shute, 1823).

37. Ethan Smith, *View of the Hebrews; or the Tribes of Israel in America: Exhibiting Chap. I. The Destruction of Jerusalem, Chap. II. The Certain Restoration of Judah and Israel, Chap. III. The Present State of Judah and Israel, Chap. IV. An Address of the Prophet Isaiah to the United States Relative to Their Restoration*, 2d ed. (Poultney, VT: Smith and Shute, 1825).

38. John L. Sorenson, "Digging into the Book of Mormon: Our Changing Understanding of Ancient America and its Scripture," *The Ensign* 14 (September 1984): 28, incorrectly described Ethan Smith's *View of the Hebrews* as a "romantic novel."

39. Emily A. Ross, letter to William M. Powell, 22 April 1976, Manuscript 7101, Archives, Historical Department, The Church of Jesus Christ of Latter-day Saints, Salt Lake City.

40. Ethan Smith, *The Blessing of Abraham Come on the Gentiles: A Lecture on Infant Baptism Delivered at Bolton, N.Y., August 3, 1818*, 3d ed. (Poultney, VT: Smith and Shute, 1824) and *View of the Trinity; A Treatise on the Character of Jesus Christ, and on the Trinity in Unity of the Godhead, with Quotations from the Primitive Fathers*, 2d ed. (Poultney,

VT: Smith and Shute, 1824). Earlier Ethan published two other books: *A Key to the Figurative Language Found in the Sacred Scriptures, in the Form of Questions and Answers* (Exeter, [NH]: C. Morris, 1814) and *A Dissertation on the Prophecies relative to Antichrist and the Last Times; Exhibiting the Rise, Character, and Overthrow of That Terrible Power; and a Treatise on the Seven Apocalyptic Vials*, 2d ed. (Boston: S. T. Armstrong, 1814).

41. Ferguson, letter to James D. Still, 3 December 1979, in Ferguson Collection, UU. For a reproduction of this letter, see C. M. Larson, *By His Own Hand*, 186.

42. This applies equally well to the lack of knowledge concerning other works written previous to 1830 about the origins of the Indians, which Joseph Smith may or may not have read or heard discussed. Robert N. Hullinger, *Joseph Smith's Response to Skepticism* (Salt Lake City: Signature Books, 1992), 187, said that "the Israelite theory of native American origins was there as a source for Joseph Smith to use in defending God against the forces of deism and rationalism." Stuart J. Fiedel, *Prehistory of the Americas*, 2d ed. (New York: Cambridge University Press, 1992), 3, went beyond the available evidence when he concluded the following concerning Joseph Smith: "[Thomas] Jefferson tentatively concluded that the Indians' ancestors had raised the mounds and buried their dead in them. However, other attributed the mounds to a vanished civilized race, who had been exterminated by the Indians. The discovery of mounds in the Ohio and Mississippi valleys, which were larger and more complex than those previously known in the east, intensified the debate over the mound-builders' identity, and the mounds became the focus of a wildly imaginative literature in the early nineteenth century. . . . One avid reader of mound-builder fantasies was Joseph Smith, whose Book of Mormon, with its account of Israelite migrations to North America [*sic*], seems to reflect his familiarity with this literature."

43. John Phillip Walker, ed., *Dale Morgan on Early Mormonism: Correspondence and a New History* (Salt Lake City: Signature Books, 1986), 313. Morgan continued: "That this should be the character of Joseph's book, that it should exemplify as truly as *View of the Hebrews* a state of mind and a complex of ideas, the concepts of its time embedded in its pages like so many oysters in a stratum of limestone, is more significant in the evaluation of the Book of Mormon than any question of literary derivation, however decisive its bearing may be upon what the book claims to be. For, painful as such a finding may be to the sensibilities of those to whom the historicity of the Book of Mormon is a matter of the greatest importance, Joseph's book is a great deal more useful to a student of the intellectual preoccupations and the folkways of New York State in the third decade of the nineteenth century than to a scholar who would reconstruct the pre-Columbian history of America."

44. "From Priest's *American Antiquities*," *Times and Seasons* 3 (1 June 1842): 813-14. Josiah Priest, *American Antiquities and Discoveries*

in the West 2d ed. rev. (Albany, NY: Hoffman and White, 1833), quoted from the second edition of *View of the Hebrews*.

45. See the author's "'A Most Sacred Possession': The Original Manuscript of the Book of Mormon," *The Ensign* 7 (September 1977): 87. Cf. Richard P. Howard, *Restoration Scriptures: A Study of Their Textual Development*, 2d ed., rev. and enl. (Independence, MO: Herald Publishing House, 1995), 11-12.

46. David Persuitte, *Joseph Smith and the Origins of the Book of Mormon* (Jefferson, NC: McFarland and Co., 1985), 57. Persuitte added that "Mary Gates, a cousin of Joseph's maternal grandmother (Lydia Gates Mack) was married to Nathaniel Cowdery, Jr., the brother of William Cowdery, Oliver's grandfather." Phillip R. Legg, *Oliver Cowdery: The Elusive Second Elder of the Restoration* (Independence, MO: Herald Publishing House, 1989), 16, quoted both of these statements by Persuitte (changing only "Joseph's mother" to "Joseph Smith, Jr.'s mother"), but did not enclose them within quotation marks.

47. Ferguson, letter to Still, 3 December 1979. Quinn, *Early Mormonism*, 31, 87-89, using contemporary census documents and later reminiscence, suggested that the Joseph Smith Sr. family made "a temporary move . . . from Tunbridge to Poultney in 1800." Even if the Joseph Smith Sr. family lived in Poultney for a time, it provides no connection with Ethan Smith, since his pastorate in Poultney did not begin until almost twenty years later.

48. Persuitte, *Joseph Smith*, 7.

49. Ferguson, letter to Ronald Barney, 10 January 1983, in Ferguson Collection, UU. Ferguson listed the subject of the letter as: "Oliver Cowdery--possible member of Ethan Smith congregation, Poultney, Vt."

50. Ross, letter to Powell, 22 April 1976.

51. Claude Heater, letter to author, 13 June 1994, in author's possession. Cf. the discussion of Ethan Smith and *View of the Hebrews* in Dan Vogel, *Indian Origins and the Book of Mormon: Religious Solutions from Columbus to Joseph Smith* (Salt Lake City: Signature Books, 1986), 9, 42-43, 76n16, 81n50, 98n90.

52. Barney, interview with Ferguson, typed on 19 April 1984. John L. Brooke, *The Refiner's Fire: The Making of Mormon Cosmology, 1644-1844* (New York: Cambridge University Press, 1994), 361n41, suggested--without any definite evidence--that Cowdery may have worked in the shop that printed Ethan Smith's book.

53. The author's "Conjectural Emendation and the Text of the Book of Mormon," *Brigham Young University Studies* 18 (1978): 564, pointed out that "the presence of such errors [of hearing] in the Original MS of the Book of Mormon actually supports the position that Joseph Smith dictated to his scribe. Such difficulties are a natural product of the dictation process and are evidence that there was no collusion between the dictator and the scribe."

54. B. H. Roberts, "A Parallel," typescript, 1927, in the B. H. Roberts Collection, Manuscript 106, Box 16, Fd 3, Manuscripts

Division, J. Willard Marriott Library, University of Utah, Salt Lake City; hereafter abbreviated to Roberts Collection. See Brigham D. Madsen, ed., *B. H. Roberts: Studies of the Book of Mormon* (Urbana and Chicago: University of Illinois Press, 1985; reprint, Salt Lake City: Signature Books, 1992), 321-44. For widely contrasting reviews of the publication of Roberts's manuscripts, compare John W. Welch, "New B. H. Roberts Book Lacks Insight of His Testimony," review of *B. H. Roberts: Studies of the Book of Mormon*, edited by Brigham D. Madsen, in *Deseret News, LDS Church News*, 15 December 1985, 11, and Joel B. Groat, "B. H. Roberts' Doubts," review of *B. H. Roberts: Studies of the Book of Mormon*, edited by Brigham D. Madsen, in *Heart and Mind: The Newsletter of Gospel Truths Ministries* (January-March 1995): 5-6.

55. B. H. Roberts, "A Book of Mormon Study," part I, chap. xiii, 19-20, typescript, 1922, in Box 9, Book 2, Roberts Collection; Madsen, *Roberts: Studies*, 240. Having discovered this long-lost manuscript in October 1973 in the possession of one of Roberts's grandsons, H. Grant Ivins, letter to Lowry and Florence [Nelson], 4 November 1973, in H. Grant Ivins Collection, Ms 362, Box 1, Fd 14, explained: "When the Church people talked Ben Roberts out of publishing this material, they told him that to publish would ruin his father's reputation as a historian and as a 'defender of the Church.' In my opinion, the reverse is true. This book would establish him as an honest historian, really seeking the truth, no matter what it did to his other works." For two opposing views on the significance of B. H. Roberts's comparison of the Book of Mormon and *View of the Hebrews*, see Madison U. Sowell, "Defending the Keystone: The Comparative Method Reexamined," *Sunstone* 6 (May-June 1981): 44, 50-54, and George D. Smith, "Defending the Keystone: Book of Mormon Difficulties," *Sunstone* 6 (May-June 1981): 45-50.

56. Even though this post-it note written by Ferguson was attached to the copy of *One Fold and One Shepherd* that Warren used, Warren never mentioned the subject of Ethan Smith in Bruce W. Warren and Thomas Stuart Ferguson [*sic*], *The Messiah in Ancient America* (Provo, UT: Book of Mormon Research Foundation, 1987). For an analysis of the reputed coauthorship between Warren and Ferguson, see the author's "The Odyssey of Thomas Stuart Ferguson," *Dialogue: A Journal of Mormon Thought* 23 (Spring 1990): 84n6, and Appendix B, "Examining the Authorship of *The Messiah in Ancient America*," below.

57. George D. Smith, "Orthodoxy and Encyclopedia," *Sunstone* 16 (November 1993): 50.

58. Barney, interview with Ferguson, typed on 19 April 1984.

59. Ronald O. Barney, interview with Ferguson, 4 January 1983, written in Barney's journal on 15 February 1983, in Box 77, Fd 13, Marquardt Collection.

60. John W. Rigdon, "Lecture Written by John W. Rigdon on the Early History of the Mormon Church," typescript, 1906, in John W. Rigdon Collection, Manuscript 354, Manuscripts Division, J. Willard Marriott Library, University of Utah, Salt Lake City. For Ferguson's

copy of this document to which he added annotations and post-it notes, see Ferguson Collection, UU.

61. Josephine Rigdon Secord, letter to Arlene Hess, 27 February 1967, in Arlene Hess Collection, Manuscript 1281, Special Collections and Manuscripts, Harold B. Lee Library, Brigham Young University, Provo, UT.

62. F. Mark McKiernan, *The Voice of One Crying in the Wilderness: Sidney Rigdon, Religious Reformer, 1793-1876* (Lawrence, KS: Coronado Press, 1971).

63. An overprotective friend of Ferguson allowed the author only a few seconds to look at the 20 January 1982 letter of Ferguson to McKiernan, when it was yanked out of sight and thrown dramatically onto the pile of documents on the floor that were soon to be destroyed. This friend justified his action with the comment that people should not see Ferguson's criticism. The author, knowing the name McKiernan, memorized the date of 20 January 1982 and contacted McKiernan to get a copy of the letter. However, McKiernan does not keep old correspondence. F. Mark McKiernan, letter to author, 11 May 1994, in author's possession, looking back at his letter and phone call with Ferguson, explained that Ferguson "was unhappy with my views of Rigdon's [lack of] participation in the origins of the Book of Mormon. I considered him a crank with a point to prove and dismissed the exchange."

64. Ferguson, research notes, conversation with Lloyd J. Neuffer, [4 January 1983], in Ferguson Collection, UU.

65. Lloyd J. Neuffer, letter to author, 26 December 1988, in author's possession.

66. Ronald O. Barney, letter to Ferguson, 17 January 1983, in Ferguson Collection, UU.

67. Ferguson, letter to Barney, 10 January 1983.

68. Richard S. Van Wagoner and Steven Walker, "Joseph Smith: The Gift of Seeing," *Dialogue: A Journal of Mormon Thought* 15 (Summer 1982): 48-68; William D. Russell, "A Further Inquiry into the Historicity of the Book of Mormon," *Sunstone* 7 (September-October 1982): 20-27.

69. Ferguson, letter to Ronald Barney, 1 February 1983, in Ferguson Collection, UU.

70. Barney, letter to Ferguson, 17 January 1983.

71. Samuel M. Ellis, letter to Lloyd J. Neuffer, 13 November 1933, in Lloyd J. Neuffer Collection, Manuscript 7364, Archives, Historical Department, The Church of Jesus Christ of Latter-day Saints, Salt Lake City. Linda King Newell and Valeen Tippetts Avery, *Mormon Enigma: Emma Hale Smith, Prophet's Wife, "Elect Lady," Polygamy's Foe, 1804-1879* (Garden City, NY: Doubleday and Co., 1984), 111, described this episode as follows: "In mid-April [1842] Joseph had asked Sidney Rigdon's nineteen-year-old daughter Nancy to become his plural wife. [John C.] Bennett had his own eye on the girl and forewarned her, so she refused Joseph. The following day Joseph dictated a letter to her

with Willard Richards acting as scribe. It read in part, 'Happiness is the object and design of our existence; and will be the end thereof, if we pursue the path that leads to it; and this path is virtue, uprightness, faithfulness, holiness, and keeping all the commandments of God. . . . That which is wrong under one circumstance, may be, and often is, right under another. . . . Whatever God requires is right, no matter what it is, although we may not see the reason thereof till long after the events transpire.' Nancy Rigdon showed the letter to her father. Rigdon immediately sent for Joseph, who reportedly denied everything until Sidney thrust the letter in his face."

72. Richard S. Van Wagoner, *Sidney Rigdon: A Portrait of Religious Excess* (Salt Lake City: Signature Books, 1994), 132-41.

73. Gerald Clarke, "Needed: New Myths for Modern Man," *Reader's Digest* 107 (December 1975): 177-80.

74. Ferguson, letter to Mr. and Mrs. Harold W. Lawrence, 9 February 1976, in Ferguson Collection, UU. For a reproduction of this letter, see C. M. Larson, *By His Own Hand*, 184-85.

75. Ferguson, letter to Lawrences, 9 February 1976.

76. Ibid.

77. Jessee, "First Vision," 275-94. Jerald Tanner and Sandra Tanner, *Mormonism: Shadow or Reality*, 2d ed. (Salt Lake City: Modern Microfilm Co., 1972). Eric Hoffer, *The True Believer: Thoughts on the Nature of Mass Movements* (New York: Harper and Row, 1951). Fawn M. Brodie, *No Man Knows My History: The Life of Joseph Smith, The Mormon Prophet*, 2d ed., rev. and enl. (New York: Alfred A. Knopf, 1971. Fifty years after her book first appeared in 1945, Sterling M. McMurrin, Leonard J. Arrington, Newell G. Bringhurst, Roger D. Launius, Mario S. DePillis, Lavina Fielding Anderson, Mauricio Mazon, Todd Compton, and William Mulder discussed its impact on Mormon studies, at the 9 August 1995 Sunstone Symposium.

78. Ferguson, letter to Wesley P. Walters, 6 July 1971, in Ferguson Collection, UU.

79. Ferguson [signed by "bh"], letter to Harold H. Hougey, 26 June 1975, in Ferguson Collection, UU.

80. Ibid.

81. Ferguson, letter to Still, 3 December 1979.

82. Ibid.

83. Harold Bloom, *The American Religion: The Emergence of the Post-Christian Nation* (New York: Simon and Schuster, 1993), 82, quoted in Edwin O. Haroldsen, "'Good and Evil Spoken of,'" *The Ensign* 25 (August 1995): 8.

84. J. Don Cerchione, letter to Ferguson, with handwritten response by Ferguson, 21 July 1976, in Ferguson Collection, UU.

85. Ferguson, letter to Burt Stride, 15 September 1981, in Ferguson Collection, UU.

86. Ferguson, letter to Rosemary Brown, 23 October 1980, in Ferguson Collection, UU. For a reproduction of this letter, see Robert L. Brown and Rosemary Brown, *They Lie in Wait to Deceive: "A Study*

of Anti-Mormon Deception" (Mesa, AZ: Brownsworth Publishing Co., 1981), 1:228.

87. Ferguson, letter to Mr. and Mrs. Robert L. Brown, 17 November 1980, in Ferguson Collection, UU.

88. Ferguson, letter to Still, 3 December 1979. Elsewhere Ferguson used the terminology "myth-fraternity" and "great fraternity" in referring to the LDS Church (Ferguson, letter to Lawrences, 9 February 1976; Barney, interview with Ferguson, typed on 19 April 1984).

89. Ferguson, handwritten response to James D. Still, letter to Ferguson, 5 December 1979, in Ferguson Collection, UU.

90. Ferguson, letter to Stride, 15 September 1981.

91. Ibid.

92. Tanner and Tanner, *Ferguson's Manuscript*, 5.

93. Neuffer, letter to author, 26 December 1988.

94. Barney, interview with Ferguson, written on 15 February 1983.

95. Fred W. Nelson, Jr., "In Honor of Thomas Stuart Ferguson, 1915-1983," *Newsletter and Proceedings of the S.E.H.A.* [Society for Early Historic Archaeology], no. 161 (May 1987): 2.

96. Bach Interview, 25 May 1993.

97. Roberts, "Book of Mormon Study," part I, chap. xiv, 13, in Roberts Collection; Madsen, *Roberts: Studies*, 250.

98. Terrence L. Szink, review of *The Messiah in Ancient America*, by Bruce W. Warren and Thomas Stuart Ferguson, in *Review of Books on the Book of Mormon* 1 (1989): 132.

99. David S. King, "'Proving' the Book of Mormon: Archaeology vs. Faith," *Dialogue: A Journal of Mormon Thought* 24 (Spring 1991): 144-45.

100. Dee F. Green, "Book of Mormon Archaeology: The Myths and the Alternatives," *Dialogue: A Journal of Mormon Thought* 4 (Summer 1969): 79.

101. It may be merely a quirk of history as to which of Ferguson's letters have been preserved or it may be a significant reflection of Ferguson's temporary reticence on speaking out against the Book of Mormon, but the gap in the years 1973, 1974, and 1975 correspond to the time when his son, Larry S. Ferguson, served an LDS mission.

102. Ferguson published only one non-Book-of-Mormon study during his lifetime. See Ferguson, "Do You Know How to Read?" *The Improvement Era* 51 (January 1948): 20, 59-61.

103. Larry S. Ferguson, "The Most Powerful Book," letter to the editor, *Dialogue: A Journal of Mormon* Thought 23 (Fall 1990): 9.

104. Sorenson, "Addendum," 119.

105. Barney, interview with Ferguson, typed on 19 April 1984, said the following: "Lastly, I was bothered by Ferguson's claims that he liked the Church very much and intended to stay in it to the end of his life. He saw no need to quit the Church as so many do because he didn't see God in any of the churches. So, the Mormon Church was in the same category as the rest of the religions that professed divine favor. He referred to the Church as a 'great fraternity.' The most disconcert-

ing thing about this position was that he said that he had just been in Provo on the previous weekend giving a new grandchild 'a name and a blessing.' That, of course, would require the use of the priesthood. I thought that was quite hypocritical on Ferguson's part."

106. Jerald Tanner and Sandra Tanner, "Ferguson's Two Faces: Mormon Scholar's 'Spoof' Lives on after His Death," *Salt Lake City Messenger*, no. 69 (September 1988): 1-10.

107. Ferguson, letter to Lawrences, 9 February 1976. Technically, Ferguson is proposing a hypocritical practice to the Lawrences, rather than admitting his own such course.

108. Barney, interview with Ferguson, written on 15 February 1983. Barney's unintentional second occurrence of "once" in this sentence has been eliminated.

109. Barney, interview with Ferguson, typed on 19 April 1984.

110. Ferguson, letter to Barney, 10 January 1983.

111. Ferguson, letter to Barney, 1 February 1983.

112. The Wesley P. Lloyd Collection, Accession 1338, Manuscripts Division, J. Willard Marriott Library, University of Utah, Salt Lake City; part of the Lloyd diary entry is printed in Madsen, *Roberts: Studies*, 22-24. In an effort to distance an LDS General Authority, B. H. Roberts, from this liberal viewpoint, Truman G. Madsen and John W. Welch, *Did B. H. Roberts Lose Faith in the Book of Mormon?* (Provo, UT: Foundation for Ancient Research and Mormon Studies, 1985), 35, said that Wesley P. Lloyd "is not reliable as a reporter." This disparagement of Lloyd was deleted in a later printing.

113. Michael D. Coe, Dean Snow, and Elizabeth Benson, *Atlas of Ancient America* (New York: Facts On File Publications, 1986), 24, stated: "In the racist and generally anti-Indian thought of the day it was felt that these [Moundbuilders] could not have been the dark-skinned Indians but a white race which had disappeared long ago. The idea that white people had been in America long before Columbus also took off from the late and largely spurious legend of Madoc, the Welsh chieftain who had supposedly journeyed west to the New World. It was long believed, and still is by some, that there were 'white' Indians among Plains tribes like the Mandan, descended from Madoc's Welsh immigrants. Such notions surely influenced Joseph Smith, Jr. (1805-44), the founder of the Mormon religion."

5

Book of Mormon Archaeological Tests

Knowing the value of responding to people who sought his advice, Ferguson answered many letters during the 1970s and early 1980s. Late in 1974 a request of a different sort was made of him, which led him--after a lifetime of studying the Book of Mormon--to write a twenty-nine-page analysis of what he felt were the most important archaeological problems relating to its historicity.

Written Symposium
on the Book of Mormon

David A. Palmer, a chemical engineer with an interest in the Book of Mormon, felt that the time was right for LDS students of the Book of Mormon to try to reach a general agreement concerning the main aspects of its geography. In 1974 Palmer proposed a two-stage written symposium to tackle this problem. In the first stage V. Garth Norman[1] and John L. Sorenson[2] were to make fresh revisions of their varying geographical theories. In the second stage selected LDS scholars were to offer constructive criticism of these two geographies in a "Book of Mormon Non-Conference Symposium" and mail their response to the other participants.[3] Palmer enlisted the following individuals to join him in this unique symposium: B. Keith Christensen, a commercial illustrator; Thomas Stuart Ferguson, founder of the New World Archaeological Foundation; Fred W. Nelson, Jr., a chemist and archaeologist; V. Garth Norman, an NWAF archaeologist; John L. Sorenson, a BYU professor of anthropology; Calvin D. Tolman, an offset pressman at the Deseret News; Bruce W. Warren, a doctoral student in anthropology; and J. Nile Washburn, a writer on Book of Mormon geography. Palmer required each participant to "make a *substantive* evaluation" of both geographical theories.[4]

In his March 1975 contribution to this symposium Ferguson focused more attention on the position paper of John L. Sorenson:

> Sorenson lays down some factual requirements that the correlation of Jaredite-Nephite places must meet to be valid and acceptable: (1) configuration, (2) dimensions, (3) directions, (4) topography, (5) plant life, (6) animal life, (7) climate . . . . These are objective tests. To Sorenson's list of requirements--his "test" list--I think there should be added two additional items, (1) metals and (2) scripts, bringing the list of requirements to nine. He gives but one paragraph to his first test, "configuration." . . . He gives seven full pages to item two, "dimensions." . . . Four and a half pages are devoted to his test three, "directions." Sorenson's discussion of test four, "topography," encompasses seven pages. He quits after covering his first four items.
>
> In my opinion, the most demanding and exacting tests (and therefore the most substantial) are "plant life," "animal life," "metals," and "scripts." Neither Norman nor Sorenson applies any of these more significant and truth-testing factors to their hypotheses. This is my main criticism of each of the papers.[5]

While Ferguson's initial assignment was to respond to the Norman and Sorenson geographical theories, his paper addressed more broadly what he saw as the critical difficulties in Book of Mormon archaeology. He divided these problems into four areas: the Plant-Life Test, the Animal-Life Test, the Metallurgy Test, and the Script Test. This insightful document reveals Ferguson's perception of what he termed "the big weak spots" involved in attempting to authenticate the Book of Mormon through archaeology.[6] Ferguson also described his paper for the symposium as being a study "pointing up Book of Mormon problems raised by archaeology."[7]

Ferguson became aware of the earlier investigation into similar problems of the Book of Mormon made by B. H. Roberts, a member of the LDS First Council of Seventy, when the Tanners published the text in 1980. In 1921 William E. Riter of Salina, Utah, wrote to Apostle James E. Talmage for an answer to five questions which a friend of his in Washington, D.C., had asked about the Book of Mormon. The questions concerned the development of native American languages, the presence of the horse in the New World, knowledge of steel and metallurgy, use of metal swords and cimiters, and possession of silk. Talmage passed this letter on to Roberts for his answer. Roberts wrote a 141-page study entitled "Book of Mormon Difficulties: A Study," which discussed these five problems in three chapters.[8] In January 1922 Roberts presented this paper to the First Presidency and the Twelve Apostles, but their only response was silence. The following month Roberts condensed these problems into a short, positive letter in reply to Riter, not discussing any of the difficulties he had found in the Book of Mormon. Roberts felt very unsatisfied, and during the first three months of 1922 he delved further and wrote "A Book of Mormon Study," which discussed the controversial idea that Joseph Smith might have produced the Book of Mormon himself, using his own creative imagination and possibly Ethan Smith's *View of the Hebrews*.[9] This was followed in October 1927 by "A Parallel," which condensed "A Book of Mormon Study" into eighteen comparisons between the *View of the Hebrews* and the Book of Mormon.[10] Many LDS students consider these controversial analyses by Roberts concerning problems in the Book of Mormon to be thought-provoking, even though Roberts wrote them over seventy years ago. Because Ferguson did not become aware of Roberts's study until at least five years after his own, it provides a comparative analysis.

The written criticisms by Ferguson and the others participating in the 1975 symposium were taken into account by both Norman and Sorenson. Norman chose not to publish his geographical position. However, after careful revision Sorenson published his viewpoint a decade later as *An Ancient American Setting for the Book of Mormon*.[11] Deanne G. Matheny, who formerly taught anthropology at BYU, reviewed Sorenson's book in 1993.[12] Sorenson himself (then a BYU emeritus professor) responded to Matheny the following year.[13] Ferguson's study is now twenty-one years old, but using all these sources and the most current archaeological and historical evidence provides an opportunity to place the problems he raised into better perspective and to update the discussion to the present.

Before discussing the four types of tests, Ferguson made a plea to consult the Book of Mormon text in order to find out precisely what it contains:

> What are the demands of the text of the Book of Mormon for the dirt, soil, earth, and ground of Book of Mormon places? Let's turn to the text of the Book of Mormon for some of the specific things that must be found in the ground occupied 2500 years by people from Iraq and for 1000 years by people from Israel.[14]

The Book of Mormon account of the Jaredites, Nephites, Lamanites, and other groups reveals a diverse record of their material cultures. Though such details are not the purpose of the Book of Mormon, there is enough incidental information provided to enable these important tests of its authenticity. Ferguson's goal was to produce a dispassionate analysis of the perceived problems of the Book of Mormon, approached from four different angles.

No. 1--The Plant-Life Test
of the Book of Mormon

In what Ferguson called the "Plant-Life Test," he presented quotations from the Book of Mormon that mention wheat, barley, figs, and grapes, then repeated the same list and attached the word "none" to each in order to indicate that no known evidence supports the existence of these plants in Mesoamerica. Ferguson then continued:

> This negative score on the plant-life test should not be treated too lightly. An abundance of evidence supporting the existence of these plants has been found in other parts of the world of antiquity. The existence of numerous non-Book-of-Mormon plants (maize,[15] lima beans, tomatoes, squash, etc.) has been supported by abundant archaeological findings. . . . Art portrayals in ceramics, murals, and sculptured works--of ancient plant life--are fairly commonplace. Thousands of archaeological holes in the area proposed have given us not a fragment of evidence of the presence of the plants mentioned in the Book of Mormon--the holes include the great one dug by Edwin Shook at Tehuacán, Puebla, Mexico. He excavated a cave--going down and back to 5,000 B.C., finding most of the major plants of the area. But no wheat, barley, figs, or grapes.[16]

To his credit Ferguson showed awareness--both here and in his discussion of the animal-life and the metallurgy tests--of the difference between the direct evidence of archaeological discoveries and the indirect evidence derived from sculptural and pictorial representations.

However, Ferguson did not explain that all of the occurrences of "grapes" and "figs" in the Book of Mormon are contained in biblical quotations. It could conceivably be argued that such quotations refer only to the Old World plants. The four instances of the term "grapes" in 2 Ne. 15:2-4 are imbedded within a thirteen-chapter-long quotation from Isaiah. Also, in the Book of Mormon the resurrected Jesus asked the people at Bountiful: "Do men gather grapes of thorns, or figs of thistles?"

(3 Ne. 14:16), using the same wording as found at Matthew 7:16. Native grapes were used in northern Mexico.[17] In the sixteenth century Diego de Landa mentioned the existence of wild vines with edible grapes, though Mayan wine or *balche* was made by fermenting tree bark, honey, and water.[18] Evidence of a wild fig has been discovered at Don Martín in Chiapas.[19] Accordingly, Ferguson was mistaken both when he assumed that grapes and figs were Book of Mormon plants and when he asserted that no varieties of grapes or figs were known in Mesoamerica.

For archaeological confirmation of the Book of Mormon to be significant, it must come from both the right time period and the right place. The site at Don Martín, near Santa Rosa (which Sorenson identified as Zarahemla) has produced plant remains dating to the Late Preclassic time (200 B.C. to A.D. 200). Deanne G. Matheny, wife of and fellow archaeologist with Raymond T. Matheny, said the following concerning the discovered plants at this site:

> The seeds of more than fifty species of plants and other plant parts were among the remains recovered from the pits [at Don Martín]. . . . Several of those identified were domesticates, including the jack bean (*Canavalia*), manioc (*Manihot*), two species of maize (*Zea mays*), and two species of common bean (*Phaseolus*). Other species that may have been cultivated include amaranth (*Amaranthus*), chili pepper (*Capsicum*), goose foot (*Chenopodium*), sunflower (*Helianthus*), tobacco (*Nicotiana*), and *Crescentia*, *Acromia mexicana*, and *Sideroxylon tempisque*. Five wild plants were gathered: fig, palm, *portulaca*, *vitis*,[20] and *annonaceae*.
>
> At other archaeological sites in Mesoamerica dating to pre-Columbian times, pollen studies and studies of seeds and other plants have revealed similar plant assemblages. But thus far no Old World plants have been identified by the presence of their pollens or other remains.[21]

Mesoamerican plant remains have thus been discovered in the archaeological record during the stated times of the Book of Mormon, showing the domestication of maize, beans, squash, avocado, chili peppers, and the bottle gourd.[22] John A. Price, professor of anthropology at York University, summarized the evidence for New World plants:

No Native Americans made grape wine or wheat bread. Instead, native plants . . . were domesticated: corn, beans, squashes, potatoes, tomatoes, manioc, . . . The Jaredites and Nephites are portrayed as having had plow agriculture of wheat and barley . . . , but nothing remotely resembling this kind of culture has ever been found, either archaeologically or ethnographically, in the aboriginal New World. . . . This was not plow agriculture; the animal-drawn plow was absent in the pre-Columbian world. It was hand agriculture of corn or manioc or potatoes, not wheat or barley.[23]

Wheat is mentioned at Mosiah 9:9 in a list of other seeds, and occurs metaphorically in the words of the resurrected Jesus to a multitude, warning them to avoid temptation since Satan wanted to "sift you as wheat" (3 Ne. 18:18). Since there are several other cultural adaptations--such as the replacement of "farthing" by "senine" (3 Ne. 12:26; cf. Matt. 5:26)--it should be assumed that, if the Nephites in first century A.D. did not have wheat, Jesus would have substituted it with a more appropriate plant name. Barley occurs four times--at Mosiah 7:22; 9:9 and Alma 11:7, 15.

Ferguson pointed out the lack of verification for the existence of wheat and barley during Book of Mormon times in Mesoamerica. B. H. Roberts also listed these two plants.[24] John L. Sorenson, professor of anthropology at BYU, reported that in 1982 some domesticated barley was discovered in Arizona.[25] Raymond T. Matheny, another professor of anthropology at BYU, countered that this was an indigenous American species in the Hohokam culture (dated about A.D. 900), and "has nothing to do with the Old World horticum [*Hordeum*] barley."[26] However, the Book of Mormon does not specify whether the barley referred to was an Old World transplant they brought in the form of seeds to the New World or a native variety they found at or soon after their arrival here. More recently Sorenson reported the discovery of this North American barley in Illinois and Oklahoma.[27] The lack of evidence for the existence of wheat in the New World remains a major difficulty in verifying the antiquity of the Book of Mormon.[28]

No. 2--The Animal-Life Test
of the Book of Mormon

In the "Animal-Life Test" Ferguson presented Book of Mormon quotations for the ass, bull, calf, cattle, cow, goat, horse, ox, sheep, sow (swine), and elephant. After citing the relevant passages for each of these items, Ferguson repeated the same list of names, emphatically adding the word "none" with each. Ferguson then commented:

> Evidence of the foregoing animals has not appeared in any form--ceramic representations, bones or skeletal remains, mural art, sculptured art, or any other form. However, in the regions proposed by Norman and Sorenson, evidence has been found in several forms of the presence in Book of Mormon times of other animals--deer, jaguars, dogs, turkeys, etc. The zero score presents a problem that will not go away with the ignoring of it. Non-LDS scholars of first magnitude, some who want to be our friends, think we have real trouble here. That evidence of the ancient existence of these animals is not elusive is found in the fact that proof of their existence in the ancient old-world is abundant. The absence of such evidence in the area proposed for our consideration in this symposium is distressing and significant, in my view.[29]

Pre-Columbian Mayan hieroglyphs and ceramic art depict various mammals, such as jaguars (fig. 29), tapirs, deer, monkeys,[30] dogs, peccaries, coatimundis, armadillos, rabbits, gophers, and leaf-nosed bats.[31] The largest mammals alive in Mesoamerica when the Europeans arrived were jaguars, pumas, tapirs, and deer. After quoting numerous passages listing various Book of Mormon animals, B. H. Roberts of the LDS First Council of Seventy stated that this "unequivocally commits the Book of Mormon to the existence and use of the horse and the other Old World domestic animals mentioned above--horses, asses, oxen, cows, sheep, goats, swine (the last, however, only among the Jaredites)."[32]

In the second century B.C. the Lamanites mistreated the people of Limhi, with the Book of Mormon stating that they "began to put heavy burdens upon their backs, and drive them as they would a dumb ass" (Mosiah 21:3). However, Roberts quoted an early twentieth-century authority to the effect that "before the time of Columbus, *no tribe had an animal able to carry a man*."[33] No asses or other domesticated animals could be used to transport either humans or heavy loads, because "no animals large enough to carry cargo lived in Mesoamerica before the coming of the Spanish."[34]

Enos, a nephew of the Nephi who was one of the original colonists, provided an early description of the domesticated animals among the Nephites:

> And it came to pass that the people of Nephi did till the land, and raise all manner of grain, and of fruit, and flocks of herds,[35] and flocks of all manner of cattle of every kind, and goats, and wild goats, and also many horses (Enos 1:21).

Many times in the Book of Mormon "flocks" and "herds" are mentioned. However, unless there is some specification as to what animal is actually being referred to in that particular flock or herd, it is useless to speculate as to the intended animal. For example, John L. Sorenson proposed that the Book of Mormon "flocks" and "herds" might have consisted of any one of the following twenty animals: deer, peccaries, turkeys, Muscovy

Fig. 29--Jaguar, Panthera onca. Reproduced from National Geographic Book Service, *Wild Animals of North America* (1987), courtesy of National Geographic Society.

ducks, Tinamou ducks,[36] quail, pheasants, partridges, doves, *curassow, cotinga,* roseate spoonbills, macaws, *chachalaca,* parrots, hares, rabbits, *paca, agouti,* and fattened dogs.[37] In this menagerie of possible animals to be considered as part of a flock, the only animal actually mentioned in the Book of Mormon is the dog. The domestic dog certainly may have been a source of food,[38] but in the Book of Mormon the dog serves as an example in metaphors: people should not throw holy things to dogs (3 Ne. 14:6), nor should they depart from righteousness and turn to iniquity like a dog which eats his own vomit (3 Ne. 7:8).

The Book of Mormon mentions sheep a total of twenty-six times. There are also twenty-two instances of shepherd and one reference to wool at 2 Ne. 8:8, which is a quotation from Isa. 51:8. Sheep, however, are not native American animals.[39] All the various animals mentioned in the Book of Mormon must be compared with the evidence available concerning animals in the Americas. Careful examination of many thousands of New World images on pottery and stone reveals no artistic renditions of Old World domestic animals. In the 1960s Sidney B. Sperry, professor of religion at BYU, admitted that "the problem of demonstrating the use of domestic animals among ancient American peoples is the most difficult scientific problem faced by Book of Mormon scholars at the present time."[40] Because considerable study has been done on the elephant and the horse, these two animals are examined in some detail.

Elephants among the Jaredites

In Ferguson's list of the various animals in the "Animal-Life Test" he qualified the negative verdict on elephants by explaining that there are "none contemporary with [the] Book of Mormon."[41] It seems justifiable for Ferguson to understand the meaning of the word "elephant" to include the extinct mammoth and mastodon of North America. The Book of Mormon contains the following reference to elephants: "and they also had horses, and asses, and there were elephants and cureloms and cumons; all of which were useful unto man, and more especially the elephants and cureloms and cumoms" (Ether 9:19). This indicates that the Jaredites found the elephants to be particularly helpful. However, it should be kept in mind that this solitary verse with its two occurrences of elephants is comparatively early in their history, since Emer is estimated to have lived about 2500 B.C.[42]

Jean Frédéric Waldeck, who lived for a year in the Mesoamerican jungles during the early 1830s, published drawings of various Mayan hieroglyphic inscriptions. Waldeck's conviction that the Mayan culture was derived from the Old World "distorted his perceptions and drove him to see non-existent" influences in the hieroglyphs.[43] Waldeck drew two elephant heads in his creative rendition of the middle panel of glyphs in the Temple of the Inscriptions at Palenque (fig. 30).[44] This should be compared with

Fig. 30--Alleged representation of elephant heads (1st row, 3d glyph and 2d row, 1st glyph), The Temple of the Inscriptions, Palenque, Mexico. Reproduced from drawing by Jean Frédéric Waldeck, in Claude F. Baudez, Jean-Frédéric Waldeck (1993), courtesy of Fernand Hazan Editions.

Fig. 31--Same set of glyphs, The Temple of the Inscriptions, Palenque, Mexico. Reproduced from drawing by Annie Hunter, in Alfred P. Maudslay, Archaeology (1889-1902).

Annie Hunter's more accurate drawings of the same set of glyphs (fig. 31).[45] John L. Sorenson cited Albert S. Gatschet's 1887 article on "Elephants in America," in which Gatschet quoted Davyd Ingram's sixteenth-century fanciful description of elephants supposedly seen roaming in the eastern part of North America.[46] Ingram showed his lack of dependability as an eyewitness in his description of a grotesque headless animal purportedly sighted on this same journey:

> He [Ingram] did alsoe see one other Straunge Beaste bigger than a Beare, yt had nether heade nor necke, his eyes and mouthe weare in his breast; this beaste is verye ouglie to beholde and Cowardlie of kynde, yt beareth a very fyne skynne like a Ratte, full of sylver heare.[47]

Sorenson commented that Ingram's account "at the least, shows some of the difficulty eye-witnesses and non-eye-witnesses have with perception and labeling."[48] It seems rather that this account illustrates how an unreliable observer with a vivid imagination can embellish a genuine travel narrative. Informed writers real-

Fig. 32--Skeleton of the Columbian mammoth, Mammuthus columbi, at Temple Hill, New York. Reproduced from Chris A. Hartnagel and Sherman C. Bishop, "Mastodons, Mammoths, and Other Pleistocene Mammals," *New York State Museum Bulletin* (1921).

ized that the mammoth had been extinct for a long time. A New York writer in the 1823 *Palmyra Herald* showed such awareness: "What wonderful catastrophe destroyed at once the first inhabitants, with the species of mammoth, is beyond the researches of the best scholar and greatest antiquarian."[49]

Numerous reasons have been proposed to explain the extinction of the large mammals during the late Pleistocene era.[50] The two major theories to account for this extinction are climatic changes and human hunting.[51] In North America prehistoric remains of the Columbian mammoth (*Mammuthus columbi*, fig. 32) and the American mastodon (*Mammut americanum*, fig. 33) have been found.[52] Gary Haynes, professor of anthropology at the University of Nevada, Reno, pointed out that mammoths and mastodons disappeared during the late Pleistocene from 10,000 to 12,000 years ago.[53]

In the last four decades numerous refinements in carbon-14 dating have shown that not all radiocarbon dates are equally

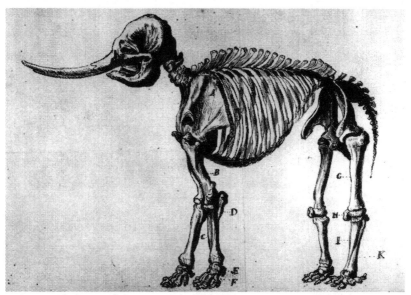

Fig. 33--Skeleton of the American mastodon, Mammut americanum.
Drawing by Rembrandt Peale, reproduced from Lillian B. Miller, *In Pursuit of Fame: Rembrandt Peale* (1992), courtesy of American Philosophical Society.

valid. Since their accuracy varies according to type of material being dated and the possibilities of contamination, Donald K. Grayson, professor of archaeology at the University of Washington, analyzed the thirty-eight genera of mammals that supposedly became extinct during the late Pleistocene period and found that only seven genera have the very best radiocarbon dates. Two of these seven are the mammoth and mastodon, with twenty-five good dates ranging from 10,395 ± 100 years ago back to more than 33,000 years ago, scattered over thirteen different archaeological sites.[54] In 1993 three Russian scientists announced that Old World woolly mammoths (*Mammuthus primigenius*), which were stranded on Wrangel Island in the East Siberian Sea off northeastern Siberia, evolved into midget mammoths only four to six feet high and survived until about 3700 years ago.[55] However, the evidence that neither the mammoth nor the mastodon of North America survived the last Ice Age is strong; accordingly, these animals had been extinct thousands of years before the Jaredites, the earliest Book of Mormon people, lived in the New World.

Horses in the Book of Mormon

Several references to horses are scattered throughout the Book of Mormon. First of all, after leaving Jerusalem, living in the wilderness for eight years, and sailing across the ocean, Nephi described what wild animals their small colony encountered as they arrived in the New World:

> And it came to pass that we did find upon the land of promise, as we journeyed in the wilderness, that there were beasts in the forests of every kind, both the cow and the ox, and the ass and the horse, and the goat and the wild goat, and all manner of wild animals, which were for the use of men. And we did find all manner of ore, both of gold, and of silver, and of copper (1 Ne. 18:25).

These indigenous animals were found--not brought--by the Nephites.[56] In the first century B.C. the Lamanite king Lamoni gave orders to his servants to prepare "his horses and chariots" (Alma 18:9; 20:6) for two trips. Under the direction of Lachoneus, their governor, and Gidgiddoni, the chief captain of their army, in A.D. 17 the Nephites gathered "their horses, and their chariots, and their cattle, and all their flocks and their herds" (3 Ne. 3:22) into the lands of Zarahemla and Bountiful in defense against the Gadianton robbers. The Nephite plan was to assemble enough "provisions, and horses and cattle, and flocks of every kind, that they might subsist" (3 Ne. 4:4) for seven years. A possible interpretation of this verse is that they ate horse meat during this period.[57] However, nine years later there were still horses alive among the people, for in A.D. 26 the Nephites returned to their original lands, "every man, with his family, his flocks and his herds, his horses and his cattle" (3 Ne. 6:1). The Jaredites, who date from the third millennium B.C., also had horses (Ether 9:19).

Several species of horses existed in prehistoric America, including the Pleistocene horse, *Equus scotti* (fig. 34).[58] At least

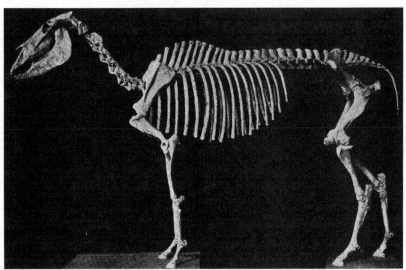

Fig. 34--Skeleton of a Pleistocene horse, Equus scotti, at Rock Creek, Texas. Reproduced from Henry F. Osborn, *The Horse* (1913).

130 individuals of *Equus occidentalis* were trapped in the La Brea tar pits.[59] B. H. Roberts warned that these Pleistocene finds at Rancho La Brea cannot be used to sustain the Book of Mormon claim concerning horses, since there is "positive and well nigh universal testimony about the absence of the horse from America within historic times."[60] More recently Bruce J. MacFadden, curator of the Florida Museum of Natural History at the University of Florida, stated that the extinction of the horse in the Americas occurred about 11,000 years ago at the close of the Pleistocene era.[61] This is supported by fifteen good radiocarbon dates, with the youngest being 10,370 ± 350 years ago.[62] The extinction of the horse before the growth of civilization in Mesoamerica is also supported by the fact that no depictions of the horse occur in any pre-Columbian art.[63]

Ferguson was aware that there was no support for the existence of the horse during Book of Mormon times.[64] Just as the discredited Jean Frédéric Waldeck saw elephants depicted in Mayan ruins, so Milton R. Hunter, an LDS General Authority in the First Council of Seventy, saw horses; and in his *Archaeology and the Book of Mormon* he displayed a photograph of a carved stone showing a bearded man standing by a horse on the Temple of Wall Panels in Chichén Itzá (fig. 35).[65] However, this reputed "horse" reaches only to the height of the man's waist, and John L. Sorenson rightly suggested that Hunter's animal is probably a deer.[66]

Sorenson, in an effort to support his position that the horse might have survived into Book of Mormon times, stated the following:

> Archaeologist Paul S. Martin, for example, saw no theoretical reason why "pockets" of horses and other Pleistocene fauna could not have survived as late as 2000 B.C. Dr. Ripley Bullen thought horses could have lasted until 3000 B.C. in Florida, and J. J. Hester granted a possible 4000 B.C. survival date.[67]

Let us examine Sorenson's three assertions. (1) Paul S. Martin, professor of geosciences at the University of Arizona, was quoted out of context, for after expressing the theoretical possibility that

Sorenson referred to, Martin then made the following strong statement: "But in the past two decades concordant stratigraphic, palynological [relating to the study of pollen], archaeological, and radiocarbon evidence to demonstrate beyond doubt the post-glacial survival of an extinct large mammal has been confined to extinct species of *Bison*."[68] (2) Ripley Bullen spoke in general of the extinction of mammals in Florida and not specifically of the horse as Sorenson asserted.[69] (3) James J. Hester, professor of anthropology at the University of Colorado, did not suggest that the horse survived until 4000 B.C., but rather used a date more than two thousand years earlier.[70] Hester's date of 8240 years before the present (with a variance of ± 960 years) was published in 1967, but the validity of the radiocarbon dating for these horse remains at Whitewater Draw, Arizona, has been questioned. The next youngest horse date of 10,370 ± 350 years ago has a better quality of material being dated and stronger association between

Fig. 35--Alleged representation of a horse, Temple of Wall Panels, Chichén Itzá, Mexico, as interpreted by Milton R. Hunter. Reproduced from Milton R. Hunter, *Archaeology and the Book of Mormon* (1956), courtesy of Deseret Book Co.

the material actually being tested and the extinct genus.[71] Clearly, Sorenson's three arguments for a late survival of the horse do not hold up under scrutiny.[72] Certain now extinct species may have survived in particular areas after the Ice Age. For example, one scholar recently stated that "in one locality in Alberta, *Equus conversidens* [a short-legged, small horse] may still have been in existence about 8,000 B.P. [before present]."[73] While there may have been small "pockets" of horses surviving after the Late Pleistocene extinctions, the time period for such survivals would still be long before the earliest Jaredites of the Book of Mormon.

John W. Welch, professor of law at BYU, referred to the find in Mayapán of horse remains which were "considered by the zoologist studying them to be pre-Columbian."[74] Examination of Welch's citation reveals that he misrepresented the evidence, which does not date to pre-Columbian times (and hence potentially to the Book of Mormon period) but rather to prehistoric Pleistocene times. This find at Cenote Ch'en Mul consists of one complete horse tooth and fragments of three others, which were found six feet below the surface in black earth and were "heavily mineralized [fossilized], unlike any other material in the collections."[75] Thousands of bones and teeth were examined at Mayapán, which is a Late Post-Classic site established in the thirteenth century A.D., but these four horse teeth were the only ones fossilized. The reporting scholar did not suggest that the Mayan people had ever seen a pre-Columbian horse, but that in Pleistocene times horses lived in Yucatán, and that "the tooth fragments reported here could have been transported in fossil condition" by the Maya as curiosities.[76] Thus, Welch's assertion about pre-Columbian horses must be corrected to refer to ancient Pleistocene horses, since these fossilized horse teeth at Mayapán date to thousands of years before the Jaredites.

Faced with strong evidence of the prehistoric extinction of the horse in the New World at the end of the last Ice Age, Sorenson sidestepped the issue by suggesting that Joseph Smith used the term "horse" to translate a word on the plates for either a tapir or a deer.[77] Deanne Matheny responded to this suggestion:

It seems unlikely that both Jaredites and Nephites, who were well-acquainted with horses, would have mistaken a deer or a tapir for a horse. Their experience in the Old World should have led them to categorize the small New World deer and the squat stout tapir as animals considerably different from the horse.[78]

The endangered Baird's tapir, ranging in the wild from Mexico to Ecuador, is "well suited for movement through the dense vegetation along the banks of rivers and the edges of forests, which are its favorite grazing areas."[79] This rarely-seen tapir seems an unlikely candidate for the Book of Mormon horse. Ferguson had earlier rejected the possibility of identifying the horse with the tapir.[80] When the Maya first saw the European horse or cow, they called it by the name of the largest animal they knew--the tapir. Glenna Nielsen Grimm, who received her Ph.D. in anthropology at the University of Utah, contrasted the differing naming techniques of the Maya and the Spaniards:

> They [the Maya] did not have a word for the horse. They didn't have a word for the cow. They weren't familiar with these animals. However, the Spaniards who knew what a horse looked like and what a cow looked like, when they saw the tapir . . . they called it a pig. Now they were familiar with pigs from the Old World and they were familiar with horses, so they didn't call it a horse--it doesn't look like a horse--and being a nocturnal animal I don't know that it [the tapir] could ever fulfill the usage that people put horses to.[81]

When people confront a previously unknown animal, they often name it according to a characteristic feature or similarity to another animal. However, the Book of Mormon does not say "like a horse" or "similar to a cow," so there is no evidence that the names of animals refer merely to similar animals.[82]

Sorenson has dropped his advocacy of the tapir as the animal that the Nephites and Jaredites called the "horse" and in 1994 focused on the deer, suggesting the possibility that deer may have been ridden in Mesoamerica. Sorenson pointed out that, when first seeing Spanish horses, the Aztecs called them "the deer-which-carried-men-upon-their-backs." Sorenson concluded that "such information shows that there is nothing inherently implausible in the idea" of Mesoamerican men riding deer.[83] However, Stephen E. Thompson, an LDS Egyptologist at Brown University, questioned Sorenson's logic, saying that "if this is the way Aztecs referred to horses, then obviously the major difference between deer and horses was that horses carried men, while deer did not."[84] Also, the Mesoamerican subspecies of the white-tailed deer, which rarely weighs more than 110 pounds, is much smaller than those found further north in North America.[85]

As further support for understanding the Book of Mormon horse as a deer, Sorenson stated that in the Quiché Maya language the word *keh* means "deer or horse" and the related word *kieh* means "horse."[86] However, Sorenson misused his source, the *Quiché-English Dictionary*, for it specifies that the term *kieh* is the twentieth-century word for the modern horse in the central and western area of native Quiché speakers, while the term *keh* indicates the native white-tailed deer during all time periods and also refers to the European horse introduced by the Spaniards in the sixteenth century.[87] The pre-Columbian Quiché term *keh* did not mean horse because there were no horses to provide names for. Raymond Matheny suggested that proposing various substitute terms is "a weak way to try to explain the presence of these names in the Book of Mormon."[88]

It was an assumption by common people in early nineteenth century America that horses--as well as asses, oxen, cows, sheep, goats, and swine--were native to America, though serious scholars were aware that these animals had been imported by the Europeans.[89] After surveying the most up-to-date evidence, Deanne Matheny concluded that "at this point then there is no convincing evidence that the horse survived until the period of the Mesoamerican civilizations."[90] B. H. Roberts referred to the difficulties of establishing the existence of the horse in America during historic times as "our embarrassing problems."[91] The absence of support for the animals mentioned in the Book of Mormon--at the same time as there exists clear evidence of what the Mesoamerican animals actually were--constitutes a serious obstacle to verifying the historicity of the Book of Mormon.

No. 3--The Metallurgy Test
of the Book of Mormon

In the "Metallurgy Test" Ferguson quoted numerous passages from the Book of Mormon that refer to bellows, brass, breastplates, chains, copper, engravings, gold, hilts, iron, ore, plowshares, silver, steel, and swords, and then repeated each metal, object used in the metallurgical process, or metallic product, with the added comment that there is no evidence for that item. He then remarked:

> Metallurgy does not appear in the region under discussion until about the ninth century A.D. None of the foregoing technical demands are met by the archaeology of the region proposed as Book of Mormon lands and places. I regard this as a major weakness in the armor of our proponents and friends. (It is just as troublesome to the authors of the other correlations--those [who] have gone before--including Tom Ferguson.)
> I doubt that the proponents will be very convincing, if they contend that evidence of metallurgy is difficult to find and a rarity in archaeology. Where mining was practiced--as in the Old Testament world--mountains of ore and tailings have been found. Artifacts of metal have been found. Art portrays the existence of metallurgical products. Again, the score is zero. In view of the magnitude of metallurgical skills and usage in the Book of Mormon, . . . plenty of evidence should have turned up by now in the regions pointed to in the primary papers of this symposium, if our friends have things pinpointed.[92]

William J. Hamblin, professor of history at BYU, criticized those who see "large-scale metal 'industries'" among Book of Mormon peoples, affirming that the text "claims only that certain metals were known to the Nephites."[93] However, the Book of Mormon attributes advanced metallurgical skills to both Jaredites and Nephites. Glenna Nielsen Grimm said that "sophisticated metallurgical processes were engaged in that involved the mining and refining of both ferrous [i.e., iron] and non-ferrous ores."[94] Consider the impressive description of metallurgical technology during the time of Kish, a Jaredite king about 1500 B.C.:[95]

> And they did work in all manner of ore, and they did make gold, and silver, and iron, and brass, and all manner of metals; and they did dig it out of the earth; wherefore, they did cast up mighty heaps of earth to get ore, of gold, and of silver, and of iron, and of copper. And they did work all manner of fine work (Ether 10:23).

One must keep in mind the important distinction between mere metalworking and true metallurgy. Metalworking means the cold hammering and shaping of metal,[96] while metallurgy requires temperatures of 700° to 800° C and involves some or all of the following technological processes: smelting, casting, gilding, annealing, soldering, and alloying.[97] The Book of Mormon does specify the practice of smelting among the Jaredites, for Ether explained that Shule "did molten out of the hill, and made swords out of steel" (Ether 7:9).

Raymond Matheny described the metallurgical technology needed to produce iron objects:

> A ferrous industry is a whole system of doing something. It's just not an esoteric process that a few people are involved in, but ferrous industry--that means mining iron ores and then processing these ores and casting these ores into irons and then making steels and so forth--this is a process that's very complicated. . . . In other words, society would have to be organized at a certain level before ferrous industry would be feasible.
>
> The technology of mining is problematical for the Book of Mormon. Where do you find iron ores in sufficient quantity to create an industry? . . . No evidence has been found in the New World for a ferrous metallurgical industry dating to pre-Columbian times. And so this is a king-size kind of problem, it seems to me, for so-called Book of Mormon archaeology. This evidence is absent.[98]

Matheny also pointed out that the extraction of iron from ore needs high temperatures and various fluxing substances which produce slag, which in turn become indestructible rock forms. In the 1920s B. H. Roberts summarized the situation, saying that "there is nothing on which the later investigators of our American antiquities are more unanimously agreed upon than the matter of the absence of the knowledge of, and hence the non-use of, iron or steel among the natives of America."[99] This condition concerning the complete absence of iron still exists today. The metalsmiths in Peru--not Mesoamerica--developed skills in gold and silver by 1000 B.C., with copper working appearing about A.D. 500, but no pre-Columbian iron metallurgy developed anywhere in the New World.[100]

Historical and comparative linguistics of various Meso-american languages sometimes suggests the existence of a word for metal during the period from ca. 2500 B.C. to A.D. 400.[101] Citing a study which proposed a word for metal in the reconstructed Proto-Mixtecan language, Sorenson said that "the researchers were puzzled by the fact that a word for 'metal' seemed to have existed in the protolanguage at about 1000 B.C."[102] Sorenson misrepresented his source, since the linguists, Robert E. Longacre and René Millon, actually said:

> The linguistic evaluation of a set provides the framework for its cultural evaluation, but however strong it may be linguistically this does not provide proof that the specific aspect of Proto-Mixtecan or Proto-Amuzgo-Mixtecan life it represents actually existed on that horizon. . . . For example, one set, linguistically evaluated as solid, reconstructs in Proto-Mixtecan with the meaning *bell* or perhaps *metal*. . . . The existence of metal or metal bells at this early date is highly improbable on the basis of existing archaeological evidence. Examination of the set suggests that the original meaning may have been *rattle* but it is impossible to be certain of this.[103]

Longacre and Millon explained that greater certainty is obtained when a group of related vocabulary terms describing a specific cultural practice is reconstructed for the protolanguage. The likelihood of the same "semantic shifts" having occurred in all of the words associated with such a practice is highly improbable. Longacre and Millon discussed six strong complexes of related terms: the Maize Complex, the Maguey Complex, the Agricultural Complex, the Masa Preparation Complex, the Weaving Complex, and the Palm Complex, but they referred again to the conjectured word for "metal" in a list of six terms excluded for various reasons.[104] This effort to determine vocabulary items in the Proto-Mixtecan language brought forth merely a conjectured word for either metal, or a bell, or a rattle, and not a group of related metallurgical terms. This certainly does not reveal names for many different kinds of metal, such as the numerous metals required by the Book of Mormon--(1) gold, (2) silver, (3) iron, (4) steel, (5) copper, (6) brass, and (7) an unknown substance named "ziff."

Sorenson suggested possible instances of early metal in Mesoamerica. The earliest copper known consists of a piece of sheeting from Cuicuilco in the Valley of Mexico, which according to Sorenson probably dates to about the first century B.C.[105] However, Emil W. Haury, one of the archaeologists on the original project but not the one who actually removed the copper artifact from the ground, believed that "the Cuicuilco copper is assignable to the late period of Aztec dominance of the Valley of Mexico," as hinted by a mingling of Aztec pottery with Preclassic pottery on the mound, as well as the fact that copper sheeting and copper nails indicate later developments in metallurgy.[106]

In his annotated bibliography on Book of Mormon metals Sorenson classified each instance of metal in one of five groups as to the certainty of the identification, analysis, and dating.[107] These range from an "A" category, in which the item was uncovered by a professional archaeologist in a datable context, successively down to the fifth category, in which incomplete information made a reliable assessment difficult. Only two examples in Sorenson's "A" category fall within Book of Mormon times. The first find, which contains iron and copper, is described as "a metal-resembling substance, small, irregular shaped pieces."[108] It was found at Teotihuacán and is dated from A.D. 300 to 400. The second instance is a claw-shaped bead of the gold-copper alloy known as tumbaga, which was excavated at Altun Ha in northern Belize.[109] David M. Pendergast, archaeologist at the Royal Ontario Museum at Toronto, dated this metallic animal claw to "somewhat before A.D. 500," which would place it after the Book of Mormon, but Sorenson initially stretched this to include the hundred year period from A.D. 400 to 500, and then lowered it further to A.D. 350 to 450.[110] Both of these examples were found outside the area which Sorenson has proposed as Book of Mormon lands.

Deanne Matheny remarked concerning Sorenson's bibliographic study on metals:

> The question that has again not been considered [by Sorenson] is whether the specimens were of local manufacture or represent trade pieces from lower Central America. The majority of the specimens date to Late Classic times falling outside of the Book of Mormon period. The few that are genuinely Early Classic or slightly earlier seem to be trade pieces not produced in the area. We are still left with virtually the entire span of time covered by Book of Mormon events with no metallurgy in the area chosen by Sorenson.[111]

When metallurgy began in Mesoamerica during the Terminal Classic Period about the ninth century A.D., the tools and techniques were borrowed from Costa Rica and the Isthmus of Panama and ultimately from Andean South America.[112] From the third century A.D. onwards various metal objects were imported as trade goods into Mesoamerica from this southeastern place of manufacture. There is no evidence of pre-Columbian metallurgical production in Mesoamerica before the ninth century A.D.[113] Even though the use of metal is usually considered to be an important aspect in the growth of culture, all the civilizations in Mesoamerica developed without the use of metal.[114] By the time metal appeared the culture was beginning to decline.[115]

Metal Swords in the Book of Mormon

Because of the absence of metal swords in Mesoamerica, William J. Hamblin and the late A. Brent Merrill, who served as a major in the U. S. Air Force, proposed that "the most likely candidate for the Book of Mormon sword is the weapon known in Nahuatl as the *macuahuitl* or *macana*."[116] Hamblin and Merrill presented a number of parallels between the wooden *macuahuitl* (fig. 36) and Book of Mormon swords, but they attempted to explain away specific statements that the latter swords were made of steel.[117] The Book of Mormon makes numerous references to swords, but most of these are ambiguous in the sense that they do not indicate the material from which the swords were made. The critical question is the type of material used for the sword--not whether the Aztec *macuahuitl* is defined as a sword, a broad-sword, or a club.[118] Early in Nephite history one of the original colonizers, Nephi, described his own sword-making activities and instructed his relatives and descendants how to work in various metals, including steel:

> And I, Nephi, did take the sword of Laban, and after the manner of it did make many swords, lest by any means the people who were now called Lamanites should come upon us and destroy us. . . . And I did teach my people to build buildings, and to work in all manner of wood, and of iron, and of copper, and of brass, and of steel, and of gold, and of silver, and of precious ores, which were in great abundance (2 Ne. 5:14-15).

Thus, Nephite weapons included metal swords fashioned after Laban's sword. It is fortunate that there exists a detailed description of that sword:

> And I [Nephi] beheld his [Laban's] sword, and I drew it forth from the sheath thereof; and the hilt thereof was of pure gold, and the workmanship thereof was exceeding fine, and I saw that the blade thereof was of the most precious steel (1 Ne. 4:9).[119]

Both the sharpness and the relative shortness of this steel-bladed sword is demonstrated by Nephi's grabbing the hair of Laban's head with one hand and decapitating him with his other hand wielding the sword (1 Ne. 4:18). Laban's early sixth century steel sword is consistent with what is known about the technology in the Near East, where carburizing and quenching iron was practiced to produce steel since about 800 B.C.[120] Jarom, though only a great-grandson of Lehi, lived at least until 238 years after Lehi had departed from Jerusalem. Jarom provided a description of the cultural achievements of his people in the fourth century B.C.:

Fig. 36--A Maya warrior, brandishing a wooden macuahuitl sword with obsidian blades. Reproduced from Ferdinand Anders, *Codex Ixtlilxochitl* (1976), courtesy of Bibliothèque Nationale de France.

> And we [the Nephites] multiplied exceedingly, and spread
> upon the face of the land, and became exceeding rich in
> gold, and in silver, and in precious things, and in fine
> workmanship of wood, in buildings, and in machinery,
> and also in iron and copper, and brass and steel, making all
> manner of tools of every kind to till the ground, and
> weapons of war--yea, the sharp pointed arrow, and the
> quiver, and the dart, and the javelin, and all preparations
> for war (Jarom 1:8).

The much earlier account of the Jaredites is recorded in the
Book of Ether. Jared, one of the original colonists, had a great-
grandson named Shule, whose time period has been estimated at
ca. 2800 B.C., which is much earlier than the Iron Age in the Old
World. Ether indicated the metallurgical skills during this era:

> Wherefore, he [Shule] came to the hill Ephraim, and he did
> molten out of the hill, and made swords out of steel for
> those whom he had drawn away with him; and after he
> had armed them with swords he returned to the city
> Nehor, and gave battle unto his brother Corihor, by which
> means he obtained the kingdom and restored it unto his
> father Kib (Ether 7:9).

Shule smelted suitable ore to make steel swords, so there is no
rational way to interpret this passage as referring to wooden
swords.[121] That Jaredite swords over two thousand years later at
the end of their history were still made of metal blades is confirmed by an account elsewhere in the Book of Mormon. An
exploratory party of forty-three Nephites discovered the remains
of the Jaredites in the early second century B.C. King Limhi
described what they found:

> And for testimony that the things that they had said are
> true they have brought twenty-four plates which are filled
> with engravings, and they are of pure gold. And behold,
> also, they have brought breastplates, which are large, and
> they are of brass and of copper, and are perfectly sound.
> And again, they have brought swords, the hilts thereof
> have perished, and the blades thereof were cankered with
> rust (Mosiah 8:9-11).

These Nephites discovered the land where more than two million
Jaredites over a period of years lost their lives (Ether 15:1). In the

Fig. 37--Sacrificial knife with chipped flint blade and wooden handle, depicting intertwined serpents, Sacred Cenote, Chichén Itzá, Mexico.
Reproduced from Clemency C. Coggins and Orrin C. Shane, *Cenote of Sacrifice* (1984), courtesy of Peabody Museum of Archaeology.

end, only the historian Ether survived to write the story. Consequently, this description of the discovered remains of their armor and weapons provides a glimpse into the level of their technology near the end of their civilization. The handles of their swords, presumably made of wood, had disintegrated, but the metal blades had merely rusted. Thus, whether these Jaredite blades were made of iron, steel, or copper, metal swords were used among the Jaredites from about 2800 B.C. to the end of their civilization.[122] B. H. Roberts observed that "the Book of Mormon thoroughly commits us to the fact of the use of iron and steel among Book of Mormon peoples."[123]

The Maya in Mesoamerica were Stone Age people with offensive weapons such as knives (fig. 37), spears, lances, javelins, broadswords, battle-axes, war-clubs, and even a combination mace-dagger. The points or blades for these weapons were manufactured either from flint found in limestone beds or from obsidian located in volcanic lava flows. The weapons used by Mayan warriors can be documented from stone monuments, artwork on vases, ceramic statuettes, and surviving artifacts. The Mayan broadswords, which by the later Aztecs were called *macuahuitls*, were a "long and heavy double-edged flint-swords apparently designed to be held with two hands to be applied in close combat."[124] The small flint or obsidian blades were inserted into grooves on opposite sides of the wooden club, which in battle could be as deadly as a metal sword. The Aztec oak broad-sword (*macuahuitl*), which was two feet eight inches long, most likely was developed in the mid-fourteenth century.[125] When a Spanish conquistador armed with his steel sword fought an Aztec warrior with his wooden *macuahuitl* the similarity was immediately noticed and "the Aztec term *tepuzmacuahuitl* ('metal macuahuitl') was soon applied to the import."[126]

After examination of both the physical evidence in Mesoamerican archaeology and the textual evidence in the Book of Mormon, Deanne Matheny commented:

> [Prescott] Follett notes in his study of Maya weapons that what he classifies as the standard type of Maya *macuahuitl* is "more in the nature of a war-club or mace than the true broad-sword type of *macuahuitl*." . . . I am aware of no evidence presently available suggesting the existence of the sword type of *macuahuitl* during the period covered by the Book of Mormon.
> . . . There is never any indication in the Book of Mormon that metal swords are not being referred to, and metal swords are the only type ever specifically mentioned.[127]

Accordingly, Ferguson's statement in his "Metallurgy Test" that the archaeology of Mesoamerica does not support the presence of metal implements during the Book of Mormon era still stands. The absence of Mesoamerican copper/bronze/brass metallurgy during Book of Mormon times and the complete absence of Mesoamerican iron metallurgy during any pre-Columbian time period constitute a major problem for the historicity of the Book of Mormon. This is especially the case since it is known what kinds of stone weapons were used in Preclassic Mesoamerica.

No. 4--The Script Test
of the Book of Mormon

The last major test--the "Script Test"--involves the identification of translatable inscriptions of a people. This is a crucial test, since a developed writing system is a hallmark of civilization. Ferguson felt that the "Script Test" was "the most exacting and definitive and precise of all,"[128] and suggested that New

World inscriptions ought to be found in cuneiform (for the Jaredites) and Hebrew and Egyptian (for the Nephites). Nephi made the following statement at the beginning of the Book of Mormon:

> Yea, I make a record in the language of my father, which consists of the learning of the Jews and the language of the Egyptians. And I know that the record which I make is true; and I make it with mine own hand; and I make it according to my knowledge (1 Ne. 1:2-3).

Two divergent interpretations of this statement have been made by LDS scholars. Hugh Nibley, professor of history and religion at BYU, understood it to mean that the Nephite record was kept in the Egyptian language,[129] while John L. Sorenson interpreted it to indicate that the records were kept in the Hebrew language using Egyptian characters.[130] In the early fifth century A.D. Moroni explained about the records kept:

> And now, behold, we have written this record according to our knowledge, in the characters which are called among us the reformed Egyptian, being handed down and altered by us, according to our manner of speech. And if our plates had been sufficiently large we should have written in Hebrew; but the Hebrew hath been altered by us also; and if we could have written in Hebrew, behold, ye would have had no imperfection in our record (Morm. 9:32-33).

In 1971 Ferguson felt that a friend of his had succeeded in deciphering the Mayan hieroglyphs as a result of comparisons with the cuneiform texts of the ancient Assyrian language, but this premature finding was not confirmed by further research.[131] No cuneiform inscriptions have ever been discovered anywhere in the Americas.[132]

Ferguson discussed the evidence for Hebrew mentioned in a letter from George F. Carter, professor of geography at Texas A&M University: "A seal found at Tlatilco, a suburb of Mexico City, bears the Hebrew name, *Hiram,* apparently in Egyptian script! . . . A cylinder seal found at Tlatilco, Mexico, bearing a Hebrew name, *Hiram!* Wow!"[133] Ferguson accepted the Tlatilco seal as having Hebrew inscriptions, but there are serious problems in reading it as a Hebrew text. Carter quoted in his letter to Ferguson the entire proposed translation of the Tlatilco roller stamp as made by the maverick scholar Barry Fell: "Seal of King Shishak Hiram. Forgers will be decapitated."[134] Fell's identification and supposed translation have not passed the scrutiny of other scholars.[135] Though Carter originally accepted Fell's translation, he changed his mind and in 1989 affirmed that the Tlatilco seal did not contain the Hebrew word "Hiram."[136] Consequently, the purported evidence from Tlatilco must be ignored. By 1982 even Ferguson had concluded that there is no evidence of Hebrew in pre-Columbian America.[137]

Ferguson next discussed Egyptian inscriptions:

> Three glyphs on a three-inch cylinder seal, found at Chiapa de Corzo, state of Chiapas, Mexico, by the New World Archaeological Foundation. Identified as Egyptian by only one great scholar, William Foxwell Albright (now deceased). Identification seriously questioned by other great scholars--because of the limited number of glyphs in the find. (Probably the biggest strike so far in support of our proponents--and the *only one* in this technical and demanding testing of their hypotheses).[138]

Ferguson admitted that this identification of Egyptian hieroglyphs in Mesoamerica is strongly questioned by other scholars.

Calendar Dates and Hieroglyphics Deciphered

In 1841 the American explorer John Lloyd Stephens said concerning the ruins of one of the Mayan cities:

> One thing I believe, that its history is graven on its monuments. No Champollion has yet brought to them the energies of his inquiring mind. Who shall read them?[139]

After years of intense study of the fourteenth-century Codex Dresden, the clue written by a native Mayan scribe in the margin of the *Book of Chilam Balam of Mani* that a bar was the number five and a dot was the number one, and Alfred P. Maudslay's accurate drawings of the Copán stelae, the German scholar,

Ernst W. Förstemann, first decoded complex Mayan calendrical texts in the 1880s. In 1905 J. Thomas Goodman proposed a correlation of Mayan dates to the European calendar.[140] For decades there were several competing theories concerning how the two dating systems should be aligned to each other.[141] However, the Goodman-Martínez-Thompson correlation, which was slightly revised from Goodman's original correlation, has won general acceptance since it has been independently confirmed by the latest refinement in radiocarbon dating.[142] In the Mayan system of bar-and-dot arithmetic the numbers were indicated using three symbols: the dot for one, the bar for five, and a stylized shell for zero. The Mayan had two systems of counting days. The *haab* or

Fig. 38--The eighteen twenty-day months of Haab, and the five unlucky days of Uayeb. Reproduced from British Museum's *Guide to the Maudslay Collection* (1938), courtesy of Trustees of the British Museum.

vague year consists of eighteen named months (fig. 38) of twenty days each, with five extra days added at the end to make a 365-day year. The *tzolkin* or Sacred Round consists of twenty named days associated with thirteen consecutive numbers or a 260-day cycle. Meshing the vague year with the Sacred Round produced the Calendar Round. Since there are 18,980 possible combinations between the two systems, the same sequence did not return until every fifty-two years. The basic unit in the Mayan Long

Count (also called the Initial Series) was the day or *kin*. The multiples of days is as follows:

20 *kins*	=	1 *uinal* (20 days)
18 *uinals*	=	1 *tun* (360 days)
20 *tuns*	=	1 *katun* (7200 days)
20 *katuns*	=	1 *baktun* (144,000 days)

A Long Count date included these five divisions, along with the position in the Calendar Round when the date ended. The calendrical dates on Mayan monuments can be confidently read and correlated to our calendar.[143] The Mayan calendar can indicate extremely large numbers. For example, on Stela 1 at the ruins of Cobá in Quintana Roo appears the rare expanded date for the Mayan creation, which is so phenomenally large that 40,000,000,000,000,000,000,000,000,000,000 years--that's 40 octillion years--would have to pass away before the cycle would come around again![144]

Förstemann's solving of the Mayan calendar system was only the first stage in breaking the code of the Mayan hieroglyphics. By the mid-twentieth century several discoveries moved studies dramatically forward. In the early 1950s Yuri V. Knorosov, a Russian epigrapher, began to decipher Mayan hieroglyphs when he discovered that the hieroglyphs were mixed with both words and syllables.[145] In 1958 Heinrich Berlin, a German epigrapher, discovered what he called "emblem glyphs" or hieroglyphic symbols indicating the names of particular cities or possibly the dynastic family ruling them for several generations.[146] Each emblem glyph

Fig. 39--Quiriguá emblem glyph, prefix T36 with kan cross k'ul, superfix T168 ahpo, subfix T130 wa, and main sign T559, a tree with pod. Reproduced from drawing by Annie Hunter, in Alfred P. Maudslay, *Archaeology* (1889-1902).

functions similar to the way an image of the space needle identifies the city of Seattle in American culture since the 1960s. Emblem glyphs have been identified for a number of Meso-american sites (fig. 39).[147]   In 1960 Tatiana Proskouriakoff, another Russian scholar, revealed the historical content of the Mayan inscriptions at Piedras Negras to such an extent that it can now be stated that "the figures which appear in Classic reliefs are not gods and priests but dynastic autocrats and their spouses, children, and subordinates."[148] In a very real sense carved representations which formerly were considered to be gods and under-world lords were transformed into actual people who had a place in Mayan history. In December 1973 the First Palenque Round Table became a landmark Mayan conference, due to the unique chemistry resulting from bringing the traditional dirt archae-ologists together with epigraphers, art historians, and astron-omers at the very site of the Mayan ruins.[149] At this conference Linda Schele and Peter Mathews announced that they had identi-fied the dynastic successions of all Palenque rulers extending back to A.D. 465. With these important developments in deciphering Mayan hieroglyphics--not just calendar dates--year by year more glyphs are being translated.[150]

In his "Book of Mormon Difficulties" B. H. Roberts quoted Frederick S. Dellenbaugh to the effect that "no authentic trace of any Old World language thus far has been found on this [the American] continent."[151] In comparing Mesoamerican hiero-glyphic writing with Egyptian hieroglyphs Linda Miller Van Blerkom of the anthropology department at the University of Colorado stated that "all six classes of signs which are found in word-syllabic writing systems [such as Egyptian] can be demon-strated for the Maya."[152] Such a comparison did not imply that the two languages are in any way related. Likewise, Joyce Mar-cus compared Egyptian writing and Mesoamerican writing merely "in its format and in its function"--but not as related writing systems.[153] Scholars today see no linguistic relationship between any native American language or script and "ancient

Fig. 40--Maya hieroglyphs on stairs of east court, House C, Palenque, Mexico. Reproduced from Eduard Seler, "Studien in den Ruinen von Palenque," *Abhandlungen der königlich preussischen Akademie der Wissenschaften* (1915).

Egyptian, Sumerian/Akkadian, or Hebrew languages or writing systems."[154] Gordon R. Willey, formerly on the board of directors of NWAF, stated that no relationships have been established between a native American Indian language and any Old World language.[155]

The four main Mesoamerican writing systems are the Aztec, Mixtec, Zapotec, and Maya. However, both the Mixtec and Aztec developed in the Post-Classic Period, which dates from the tenth century A.D.[156] The origins of the Mayan hieroglyphic system are unclear but it is often considered the most significant cultural achievement in the New World. The hieroglyphs inscribed on stone monuments (fig. 40) are a later development of inscriptions on other media. There are indications that an ancient place name has survived up to the modern times.[157] However, no personal or place names found in the Book of Mormon have been discovered or deciphered--except biblical names discovered in Old World archaeological sites. Especially now that the Mayan writing system can be understood to a great degree, this lack of confirmation has become a serious problem for the Book of Mormon.

Ferguson's Dilemma
about the Book of Mormon

Ferguson's 1975 listing of problems remains unanswered twenty-one years later. Thus, these points still stand as serious obstacles to authenticating the Book of Mormon. In his study Ferguson remarked that no one "from Joseph Smith to the present day, has put his finger on a single point of terrain that was a Book of Mormon geographical place."[158]

Hugh Nibley explained concerning the Book of Mormon:

> We can never prove absolutely that the Book of Mormon is what it claims to be; but any serious proven fault in the work would at once condemn it. If I assume the Book of Mormon to be fraudulent, then whatever is correct in it is merely a lucky coincidence, devoid of any real significance. But if I assume that it is true, then any suspicious passage is highly significant and casts suspicion on the whole thing, no matter how much of it is right.[159]

In establishing the ambitious NWAF program Ferguson essentially followed the procedure outlined by Nibley, in which one began with the assumption that the Book of Mormon was true.[160]

Ferguson concluded his study for this written symposium with the remark that the meager amount of specific support for the Book of Mormon left him in a real dilemma. Ferguson then referred to Dee F. Green, assistant professor of anthropology at Weber State College, who made the following declaration:

> The first myth we need to eliminate is that Book of Mormon archaeology exists. Titles on books full of archaeological half-truths, dilettanti on the peripheries of American archaeology calling themselves Book of Mormon archaeologists regardless of their education, and a Department of Archaeology at BYU devoted to the production of Book of Mormon archaeologists do not insure that Book of Mormon archaeology really exists. The Book of Mormon is really there so we *can* have Book of Mormon studies, and archaeology is really there so we can study archaeology, but the two are not wed. *At least they are not wed in reality since no Book of Mormon location is known with reference to modern topography.*[161]

Concerning this statement about there being no real archaeology of the Book of Mormon, Ferguson wishfully remarked: "I, for one, would be happy if Dee were wrong."[162]

Ferguson told Ronald O. Barney, an employee of the LDS Church's Historical Department, about the following episode which occurred during a board meeting of NWAF sometime after 1967, and probably after Ferguson had prepared his 1975 archaeological study. In Barney's words:

> Ferguson felt that he really made a point in telling me about his experience with the New World Archaeological Foundation after rejecting the Book of Mormon. He said that at one of their professional meetings he presented a list of some claims that the Book of Mormon made concerning the material culture that ought to have remained if there really was a Book of Mormon people in Central or South America. . . . He said that the leading men there could offer no explanation as to why these things did not exist in archaeological digs. The lack of these artifacts was a very important evidence to him that the Book of Mormon was a fanciful attempt at creating the divine here on the earth.[163]

Along with his 1976 letter to Harold W. Lawrence Ferguson sent a copy of his 1975 "Written Symposium on Book of Mormon Geography," and explained concerning the Book of Mormon that "what is in the ground [archaeologically] will never conform to what is in the book" because it is fiction produced by Joseph Smith.[164]

John L. Sorenson, who did not indicate whether or not he was referring specifically to Ferguson's 1975 analysis, expressed his opinion concerning Ferguson:

> He was not one whose careful "study" led him to see greater light, light that would free him from Latter-day Saint dogma, as [Charles M.] Larson represents. Instead he was just a layman, initially enthusiastic and hopeful but eventually trapped by his unjustified expectations, flawed logic, limited information, perhaps offended pride, and lack of faith in the tedious research that real scholarship requires. The negative arguments he used against the Latter-day Saint scriptures in his last years display all these weaknesses.[165]

Sorenson's rather harsh indictment of Ferguson's efforts requires some comment. True, Ferguson was not a professional archaeologist, but he was convinced that his expectations were justified. Also, Ferguson would disagree vehemently with Sorenson's criticism about his lacking "faith in the tedious research that real scholarship requires," since it was Ferguson's strong belief in the value of the careful research carried out by competent scholars that helped him form his arguments concerning the archaeological problems of the Book of Mormon.

Sorenson's characterization ignored Ferguson's deep-seated desire to follow the truth wherever it led him--even if it took him far from the fervent convictions of his youth. On the other hand, Jerald and Sandra Tanner overstated the case when they asserted that "Ferguson believed that archaeology *disproved* the Book of Mormon."[166] For Ferguson, when asked if it was really true that he had found no evidence for the Book of Mormon, responded by saying that the question was too general, since "some [archaeological] findings tend to support--some tend to contradict" the Book of Mormon and "archaeology casts grave doubt on Bk. of Abraham and some doubt on Bk. of Mormon."[167] So, while the absence of archaeological evidence can never disprove the Book of Mormon, it does cast some suspicion on it, especially since the plant, animal, technological, and literary evidence during the Preclassic time period in Mesoamerica paints a clearer picture year by year.

Sorenson classified his own Book of Mormon geography as sometimes being "probable," and then added "if the shoe fits, wear it."[168] Deanne Matheny concluded her critique of Sorenson:

> For me these models [by Hauck and Sorenson] require too many changes and arbitrary interpretations, too many deviations from the plain meaning of the words in the text of the Book of Mormon, for either of them to achieve even a partial fit with the geographical and archaeological evidence. . . .
>
> Does the shoe fit for the current Limited Tehuántepec theory models? Rather than a comfortable "Cinderella" fit, it is more like a "step-sister" mismatch, requiring considerable remodeling of shoe and foot.[169]

Likewise, Ferguson responded to Sorenson's earlier geographical study--which was titled with the question "Where in the World?"--by answering that Book of Mormon geography exists nowhere in the real world. Describing his own 1975 study, Ferguson divulged that "the real implication of the paper is that you can't set Book of Mormon geography down anywhere--because it is fictional and will never meet the requirements of the dirt-archaeology."[170] In his view the Book of Mormon is not a translated account of historical peoples, but a fictional story concocted by Joseph Smith, perhaps with the assistance of one or two others. In what is essentially a response to Ferguson's skepticism, David A. Palmer said: "To say that there is no Book of Mormon geography is to me absurd. There is a geography. I believe that the Book of Mormon history occurred in real time and space."[171] Sorenson was also aware of Ferguson's liberal position and expressed the options as follows: "Either the Book of Mormon promised land was in some portion of Mesoamerica or it was nowhere."[172]

At the Sunstone Symposium in 1984 Raymond Matheny summarized the Book of Mormon problem in a way very much like Ferguson's assessment:

> All these [Book of Mormon cultural traits] paint a scene that seem[s] to be quite foreign to what I am familiar with in the archaeological record of the New World. . . . And the terminologies and the language used and the methods of explaining and putting things down are nineteenth century literary concepts and cultural experiences one would expect Joseph Smith and his colleagues would experience. . . . If I were doing this cold like John Carlson is here, I would say in evaluating the Book of Mormon that it had no place in the New World whatsoever. . . . It seems like these are anachronisms. It seems like the items are out of time and place, in trying to put them into the New World. And I think there's a great difficulty here for we Mormons in understanding what this book [of Mormon] is all about.[173]

B. H. Roberts, after demonstrating in the Book of Mormon the similarity of the character traits of the three anti-Christs named Sherem, Nehor, and Korihor, reluctantly stated:

They are all of one breed and brand; so nearly alike that one mind is the author of them, and that a young and undeveloped, but piously inclined mind. The evidence I sorrowfully submit, points to Joseph Smith as their creator. It is difficult to believe that they are the product of history, that they come upon the scene separated by long periods of time, and among a race which was the ancestral race of the red man of America.[174]

Michael D. Coe, professor of anthropology at Yale University, offered some suggestions to Mormons:

Forget the so-far fruitless quest for the Jaredites, Nephites, Mulekites, and the lands of Zarahemla and Bountiful: there is no more chance of finding them than of discovering the ruins of the bottomless pit described in the book of Revelation. . . . Continue the praiseworthy excavations in Mexico, remembering that little or nothing pertaining to the Book of Mormon will ever result from them.[175]

Likewise, Ferguson found that the known archaeology of Mesoamerica does not fit the requirements of the Book of Mormon. This raised for him serious questions about the antiquity of the volume. From his youth he had assumed that the Book of Mormon was historical--and had believed in it intensely--but during the last thirteen years of his life Ferguson maintained that that assumption was wrong and the best explanation was found in Joseph Smith and his nineteenth century environment.[176]

The Contributions
of Tom Ferguson

Ferguson's odyssey was an attempt at verification of the historical claims of the Book of Mormon. His early faith concerning the Book of Mormon is exemplified in a 1957 assessment addressed to the LDS First Presidency: "To me, the Book of Mormon is like a sleeping volcano, ready to burst forth with knowledge of greatest import for the whole world."[177] This book was the love of his life--second only to his family. Providing archaeological support for the Book of Mormon, Ferguson explained, was his own "magnificent obsession" in life.[178]

Fred W. Nelson, Jr., radiation safety officer at BYU, described Ferguson's effect on how Mormons relate Meso-american cultures with the Book of Mormon:

> It would be fair to say that his books, along with the many lectures he gave throughout his life, have had a great influence on the general membership of the LDS Church with regard to how they relate the Book of Mormon and archaeology.[179]

Ferguson possessed a dynamic personality and an enthusiasm that was contagious among the people with whom he worked. Though he was only an amateur archaeologist, he was an independent thinker who plunged seriously into his cause. Ferguson was the indispensable force behind the founding of NWAF in 1952.[180] In spite of the fact, as one Mormon scholar said, that "there have been no spectacular finds (from the Book of Mormon point of view), no Zarahemlas discovered, no gold plates brought to light, no horses uncovered, and King Benjamin's tomb remains unexcavated,"[181] still Ferguson's key involvement with NWAF will be his lasting accomplishment, for it became a major force in the Preclassic archaeology of Mesoamerica. The non-Mormon archaeologist Michael D. Coe expressed admiration concerning the role that Ferguson played:

> While the guiding light of this [NWAF] endeavor, Ferguson, was also an Iron Rod, from the beginning everything was put on what non-Mormons would consider a scholarly underpinning. . . . There can be no question that the New World Archaeological Foundation's program has been an unqualified success. . . . Credit for this goes to the foresight of Ferguson and the original directors. . . .[182]

The professional archaeological investigations of the now-essentially-defunct NWAF into the origins of Mesoamerican civilization owe much to the work of Ferguson. It is unfortunate that--just because archaeological confirmation of the Book of Mormon has not come forth as anticipated by both Ferguson and the Mormon Church leaders who funded the foundation--the Church has decided to reduce NWAF to a token organization.

Ferguson's Resolution
of the Dilemma

Ferguson's quest did not follow a straight course. He lived his life as a dedicated Latter-day Saint, expecting with the certainty of the true believer that he would find archaeological proof of the historical authenticity of the Book of Mormon. However, the physical evidence he looked so diligently for did not come forth. In the end, Ferguson was theologically shipwrecked less by the failure to find persuasive archaeological support for the Book of Mormon than by his encounter with independent translations of the Joseph Smith Egyptian papyri. Though his ship ran aground, it did not sink, and he managed to salvage what he felt were its essentials. Ferguson himself used nautical imagery, saying that he wanted "to stay aboard the good ship, Mormonism--for various reasons that I think valid."[183]

Ferguson's odyssey traversed the whole gamut of firm faith, exciting exploration, devastating doubt, and calm contentment. Garth N. Jones, speaking at the 1989 Sunstone Symposium held at the University of Utah, summarized Ferguson's point of view near the end of his life:

> Ferguson experienced an odyssey with all of its serendipitous beauties and qualities. He died a wise and tolerant person, understanding the importance of myth in human affairs. . . . Ferguson understood and appreciated the good qualities of the LDS Church and its community of believers.[184]

Throughout the last thirteen years of his life Ferguson was a broad-minded humanist. In the most-recent Ferguson letter to have been discovered, he explained his position:

> Now that my eyes have been opened . . . , I see more clearly into many other conflicts and problems the Prophet [Joseph Smith] had, and have conviction that he was a phony with lots of meritorious ideas. I have decided not to attack him openly--in my opinion, now, all religions are man-made, and most of them do more good than harm--so let them be.[185]

If one were a satisfied, active Mormon, Ferguson would not want that person to change. If one decided that the Book of Mormon was composed by Joseph Smith, he counseled him/her to stay in the LDS Church and keep quiet, in order to enjoy the benefits of being a member. If one could not follow this path but felt the need to leave the LDS Church, he encouraged that person to do so. If one were happy as an orthodox Christian, his advice was, stay that way. The bottom line of Ferguson's position was that whatever works for a person and gives meaning to life was, by definition, good for that person.

One may feel that Ferguson's ideas are completely mistaken, or one may feel that his reconciliation of the conflict between faith and reason is a worthwhile solution. Given Ferguson's own disillusionment, one must give him credit for having resolved the dilemma to his personal satisfaction, for he was at peace with himself and often spoke of the need to consider the Big Picture. However, it would be unfair to Ferguson to say that he completely lost faith in Mormonism. He continued his church activity and he justified his sometimes waffling behavior on various social and cultural grounds. He saw many beneficial things in the religions of mankind, and Mormonism was to him the most useful--but not ultimately true. Though Ferguson doubted that Joseph Smith could translate Egyptian texts, though he repudiated the antiquity of the Book of Abraham, though he rejected the authenticity of the Book of Mormon, though he questioned that Joseph Smith or anyone else was a true prophet of God--still he considered the LDS Church to be a wonderful fraternity, valued church activity and fellowship, sang in his ward choir, appreciated the moral principles of the Book of Mormon, developed a more tolerant attitude about the opinions of others, felt that religion served a genuine need in human life, found relaxation in working in the garden, and enjoyed life immensely. In fact Thomas Stuart Ferguson was playing tennis when a massive heart attack brought immediate death on 16 March 1983 at the age of sixty-seven.[186] His legacy is a commitment to the search for truth.

Notes

1. V. Garth Norman, "Book of Mormon Geography Study on the Narrow Neck of Land Region," Book of Mormon Geography Working Paper, no. 1, typescript, 1966, rev. 1972, and "Reconstruction and Correlation of the Geography of the Land Southward, Border Regions of the Book of Mormon," Book of Mormon Geography Working Paper, no. 2, typescript, 1975; both of which are located in the Calvin D. Tolman Collection, Accession 1445, Manuscripts Division, J. Willard Marriott Library, University of Utah, Salt Lake City; hereafter abbreviated to Tolman Collection.

2. John L. Sorenson, "Where in the World? Views on Book of Mormon Geography," Book of Mormon Working Paper, no. 8, typescript, 1974, in Tolman Collection.

3. David A. Palmer, form letter, 8 September 1974, in Tolman Collection.

4. David A. Palmer, letter to Geography Symposium Participants, 20 December 1974, with emphasis in original, in Tolman Collection.

5. Thomas Stuart Ferguson, "Written Symposium on Book of Mormon Geography: Response of Thomas S. Ferguson to the Norman and Sorenson Papers," typescript, 12 March 1975, 1-2, in the Thomas Stuart Ferguson Collection, Accession 1350, Manuscripts Division, J. Willard Marriott Library, University of Utah, Salt Lake City; hereafter abbreviated to Ferguson Collection, UU. The text of Ferguson's study is reproduced in Appendix A, "Thomas Stuart Ferguson on Book of Mormon Archaeology," below. It was first published in Jerald Tanner and Sandra Tanner, eds., *Ferguson's Manuscript Unveiled* (Salt Lake City: Utah Lighthouse Ministry, 1988).

6. Ferguson, letter to Mr. and Mrs. Harold W. Lawrence, 9 February 1976, in Ferguson Collection, UU.

7. Ferguson, handwritten response on letter of J. Don Cerchione to Ferguson, 21 July 1976, in Ferguson Collection, UU.

8. B. H. Roberts, "Book of Mormon Difficulties: A Study," typescript, 1921, in the B. H. Roberts Collection, Manuscript 106, Box 9, Book 1, Manuscripts Division, J. Willard Marriott Library, University of Utah, Salt Lake City; hereafter abbreviated to Roberts Collection. The incomplete manuscript (missing part II of "Difficulties") was reproduced in Jerald Tanner and Sandra Tanner, eds., *Roberts' Manuscripts Revealed: A Photographic Reproduction of Mormon Historian B. H. Roberts' Secret Studies on the Book of Mormon* (Salt Lake City: Modern Microfilm Co., 1980) and the complete manuscript was published in Brigham D. Madsen, ed., *B. H. Roberts: Studies of the Book of Mormon*, (Urbana and Chicago: University of Illinois Press, 1985; reprint, Salt Lake City: Signature Books, 1992), 61-148.

9. B. H. Roberts, "A Book of Mormon Study," typescript, 1922, in Box 9, Books 2-3, Roberts Collection; Madsen, *Roberts: Studies*, 149-319.

10. B. H. Roberts, "A Parallel," typescript, 1927, in Box 16, Fd 3,

Roberts Collection, UU; Madsen, *Roberts: Studies*, 321-44. John W. Welch, *Finding Answers to B. H. Roberts' Questions and "An Unparallel"* (Provo, UT: Foundation for Ancient Research and Mormon Studies, 1985), responded to the problems proposed in Roberts's studies.

11. John L. Sorenson, *An Ancient American Setting for the Book of Mormon* (Salt Lake City: Deseret Book Co., 1985; Provo, UT: Foundation for Ancient Research and Mormon Studies, 1985). Citing BYU Religious Instruction Administrative Council Minutes for 31 May 1978, Gary James Bergera and Ronald Priddis, *Brigham Young University: A House of Faith* (Salt Lake City: Signature Books, 1985), 86, 408n73, indicated that Sorenson's manuscript "was rejected for publication by BYU's Religious Studies Center because Elder Mark E. Petersen found the topic to be 'too touchy,'" and only after Petersen died did the Deseret Book Company and F.A.R.M.S. jointly publish the book.

12. Deanne G. Matheny, "Does the Shoe Fit? A Critique of the Limited Tehuántepec Geography," in *New Approaches to the Book of Mormon: Explorations in Critical Methodology*, ed. Brent Lee Metcalfe (Salt Lake City: Signature Books, 1993), 269-328.

13. John L. Sorenson, "Viva Zapato! Hurray for the Shoe!" review of "Does the Shoe Fit?" by Deanne G. Matheny, in *Review of Books on the Book of Mormon* 6, no. 1 (1994): 297-361.

14. Ferguson, "Symposium," 4-5.

15. Ferguson's statement that "maize" is a non-Book-of-Mormon plant is incorrect, for the three instances of "corn" at Mosiah 7:22; 9:9, 14, correspond with the known staple food. Jeremy A. Sabloff, *The New Archaeology and the Ancient Maya* (New York: Scientific American Library, 1990), 114, stated that Mesoamerican people of the Preclassic period "grew maize as their principal subsistence crop."

16. Ferguson, "Symposium," 6-7.

17. Weston La Barre, "Native American Beers," *American Anthropologist* 40 (April-June 1938): 232, quoted in Sorenson, "Viva," 336.

18. Diego de Landa, *Landa's Relación de las cosas de Yucatán*, ed. and trans. by Alfred M. Tozzer (Cambridge, MA: Peabody Museum, Harvard University, 1941), 92, 198.

19. Alejandro Claudio Martínez Muriel, "Don Martín, Chiapas: Inferencias Economico-sociales de una Communidad Arqueologica" (M.A. thesis, Escuela Nacional de Antropología e Historia, Mexico, 1978), 104, quoted in D. G. Matheny, "Critique," 302.

20. Sorenson, ibid., 339, pointed out that "when Matheny wrote out the names of some of Martínez's plants, she put down '*vitis*,' apparently unable to bring herself to say 'grape'!"

21. D. G. Matheny, "Critique," 301-302.

22. Richard E. Blanton et alia, *Ancient Mesoamerica: A Comparison of Change in Three Regions*, 2d ed. (Cambridge, England: Cambridge University Press, 1993), 40, explained that the bottle gourd was never eaten, but was used "as a container for carrying water."

23. John A. Price, "The Book of Mormon vs. Anthropological Prehistory," *The Indian Historian* 7 (Summer 1974): 38. Though Price

was LDS, he had been away from Mormon culture for years and his article exhibits several errors characteristic of non-Mormon treatments.

24. Roberts, "Difficulties," chap. ii, 1, in Roberts Collection; Madsen, *Roberts: Studies*, 95.

25. Sorenson, *Setting*, 184.

26. Raymond T. Matheny, "Book of Mormon Archaeology: Sunstone Symposium #6, Salt Lake Sheraton Hotel, August 25, 1984," typescript, 1984, in the David J. Buerger Collection, Manuscript 622, Box 33, Fd 17, Manuscripts Division, J. Willard Marriott Library, University of Utah, Salt Lake City; hereafter abbreviated to Buerger Collection. Matheny's remarks were transcribed without permission.

27. Sorenson, "Viva," 341.

28. Because no pre-Columbian wheat has been found anywhere in the Americas, Sorenson tried to get out of the difficulty by suggesting that perhaps Joseph Smith may have dictated the mistranslation "wheat" for the native plant "amaranth." Then Sorenson, *Setting*, 185-86, quoted with approval the identification of the Book of Mormon plant *sheum* with the Akkadian *s(h)e'um* "barley." However, since both *barley* and *sheum* are mentioned in the same verse (Mosiah 9:9), Sorenson admitted that reference is made to two different grains. Then, curiously, he suggested that amaranth might be the Book of Mormon *sheum*. But amaranth can not be used to identify *sheum* and to solve the problem of the absence of wheat. Clearly, there is a problem here that no amount of linguistic gymnastics in lexicons can solve. William J. Hamblin, "Basic Methodological Problems with the Anti-Mormon Approach to the Geography and Archaeology of the Book of Mormon," *Journal of Book of Mormon Studies* 2 (Spring 1993): 191-93, handled the absence of wheat in another way. After quoting Luke P. Wilson's criticism that the lack of wheat, barley, linen (presumably from flax), grapes, and olives is a problem for the Book of Mormon, Hamblin then examined possibilities concerning each of these items--except wheat. That topic is completely avoided, both in Hamblin's text and footnotes. Cf. Luke P. Wilson, "The Scientific Search for Nephite Remains," *Heart and Mind: The Newsletter of Gospel Truths Ministries* (Fall 1992): 2-3, 5.

29. Ferguson, "Symposium," 12-13.

30. Mary Baker, "Capuchin Monkeys (*Cebus capucinus*) and the Ancient Maya," *Ancient Mesoamerica* 3 (Fall 1992): 219-28, suggested that the hieroglyphic depictions represent capuchin monkeys rather than howler monkeys or spider monkeys.

31. J. Eric S. Thompson, *A Catalog of Maya Hieroglyphs* (Norman, OK: University of Oklahoma Press, 1962), 336, 340-41, 336, 343, 366, 375, 379-81; Robert J. Sharer, *The Ancient Maya*, 5th ed. (Stanford, CA: Stanford University Press, 1994), 623, 628; and Jeanette Favrot Peterson, *Precolumbian Flora and Fauna: Continuity of Plant and Animal Themes in Mesoamerican Art* (San Diego: Mingei International Museum of World Folk Art, 1990), passim.

32. Roberts, "Difficulties," chap. ii, 6, in Roberts Collection; Madsen, *Roberts: Studies*, 98.

33. Roberts, "Difficulties," chap. ii, 8, in Roberts Collection; Madsen, *Roberts: Studies*, 99. B. H. Roberts is here quoting Clark Wissler, *The American Indian: An Introduction to the Anthropology of the New World* (New York: Douglas C. McMurtrie, 1917), 37, with Roberts adding the emphasis to Wissler's wording.

34. Linda Schele and David Freidel, *A Forest of Kings: The Untold Story of the Ancient Maya* (New York: William Morrow, 1990), 60.

35. This enigmatic Book of Mormon phrase occurs only here.

36. D. G. Matheny, "Critique," 303n20, pointed out that the Tinamou is not a duck, but " belongs to the family Tinamidae."

37. Sorenson, *Setting*, 292-93.

38. Richard E. W. Adams, *Prehistoric Mesoamerica*, rev. ed. (Norman, OK: University of Oklahoma Press, 1991), 37, explained that domesticated dogs were eaten, but were "no substitute for cattle, sheep, goats, or pigs, all of which were important in the Old World Neolithic but lacking in the New World."

39. Sorenson, *Setting*, 296-97, asserted that "real sheep's wool was found in a burial site at Cholula," but examining Sorenson's source one finds that Sigvald Linné, *Mexican Highland Cultures: Archaeological Researches at Teotihuacán, Calpulalpan, and Chalchicomula in 1934-35*, (Stockholm: Ethnographical Museum of Sweden, 1942), 156, indicated that "the grave is not with certainty stated to be pre-Spanish."

40. Sidney B. Sperry, *Answers to Book of Mormon Questions (formerly Problems of the Book of Mormon)* (Salt Lake City: Bookcraft, 1967), 164.

41. Ferguson, "Symposium," 13.

42. Sorenson, *Setting*, 119, 298.

43. The editors of Time-Life Books, *The Magnificent Maya*, Lost Civilizations (Alexandria, VA: Time-Life Books, 1993), 21.

44. Claude François Baudez, *Jean-Frédéric Waldeck, peintre: le premier explorateur des ruines mayas* ([Paris]: Fernand Hazan Editions, 1993), 127, fig. 23.

45. Alfred P. Maudslay, *Archaeology*, in *Biologia Centrali-Americana; or, Contributions to the Knowledge of the Fauna and Flora of Mexico and Central America*, ed. F. Ducane Godman and Osbert Salvin (London: R. H. Porter, and Dulau and Co., 1889-1902), vol. 4, pl. 61.

46. John L. Sorenson, *Animals in the Book of Mormon: An Annotated Bibliography* (Provo, UT: Foundation for Ancient Research and Mormon Studies, 1992), 12.

47. Albert S. Gatschet, "Elephants in America," *The American Antiquarian and Oriental Journal* 9 (1887): 202-203.

48. Sorenson, *Animals*, 12.

49. *Palmyra Herald*, 19 February 1823, quoted in Dan Vogel, *Indian Origins and the Book of Mormon: Religious Solutions from Columbus to Joseph Smith* (Salt Lake City: Signature Books, 1986), 47.

50. Björn Kurtén and Elaine Anderson, *Pleistocene Mammals of North America* (New York: Columbia University Press, 1980), 357.

51. T. Douglas Price, "The View from Europe: Concepts and Ques-

tions about Terminal Pleistocene Societies," in *The First Americans: Search and Research*, ed. Tom D. Dillehay and David J. Meltzer (Boca Raton, FL: CRC Press, 1991), 196.

52. Adrian Lister and Paul Bahn, *Mammoths* (New York: Macmillan, 1994), 31, indicated that the range of the woolly mammoth (*Mammuthus primigenius*) was limited to Alaska, Canada, and northern United States. John M. Harris and Shelley M. Cox, "Rancho La Brea Mammoths," *Current Research in the Pleistocene* 10 (1993): 97, pointed out that earlier authorities concluded that both the imperial mammoth (*Mammuthus imperator*) and the Columbian mammoth were found at the La Brea tar pits, while more recently scholars have identified these remains as either the imperial mammoth or the Columbian mammoth, adding that probability favors the single species being the latter.

53. Gary Haynes, *Mammoths, Mastodonts, and Elephants: Biology, Behavior, and the Fossil Record* (Cambridge, England: Cambridge University Press, 1991), 198, 264. Hugh Nibley, *Since Cumorah: The Book of Mormon in the Modern World*, 2d ed., The Collected Works of Hugh Nibley, ed. John W. Welch (Salt Lake City: Deseret Book Co., 1988; Provo, UT: Foundation for Ancient Research and Mormon Studies, 1988), 7:225, overstated the period during which archaeologists date the extinction of the mammoth and mastodon in North America: "The guesses of scientists range all the way from hundreds of thousands to mere hundreds of years ago."

54. Donald K. Grayson, "The Chronology of North American Late Pleistocene Extinctions," *Journal of Archaeological Science* 16 (March 1989): 158-59.

55. S. L. Vartanyan, V. E. Garutt, and A. V. Sher, "Holocene Dwarf Mammoths from Wrangel Island in the Siberian Arctic," *Nature* 362 (25 March 1993): 337-40.

56. In spite of the statement that the Nephites "found" animals in the New World, Hamblin, "Problems," 193, explained the absence of archaeological evidence for such animals by suggesting that "a species may have existed only in small numbers--introduced by, and limited to the civilizations of the Nephites--which subsequently became extinct."

57. Diane E. Wirth, *A Challenge to the Critics: Scholarly Evidences of the Book of Mormon* (Bountiful, UT: Horizon Publishers, 1988), 56. However, D. G. Matheny, "Critique," 303-304, pointed out that if the Nephites were living the Mosaic dietary laws, they would not be allowed to eat horses, since they "divide not the hoof."

58. Chester Stock, *Rancho La Brea: A Record of Pleistocene Life in California*, 7th ed., rev. by John M. Harris, Science Series, no. 37 (Los Angeles: Natural History Museum of Los Angeles County, 1992), 39.

59. John M. Harris and George J. Jefferson, *Rancho La Brea: Treasures of the Tar Pits*, Science Series, no. 31 (Los Angeles: Natural History Museum of Los Angeles County, 1985), 32.

60. Roberts, "Difficulties," chap. ii, 18, in Roberts Collection; Madsen, *Roberts: Studies*, 104.

61. Bruce J. MacFadden, *Fossil Horses: Systematics, Paleobiology, and*

Evolution of the Family Equidae (Cambridge, England: Cambridge University Press, 1992), 3. MacFadden added: "In a minority view, Clutton-Brock . . . believes that they may have persisted into historical times." In fairness one must clarify that Juliet Clutton-Brock, *Domesticated Animals from Early Times* (Austin, TX: University of Texas Press, 1981; London: British Museum, 1981), 81, did not take that position, but simply referred to others who did: "In America the horse may have been extinct 8000 years ago although some people believe it lingered on until the post-Columbian period." In the reprint eight years later Juliet Clutton-Brock, *A Natural History of Domesticated Animals* (Austin, TX: University of Texas Press, 1989), 81, deleted the last eleven words.

62. Grayson, "Chronology," 158. Hamblin, "Problems," 194, stated that the horse is "generally thought to have been extinct by the end of Pre-Classic times (before A.D. 300)." Hamblin confused the generally accepted period for the extinction of the horse on the American continents, missing the date by over 8,000 years.

63. Millard Sheets, *The Horse in Folk Art* (La Jolla, CA: Mingei International Museum of World Folk Art, 1984), 12.

64. Ferguson, letter to Chris B. Hartshorn, 18 April 1962, in Ferguson Collection, BYU.

65. Milton R. Hunter, *Archaeology and the Book of Mormon* (Salt Lake City: Deseret Book Co., 1956), 6.

66. Sorenson, *Animals*, 15.

67. John L. Sorenson, "Once More: The Horse," in *Reexploring the Book of Mormon: The F.A.R.M.S. Updates*, ed. John W. Welch (Salt Lake City: Deseret Book Co., 1992; Provo, UT: Foundation for Ancient Research and Mormon Studies, 1992), 98-99. Daniel C. Peterson, "Book of Mormon Economy and Technology," in *Encyclopedia of Mormonism*, ed. Daniel H. Ludlow (New York: Macmillan Publishing Co., 1992), 1:173, referred to Sorenson's argument about the survival of the horse into the Book of Mormon period. Hugh Nibley, *Teachings of the Book of Mormon* (Provo, UT: Foundation for Ancient Research and Mormon Studies, 1993), 4:1-3, stated that the absence of the horse "is the strongest argument, supposedly, that has been raised against the Book of Mormon," and then answered the problem by simply asserting that the horse never became extinct in North America.

68. Paul S. Martin, "The Discovery of America," *Science* 179 (9 March 1973): 974n3.

69. Robert A. Martin and S. David Webb, "Late Pleistocene Mammals from the Devil's Den Fauna, Levy County," in *Pleistocene Mammals of Florida*, ed. S. David Webb (Gainesville, FL: University Presses of Florida, 1974), 144, quoting Ripley Bullen.

70. James J. Hester, "The Agency of Man in Animal Extinctions," in *Pleistocene Extinctions: The Search for a Cause*, ed. Paul S. Martin and H. E. Wright (New Haven, CT: Yale University Press, 1967), 183.

71. Jim I. Mead and David J. Meltzer, "North American Late Quaternary Extinctions and the Radiocarbon Record," in *Quaternary Extinctions: A Prehistoric Revolution*, ed. Paul S. Martin and Richard G.

Klein (Tucson, AZ: University of Arizona Press, 1984), 446. Mead and Meltzer, ibid., 447, explained: "When one considers only those genera for which we have demonstrably reliable dates . . . that are not derived from bone collagen (*Camelops*, *Equus*, *Mammut*, *Mammuthus*, *Nothrotheriops*, *Panthera*), a familiar pattern appears. These reliable dates . . . indicate that late Pleistocene extinctions lasted no later than 10,000 yr B.P. [before present] and possibly were complete by 10,800 yr B.P."

72. Sorenson, *Setting*, 395n63, asserted that one scholar discovered "horse remains in southwest Yucatán caves in association with artifacts." Examining Sorenson's source reveals that Henry C. Mercer, *The Hill-Caves of Yucatán: A Search for Evidence of Man's Antiquity in the Caverns of Central America* (Philadelphia: J. B. Lippincott Co., 1896), 40, 69, 170, 172, found in the Sayab cave two horse teeth which "had probably worked down from the surface in recent time," in the Chekta-leh cave he found a horse phalanx, which "must have been modern and Spanish," and in the Lara cave he also found bones of the European horse, *Equus caballus*, which had been imported into the Americas since the fifteenth century. Consequently, Sorenson's implication of finding a pre-Columbian horse is not supported.

73. Björn Kurtén, *Before the Indians* (New York: Columbia University Press, 1988), 98.

74. Welch, *Answers*, 8.

75. Harry E. D. Pollock and Clayton E. Ray, "Notes on Vertebrate Animal Remains from Mayapán," *Current Reports* (Carnegie Institution), no. 41 (August 1957): 638.

76. Clayton E. Ray, "Pre-Columbian Horses from Yucatán," *Journal of Mammalogy* 38 (May 1957): 278. The horses lived during the Pleistocene period and by Mayan times their teeth were already fossils.

77. Sorenson, *Setting*, 293-96. Sorenson, ibid., 299, suggested a known native American animal for various Book of Mormon animals, proposing that the brocket is either the Book of Mormon cow or goat, the bison is either the cow or ox, the deer is either the cow, horse, or goat, the tapir is either the horse, ox, or ass, while the llama and alpaca are either the cow, ox, ass, or sheep.

78. D. G. Matheny, "Critique," 306.

79. John F. Eisenberg, Colin P. Groves, and Kathy MacKinnon, "Tapirs," in *Grzimek's Encyclopedia of Mammals*, ed. Sybil P. Parker (New York: McGraw-Hill Publishing Co., 1990), 4:599.

80. Milton R. Hunter and Thomas Stuart Ferguson, *Ancient America and the Book of Mormon* (Oakland, CA: Kolob Book Co., 1950), 309.

81. Glenna Nielsen Grimm, "The Material Culture of the Book of Mormon," audio tape, 13 May 1992, Sunstone Book of Mormon Lecture, in the Sunstone Foundation Records, Accession A0370, Manuscripts Division, J. Willard Marriott Library, University of Utah, Salt Lake City.

82. The transliteration of the unusual animal names "cumoms" and "cureloms" (Ether 9:19) suggests that Joseph Smith normally translated the names of animals (such as the horse, cow, sheep, goat, etc.) as long

as a close equivalent was available.

83. Sorenson, "Viva," 347.

84. Stephen E. Thompson, "'Critical' Book of Mormon Scholarship," review of *New Approaches to the Book of Mormon*, ed. Brent Metcalfe, and *Review of Books on the Book of Mormon*, ed. Daniel Peterson, in *Dialogue: A Journal of Mormon Thought* 27 (Winter 1994): 204.

85. Valerius Geist, "White-tailed or Mule Deer (Genus *Odocoileus*)," in *Grzimek's Encyclopedia*, 5:215.

86. Sorenson, *Setting*, 296, 395n67.

87. Munro S. Edmonson, *Quiche-English Dictionary* (New Orleans, LA: Tulane University of Louisiana, 1965), 57-58. Munro S. Edmonson, letter to author, 18 September 1994, in author's possession, explained: "The word *keh* meant 'deer' until the arrival of Spanish horses in Guatemala in 1524. . . . At a later date some dialects changed the pronunciation of the original word to *kieh*, which means 'deer,' 'horse,' or sometimes merely 'animal.' The form *keh* meaning 'deer' does go back to at least the eighth century A.D., but has nothing to do with horses. The super-Mormons [sic] are again, alas, wrong."

88. R. T. Matheny, "Archaeology," 30.

89. Vogel, *Origins*, 46, 91n67.

90. D. G. Matheny, "Critique," 306.

91. Roberts, "Difficulties," chap. ii, 22, in Roberts Collection; Madsen, *Roberts: Studies*, 107.

92. Ferguson, "Symposium," 20-21.

93. Hamblin, "Problems," 191. Hamblin continued: "Thus it is only [Luke] Wilson's *interpretation* of the Book of Mormon claiming the existence of widespread iron *industries* in Pre-Classic Mesoamerica which cannot be reconciled with the archaeological record," with emphasis in original. Hamblin can only understand the Book of Mormon as not having metallurgy by ignoring--or re-interpreting--the passages that indicate such skills.

94. Grimm, "Culture."

95. Sorenson, *Setting*, 118.

96. David A. Palmer, *In Search of Cumorah: New Evidences for the Book of Mormon from Ancient Mexico* (Bountiful, UT: Horizon Publishers, 1981), 114, incorrectly used the term "metallurgy," since his examples related to metalworking skills; cf. D. G. Matheny, "Critique," 289.

97. Karen O. Bruhns, "The Crucible: Sociological and Technological Factors in the Delayed Diffusion of Metallurgy to Mesoamerica," in *New Frontiers in the Archaeology of the Pacific Coast of Southern Mesoamerica*, ed. Frederick Bove and Lynette Heller (Tempe, AZ: Arizona State University, 1989), 224.

98. R. T. Matheny, "Archaeology," 22-23.

99. Roberts, "Book of Mormon Study," chap. viii, 7, in Box 9, Book 2, Roberts Collection; Madsen, *Roberts: Studies*, 198. Roberts wondered if Smith's error about the existence of iron in the Book of Mormon was perhaps due to Ethan Smith: "Could it be that Ethan Smith, influenced and misled by the reported discovery of the evidence of iron and its uses

among the native Americans in ancient times, was innocently followed into this error by the author of the Book of Mormon?"

100. Robert Raymond, *Out of the Fiery Furnace: The Impact of Metals on the History of Mankind* (University Park, PA: Pennsylvania State University Press, 1986), 22. The hammering of unsmelted meteoric iron is metalworking, not metallurgy.

101. Roberto Escalante, "El vocabulario cultural de las lenguas de Mesoamérica," in *La validez teórica del concepto Mesoamérica*, XIX Mesa Redonda (Mexico City: Instituto Nacional de Antropología e Historia and Sociedad Mexicana de Antropología, 1990), 156-61, concerning the reconstructed Proto-Mayan, Proto-Havean, and Proto-Otomanguean languages. Lyle Campbell and Terrence Kaufman, "A Linguistic Look at the Olmecs," *American Antiquity* 41 (January 1976): 85, 87-88, concerning the reconstructed Proto-Mixe-Zoquean language of about 1500 B.C. Both of these sources are quoted in Sorenson, "Viva," 320.

102. Sorenson, *Setting*, 279.

103. Robert E. Longacre and René Millon, "Proto-Mixtecan and Proto-Amuzgo-Mixtecan Vocabularies: A Preliminary Cultural Analysis," *Anthropological Linguistics* 3 (April 1961): 22.

104. Ibid., 24-25, 29.

105. Sorenson, *Setting*, 278.

106. Emil W. Haury, "Cuicuilco in Retrospect," *The Kiva* 41 (Winter 1975): 199, quoted in D. G. Matheny, "Critique," 288.

107. John L. Sorenson, *Metals and Metallurgy relating to the Book of Mormon Text* (Provo, UT: Foundation for Ancient Research and Mormon Studies, 1992), passim.

108. Linné, *Cultures*, 132.

109. David M. Pendergast, "Tumbaga Object from the Early Classic Period, Found at Altun Ha, British Honduras (Belize)," *Science* 168 (3 April 1970): 117.

110. Cf. variant dates in Sorenson, *Metals*, 40, 69.

111. D. G. Matheny, "Critique," 291.

112. Bruhns, "Crucible," 221.

113. Dorothy Hosler, *The Sounds and Colors of Power: The Sacred Metallurgical Technology of Ancient West Mexico* (Cambridge, MA: The Massachusetts Institute of Technology, 1994), 12.

114. Dorothy Hosler, "Archaeometallurgy: The Development of Ancient Mesoamerican Metallurgy," *JOM [Journal of Minerals, Metals, and Materials Society]* 42 (May 1990): 44.

115. Welch, *Answers*, 9, who would like to have metallurgy in Mesoamerica during Book of Mormon times, misrepresented an article in *Scientific American*, referring to "the degree of sophistication now observable in the craftsmanship of ancient Mesoamerican metallurgists." However, Heather Lechtman, "Pre-Columbian Surface Metallurgy," *Scientific American* 250 (June 1984): 56-63, said nothing about Mesoamerican metallurgy, but rather dealt exclusively with the Chavín, the Moche, and the Chimú cultures of Andean South America.

116. William J. Hamblin and A. Brent Merrill, "Swords in the Book

of Mormon," in *Warfare in the Book of Mormon*, ed. Stephen D. Ricks and William J. Hamblin (Salt Lake City: Deseret Book Co., 1990; Provo, UT: Foundation for Ancient Research and Mormon Studies, 1990), 338. Cf. D. G. Matheny, "Critique," 292-97.

117. Hamblin and Merrill, "Swords," 342-43, also misinterpreted a metaphorical reference at Alma 24:12, which works perfectly well with steel swords, concerning the stains of sin being removed by God.

118. William J. Hamblin, "An Apologist for the Critics: Brent Lee Metcalfe's Assumptions and Methodologies," review of "Apologetic and Critical Assumptions about Book of Mormon Historicity," by Brent Lee Metcalfe, in *Review of Books on the Book of Mormon* 6, no. 1 (1994): 481-83. Summarizing Hamblin's research, Daniel C. Peterson, "LDS Scholars Refute Attacks on the Book of Mormon," *This People* 15 (Summer 1994): 31, sidestepped the issue of the metal swords of the Book of Mormon.

119. Hamblin and Merrill, "Swords," 343, suggested that "a possible difficulty with interpreting the *macuahuitl* as the Book of Mormon sword concerns the five references in the Book of Mormon to drawing a sword." The passage of 1 Ne. 4:9 specifically mentions that the sword was drawn from its sheath, but Hamblin and Merrill discounted its applicability since reference is being made to Laban's sword from the Near East. The four other Book of Mormon passages have the wording "drew his sword" and for these cases they argued that "these references could describe grasping or brandishing a sword before combat rather than actually 'drawing' it from a sheath." Since it was published just one year before the Book of Mormon was dictated, Noah Webster, *An American Dictionary of the English Language*, 2 vols. (New York: S. Converse, 1828), provides a good indication of contemporary meanings. Webster gave as one of his forty definitions of the transitive verb "draw" the following: "to pull out, as to *draw* a sword or dagger from its sheath; to unsheathe," but not the meaning of brandishing a sword.

120. Kenneth C. Barraclough, *Steelmaking before Bessemer* (London: Metals Society, 1984), 1:13.

121. Hamblin and Merrill, "Swords," 347, suggested that one might "equate this Jaredite steel with the 'steel' of the King James translation of the Old Testament, which actually refers to the Hebrew word for 'bronze.'" According to Koehler and Baumgartner, *Lexikon*, 3:647-48, 653, the Hebrew words $n^e ch\hat{u}sh\bar{a}h$ and $n^e chosheth$ mean copper, bronze, or brass. It is not clear why the KJV mistranslation would justify Joseph Smith mistranslating in the same way. Cf. Mark D. Thomas, "Swords Cankered with Rust," review of *Warfare in the Book of Mormon*, ed. Stephen D. Ricks and William J. Hamblin, in *Sunstone* 15 (September 1991): 62, and William J. Hamblin, "Sharper Than a Two-edged Sword," *Sunstone* 15 (December 1991): 54-55.

122. D. G. Matheny, "Critique," 285, assumed that the blades of the Jaredite swords were made "of ferrous metal." Sorenson, "Viva," 324, countered Matheny, correctly pointing out that the blades "could just as well have been copper, which also rusts."

123. Roberts, "Difficulties," chap. ii, 22, in Roberts Collection; Madsen, *Roberts: Studies*, 107. The use of metal swords does not imply that the Book of Mormon peoples did not also have wooden weapons, for clubs are mentioned--probably made of wood. Both Nephites and Lamanites used clubs: Zeniff used them against the Lamanites (Mosiah 9:16), certain Lamanite prisoners employed clubs in an escape attempt (Alma 57:14), and some Lamanite robbers used clubs (Alma 17:36-37).

124. Francis Robicsek, "The Weapons of the Ancient Maya," in *Circumpacifica*, ed. Bruno Illius and Matthias Laubscher (Frankfurt am Main: Peter Lang, 1990), 372.

125. Ross Hassig, *Mexico and the Spanish Conquest*, Modern Wars in Perspective (London and New York: Longman, 1994), 25. Cf. Ross Hassig, *War and Society in Ancient Mesoamerica* (Berkeley and Los Angeles and Oxford: University of California Press, 1992), 112, 231n27.

126. Michael D. Coe, "Pre-Conquest America," in *Swords and Hilt Weapons*, ed. Anne Cope (London: Multimedia Books, 1993), 222.

127. D. G. Matheny, "Critique," 296-97.

128. Ferguson, "Symposium," 26.

129. Hugh Nibley, *Lehi in the Desert and the World of the Jaredites* (Salt Lake City: Bookcraft, 1952), 13-20; reprinted in *Lehi in the Desert, The World of the Jaredites, There Were Jaredites*, The Collected Works of Hugh Nibley, ed. John W. Welch (Salt Lake City: Deseret Book Co., 1988; Provo, UT: Foundation for Ancient Research and Mormon Studies, 1988), 5:13-19.

130. Sorenson, *Setting*, 74-81.

131. Ferguson, letter to J. Willard Marriott, 30 March 1971, in the John Willard and Alice Sheets Marriott Collection, Manuscript 164, Box 17, Fd 15, Manuscripts Division, J. Willard Marriott Library, University of Utah, Salt Lake City.

132. For Jean Frédéric Waldeck's artistic creation of cuneiform markings, see the bottom right glyph in fig. 30, above.

133. Ferguson, "Symposium," 24, with emphasis in original.

134. George F. Carter, letter to Ferguson, 6 March 1975, in Ferguson Collection, UU. One's confidence in Fell's ability must plummet since he claimed to have translated the first line of a new version of the Anthon Transcript (this version was "discovered" in 1980, but was later revealed to be a forgery of Mark Hofmann), as follows: "Revelation of Nefi: I have written these things, I, Nefi, a son born to sagacious parents." Compare 1 Ne. 1:1, and see Barry Fell, "An Enciphered Ancient Moorish Text," typescript, 1980, in the H. Michael Marquardt Collection, Accession 900, Box 105, Fd 6, Manuscripts Division, J. Willard Marriott Library, University of Utah, Salt Lake City; hereafter abbreviated to Marquardt Collection.

135. Michael D. Coe, letter to author, 26 April 1988, in author's possession, said concerning Fell's translation: "As for the Tlatilco 'seal' (i.e., roller stamp), no reputable archaeologist believes that it has the name 'Hiram' on it--nor do they have any faith in any of Barry Fell's other dubious claims."

136. George F. Carter, "Mexican Sellos: Writing in America, or the Growth of an Idea," in *Diffusion and Migration: Their Roles in Cultural Development*, ed. P. G. Duke et alia (Calgary: Chacmool, University of Calgary Archaeological Association, 1978), 187, 192, 201. George F. Carter, letter to author, 3 July 1989, in author's possession.

137. Ferguson, letter to Robert M. Carmack, 7 January 1982, in Ferguson Collection, UU. William J. Hamblin, review of *Archaeology and the Book of Mormon*, by Jerald Tanner and Sandra Tanner, in *Review of Books on the Book of Mormon* 5 (1993): 260, 270-71, overstated the case when he claimed that "the Bat Creek inscription is now widely accepted as a Hebrew text." For the controversy concerning the authenticity of this A.D. 100 to 200 Hebrew inscription in Tennessee, see J. Huston McCulloch, "The Bat Creek Inscription: Did Judean Refugees Escape to Tennessee?" *Biblical Archaeology Review* 19 (July-August 1993): 46-53, 82-83; and P. Kyle McCarter, Jr., "Let's Be Serious about the Bat Creek Stone," *Biblical Archaeology Review* 19 (July-August 1993): 54-55, 83.

138. Ferguson, "Symposium," 24, with emphasis in original. In chap. 2, pp. 61-62, above, the opinions of Matthew W. Stirling, J. Alden Mason, and David H. Kelley are quoted concerning this roller stamp.

139. John Lloyd Stephens, *Incidents of Travel in Central America, Chiapas, and Yucatán* (New York: Harper and Brothers, 1841), 1:159-60.

140. J. Thomas Goodman, "Maya Dates," *American Anthropologist* 7 (October-November 1905): 642-47.

141. Sharer, *Ancient Maya*, 575, pointed out that Herbert Spinden reduced all Mayan dates of the Goodman-Martínez-Thompson correlation by 256 years, George Vaillant added 256 years to such dates, and several correlations were based on the almanac in the Dresden Codex.

142. A correlation problem of a different sort confronts students of the Book of Mormon. John L. Sorenson, "The Book of Mormon as a Mesoamerican Codex," *Newsletter and Proceedings of the S.E.H.A.*, no. 139 (December 1976): 8n55, explained the problem: "Nephite record allots just over '600 years' for the span in secular time from 597/6 B.C., Zedekiah's first regnal year, to 6/5 B.C., probably Christ's birth. If 600 360-day (Maya) tuns (i.e., one and one-half baktuns) is meant, the 591.36 sidereal years is covered quite precisely. If not, the chronology is inexplicable." However, the Mayan "tun" of eighteen twenty-day months does not fit the Book of Mormon pattern of months within a year, since at Alma 49:1, 29, the eleventh month is near the end of the year, indicating a twelve-month year not an eighteen-month year. In order to cover the period from leaving Jerusalem in 587 (not 597) B.C. to the birth of Jesus in 5 B.C., Randall P. Spackman, *Introduction to Book of Mormon Chronology: The Principal Prophecies, Calendars, and Dates* (Provo, UT: Foundation for Ancient Research and Mormon Studies, 1993), 4, 15, 17, 28, 30, proposed that Lehi's prophecy of 600 years refers to twelve-moon years of 354 days each, reducing the period to 582 years. Spackman, ibid., 61, then suggested that from the birth of Jesus they used a 365-day solar year. Spackman's 354-day year has no parallel

in Mesoamerica.

143. Munro S. Edmonson, *The Book of the Year: Middle American Calendrical Systems* (Salt Lake City: University of Utah Press, 1988), 27, gave the earliest Long Count date as 36 B.C., which was discovered by Gareth Lowe at Chiapa de Corzo. Sharer, *Ancient Maya*, 622, indicated that the earliest known lowland Mayan inscription is the Tikal Stela 29 date of 292 B.C., but this is a typographical error for A.D. 292.

144. George E. Stuart, "The Calendar," in Gene S. Stuart and George E. Stuart, *Lost Kingdoms of the Maya* (Washington, D.C.: National Geographic Society, 1993), 177. Stuart provided an analogy to help understand this huge span of years: "The interval is approximately equal to the fifteen-billion-year span that separates us from the cosmic 'big bang' multiplied almost 3,000,000,000,000,000,000 times!"

145. [Michael West, ed.,] "Knorosov in Mexico," *Institute of Maya Studies Newsletter* 24 (October 1995): 6.

146. Charles Gallenkamp, *Maya: The Riddle and Rediscovery of a Lost Civilization*, 3d rev. ed. (New York: Viking, 1985), 118-19.

147. Peter Mathews, *The Proceedings of the Maya Hieroglyphic Weekend, October 27-28, 1990, Cleveland State University*, ed. Phil Wanyerka (Austin, TX: Maya Hieroglyphic Weekend, 1991), 85-86, listed emblem glyphs for thirty-five sites.

148. Michael D. Coe, *The Maya*, 5th ed., fully rev. and exp., Ancient Peoples and Places (London: Thames and Hudson, 1993), 196. See Tatiana Proskouriakoff, *Maya History*, ed. Rosemary A. Joyce (Austin, TX: University of Texas Press, 1993).

149. Michael D. Coe, *Breaking the Maya Code* (New York: Thames and Hudson, 1992), 196.

150. Linda Schele and Nikolai Grube, *The Proceedings of the Maya Hieroglyphic Workshop [on] Late Classic and Terminal Classic Warfare, March 11-12, 1995*, ed. Phil Wanyerka (Austin, TX: Maya Hieroglyphic Workshop, 1995).

151. Roberts, "Difficulties," chap. I, 45, in Roberts Collection; Madsen, *Roberts: Studies*, 87. Welch, *Answers*, 7, countered Roberts's statement by mentioning the research of Brian Stubbs in comparing Hebrew and the Uto-Aztecan languages. Brian Stubbs, *Elements of Hebrew in Uto-Aztecan: A Summary of the Data* (Provo, UT: Foundation for Ancient Research and Mormon Studies, 1988), found a few unrelated correlations among thousands of grammatical possibilities.

152. Linda Miller Van Blerkom, "A Comparison of Maya and Egyptian Hieroglyphics," *Katunob* 11, no. 3 (August 1979): 6.

153. Joyce Marcus, *Mesoamerican Writing Systems: Propaganda, Myth, and History in Four Ancient Civilizations* (Princeton, NJ: Princeton University Press, 1992), 19.

154. Edward H. Ashment, "'A Record in the Language of My Father': Evidence of Ancient Egyptian and Hebrew in the Book of Mormon," in *New Approaches to the Book of Mormon: Explorations in Critical Methodology*, ed. Brent Lee Metcalfe (Salt Lake City: Signature Books, 1993), 341.

155. Gordon R. Willey, *An Introduction to American Archaeology* (Englewood Cliffs, NJ: Prentice-Hall, 1966), 1:17. Willey, ibid., 1:25 *n*20, added in an endnote that the sole exception to this statement is the Eskimo language, which "is the same in America and Siberia." Joseph H. Greenberg, *Language in the Americas* (Stanford, CA: Stanford University Press, 1987), 331, also argued for the genetic unity of New World languages, except for the Na-Dene and Eskimo-Aleut families.

156. Marcus, *Systems*, 29.

157. David Stuart, *The Yaxhá Emblem Glyph as Yax-ha* (Washington, D.C.: Center for Maya Research, 1985), 4, said: "I therefore propose that the place name Yaxha was used during the Classic Period, probably in reference to both the site and the lake which go by this same name today." See David Stuart and Stephen D. Houston, *Classic Maya Place Names* (Washington, D.C.: Dumbarton Oaks Research Library, 1994).

158. Ferguson, "Symposium," 4. T. Michael Smith, "A New Discovery and Caution," *Ancient America Foundation Newsletter*, no. 3 (December 1994): 4, also stated: "We don't yet have a verified first-ever 'Mesoamerican site to Book of Mormon text site' correspondence." For an RLDS perspective on the Book of Mormon, see the articles in Raymond C. Treat, ed., *Recent Book of Mormon Developments: Articles from the Zarahemla Record* (Independence, MO: Zarahemla Research Foundation, 1992). However, compare Alison V. P. Coutts, "Earnestly Seeking," review of *Recent Book of Mormon Developments*, by Raymond Treat, in *Review of Books on the Book of Mormon 7*, no. 2 (1995): 253-55.

159. Hugh Nibley, "New Approaches to Book of Mormon Study: Part I, Some Standard Tests," *The Improvement Era* 56 (November 1953): 831. The text quotes Nibley's words as expressed in 1953, but most of these words were intentionally deleted and replaced in the 1989 F.A.R.M.S. reprint, *The Prophetic Book of Mormon*, The Collected Works of Hugh Nibley, ed. John W. Welch (Salt Lake City: Deseret Book Co., 1989; Provo, UT: Foundation for Ancient Research and Mormon Studies, 1989), 8:56, by the revised wording: "Thus, while we can never prove absolutely that the Book of Mormon is what it claims to be, we are justified at the outset in assuming that it is what it claims to be. If one assumes that it is true, its features at least become testable." The reprint also eliminated the following analogy by Nibley concerning a counterfeit dollar bill: "The reader cannot produce absolute proof that the dollar bill in his pocket is genuine; it may look all right even to the trained eye and still contain minute evidence of counterfeiting which escape[s] the expert; but if there is anything obviously wrong with it, we then have absolute proof that it is counterfeit."

160. Ferguson's intense belief in the Book of Mormon during the 1930s, 1940s, 1950s, and early 1960s contrasts sharply with the early skepticism of Fawn M. Brodie and Dale L. Morgan. See Gary F. Novak, "Naturalistic Assumptions and the Book of Mormon," *Brigham Young University Studies* 30 (Summer 1990): 24-30.

161. Dee F. Green, "Book of Mormon Archaeology: The Myths and the Alternatives," *Dialogue: A Journal of Mormon Thought* 4 (Sum-

mer 1969): 77, with emphasis in original.
162. Ferguson, "Symposium," 29.
163. Ronald O. Barney, interview with Ferguson, 4 January 1983, typed on 19 April 1984, in Box 77, Fd 13, Marquardt Collection.
164. Ferguson, letter to Mr. and Mrs. Harold W. Lawrence, 20 February 1976, in Ferguson Collection, UU. Recently some have not considered the antiquity or modernity of the Book of Mormon as an either/or issue. For example, Blake T. Ostler, "The Book of Mormon as a Modern Expansion of an Ancient Source," *Dialogue: A Journal of Mormon Thought* 20 (Spring 1987): 66-123, argued a middle-of-the-road position that the Book of Mormon contains both translations of ancient texts and nineteenth-century "expansions" authored by Joseph Smith. For responses to Ostler, see Stephen E. Robinson, "The 'Expanded' Book of Mormon?" in *The Book of Mormon: Second Nephi, the Doctrinal Structure*, ed. Monte S. Nyman and Charles D. Tate, Jr. (Provo, UT: Religious Studies Center, Brigham Young University, 1989), 391-414; and Robert L. Millet, "The Book of Mormon, Historicity, and Faith," *Journal of Book of Mormon Studies* 2 (Fall 1993): 4, reprinted in Robert L. Millet, *The Power of the Word: Saving Doctrines from the Book of Mormon* (Salt Lake City: Deseret Book Co., 1994), 292-93.
165. John L. Sorenson, "Addendum," to John Gee's review of *By His Own Hand upon Papyrus*, by Charles M. Larson, in *Review of Books on the Book of Mormon* 4 (1992): 119.
166. Jerald Tanner and Sandra Tanner, "Ferguson's Two Faces: Mormon Scholar's 'Spoof' Lives on after His Death," *Salt Lake City Messenger*, no. 69 (September 1988): 7, with emphasis in original.
167. Ferguson, handwritten response on letter of J. Don Cerchione to Ferguson, 21 July 1976, in Ferguson Collection, UU.
168. Sorenson, *Setting*, 188.
169. D. G. Matheny, "Critique," 321-22. Sorenson, "Viva," 301, remained unconvinced by D. G. Matheny's review and answered her by saying, "Yes, the shoe fits--a little stiffly but about as well as most new shoes that need getting used to."
170. Ferguson, letter to Lawrences, 20 February 1976.
171. David A. Palmer, "Symposium on Book of Mormon Geography: Response of David A. Palmer to Papers by V. G. Norman and J. L. Sorenson," typescript, April 1975, 13, in Tolman Collection.
172. John L. Sorenson, quoted in Bergera and Priddis, *Brigham Young University*, 85. In a similar manner Sorenson, *Setting*, 31, stated: "One point needs to be emphasized: the Book of Mormon account actually did take place *some*where," with emphasis in original.
173. R. T. Matheny, "Archaeology," 25-26, 30-31. The typescript has "and trying to put them into the New World," but to make sense the "and" has been changed to an "in." R. T. Matheny, in a 1992 letter quoted in Hamblin, "Problems," 190, explained that "the question [to which he was asked to respond at the 1984 Sunstone Symposium] dealt with how does a non-Mormon archaeologist evaluate the Book of Mormon in terms of its cultural content and claims. My answer to the

question was an *ad hoc* response where I tried to put myself in a non-Mormon's professional shoes and talked about the nature of the problems that the Book of Mormon poses for the archaeologist."

174. Roberts, "Book of Mormon Study," part II, chap. iii, 13-14, in Roberts Collection; Madsen, *Roberts: Studies*, 271. For a reproduction of a page from Roberts's "Book of Mormon Study," see fig. 27, above. A little later, after comparing the final battles of the Jaredites and Nephites, B. H. Roberts, "Book of Mormon Study," part II, chap. iv, 17; Madsen, *Roberts: Studies*, 283, asked: "Is all this sober history inspired written and true, representing things that actually happened? Or is it a wonder-tale of an immature mind, unconscious of what a test he is laying on human credulity when asking men to accept his narrative as solemn history?"

175. Michael D. Coe, "Mormons and Archaeology: An Outside View," *Dialogue: A Journal of Mormon Thought* 8, no. 2 (1973): 48, with Coe's plural "Revelations" having been corrected. For an explanation of the methods and theory of archaeology, see Wendy Ashmore and Robert J. Sharer, *Discovering Our Past: A Brief Introduction to Archaeology*, 2d ed. (Mountain View, CA: Mayfield Publishing Co., 1996).

176. For a criticism of an environmental explanation of the Book of Mormon, see Gary F. Novak, "Examining the Environmental Explanation of the Book of Mormon," review of *Joseph Smith's Response to Skepticism*, by Robert N. Hullinger, in *Review of Books on the Book of Mormon* 7, no. 1 (1995): 139-54.

177. Ferguson, letter to the First Presidency, 22 November 1957, in Ferguson Collection, BYU.

178. Ferguson, letter to Allie [Alice] Marriott, 7 September 1954, in Ferguson Collection, BYU, alluding to the 1954 Universal motion picture, based on Lloyd C. Douglas's novel, *Magnificent Obsession*.

179. Fred W. Nelson, Jr., "In Honor of Thomas Stuart Ferguson," *Newsletter and Proceedings of the S.E.H.A.*, no. 161 (May 1987): 2.

180. For a bibliography of publications of the New World Archaeological Foundation, see Thomas A. Lee, Jr., *New World Archaeological Foundation Obra, 1952-1980* (Provo, UT, and San Cristóbal de las Casas, Chiapas: New World Archaeological Foundation, 1981).

181. Green, "Myths," 77. The horses which have been discovered are either Pleistocene fossils or post-Conquest bones, but not during the Book of Mormon time span.

182. Coe, "Archaeology," 45-46.

183. Ferguson, letter to Lawrences, 9 February 1976.

184. Garth N. Jones, response to the author's "Odyssey of Thomas Stuart Ferguson," typescript, 1989, 2-3, in the Garth N. Jones Collection, Accession 1557, Manuscripts Division, J. Willard Marriott Library, University of Utah, Salt Lake City.

185. Ferguson, letter to George F. Carter, 24 May 1977, in Ferguson Collection, UU, which letter was donated in January 1996.

186. His death certificate gave the cause of death as "arteriosclerotic heart disease and hypertension."

Appendix A

Thomas Stuart Ferguson on Book of Mormon Archaeology[1]

David A. Palmer tells us to "correct our errors . . . give constructive criticism . . . apply our knowledge of American cultures, archaeology, mythology, languages, ethnohistory, etc. . . . indicate how your knowledge or analysis supports or challenges the [V. Garth] Norman and [John L.] Sorenson papers . . . show how they fail to satisfy the requirements of the text."

Thus, it is clear to all of us that we should be forthright in this discussion. Certainly it is no time for turning off the mind.

Garth Norman emphasizes "unbiased scholarly inquiry" (at page seven of his first paper). John Sorenson says we must be "reality based" (Appendix, p. 29). "No correlation is acceptable which exhibits major flaws . . ." (Appendix, p. 1). Sorenson lays down some factual requirements that the correlation of Jaredite-Nephite places must meet to be valid and acceptable: (1) configuration, (2) dimensions, (3) directions, (4) topography, (5) plant life, (6) animal life, (7) climate (p. 1). These are objective tests.

To Sorenson's list of requirements--his "test" list--I think there should be added two additional items, (1) metals and (2) scripts, bringing the list of requirements to nine. He gives but one paragraph to his first test, "configuration" (p. 1). He gives seven full pages to item two, "dimensions" (pp. 1-8). Four and a half pages are devoted to his test three, "directions." Sorenson's discussion of test four, "topography," encompasses seven pages. He quits after covering his first four items.

In my opinion, the most demanding and exacting tests (and therefore the most substantial) are "plant life," "animal life," "metals," and "scripts." Neither Norman nor Sorenson applies any of these more significant and truth-testing factors to their hypotheses. This is my main criticism of each of the papers.

Hundreds of pages have been written heretofore of material similar to the Norman-Sorenson papers. Those discussions begin with Col. Willard Young--the grandfather of the "Central American Theory."[2] He carefully studied for years configuration, dimensions, directions, and topography, trying to hit upon the location of Book of Mormon places. He had the Jaredites cross the Atlantic and land in the Bay of Honduras. To him, the Jaredites lived out their existence in Honduras and Guatemala ("land northward"). Lehi landed, according to Colonel Young's views, in El Salvador. The land of Nephi he placed in the upper valley of the Humuya River in Honduras. The land of Zarahemla was put on the west side of the Ulúa River in Honduras. The "land southward" was to Col. Willard Young, Honduras, El Salvador, and Guatemala. Cumorah-Ramah was in Guatemala (near Chiquimula). Mulek crossed the Atlantic and landed on the coast of Honduras near the mouth of the Ulúa River.

Norman C. Pierce, in the little book entitled *Another Cumorah, Another Joseph*, published in 1954, placed Nephi near Tegucigalpa, Honduras, and Zarahemla on the westerly side of the Ulúa River (which is his "Sidon"--as it was to Colonel Young long before 1954).[3] Pierce places Cumorah in southeastern Guatemala. Although Pierce published his book in 1954, he had it all figured out and on a relief map in 1923. (His map was drawn for him by Jean R. Driggs in 1923,[4] who acknowledged receiving help from Col. Willard Young.)

In 1927 J. M. Sjodahl published his very scholarly and comprehensive book, *An Introduction to the Study of the Book of Mormon*, with wonderfully detailed things having to do with configuration, dimensions, directions, and topography.[5] He includes the data from all the very early Book of Mormon geography experts, including Joel Ricks[6] of Logan, Utah; Col. Willard Young; Stuart Bagley;[7] and Sjodahl himself. All had done extensive work more than fifty years ago. Bagley landed the Jaredites on the coast of Yucatán. His Zarahemla was on a fork of the Usumacinta River, which was his Sidon River--as it is Norman's (second paper, p. 2). He put Bountiful in Chiapas, the City Bountiful being at the site we know today as Palenque. His Desolation was the area north of Tehuántepec. Others have already pushed for Costa Rica and Nicaragua. An acquaintance of mine who lives in Nevada is certain it all happened in Costa Rica and Nicaragua.

Sjodahl, incidentally, in his 1927 book locates the "narrow pass" exactly where Norman now locates it, on the Pacific side of the Isthmus of Tehuántepec (see his map at p. 420).

Brother [J. Nile] Washburn, do not feel bad or sad because your 1939 book[8] has not been mentioned or cited by the principal panelists of this discussion--my books aren't referred to either --and it matters not. In his 1959 *Geography of the Book of Mormon*, Fletcher B. Hammond did an outstanding job and he is not mentioned.[9] M. Wells Jakeman has labored prodigiously for a lifetime on the project.[10] We have come late to the "configuration-dimension-direction-topography" struggle. With all of these great efforts, it cannot be established factually that anyone, from Joseph Smith to the present day, has put his finger on a single point of terrain that was a Book of Mormon geographical place. And the hemisphere has been pretty well checked out by competent people. Thousands of sites have been excavated. This panel can now point to little that is new in Book of Mormon geography. Even the proposal that the "narrow pass" was on the

Pacific side of Tehuántepec is old.

To the numerous writers already mentioned, can be added other late comers who have had the fun of making an effort with the configuration-dimension-direction-topography data: Riley L. Dixon, *Just One Cumorah* (1958)[11] and E. Cecil McGavin and Willard Bean, *Book of Mormon Geography* (1948)[12] are two more examples of those who have tried and failed.

In failing to apply the more severe and demanding tests--plant life, animal life, metals, and script--Norman and Sorenson just add their names and papers to the long list of those who have gotten nowhere. Each has used sophisticated, up-to-date archaeological terminology--"Pre-Classic," "Early Classic," etc., but this doesn't do the job of establishing Book of Mormon locations. The "digging" must go deeper.

What are the demands of the text of the Book of Mormon for the dirt, soil, earth, and ground of Book of Mormon places? Let's turn to the text of the Book of Mormon for some of the specific things that must be found in the ground occupied 2500 years by people from Iraq and for 1000 years by people from Israel.

Plant-Life Test

The text of the Book of Mormon requires the finding of evidence of some or all of the following plants in regions proposed as Nephite-Lamanite country:

BARLEY[13]

Mosiah 7:22	One half of our corn, and our *barley*
Mosiah 9:9	With seeds of corn . . . and of *barley*
Alma 11:7	And either for a measure of *barley*
Alma 11:15	A shiblon for half a measure of *barley*

FIGS

3 Ne. 14:16	Gather grapes of thorns, or *figs* of thistles

GRAPES

2 Ne. 15:2	He looked that it should bring forth *grapes*

2 Ne. 15:2	And it brought forth wild *grapes*
2 Ne. 15:4	I looked that it should bring forth *grapes*
2 Ne. 15:4	It brought forth wild *grapes*
3 Ne. 14:16	Do men gather *grapes* of thorns, or figs of

WHEAT

| Mosiah 9:9 | With seed of corn, and of *wheat* |
| 3 Ne. 18:18 | To have you: that he may sift you as *wheat* |

Evidence support the existence of these forms of plant life in the regions proposed by Norman and Sorenson stands at this time as follows:

Barley:	None
Figs:	None
Grapes:	None
Wheat:	None

This negative score on the plant-life should not be treated too lightly. An abundance of evidence supporting the existence of these plants has been found in other parts of the world of antiquity. The existence of numerous non-Book-of-Mormon plants (maize, lima beans, tomatoes, squash, etc.) has been supported by abundant archaeological findings. I participated in excavating a trench at the edge of the Grijalva River with Edwin Shook, in which we found a ceramic vessel in a stratum dating to about 200 B.C. The vessel contained lima beans that had been burned anciently and discarded--pot and beans--as too badly burned to be edible. And yet they were still in their pristine and perfect form. The beans were carbon-14 dated--helping to place the whole stratum on the true time scale. Art portrayals in ceramics, murals, and sculptured works--of ancient plant life--are fairly commonplace. Thousands of archaeological holes in the area proposed have given us not a fragment of evidence of the presence of the plants mentioned in the Book of Mormon--the holes included the great one dug by Edwin Shook at Tehuacán, Pueblo, Mexico. He excavated a cave--going down and back to 5,000 B.C.--finding most of the major plants of the area. But no wheat, barley, figs, or grapes.

Animal-Life Test

The text of the Book of Mormon requires the finding of evidence of some or all of the following animals in the regions proposed as Jaredite-Nephite-Lamanite country:

ASS

1 Ne. 18:25	The ox and the *ass* and the horse
Mosiah 5:14	Doth a man take an *ass* which belongeth?
Mosiah 12:5	They shall be driven before like a dumb *ass*
Mosiah 13:24	His maid servant, nor his ox, nor his *ass*
Mosiah 21:3	And drive them as they would a dumb *ass*

ASSES

Ether 9:19	They also had horses, and *asses*

BULL

2 Ne. 8:20	As a wild *bull* in a net

CALF

2 Ne. 21:6	The *calf* and the young lion and fatling
2 Ne. 30:12	The *calf*, and the young lion, and the fatling

CALVES

1 Ne. 22:24	The righteous must be led up as *calves* of
3 Ne. 25:2	Go forth and grow up as *calves* in the stall

CATTLE

2 Ne. 17:25	And the treading of *lesser cattle* [sheep][14]
Enos 1:21	Flocks of all manner of *cattle* of every kind
Mosiah 13:18	Nor thy maid-servant, nor they *cattle*, nor
3 Ne. 3:22	Their horses, and their chariots, and their *cattle*
3 Ne. 4:4	Provisions, and horses, and *cattle*, and flocks
3 Ne. 6:1	Flocks, and his herds, his horses and his *cattle*
Ether 9:18	Also all manner of *cattle*, of oxen, and cows

COW

1 Ne. 18:25	Both the *cow* and the ox and the ass
2 Ne. 17:21	A man shall nourish a young *cow* and two
2 Ne. 21:7	And the *cow* and the bear shall feed
2 Ne. 30:13	And the *cow* and the bear shall feed

COWS
Ether 9:18   All manner of cattle, of oxen, and *cows*

BUTTER
2 Ne. 17:15   *Butter* and honey shall he eat
2 Ne. 17:22   He shall eat *butter*
2 Ne. 17:22   For *butter* and honey shall every one eat

MILK
2 Ne. 9:50   Come buy wine and *milk* without money
2 Ne. 17:22   For the abundance of *milk* they shall give
2 Ne. 26:25   Buy *milk* and honey, without money and

FATLING
2 Ne. 21:6   And the young lion and the *fatling* together
2 Ne. 30:12   And the young lion, and the *fatling*, together

FATLINGS
Mosiah 11:3   And a fifth part of their *fatlings*
Alma 1:29   Flocks and herds, and *fatlings* of every kind
Hel. 6:12   Raise many flocks and herds, yea, many *fatlings*

FIRSTLINGS
Mosiah 2:3   Also took of the *firstlings* of their flocks

FLOCKS
His Flocks--
Mosiah 5:14   Suffer that he shall feed among his *flocks*
Alma 18:2   Faithfulness of Ammon in preserving his *flocks*
3 Ne. 6:1   Every man, with his family, his *flocks*

Our Flocks--
Mosiah 7:22   One-half of the increase of our *flocks*
Mosiah 22:8   We will depart with our women . . . our *flocks*
Alma 17:28   Behold our *flocks* are scattered already
Alma 17:33   With these men who do scatter our *flocks*

Their Flocks--
Mosiah 2:3   Also took of the firstlings of their *flocks*
Mosiah 9:14   Were watering and feeding their *flocks*
Mosiah 9:14   Began to slay them, and to take off their *flocks*
Mosiah 10:21   My people began to tend their *flocks*
Mosiah 11:16   And while they were tending their *flocks*
Mosiah 11:17   Drove many of their *flocks* out of the land
Mosiah 21:18   And secured their grain and their *flocks*
Mosiah 22:2   To take their women . . . and their *flocks*
Mosiah 22:6   They gather together their *flocks* and herds
Mosiah 22:10   His people should gather their *flocks* together

Mosiah 22:11   Depart . . . into the wilderness with their *flocks*

Mosiah 23:1   They gathered together their *flocks*, and took

Mosiah 24:18   In the night time, gathered their *flocks* together

Mosiah 24:18   Night time were they gathering their *flocks*

Alma 2:25   Are fleeing before them with their *flocks*

Alma 3:2   Also many of their *flocks* and their herds

Alma 4:2   Also for the loss of their *flocks* and herds

Alma 17:26   Going forth with their *flocks* to the place

Alma 17:26   And all the Lamanites drive their *flocks* hither

Alma 17:27   Were driving forth their *flocks* to this place

Alma 17:27   The Lamanites, who had been with their *flocks*

Alma 17:28   Because their *flocks* were scattered by

Alma 17:33   Those men again stood to scatter their *flocks*

Alma 17:39   They watered their *flocks* and returned them

Alma 18:6   Because their brethren had scattered their *flocks*

Alma 18:6   Because they had had their *flocks* scattered

Alma 19:20   Their *flocks* scattered at the waters of Sebus

Alma 27:14   Did gather together all their *flocks*

Hel. 12:2   In the increase of their fields, their *flocks*

3 Ne. 3:13   They should gather . . . their *flocks* and their

3 Ne. 3:22   They had taken . . . all their *flocks* and their

3 Ne. 4:3   Lands desolate, and had gathered their *flocks*

Ether 2:1   With their *flocks* which they had gathered

Ether 6:4   Also food for their *flocks* and herds

Ether 9:31   Their *flocks* began to flee before the poisonous

Flocks--

Enos 1:21   *Flocks* of herds and *flocks* of all manner

Mosiah 9:12   Feast themselves upon the *flocks* of our fields

Mosiah 10:2   Thus I did guard my people and my *flocks*

Mosiah 21:16   Raise grain more abundantly, and *flocks*

Alma 1:29   And abundance of *flocks* and herds

Alma 4:6   Because of their many *flocks* and herds

Alma 7:27   Peace of God rest upon you . . . upon your *flocks*

Alma 17:25   He was set . . . to watch the *flocks* of Lamoni

Alma 17:27   Stood and scattered the *flocks* of Ammon

Alma 17:29   In restoring these *flocks* unto the king

Alma 17:31   And let us go in search of the *flocks*

Alma 17:31   We will preserve the *flocks* unto the king

Alma 17:32   That they went in search of the *flocks*

Alma 17:32   And did head the *flocks* of the king

Alma 17:33   Encircle the *flocks* round about that they

Alma 17:35   They stood to scatter the *flocks* of the king

Alma 18:3   Neither can they scatter the king's *flocks*

Alma 18:7   Waters of Sebus, to scatter the *flocks*

Alma 18:16   And I defended thy servants and thy *flocks*

Alma 18:16   In order to defend thy *flocks* and thy servants

Alma 18:20	Arms of my brethren that scattered my *flocks*
Alma 19:21	At the waters of Sebus, and scattered the *flocks*
Alma 19:21	While defending the *flocks* of the king
Alma 34:20	Cry unto him . . . over all your *flocks*
Alma 34:25	Cry over the *flocks* of your fields
Alma 62:29	Raising all manner of grain, and *flocks*
Hel. 6:12	And they did raise many *flocks* and herds
3 Ne. 4:4	Reserved . . . cattle, and *flocks* of every kind
3 Ne. 20:16	A young lion among the *flocks* of sheep
3 Ne. 21:12	A young lion among the *flocks* of sheep
Ether 1:41	Go to and gather together thy *flocks*
Ether 10:12	Became exceeding rich . . . in *flocks*, and herds

GOAT

1 Ne. 18:25	The horse, and the *goat* and the wild *goat*
Alma 14:29	As a *goat* fleeth with her young from two

GOATS

Enos 1:21	*Goats*, and wild *goats*, and also many horses
Ether 9:18	Also all manner of cattle . . . of swine, and of *goats*

HERDS

2 Ne. 5:11	And we began to raise flocks, and *herds*
Enos 1:21	Flocks of *herds*, and flocks of all manner
Mosiah 7:22	One half of the increase of our . . . *herds*
Mosiah 21:16	Grain more abundantly, and flocks, and *herds*
Mosiah 22:2	Children, and their flocks, and their *herds*
Mosiah 22:6	Gather together their flocks and *herds*
Mosiah 22:8	Our flocks, and our *herds* into the wilderness
Mosiah 22:11	Wilderness with their flocks and their *herds*
Alma 1:29	And abundance of flocks and *herds*
Alma 3:2	Also many of their flocks and their *herds*
Alma 4:2	Also for the loss of their flocks and *herds*
Alma 4:6	Because of their many flocks and *herds*
Alma 7:27	Peace . . . rest . . . upon your flocks, and *herds*
Alma 27:14	Gather together all their flocks and *herds*
Alma 62:29	Grain, and flocks, and *herds* of every kind
Hel. 6:12	They did raise many flocks and *herds*[15]
Hel. 12:2	Increase of . . . their flocks and their *herds*
3 Ne. 3:13	They should gather . . . their flocks and their *herds*
3 Ne. 3:22	All their flocks, and their *herds*, and their
3 Ne. 4:3	And had gathered their flocks, and their *herds*
3 Ne. 6:1	Every man, with his family . . . and his *herds*
Ether 6:4	Also food for their flocks and *herds*
Ether 10:12	In raising grain, and in flocks and *herds*

HORSE

1 Ne. 18:25   Cows and the ox, and the ass and the *horse*

HORSES

2 Ne. 12:7   Their land is also full of *horses*
2 Ne. 15:28   Their *horses'* hoofs shall be counted like flint
Enos 1:21   And wild goats, and also many *horses*
Alma 18:9   Behold, he is feeding thy *horses*
Alma 18:9   They should prepare his *horses* and chariots
Alma 18:10   Heard that Ammon was preparing his *horses*
Alma 18:12   When Ammon had made ready the *horses*
Alma 20:6   His servants should make ready his *horses*
3 Ne. 3:22   Taken their *horses*, and their chariots, and
3 Ne. 4:4   Reserved for themselves provisions, and *horses*
3 Ne. 6:1   His *horses* and his cattle, and all things
                     whatsoever
3 Ne. 21:14   I will cut off thy *horses* out of the midst of
Ether 9:19   And they also had *horses* and asses

OX

1 Ne. 18:25   Both the cow and the *ox*, and the ass
2 Ne. 21:7   And the lion shall eat straw like the *ox*
2 Ne. 30:13   And the lion shall eat straw like the *ox*
Mosiah 13:24   Nor his maid-servant, nor his *ox*, nor his

OXEN

2 Ne. 17:25   But it shall be for the sending forth of *oxen*
Ether 9:18   All manner of cattle, of *oxen*, and cows

SHEEP
My Sheep--

Mosiah 26:20   And shalt gather together my *sheep*
Mosiah 26:21   He that will hear my voice shall be my *sheep*
3 Ne. 15:24   And ye are my *sheep* and ye are numbered
3 Ne. 16:3   And shall be numbered among my *sheep*
3 Ne. 18:31   I know my *sheep*, and they are numbered

Sheep--

1 Ne. 22:25   He numbereth his *sheep*, and they know him
1 Ne. 22:25   He shall feed his *sheep*, and in him they
2 Ne. 17:21   A man shall nourish a young cow and two *sheep*
2 Ne. 23:14   And as a *sheep* that no man taketh up
Mosiah 14:6   And we, like *sheep*, have gone astray
Mosiah 14:7   And as a *sheep* before her shearers is dumb
Mosiah 15:6   As a *sheep* before the shearer is dumb
Alma 5:37   Gone astray, as *sheep* having no shepherd
Alma 5:38   Ye are not the *sheep* of the good shepherd
Alma 5:39   If ye are not the *sheep* of the good shepherd

Alma 5:59	Is there among you having many *sheep*?
Alma 5:60	Bring you into the fold, and ye are his *sheep*
Alma 25:12	Even as a *sheep* having no shepherd is driven
Hel. 15:13	True shepherd, and be numbered among his *sheep*
3 Ne. 14:15	False prophets, who come unto you in *sheep's*
3 Ne. 15:17	Other *sheep* I have, which are not of this
3 Ne. 15:21	Other *sheep* I have, which are not of this
3 Ne. 16:1	I have other *sheep*, which are not of this
3 Ne. 20:16	As a young lion among the flocks of *sheep*
3 Ne. 21:12	As a young lion among the flocks of *sheep*
Ether 9:18	Also all manner of cattle . . . and of *sheep*

SHEARER

Mosiah 15:6	As a sheep before the *shearer* is dumb

SOW (Swine)

3 Ne. 7:8	Or like the *sow* to her wallowing in the mire

SWINE

3 Ne. 14:6	Neither cast ye your pearls before *swine*
Ether 9:18	Cows, and of sheep, and of *swine*, and of

ELEPHANTS

Ether 9:19	And there were *elephants* and cureloms
Ether 9:19	More especially the *elephants*, and cureloms

Evidence supporting the existence of these forms of animal life in the regions proposed by Norman and Sorenson stands at this time as follows:

Ass:	None
Bull:	None
Calf:	None
Cattle:	None
Cow:	None
Goat:	None
Horse:	None
Ox:	None
Sheep:	None
Sow:	None
Elephants:	None (contemporary with Book of Mormon)

Evidence of the foregoing animals has not appeared in any form--ceramic representations, bone or skeletal remains, mural art, sculptured art, or any other form. However, in the regions proposed by Norman and Sorenson, evidence has been found in several forms of the presence in Book-of-Mormon times of other animals--deer, jaguars, dogs, turkeys, etc. The zero score presents a problem that will not go away with the ignoring of it. Non-LDS scholars of first magnitude--some who want to be our friends--think we have real trouble here. That evidence of the ancient existence of these animals is not elusive is found in the fact that proof of their existence in the ancient Old World is abundant. The absence of such evidence in the area proposed for our consideration in this symposium is distressing and significant, in my view.

Metallurgy Test

The text of the Book of Mormon requires the finding of evidence of some or all of the following metals and metallurgical skills and products in the regions proposed as Nephite-Lamanite-Jaredite-Mulekite country:

BELLOWS

1 Ne. 17:11	I, Nephi, did make a *bellows*
1 Ne. 17:11	And after I had made a *bellows*

BRASS
Engraven on (or upon) the Plates of Brass--
1 Ne. 3:3,12,24; 4:16; 5:10; 19:22; 22:1; 2 Ne. 4:15; 5:12; Mosiah 1:3,16; 10:16; 28:11

Plates of Brass--

1 Ne. 4:24	The engravings which were upon the plates of *brass*
1 Ne. 4:38	We took the plates of *brass* . . . into the wilderness
1 Ne. 5:14	Lehi, also found upon the plates of *brass*, a
1 Ne. 5:18	These plates of *brass* should go forth
1 Ne. 5:19	These plates of *brass* should never perish
1 Ne. 13:23	Engravings which are upon the plates of *brass*
1 Ne. 19:21	They are written upon the plates of *brass*
1 Ne. 22:30	Which have been written upon the plates of *brass*

2 Ne. 4:2	And they are written upon the plates of *brass*
Omni 1:14	Sent the people of Mosiah, with the plates of *brass*
Mosiah 28:20	He took the plates of *brass*, and all the things
Alma 37:3	These plates of *brass* which contain these
3 Ne. 1:2	Concerning the plates of *brass*
3 Ne. 10:7	Are they not written upon the plates of *brass*?

Brass--

1 Ne. 16:10	And it [the ball] was of fine *brass*
1 Ne. 20:4	Thy neck was an iron sinew, and thy brow *brass*
2 Ne. 5:15	To work in all manner of . . . *brass*, and of steel
Jarom 1:8	Also in iron and copper, and *brass* and steel
Mosiah 8:10	They are of *brass* and of copper
Mosiah 11:3	And of their *brass* and their iron
Mosiah 11:8	Of silver, and of iron, and of *brass*
Mosiah 11:10	Of fine wood, and of copper, and of *brass*
3 Ne. 20:19	And I will make thy hoofs *brass*
Ether 10:23	Make gold, and silver, and iron, and *brass*

BREAST-PLATES

Mosiah 8:10	They have brought *breast-plates* which are large
Alma 43:19	Moroni had prepared his people with *breast-plates*
Alma 43:21	They were not armed with *breast-plates*
Alma 43:38	Shielded from the strokes of the Lamanites by their *breast-plates*
Alma 43:44	They did pierce many of their *breast-plates*
Alma 44:9	It is your *breast-plates* . . . that have preserved you
Alma 46:13	Fastened on his head-plate and his *breast-plates*
Alma 49:6	With shields, and with *breast-plates*
Alma 49:24	Shielded by their shields, and their *breast-plates*
Hel. 1:14	Armed them with . . . head-plates, and with *breast-plates*
Ether 15:15	Having shields, and *breast-plates*, and head-plates

CHAINS

2 Ne. 1:13	Shake off the awful *chains* by which ye are
2 Ne. 1:13	Which are the *chains* which bind the children
2 Ne. 1:23	Shake off the *chains* with which ye are bound
2 Ne. 9:45	Shake off the *chains* of him that would bind
2 Ne. 13:19	The *chains* and the bracelets, and the mufflers
2 Ne. 28:19	Will grasp them with his everlasting *chains*
2 Ne. 28:22	Until he grasps them with his awful *chains*

Alma 5:7	Bands of death, and the *chains* of hell
Alma 5:9	The *chains* of hell which encircled them
Alma 5:10	Yea, and also the *chains* of hell?
Alma 12:6	Might encircle you about with his *chains*
Alma 12:11	This is what is meant by the *chains* of hell
Alma 13:30	Ye may not be bound down by the *chains*
Alma 26:14	Loosed our brethren from the *chains* of hell
Alma 36:18	Encircled about by the everlasting *chains*

COPPER

1 Ne. 18:25	Both of gold, and of silver, and of *copper*
2 Ne. 5:15	To work in all manner of wood . . . and of *copper*
Jarom 1:8	Also in iron and *copper*, and brass and steel
Mosiah 8:10	Breast-plates . . . they are of brass and of *copper*
Mosiah 11:3	A fifth part of their ziff, and of their *copper*
Mosiah 11:8	Of brass, and of ziff, and of *copper*
Mosiah 11:10	The temple, of fine wood, and of *copper*
Ether 10:23	Mighty heaps of earth to get ore, of gold . . . and of *copper*

GOLD

1 Ne. 2:4	He left his house . . . and his *gold*, and his
1 Ne. 2:11	To leave . . . their inheritance, and their *gold*
1 Ne. 3:16	He left *gold* and silver, and all manner of
1 Ne. 3:22	We did gather together our *gold*, and our
1 Ne. 3:24	For which we would give unto him our *gold*
1 Ne. 4:9	And the hilt thereof was of pure *gold*
1 Ne. 13:7	I also saw *gold*, and silver, and silks, and
1 Ne. 13:8	Behold the *gold*, and the silver, and the silks
1 Ne. 18:25	We did find all manner of ore, both of *gold*
2 Ne. 5:15	To work in all manner of wood . . . and of *gold*
2 Ne. 12:7	Their land is also full of silver and *gold*
2 Ne. 12:20	His idols of *gold*, which he hath made
2 Ne. 23:12	Make a man more precious than fine *gold*
2 Ne. 23:17	Which shall not regard silver and *gold*
Jacob 1:16	And they also began to search much *gold*
Jacob 2:12	Many of you have begun to search for *gold*
Jarom 1:8	Became exceeding rich in *gold*, and in all
Mosiah 2:12	And have not sought *gold* nor silver
Mosiah 4:19	Raiment, and for *gold*, and for silver
Mosiah 8:9	Brought 24 plates, and they are of pure *gold*
Mosiah 11:3	A fifth part of their *gold* and of their silver
Mosiah 11:8	All manner of precious things, of *gold*
Mosiah 11:9	And was ornamented with *gold* and silver
Mosiah 11:11	Seats, he did ornament with pure *gold*
Mosiah 19:15	One half of their *gold* and their silver
Mosiah 22:12	They had taken all their *gold*, and silver
Mosiah 28:11	Records which were on the plates of *gold*

Alma 1:29	Also abundance of grain, and of *gold*
Alma 4:6	Their *gold* and their silver, and all manner
Alma 11:3	The judge received . . . a senine of *gold* for a
Alma 11:3	Senum of silver, which is equal to a senine of *gold*
Alma 11:4	Names of the different pieces of their *gold*
Alma 11:5	Thus: a senine of *gold*, a seon of *gold*
Alma 11:5	A shum of *gold*, a limnah of *gold*
Alma 11:7	A senum of silver was equal to a senine of *gold*
Alma 11:8	A seon of *gold* was twice the value of a
Alma 11:9	A shum of *gold* was twice the value of a
Alma 11:10	A limnah of *gold* was the value of them
Alma 11:19	An antion of *gold* is equal to three shiblons
Alma 15:16	Amulek having forsaken all his *gold*
Alma 17:14	Their hearts were set upon . . . *gold* and silver
Alma 31:24	He saw that their hearts were set upon *gold*
Alma 31:28	Their bracelets, and their ornaments of *gold*
Hel. 6:9	They did have an exceeding plenty of *gold*
Hel. 6:11	There was all manner of *gold* in both these
Hel. 6:31	Build up unto themselves idols of their *gold*
Hel. 7:21	And that ye might get *gold* and silver
Hel. 12:2	In the increase of their fields . . . and in *gold*
Hel. 13:28	Ye will give unto him of your *gold*
3 Ne. 6:2	Their grain of every kind, and their *gold*
3 Ne. 24:3	Sons of Levi, and purge them as *gold*
3 Ne. 27:32	They will sell me for silver, and for *gold*
4 Ne. 1:46	*Gold* and silver did they lay up in store
Ether 9:17	Of *gold* and of silver, and of precious things
Ether 10:7	His fine *gold* he did cause to be refined
Ether 10:12	Became exceeding rich . . . in *gold*, and silver
Ether 10:23	They did make *gold*, and silver, and iron
Ether 10:23	Mighty heaps of earth to get ore, of *gold*

IRON
Rod of Iron--

1 Ne. 8:19	And I beheld a rod of *iron*
1 Ne. 8:20	Path, which came along by the rod of *iron*
1 Ne. 8:24	Caught hold of the end of the rod of *iron*
1 Ne. 8:24	Mist of darkness, clinging to the rod of *iron*
1 Ne. 8:30	Caught hold of the end of the rod of *iron*
1 Ne. 8:30	Continually holding fast to the rod of *iron*
1 Ne. 11:25	I beheld that the rod of *iron* which my father
1 Ne. 15:23	What meaneth the rod of *iron* which our father

Iron--

1 Ne. 13:5	Yoketh them with a yoke of *iron*
1 Ne. 20:4	And thy neck was an *iron* sinew

2 Ne. 5:15	Work in all manner of wood, and of *iron*
2 Ne. 20:34	Cut down the thickets of the forests with *iron*
Jarom 1:8	In *iron* and copper, and brass and steel
Mosiah 11:3	A fifth part of their . . . brass and their *iron*
Mosiah 11:8	All manner of precious things . . . of *iron*
3 Ne. 20:19	Yea, I will make thy horn *iron*
Ether 10:23	They did make gold, and silver, and *iron*
Ether 10:23	Get ore of gold, and of silver, and of *iron*

[METALS]¹⁶

[Hel. 6:9	Silver, and of all manner of precious *metals*]
[Ether 10:22	Iron, and brass, and all manner of *metals*]

MOULTEN

Ether 3:1	Did *moulten* out of a rock sixteen small stones
Ether 3:3	Things which I have *moulten* out of the rock
Ether 7:9	He did *moulten* out of the hill, and made swords

ORE

1 Ne. 17:9	Whither shall I go that I may find *ore*?
1 Ne. 17:10	Told me whither I should go to find *ore*
1 Ne. 17:16	I did make tools of the *ore* which I did
1 Ne. 18:25	We did find all manner of *ore*, both of
1 Ne. 19:1	Wherefore I did make plates of *ore*
Mosiah 21:27	And they were engraven on plates of *ore*
Hel. 6:11	Of silver, and of precious *ore* of every
Hel. 6:11	Workmen, who did work all kinds of *ore*
Morm. 8:5	And *ore* I have none, for I am alone
Ether 10:23	And they did work in all manner of *ore*
Ether 10:23	Did cast up mighty heaps of earth to get *ore*

ORES

2 Ne. 5:15	Of gold and of silver, and of precious *ores*
Jacob 2:12	For silver and all manner of precious *ores*

PLOW

Ether 10:25	Both to *plow* and to sow, to reap and to

PLOW-SHARES

2 Ne. 12:4	They shall beat their swords into *plow-shares*

STEEL

1 Ne. 4:9	Blade thereof was of the most precious *steel*
1 Ne. 16:18	My bow, which was made of fine *steel*
2 Ne. 5:15	To work in all manner of wood . . . and of *steel*
Jarom 1:8	Also in iron and copper, and brass and *steel*
Ether 7:9	And made swords out of *steel* for those

SILVER

1 Ne. 2:4	Gold, and his *silver*, and his precious things
1 Ne. 2:11	Their gold, and their *silver*, and their precious
1 Ne. 3:16	He left gold and *silver*, and all manner of
1 Ne. 3:22	Gather together our gold, and our *silver*
1 Ne. 3:24	Would give unto him our gold and our *silver*
1 Ne. 13:7	I also saw gold, and *silver*, and silks and scarlets
1 Ne. 13:8	Behold the gold, and the *silver*, and the silks
1 Ne. 18:25	Ore, both of gold, and of *silver*, and of copper
2 Ne. 5:15	Gold, and of *silver*, and of precious ores
2 Ne. 12:7	Their land also is full of *silver* and gold
2 Ne. 12:20	In that day a man shall cast his idols of *silver*
2 Ne. 23:17	Against them, which shall not regard *silver*
Jacob 1:16	Also began to search much gold and *silver*
Jacob 2:12	Began to search for gold, and for *silver*
Jarom 1:8	Exceeding rich in gold, and in *silver*
Mosiah 2:12	And have not sought gold nor *silver*
Mosiah 4:19	Do we not all depend . . . for *silver*, and for
Mosiah 11:3	A fifth part of their gold and of their *silver*
Mosiah 11:8	He ornamented them with . . . *silver*
Mosiah 11:9	Was ornamented with gold and *silver*
Mosiah 19:15	One half of their gold, and their *silver*
Mosiah 22:12	They had taken all of their gold and *silver*
Alma 1:29	Abundance of grain, and of gold, and of *silver*
Alma 4:6	Their *silver*, and all manner of precious things
Alma 11:3	A senum of *silver*, which is equal to a senine
Alma 11:4	Different pieces of their gold, and of their *silver*
Alma 11:6	A senum of *silver*, an amnor of *silver*
Alma 11:6	An ezrom of *silver*, and an onti of *silver*
Alma 11:7	A senum of *silver* was equal to a senine
Alma 11:11	An amnor of *silver* was as great as two senums
Alma 11:12	An ezrom of *silver* was as great as four senums
Alma 11:22	Here is six onties of *silver*, and all these
Alma 15:16	Having forsaken all his gold, and *silver*
Alma 17:14	Their hearts were set upon . . . gold and *silver*
Alma 31:24	Hearts were set upon gold, and upon *silver*
Hel. 6:9	An exceeding plenty of gold, and of *silver*
Hel. 6:11	Of *silver*, and of precious ore of every kind
Hel. 6:31	Idols of their gold and their *silver*
Hel. 7:21	And that ye might get gold and *silver*
Hel. 12:2	In gold, and in *silver*, and in all manner
Hel. 13:28	Ye will give unto him of your . . . *silver*
3 Ne. 6:2	Their *silver*, and all their precious things
3 Ne. 24:3	He shall sit as a refiner and purifier of *silver*
3 Ne. 24:3	Sons of Levi, and purge them as gold and *silver*
3 Ne. 27:32	For they will sell me for *silver* and for gold

4 Ne. 1:46	Gold and *silver* did they lay up in store
Ether 9:17	Having all manner of . . . gold, and of *silver*
Ether 10:12	People became exceeding rich . . . in gold, and *silver*
Ether 10:23	And they did make gold, and *silver*, and iron
Ether 10:23	Mighty heaps of earth to get ore . . . of *silver*

SWORDS

Our Swords--

Alma 24:12	And our *swords* have become bright
Alma 24:12	Then let us stain our *swords* no more
Alma 24:13	I say unto you, nay, let us retain our *swords*
Alma 24:13	If we should stain our *swords* again
Alma 24:15	And our *swords* are made bright
Alma 24:15	We have not stained our *swords* in the blood
Alma 24:16	We will hide away our *swords*, yea
Alma 44:8	Otherwise we will retain our *swords*
Alma 44:9	Cunning that has preserved you from our *swords*
Alma 57:9	But we did sleep upon our *swords*
Alma 57:33	We did cause that our *swords* should come
Alma 57:33	They did in a body run upon our *swords*
Alma 61:14	Let us resist them with our *swords*
Hel. 13:34	Our *swords* are taken from us in the day

Their Swords--

2 Ne. 12:4	They shall beat their *swords* into plow-shares
Alma 17:7	Zarahemla, and took their *swords*, and their
Alma 24:17	They took their *swords*, and all the weapons
Alma 43:20	They had only their *swords* and their cimeters
Alma 43:37	Heavy blows of the Nephites with their *swords*
Alma 43:38	Then a man fell among the Nephites by their *swords*
Alma 44:17	The Lamanites did contend with their *swords*
Alma 49:20	Their most strong men, with their *swords*
Alma 52:39	Those who would not deliver up their *swords*
Alma 60:16	Instead of taking up their *swords* against us
Alma 62:5	Did take up their *swords* in the defense
Hel. 15:9	And will not lift their *swords* against them
Ether 15:20	When the night came they slept upon their *swords*
Ether 15:22	And they slept again upon their *swords*
Ether 15:24	They slept upon their *swords* that night
Ether 15:24	Contended in their mights with their *swords*

By the Sword--

1 Ne. 1:13	Many should perish by the *sword*
2 Ne. 13:25	Thy men shall fall by the *sword*
2 Ne. 23:15	Is joined to the wicked, shall fall by the *sword*
Omni 1:17	Had fallen by the *sword* from time to time

Mosiah 22:2	Deliver themselves out of bondage by the *sword*
Alma 1:9	Therefore he was slain by the *sword*
Alma 1:12	Hast endeavored to enforce it by the *sword*
Alma 2:1	The man that slew Gideon by the *sword*
Alma 10:23	Famine, and by pestilence, and by the *sword*
Alma 17:39	Had been smote off by the *sword* of Ammon
Alma 50:22	Consigned to bondage, or to perish by the *sword*
Alma 50:26	They were determined by the *sword* to slay
Alma 51:19	Dissenters who were hewn down by the *sword*
Alma 51:20	Be smitten down to the earth by the *sword*
Alma 56:51	For Antipus had fallen by the *sword*
Alma 57:23	And were not all destroyed by the *sword*
Alma 58:39	And kept them from falling by the *sword*
Alma 60:5	Yea; thousands have fallen by the *sword*
Alma 60:8	Saved thousands of them from falling by the *sword*
Alma 60:12	There are many who have fallen by the *sword*
Alma 60:22	Borders of the land, who are falling by the *sword*
Alma 60:35	Of your food, even if it must be by the *sword*
Hel. 11:4	This people shall be destroyed by the *sword*
Hel. 11:5	Work of destruction did cease by the *sword*
Morm. 6:15	Did fall by the *sword*, with their ten thousand each
Ether 13:18	Many people who were slain by the *sword*
Ether 14:4	And many thousands fell by the *sword*
Ether 14:24	That Coriantumr should not fall by the *sword*
Ether 15:2	He saw that there had been slain by the *sword*
Ether 15:23	When the night came they had all fallen by the *sword*
Ether 15:28	Coriantumr, or he would perish by the *sword*
Ether 15:29	When they had all fallen by the *sword*
Moro. 9:2	And Archeantus has fallen by the *sword*

With the Sword--

1 Ne. 12:2	Great slaughters with the *sword* among my
Omni 1:2	I fought much with the *sword* to preserve
W of M 1:13	Strength of his own arm, with the *sword* of
Alma 2:20	Slain by the hand of Nehor with the *sword*
Alma 2:29	Alma fought with Amlici with the *sword*
Alma 2:31	Insomuch that he slew Amlici with the *sword*
Alma 3:2	And children had been slain with the *sword*
Alma 6:7	Slain by the hand of Nehor with the *sword*
Alma 18:16	Brethren with the sling and with the *sword*
Alma 19:22	Brother had been slain with the *sword* of
Alma 20:14	That he should slay Ammon with the *sword*
Alma 24:21	And began to slay Ammon with the *sword*
Alma 58:18	Were about to fall upon us with the *sword*
Alma 60:17	They are murdering our people with the *sword*
Alma 60:30	Zarahemla, and smite you with the *sword*
Hel. 1:23	And cut his way through with the *sword*

Hel. 10:18	And began to slay one another with the *sword*
Hel. 13:9	Yea, I will visit them with the *sword*
3 Ne. 3:6	That they should visit you with the *sword*
Morm. 2:14	Would struggle with the *sword* for their lives
Morm. 6:9	They did fall upon my people with the *sword*
Ether 15:29	And they fought again with the *sword*

His Sword--

1 Ne. 4:9	I beheld his *sword*, and I drew it forth
1 Ne. 4:18	I smote off his head with his own *sword*
1 Ne. 4:19	Smitten off his head with his own *sword*
Mosiah 19:4	He drew his *sword*, and swore in his wrath
Alma 1:9	He was wroth with Gideon and drew his *sword*
Alma 17:37	He smote off their arms with his *sword*
Alma 17:37	Smiting their arms with the edge of his *sword*
Alma 17:38	Save it were their leader, with his *sword*
Alma 19:22	Angry with Ammon, drew his *sword*, and
Alma 20:16	He drew his *sword* that he might smite him
Alma 20:22	But Ammon raised his *sword*, and said
Alma 44:8	He came forth and delivered up his *sword*
Alma 44:12	Zarahemnah retained his *sword*, and he was
Alma 44:12	Slay Moroni, but as he raised his *sword*
Alma 44:13	And laid it upon the point of his *sword*
Ether 9:27	Father; for he slew him with his own *sword*
Ether 14:1	If a man should lay his tool or his *sword*
Ether 14:2	Every man kept the hilt of his *sword* there
Ether 15:5	That he might slay him with his own *sword*
Ether 15:30	When Coriantumr had leaned upon his *sword*

By the Sword--

1 Ne. 1:13	Many should perish by the *sword*
2 Ne 13:25	Thy men shall fall by the *sword*
2 Ne. 23:15	Is joined to the wicked, shall fall by the *sword*
Omni 1:17	Had fallen by the *sword* from time to time
Mosiah 22:2	Deliver themselves out of bondage by the *sword*

Swords--

2 Ne. 5:14	After the manner of it did make many *swords*
Mosiah 8:11	They have brought *swords*, the hilts thereof
Mosiah 9:16	I did arm them with bows . . . with *swords*
Mosiah 10:8	Men armed with bows . . . and with *swords*
Alma 2:12	They did arm themselves with *swords*, and
Alma 43:18	And his people were armed with *swords*
Alma 44:18	Were exposed to the sharp *swords* of the Nephites
Alma 44:18	Fall exceeding fast before the *swords* of the
Alma 60:2	Arm them with *swords*, and with cimeters
Hel. 1:14	Armed them with *swords*, and with cimeters
Ether 7:9	Made *swords* out of steel for those whom he

Ether 7:9   And after he had armed them with *swords*

HILT

1 Ne. 4:9   And the *hilt* thereof was of pure gold
Alma 44:12   Soldiers smote it . . . and it broke by the *hilt*
Ether 14:2   Every man kept the *hilt* of his sword

HILTS

Mosiah 8:11   Swords, the *hilts* thereof have perished

TOOL

Hel. 13:34   We lay a *tool* here, and on the morrow
Ether 14:1   If a man should lay his *tool* or his sword

TOOLS

1 Ne. 17:9   That I may make *tools* to construct the
1 Ne. 17:10   I should go to find ore, that I might make *tools*
1 Ne. 17:16   I did make *tools* of the ore which I did
Jarom 1:8   *Tools* of every kind to till the ground
Ether 10:25   All manner of *tools* to till the earth
Ether 10:26   All manner of *tools* with which they did

ENGRAVE

Morm. 1:4   Ye shall *engrave* on the plates of Nephi, all

ENGRAVED

2 Ne. 5:32   I have *engraved* that which is pleasing

ENGRAVEN

Engraven on (or upon) the Plates of Brass
1 Ne. 3:3,12,24; 4:16; 5:10; 19:22; 22:1; 2 Ne. 4:15; 5:12; Mosiah 1:3,16;
10:16; 28:11

Engraven--
1 Ne. 9:3   An account *engraven* of the ministry of my people
1 Ne. 9:4   Upon the other plates should be *engraven* an
1 Ne. 19:1   I might *engraven* upon them the record of my
1 Ne. 19:1   I did *engraven* the record of my father
1 Ne. 19:1   Mine own prophecies have I *engraven* upon
1 Ne. 19:2   Proceedings in the wilderness are *engraven*
2 Ne. 5:30   Thou shall *engraven* many things upon them
2 Ne. 5:31   Upon which I have *engraven* these things
Jacob 1:1   Plates, upon which these things are *engraven*
Jacob 1:3   Should be *engraven* upon his other plates
Jacob 1:4   *Engraven* the heads of them upon these plates
Jacob 4:3   We labor diligently to *engraven* these words
Jarom 1:14   Upon them the record of our wars are *engraven*
Omni 1:11   The record of this people is *engraven* upon

Mosiah 21:27	And they were *engraven* on plates of ore
Alma 5:19	Having the image of God *engraven* upon your
3 Ne. 5:10	Record of Nephi, which was *engraven* on the plates
3 Ne. 26:11	All which were *engraven* on the Plates of Nephi

ENGRAVING

| Jacob 4:1 | Because of the difficulty of *engraving* our words |

ENGRAVINGS

1 Ne. 4:24	That I should carry the *engravings*
1 Ne. 13:23	A record like unto the *engravings* which are
2 Ne. 5:32	They will be pleased with mine *engravings*
Omni 1:20	Large stone brought unto him with *engravings*
Omni 1:20	He did interpret the *engravings* by the gift
Mosiah 1:4	Therefore he could read these *engravings*
Mosiah 8:9	Brought twenty-four plates which were filled with *engravings*
Mosiah 8:11	Or the *engravings* that are on the plates
Mosiah 21:28	Whereby he could interpret such *engravings*
Alma 37:3	Plates of brass which contain these *engravings*
Alma 63:12	*Engravings* which were in the possession of Helaman
Morm. 1:3	Deposited unto the Lord all the sacred *engravings*

Evidence supporting the existence of these metals, skills, and products in the regions proposed by Norman and Sorenson stands at this time as follows:

Bellows:	None
Brass:	None
Breast-plates:	None
Chains:	None
Copper:	None
Gold:	None
Iron:	None
Ore (mining):	None
Plow-shares:	None
Silver:	None
Swords (metal):	None
Hilts (metal):	None
Engraving:	None
Steel:	None

Metallurgy does not appear in the region under discussion until about the ninth century A.D. None of the foregoing technical demands are met by the archaeology of the region proposed as Book of Mormon lands and places. I regard this as a major weakness in the armor of our proponents and friends. (It is just as troublesome to the authors of the other correlations--those [who] have gone before--including Tom Ferguson.)[17]

I doubt that the proponents will be very convincing, if they contend that evidence of metallurgy is difficult to find and a rarity in archaeology. Where mining was practiced--as in the Old Testament world--mountains of ore and tailings have been found. Artifacts of metal have been found. Art portrays the existence of metallurgical products. Again, the score is zero. In view of the magnitude of metallurgical skills and usage in the Book of Mormon, as indicated in the citations, plenty of evidence should have turned up by now in the regions pointed to in the primary papers of this symposium, if our friends have things pinpointed.

In his newsletter, *The Interamerican*, dated January-February 1975, Carl B. Compton reports this interesting information:

> A British-backed archaeological expedition has found and excavated in the Negev Desert of Israel the oldest known underground mines. These were copper mines so enormous and sophisticated that a team of three mining engineers had to be recruited to aid [in] the excavations. The mines comprise a network of 200 shafts and galleries penetrating the white sandstone for hundreds of yards in all directions and on several levels. Each shaft has its own air shafts, permitting the use of miner's lanterns. They date from ca. 1400 B.C. The site is located near Eilat in the Timna Valley (*London Times*, 8 December 1974).

Script Test

The text of the Book of Mormon requires the finding of some or all of the following scripts in the regions proposed as Jaredite-Nephite country: *Cuneiform* (only script used in Tower of Babel times and land--oldest and first script in the world--only one in use in Tigris-Euphrates Valley from its invention about

3500 B.C. down to 600 B.C.) for the Jaredites; *Hebrew* and *Egyptian* for the Nephites.

EGYPTIAN--Reformed

The name given to the style of characters in use in the days of Mormon in which the records were engraven on the sacred plates. These characters were greatly modified from those used by Nephi and the other earlier recorders.

Morm. 9:32   Which are called among us the reformed *Egyptian*

EGYPTIANS--The people of Egypt.

1 Ne. 1:2	Learning of the Jews, and the language of the *Egyptians*
1 Ne. 4:3	And to destroy Laban, even as the *Egyptians*
1 Ne. 17:23	Led away out of the hands of the *Egyptians*
1 Ne. 17:27	We know that the *Egyptians* were drowned in
Mosiah 1:4	He having been taught in the language of the *Egyptians*
Alma 29:12	Who delivered them out of the hands of the *Egyptians*
Alma 36:28	He has swallowed up the *Egyptians* in the Red
Hel. 8:11	The waters closed upon the armies of the *Egyptians*

HEBREW--The language of the people of Israel

Morm. 9:33	We should have written in *Hebrew*
Morm. 9:33	But the *Hebrew* hath been altered by us also
Morm. 9:33	And if we could have written in *Hebrew*

WRITING

1 Ne. 6:1	Upon these plates which I am *writing*
1 Ne. 8:30	But to be short in *writing*, behold, he saw
1 Ne. 16:29	Was also written upon them, a new *writing*
2 Ne. 3:17	I will give judgment unto him in *writing*
2 Ne. 3:18	He shall write the *writing* of the fruit of
2 Ne. 33:1	Neither am I mighty in *writing*
Jacob 7:27	And I make an end of my *writing*
Jacob 7:27	Which *writing* has been small
Alma 10:2	*Writing* which was upon the wall of the temple
Alma 46:19	That all might see the *writing* which he had
3 Ne. 12:31	Let him give her a *writing* of divorcement
Ether 12:23	Because of our weakness in *writing*
Ether 12:23	Thou hast not made us mighty in *writing*
Ether 12:24	Thou hast not made us mighty in *writing*
Ether 12:40	Because of my weakness in *writing*

Ether 13:1   The people of whom I have been *writing*

WRITINGS

Jarom 1:14   According to the *writings* of the kings

WRITE
I *write*--see *I* write.
Write them, etc.--see Write *them*--unto *you*
Cannot Write--

1 Ne. 17:6   So much that we cannot *write* them all
2 Ne. 31:1   And I cannot *write* but a few things
2 Ne. 33:1   I, Nephi, cannot *write* all the things which
Jacob 4:1   And I cannot *write* but a little of my words
W of M 1:5   I cannot *write* the hundredth part of the
Morm. 8:23   Prophecies of Isaiah. Behold I cannot *write* them
Ether 12:23   Great, even that we cannot *write* them

Not Write--

1 Ne. 6:1   Wherefore I do not *write* it in this work
1 Ne. 6:5   Pleasing unto the world, I do not *write*

[Be Written--][18]
2 Ne. 30:3   Come forth, and be *written* unto the Gentiles
Jarom 1:14   Or those which they caused to be *written*
Mosiah 2:8   The words which he spake, should be *written*
Mosiah 2:9   Which he spake and caused to be *written*
Mosiah 28:11 And caused to be *written* the records which
3 Ne. 17:17   Neither can there be *written* by any man
3 Ne. 19:32   Neither can be *written* by man the words
3 Ne. 23:13   Jesus commanded that it should be *written*
3 Ne. 26:18   Things, which are not lawful to be *written*
Ether 4:16   Caused to be *written* by my servant John
Moro. 9:19   Tongue cannot tell, neither can it be *written*

Been Written--
1 Ne. 22:30   Have been *written* upon the plates of brass
Omni 1:11   No revelation, save that which has been *written*
Alma 33:12   Scriptures which have been *written* by them
3 Ne. 12:33   It hath been *written*, that whosoever shall
3 Ne. 23:12   Remembered that this thing had not been *written*
3 Ne. 27:24   Which shall be, even as hath been *written*
3 Ne. 27:25   Out of the books which have been *written*

I Have Written--
1 Ne. 10:15   For I have *written* as many of them as
1 Ne. 14:28   Things which I have *written* sufficeth me
1 Ne. 14:30   The things which I have *written* are true

1 Ne. 19:18	I, Nephi, have *written* these things unto my people
2 Ne. 8:7	In whose heart I have *written* my law
2 Ne. 11:1	Things which I have *written* sufficeth me
2 Ne. 25:1	Concerning the words which I have *written*
2 Ne. 31:2	Wherefore, the things which I have *written*
2 Ne. 33:3	But I, Nephi, have *written* what I have *written*
2 Ne. 33:4	The words which I have *written* in weakness
2 Ne. 33:5	Be angry at the words which I have *written*
Jacob 7:26	Declaring that I have *written* according to
W of M 1:3	Concerning that which I have *written*
Alma 11:46	Or this is all that I have *written*
Alma 54:5	Ammoron, I have *written* unto you somewhat
Hel. 2:14	All the account which I have *written*
3 Ne. 26:8	I have *written* them to the intent that they
Ether 4:4	I have *written* upon these plates the very things
Ether 4:5	And I have *written* them
Ether 5:1	I, Moroni, have *written* the words which we
Moro. 8:6	For this intent I have *written* this epistle
Moro. 9:25	The things which I have *written* grieve thee
Moro. 10:29	That which I have *written* is true

Have Written--

1 Ne. 14:26	Shown all things, and they have *written* them
Jacob 7:11	That none of the prophets have *written*
Jarom 1:2	Write more than my father have *written*?
Morm. 9:31	Neither them who have *written* before him
Morm. 9:32	We have *written* this record according to
Morm. 9:33	Large, we should have *written* in Hebrew
Morm. 9:33	And if we could have *written* in Hebrew
Morm. 9:34	Lord knoweth the things which we have *written*
Ether 2:12	Manifested by the things which we have *written*
Ether 12:41	Jesus of whom the prophets . . . have *written*
Moro. 1:1	I had supposed not to have *written* more
Moro. 1:4	I had supposed not to have *written* any

Is Written--

2 Ne. 2:17	An angel . . . according to that which is *written*
2 Ne. 5:12	According to that which is *written*
2 Ne. 14:3	Every one that is *written* among the living
2 Ne. 29:11	Their works, according to that which is *written*
Omni 1:11	That which is sufficient is *written*
W of M 1:11	According to the word of God which is *written*
Alma 6:8	And thus it is *written*. Amen
3 Ne. 12:21	It is also *written* before you, that thou shalt

3 Ne. 12:27	It is *written* by them of old time, that thou
3 Ne. 12:33	It is *written*, thou shalt not forswear thyself
3 Ne. 12:38	It is *written*, an eye for an eye, and a tooth
3 Ne. 12:43	It is *written* also, that thou shalt love
3 Ne. 20:36	Be brought to pass that which is *written*
3 Ne. 22:1	Then shall that which is *written* come to pass

Not Written--

1 Ne. 14:28	I have not *written* but a small part of the
1 Ne. 14:30	If all the things which I saw are not *written*
Mosiah 1:8	More things . . . which are not *written* in this
Mosiah 13:11	I perceive they are not *written* in your heart
Alma 13:31	More words . . . which are not *written* in this
Alma 33:15	It is not *written* that Zenos alone spake
Hel. 5:13	Many things which are not *written*
3 Ne. 7:17	Therefore they are not *written* in this book
3 Ne. 10:17	Are they not *written* upon the plates of brass
3 Ne. 23:11	How be it that ye have not *written* this thing
Ether 15:33	(And the hundredth part I have not *written*)

Which Were Written--

1 Ne. 14:23	The things which were *written* were plain
1 Ne. 16:27	The things which were *written* upon the ball
1 Ne. 19:3	The things which were *written* should be kept
1 Ne. 19:23	Which were *written* in the book of Moses
1 Ne. 19:24	Which were *written* unto all the house of Israel
Jacob 2:23	Because of the things which were *written* concerning David
3 Ne. 3:1	And these were the words which were *written*
Moro. 10:27	Words . . . which were *written* by this man

Were Written--

Mosiah 29:4	These were the words that were *written*
Alma 63:12	All those engravings . . . were *written*
3 Ne. 24:1	After they were *written* he expounded them

Written--

1 Ne. 1:16	Of the things which my father hath *written*
1 Ne. 1:16	For he hath *written* many things which he
1 Ne. 1:16	He also hath *written* many things which he
1 Ne. 16:29	There was also *written* upon them, a new
1 Ne. 16:29	It was *written* and changed from time to time
1 Ne. 19:23	Which was *written* by the prophet Isaiah
1 Ne. 19:24	For after this manner has the prophet *written*
2 Ne. 6:12	Gentiles, they of whom the prophet has *written*
2 Ne. 6:12	For this cause the prophet has *written* these

2 Ne. 25:8	Wherefore, for their good have I *written* them
Jacob 4:4	For this intent have we *written* these things
W of M 1:11	For there are great things *written* upon them
Mosiah 5:12	Retain the name always *written* in your hearts
Mosiah 8:1	Only a few of them have I *written* in this
Mosiah 29:4	Even a *written* word sent he among the people
Alma 9:34	The words of Amulek are not all *written*
Alma 10:2	Which was *written* by the finger of God
Alma 44:24	Record of Alma, which was *written* upon the
Alma 61:8	He hath *written* unto the king of the Lamanites
Hel. 5:6	It is said, and also *written*, that they were
Hel. 5:7	That it may be said of you, and also *written*
Hel. 5:7	Even as it has been said and *written* of them
3 Ne. 11:15	It was he, of whom it was *written* by the prophets
3 Ne. 23:13	Therefore it was *written* according as he commanded
3 Ne. 23:14	All the scriptures in one, which they had written
3 Ne. 24:16	A book of remembrance was *written* before
3 Ne. 26:8	These things have I *written*, which are a lesser
4 Ne. 1:21	And it was also *written* in the book of Nephi
Morm. 7:9	This is *written* for the intent that ye may
Morm. 8:5	And he hath *written* the intent thereof
Ether 12:40	Only a few have I *written*, because of my weakness
Moro. 8:1	Epistle of my father Mormon, *written*
Moro. 8:1	It was *written* unto me soon after my calling

WROTE

1 Ne. 1:Hd	Or in other words, I, Nephi, *wrote* this record
2 Ne. 4:2	The prophecies which he *wrote*, there are
Omni 1:9	I saw the last which he *wrote*
Omni 1:9	That he *wrote* it with his own hand
Omni 1:9	He *wrote* it in the day that he delivered
Mosiah 26:33	He *wrote* them down that he might have them
Alma 30:51	Put forth his hand and *wrote* unto Korihor
Alma 30:52	Korihor put forth his hand and *wrote*
Alma 46:12	*Wrote* upon it, in memory of our God
Alma 46:19	Might see the writing which he had *wrote*
Alma 54:4	Therefore he *wrote* an epistle, and sent it
Alma 54:4	These are the words which he *wrote* unto

Evidence supporting the existence of these forms of writing--these scripts--in the regions proposed by Norman and Sorenson stands at this time as follows:

Cuneiform: None

Hebrew: For very exciting, but meager, script data just

now (March 6, 1975) received, see the letter . . . from Professor George F. Carter, formerly of Johns Hopkins University and now of Texas A&M University. A seal found at Tlatilco (suburb of Mexico City) bears the Hebrew name, *Hiram*, apparently in Egyptian script! Carter's reference to other Old-World scripts-- Iberic, Carthaginian, and Libyan--found on the Atlantic coast of North America--are exciting. However, they don't help the Book of Mormon script test, which deals exclusively with Cuneiform, Hebrew, and Egyptian, to be found in the Norman-Sorenson designated territory. Proof of a voyage from Libya doesn't prove the Lehi voyage from Arabia--but it could relate to or even be the Mulek voyage! A cylinder seal found at Tlatilco, Mexico, bearing a Hebrew name, *Hiram*! Wow!

Egyptian: Three glyphs on a three-inch cylinder seal, found at Chiapa de Corzo, State of Chiapas, Mexico, by the New World Archaeological Foundation. Identified as Egyptian by only one great scholar, William Foxwell Albright (now deceased). Identification seriously questioned by other great scholars-- because of the limited number of glyphs in the find. (Probably the biggest strike so far in support of our proponents--and the *only one* in this technical and demanding testing of their hypotheses.) When both proponents call upon the findings of archaeology for support--with frequent references to cultures falling within the timespan of the Book of Mormon ("Pre-Classic," "Early Classic")--it seems strange that they each failed to mention the glyphs found at Chiapa de Corzo. Perhaps each is himself not convinced that the glyphs are truly Egyptian--because of the limited number found.

It is my opinion that the script test is the most exacting and definitive and precise of all. It is good that we have the two little pieces of baked clay--on this test--the seal from Chiapa de Corzo and the seal from Tlatilco. In my opinion, they lend more support to Sorenson and Norman than all of the configuration-dimension-direction-topography writing done by these two good men and all of the rest of us put together. The references from the text of the Book of Mormon (and I have only included a portion of the many having to do with the literacy of the Jaredites and Nephites) tells us that both peoples were highly literate and on a par with the ancient Sumerians of the Babel region and the Hebrews of ancient Israel. The Sumerians left literally tons of written clay tablets. In Israel have been found the wonderful Lachish letters in early Hebrew, dating to 600 B.C., written in a fortress about thirty miles from Jerusalem--while the conquering Babylonian army was approaching the fortress. If our good friend, Garth Norman, had something like the Lachish letters to identify the Tower of Sherrizah with the Oaxaca site, Giengola, we'd be thrilled for two reasons--the tough script test would have been passed with flying colors by the hypotheses of the proponents, but we would all have our very first Book-of-Mormon place identified. And what a starting point that would be.

My friend, Howard Leigh, at the Mitla Museum in Oaxaca told me that Giengola is a very late site and that it does not fall within several hundred years of our Book of Mormon time span. He probably knows as much about the site as anyone alive. There are many hilltop fortresses dating to ancient times in Mexico. It takes a lot more than configuration-dimensions-directions-topography to prove and establish factually the identity of a particular point of terrain or topography as Sherrizah or as any other specific Book-of-Mormon place. The real and honest-to-goodness ground rules are pretty well laid down by the citations being set forth from the Book of Mormon itself--right here in this simple paper. (Certainly before Bible-world scholars make positive identifications of biblical places, they are careful to meet exacting requirements such as I am proposing here. No less is required of Book-of-Mormon-world students.)

Additional Tests--Wheels, Carriages, Carts, Chariots, and Glass

The text of the Book of Mormon requires the finding of the following:

WHEELS

2 Ne. 15:28   And their *wheels* lie a whirlwind

CARRIAGES

2 Ne. 20:28   At Michmash he hath laid up his *carriages*[19]

CART

2 Ne 15:18   And sin as it were with a *cart* rope

CHARIOTS

2 Ne. 12:7   Neither is there any end of their *chariots*
Alma 18:9   They should prepare his horses and *chariots*
Alma 18:10   Was preparing his horses and his *chariots*
Alma 18:12   Had made ready the horses and the *chariots*
Alma 20:6   Make ready his horses, and his *chariots*
3 Ne. 3:22   Taken their horses, and their *chariots*
3 Ne. 21:14   And I will destroy thy *chariots*

GLASS

Ether 3:1   White and clear, even as transparent *glass*

GLASSES

2 Ne. 13:23   The *glasses*,[20] and the fine linen, and hoods

Evidence supporting the existence of these cultural elements in the regions proposed by Norman and Sorenson stands at this time as follows:

Wheels: Toys with wheels, in ceramic form, are found.
Carriages: None
Carts: None
Chariots: None
Glass: None

The ceramic toys constitute the only evidence of the wheel in ancient times for the areas designated by the proponents. The great murals of Bonampak and of Teotihuacan contain no picture of carts or chariots. The innumerable stone sculptured monuments, portraying much of the ancient way of life--including sedan chairs--give us no representation of carts or chariots. None have been found portrayed in ceramics. A visit to the Cairo Museum, to the University of Pennsylvania Museum, to the Oriental Institute of the University of Chicago, [and] to the Field Museum in Chicago reveals to visitors undisputed and powerful evidence supporting the existence of wheels (utilitarian), carts, chariot[s], and works in glass (great numbers of glass vases and dishes survive, for example from ancient Egypt) from areas referenced in the Bible. Complete chariots of wood and iron have turned up in tombs at various points in the ancient Middle East.

To my knowledge no pre-Columbian glass has been found in the regions pointed to by Norman and Sorenson. The wheeled toys and the three glyphs from Chiapa de Corzo don't give our friends much of a total score for their geographical selections.

Conclusion

The evidence supporting the geographical views of Norman and Sorenson, under the exacting tests laid down by the text of the Book of Mormon, is indeed very meager. We have the cylinder seal from Chiapa de Corzo, the cylinder seal from Tlatilco and the toys with wheels. That's about all. This paucity of specific support presents, at least to me, a dilemma. One way out of the dilemma is to say that everything was scrambled and lost because of the upheavals described in 3 Nephi for the time of the crucifixion. In my personal opinion, this is not a satisfactory escape hatch. Virtually all of the data in the Book of Mormon must be credited to Mormon and his abridgment of the "larger plates." He and Moroni, writing in the fourth century (over 300 years after the crucifixion), were responsible for the last 400 pages of the text. And it is in those 400 pages that most of the geographical data appear. Mormon doesn't say that his references to geography are useless and hopeless.

Further, innumerable excavations made in the area we are dealing with, and in the time span (3000 B.C.--400 A.D.) with which we are involved, reveal great undisturbed architectural structures, extensive relatively undisturbed ancient strata, etc., etc.--right through the time of the crucifixion.

I don't have the answer to the dilemma. I just call it up.

I'm afraid that up to this point, I must agree with Dee Green, who has told us that to date there is no Book-of-Mormon geography. I, for one, would be happy if Dee were wrong.

> Respectfully submitted,
> [signed] Thomas Stuart Ferguson
> Thomas Stuart Ferguson
> 1 Irving Lane
> Orinda, California 94563

3-12-75
[12 March 1975]

Notes

1. The text is copied from "Written Symposium on Book of Mormon Geography: Response of Thomas S. Ferguson to the Norman and Sorenson Papers," 12 March 1975, in the Thomas Stuart Ferguson Collection, Accession 1350, Manuscripts Division, J. Willard Marriott Library, University of Utah, Salt Lake City. This document was first published in Jerald Tanner and Sandra Tanner, eds., *Ferguson's Manuscript Unveiled* (Salt Lake City: Utah Lighthouse Ministry, 1988).

2. See John L. Sorenson, *The Geography of Book of Mormon Events: A Source Book*, rev. ed. (Provo, UT: Foundation for Ancient Research and Mormon Studies, 1992), 221-22.

3. Norman C. Pierce, *Another Cumorah, Another Joseph* (Salt Lake City, 1954).

4. Jean R. Driggs, *The Palestine of America* (Salt Lake City, 1928).

5. Janne M. Sjodahl, *An Introduction to the Study of the Book of Mormon* (Salt Lake City: Deseret News Press, 1927).

6. Joel Ricks, *Book of Mormon Geography* (Logan, Utah, 1940).

7. See Charles Stuart Bagley, "A Textual Geography of the Book of Mormon" and "The Limhi Expedition," in the Charles Stuart Bagley Collection, Accession 1470, Manuscripts Division, J. Willard Marriott Library, University of Utah, Salt Lake City.

8. J. A. Washburn and J. Nile Washburn, *An Approach to the Study of Book of Mormon Geography* (Provo, UT: New Era Publishing, 1939).

9. Fletcher B. Hammond, *Geography of the Book of Mormon* (Salt Lake City: Utah Printing Co., 1959).

10. M. Wells Jakeman, "The Book-of-Mormon Civilizations: Their Origin and Their Development in Space and Time," in *Progress in Archaeology: An Anthology*, ed. Ross T. Christensen (Provo, UT: The University Archaeological Society, Brigham Young University, 1963), 81-88.

11. Riley L. Dixon, *Just One Cumorah* (Salt Lake City: Bookcraft, 1958).

12. E. Cecil McGavin and Willard W. Bean, *The Geography of the Book of Mormon* (Salt Lake City: Bookcraft, 1948).

13. Throughout this "Written Symposium on Book of Mormon Geography" Ferguson quoted the list of passages from George Reynolds, *A Concordance of the Book of Mormon* (Salt Lake City, 1900), though the one-letter abbreviations used by Reynolds have here been expanded to the intended words (e.g., "b." at Mosiah 7:22 appears here as "barley"). Reynolds painstakingly compiled this concordance during 1880 and early 1881, while he was imprisoned in Salt Lake City for Mormon polygamy. See the author's *Prisoner for Polygamy: The Memoirs and Letters of Rudger Clawson at the Utah Territorial Penitentiary, 1884-87* (Urbana and Chicago: University of Illinois Press, 1993), 3, 27, 226.

14. The term "lesser cattle" is found only here in the Book of Mormon and is a quotation from Isa. 7:25. In the King James Version this two-word term translates the Hebrew word *seh*, which means a lamb or kid, i.e., the young of either sheep or goat. See Ludwig Koehler and Walter Baumgartner, *Hebräisches und aramäisches Lexikon zum Alten Testament*, ed. Johann J. Stamm, 3d ed. (Leiden: E. J. Brill, 1990), 4:1222.

15. At this point the words "Thy fault, saying, Behold *h.* is money" from Hel. 9:20 are printed in Reynolds's *Concordance*. Reynolds misplaced this line, since the *h.* refers to "here" not "herds," and this entry has accordingly been removed from Ferguson's list.

16. At this point Ferguson should have inserted the two occurrences of the word "metals." These are here added within square brackets.

17. In this parenthetical sentence Ferguson referred to himself in the third person.

18. At this point Ferguson accidentally omitted one page containing 150 scriptural passages from Reynolds's *Concordance*. These include the entries from 1 Ne. 10:15 in the subheading "Not Write" through 2 Ne. 29:10 in "Be Written."

19. The Hebrew word *keli*, which is translated as "carriages" in this quotation from Isa. 10:28, refers to "loads" not "wheeled vehicles." Accordingly, this passage should be ignored.

20. The meaning of the Hebrew word *gillāyôn*, which is translated as "glasses" in this quotation from Isa. 3:23, is unknown, but it is usually rendered as either "a hand-mirror" (i.e., a looking glass) or "a gauze robe," and not objects made of glass. Accordingly, this passage should be ignored.

Appendix B

Examining the Authorship of *The Messiah in Ancient America*

Since the title page of this 1987 book lists both Bruce W. Warren and Thomas Stuart Ferguson as authors, one must examine this posthumous attribution of coauthorship.[1] First of all, in what sense are the two individuals listed on the title page really "authors" of the book? Warren in the preface described how in the spring of 1983 Larry S. Ferguson asked him to finish the revision that his father had started of *One Fold and One Shepherd*.[2] What evidence exists that Ferguson had revised this book, and more importantly what direction did this revision take? How substantial and complete was the Ferguson manuscript of revision which Warren was asked to finish? Warren also stated that "the Ferguson family wanted the new book to be a tribute to Thomas Stuart Ferguson and his abiding testimony of the Book of Mormon and the divinity of the Messiah, Jesus the Christ."[3] Since the clear evidence in Ferguson's letters written during the last thirteen years of his life indicates that he denied the historicity of the Book of Mormon and the divinity of Jesus, it seems deceptive for Warren to speak of Ferguson's "abiding" testimony.

Paul R. Cheesman, emeritus professor of religious instruction at Brigham Young University, in the foreword to the book stated that due to the additions of Bruce W. Warren the book "should reinstate Thomas Stuart Ferguson as a source of enrichment in the fields of study concerning Mesoamerica and the Book of Mormon."[4] Why would the "additions" of one person improve one's opinion of the other? Why, indeed, does Ferguson need to be "reinstated"? Thus, the title page, the preface, and the foreword of *The Messiah in Ancient America* generate perplexing questions about exactly what, if any, was the involvement of Thomas Stuart Ferguson in the production of this book.

Bruce W. Warren, who has good academic qualifications with a Ph.D. in anthropology from the University of Arizona, should know the established conventions of scholarship in using another's words. For what one finds is that page after page of verbatim extracts from *One Fold and One Shepherd* are contained in *The Messiah in Ancient America*. Sometimes meaningless statements in the latter can be explicated by reference to the original wording in the former. For example, it is difficult to visualize what might be intended by Warren's statement that in Mexican cosmogony the end of the world's third age "is placed at the very top of the crucifixion of Christ,"[5] but the word "top" is an error produced when the words "at the very *time* of the crucifixion" were miscopied from *One Fold and One Shepherd*.[6] Another example is the unclear statement that "the glyph or day-sign for *Itzamna* was a benevolent deity, always the friend of man."[7] In this case Warren, while copying from Ferguson's *One Fold and One Shepherd*, accidentally skipped down one line into the next sentence at the word "Itzamná," omitting the intervening words shown in the following italics: "the glyph or day-sign for *Itzamna means 'king, emperor, monarch, prince, or great lord.'* Itzamna was a benevolent deity, always the friend of man."[8]

One Fold and One Shepherd is not merely reprinted in *The Messiah in Ancient America*. There are many parts rewritten and numerous sections of additions in the latter book. Is there any evidence that Ferguson worked on the new material? Warren

often employed the plural pronoun "we," hinting at joint authorship in writing portions of *The Messiah in Ancient America*. However, careful analysis sometimes delimits the reference to only
Warren or Ferguson, but not both. In a section discussing
volcanism in Mesoamerica, one finds the use of "we" in such
clauses as: "we have mentioned to this point only . . . ," "we think
it is well to remember that . . . ," and "we think we must also be
cautious about. . . ." This usage of the plural pronoun implies the
united voice of two authors, but Warren alone wrote the nine-
page section on the "Destructions in Mesoamerica at the Time of
the Crucifixion."[9] In another instance Ferguson published in *One
Fold and One Shepherd* in 1958 the statement that Floyd Carnaby
had brought to his attention a sculptured monument of the goddess Chicomecoatl with a seven-headed serpent as her head.[10]
Warren rewrote this episode by saying that this representation
"was called to our attention" by Carnaby, thus anachronistically
including Warren himself in a pre-1958 conversation between
Ferguson and Carnaby.[11] When questioned, Warren admitted
that he never met Carnaby.

Bruce W. Warren closed the first appendix of *The Messiah
in Ancient America* "with his [Ferguson's] testimony of the Book
of Mormon," which reportedly was placed during 1982 with a
photo inside copies of the Book of Mormon given to non-
Mormons. Warren then quoted the following testimony:

> We have studied the Book of Mormon for 50 years. We
> can tell you that it follows only the New Testament as a
> written witness to the mission, divinity, and resurrection
> of Jesus Christ. And it seems to us that there is no
> message that is needed by man and mankind more than
> the message of Christ. Millions of people have come to
> accept Jesus as the Messiah because of reading the Book of
> Mormon in a quest for truth. The book is the cornerstone
> of the Mormon Church.
>   The greatest witness to the truthfulness of the Book
> of Mormon is the book itself. But many are the external
> evidences that support it.[12]

What Warren did not mention to the reader is that this testimonial is typed, includes a photograph of Ferguson and his wife Ester along with their names and Orinda address, and speaks as "we," thus suggesting that it was part of the family-to-family Book of Mormon program. This testimonial reflects Ferguson's long-standing conviction of the value of the gospel of Jesus Christ for world peace. It is a positive statement for a good cause, neatly avoiding any controversial problems concerning the Book of Mormon. As we have seen, on the one hand Ferguson continued to describe the Book of Mormon to faithful Mormons as a testimony of Jesus Christ, while on the other hand Ferguson denied the historicity of the Book of Mormon in discussions with, and letters to, skeptical Mormons. So, however much weight this joint statement is given, it must be balanced with the later evidence of Ferguson's discussions with Pierre Agrinier Bach and Ronald O. Barney, as well as his final two letters--all of which occurred in 1983 before his death.

At least from the Spring of 1975 Warren was aware of Ferguson's radical views concerning the Book of Mormon, since they were both involved in the symposium concerning Book of Mormon geography, and Warren received a copy of Ferguson's controversial study. However, Warren did not utilize in *The Messiah in Ancient America* any of Ferguson's liberal analysis of Book of Mormon plants, animals, metallurgy, and scripts. In fact, Ferguson's 1975 study is never referred to in Warren's book --neither in the text nor in the bibliography.

Warren admitted that his total association with Ferguson during the last thirteen years of his life consisted of a five-minute conversation in 1979--and even this short contact was simply a friendly reminiscence and not dialogue concerning a revision of *One Fold and One Shepherd*.[13] At the time of his death in 1983 Ferguson's only work on the contemplated revision of *One Fold and One Shepherd* consisted of about twenty ideas for updating, which Ferguson had jotted on small 3M "post-it" notes and attached to the relevant pages of his own copy of the book. These notes constituted the manuscript of revision that Warren was to use to revise Ferguson's *Fold*. However, one of these notes suggested including the influence of Ethan Smith's *View of the Hebrews* on the text of the Book of Mormon. This controversial subject is not even mentioned in Warren's revision, *The Messiah in Ancient America*, even though Ferguson's having this liberal viewpoint is independently supported by his 1983 conversation with Ron Barney.[14] So, while Warren's book contains literally tens of thousands of Ferguson's words, they all represent his position when *One Fold and One Shepherd* was published in 1958 and reprinted in 1962--not his much-different ideas from 1971 to 1983.

There is an instructive parallel in the case of the attribution of coauthorship between George Reynolds and Janne M. Sjodahl for their seven-volume Book of Mormon commentary.[15] Bruce A. Van Orden, professor of church history and doctrine at BYU, found no evidence that Reynolds and Sjodahl worked together "in any way during their lifetimes," nor that there were any manuscript notes by Reynolds which could be combined with Sjodahl's manuscript.[16] But what Van Orden did find was that Philip C. Reynolds, a son of George Reynolds, quoted verbatim extracts from George Reynolds's books and introduced the plural pronouns "we" and "our" in order to imply their collaboration. Likewise, in order to understand properly Ferguson's thinking on the Book of Mormon, one must read his publications from 1941 to 1962 for his early position and his letters from 1971 to 1983 and his 1975 paper for his later views[17]--not Warren's *Messiah in Ancient America*.

One reviewer said that Warren's book "is a sentimental monument to Ferguson."[18] If Warren intended his book to be a real tribute to Ferguson, it should have been dedicated to his memory, rather than have Ferguson's name printed on the title page as if he were a genuine coauthor of the volume. *The Messiah in Ancient America* attributes fresh authorship to Ferguson, and this attempted reinstatement of the pre-Book-of-Abraham-papyri Ferguson offers an incomplete and misleading representation of his real views.

Notes

1. Bruce W. Warren and Thomas Stuart Ferguson [*sic*], *The Messiah in Ancient America* (Provo, UT: Book of Mormon Research Foundation, 1987); hereafter abbreviated to Warren, *Messiah*.

2. Thomas Stuart Ferguson, *One Fold and One Shepherd* (San Francisco: Books of California, 1958; 2d ed., Salt Lake City: Olympus Publishing Co., 1962); hereafter abbreviated to Ferguson, *One Fold*.

3. Warren, *Messiah*, xiii.

4. Paul R. Cheesman, "Foreword," in Warren, *Messiah*, xi.

5. Warren, *Messiah*, 33.

6. Ferguson, *One Fold*, 204, with the italics added to show the word miscopied.

7. Warren, *Messiah*, 85.

8. Ferguson, *One Fold*, 180, with the italics added to indicate the words omitted.

9. Warren, *Messiah*, 39-48.

10. Ferguson, *One Fold*, 95.

11. Warren, *Messiah*, 161.

12. Ibid., 283.

13. Bruce W. Warren, interview by author, 27 January 1988, notes in author's possession.

14. Ronald O. Barney, interview with Thomas Stuart Ferguson, 4 January 1983, typed on 19 April 1984, in the H. Michael Marquardt Collection, Accession 900, Box 77, Fd 13, Manuscripts Division, J. Willard Marriott Library, University of Utah, Salt Lake City.

15. George Reynolds and Janne M. Sjodahl, *Commentary on the Book of Mormon*, ed., ampl., and arr. by Philip C. Reynolds and David Sjodahl King, 7 vols. (Salt Lake City: Deseret Book Co., 1955-1961).

16. Bruce A. Van Orden, "George Reynolds and Janne M. Sjodahl on Book of Mormon Geography," typescript, 1981, 5, 13, in the Bruce A. Van Orden Collection, Accession 1388, Box 1, Fd 1, Manuscripts Division, J. Willard Marriott Library, University of Utah, Salt Lake City.

17. Ferguson's published writings from 1941 to 1962 were compiled for the author's *Register of the Thomas Stuart Ferguson Papers* (Provo, UT: Division of Archives and Manuscripts, Harold B. Lee Library, Brigham Young University, 1988), 14-15, and expanded in the selected bibliography, below. His known letters from 1971 to 1983 are available in the Thomas Stuart Ferguson Collection, Accession 1350, Manuscripts Division, J. Willard Marriott Library, University of Utah, Salt Lake City. Ferguson's 1975 "Written Symposium on Book of Mormon Geography" was published as Jerald Tanner and Sandra Tanner, eds. *Ferguson's Manuscript Unveiled* (Salt Lake City: Utah Lighthouse Ministry, 1988), and printed in Appendix A, above.

18. John Hart, review of Warren, *Messiah*, in *Deseret News, LDS Church News*, 23 January 1988, 13.

Selected Bibliography

Unpublished Works

Ferguson, Thomas Stuart. Collection, Accession 1350, Manuscripts Division, J. Willard Marriott Library, University of Utah, Salt Lake City; hereafter abbreviated to Ferguson Collection, UU.

_____. Collection, Manuscript 1549, Special Collections and Manuscripts, Harold B. Lee Library, Brigham Young University, Provo, UT.

_____. "Written Symposium on Book of Mormon Geography: Response of Thomas S. Ferguson to the Norman and Sorenson Papers." Typescript, 12 March 1975, in Ferguson Collection, UU.

Grimm, Glenna Nielsen. "The Material Culture of the Book of Mormon." Audio tape, 13 May 1992, Sunstone Book of Mormon Lecture, in the Sunstone Foundation Records, Accession A0370, Manuscripts Division, J. Willard Marriott Library, University of Utah, Salt Lake City.

Matheny, Raymond T. "Book of Mormon Archaeology: Sunstone Symposium #6, Salt Lake Sheraton Hotel, August 25, 1984." Typescript, 1984, in the David J. Buerger Collection, Manuscript 622, Box 33, Fd 17, Manuscripts

Division, J. Willard Marriott Library, University of Utah, Salt Lake City. A transcript of the entire panel discussion of this session of the Sunstone Symposium is located in Special Collections and Manuscripts, Harold B. Lee Library, Brigham Young University, Provo, UT.

Roberts, B. H. "Book of Mormon Difficulties: A Study." Typescript, 1921, in the B. H. Roberts Collection, Manuscript 106, Box 9, Book 1, Manuscripts Division, J. Willard Marriott Library, University of Utah, Salt Lake City.

_____. "A Book of Mormon Study." Typescript, 1922, in Box 9, Books 2-3, Roberts Collection.

_____. "A Parallel." Typescript, 1927, in Box 16, Fd 3, Roberts Collection.

Published Works

Adams, Richard E. W. *Prehistoric Mesoamerica.* Rev. ed. Norman, OK: University of Oklahoma Press, 1991.

Allen, Joseph L. *Exploring the Lands of the Book of Mormon.* Orem, UT: S. A. Publishers, 1989.

Ashment, Edward H. "The Book of Mormon and the Anthon Transcript: An Interim Report." *Sunstone* 5 (May-June 1980): 29-31.

_____. "'A Record in the Language of My Father': Evidence of Ancient Egyptian and Hebrew in the Book of Mormon." In *New Approaches to the Book of Mormon: Explorations in Critical Methodology,* ed. Brent Lee Metcalfe, 329-93. Salt Lake City: Signature Books, 1993.

_____. *The Use of Egyptian Magical Papyri to Authenticate the Book of Abraham: A Critical Review.* Salt Lake City: Resource Communications, 1993.

Ashmore, Wendy, and Robert J. Sharer. *Discovering Our Past: A Brief Introduction to Archaeology.* 2d ed. Mountain View, CA: Mayfield Publishing Co., 1996.

Backman, Milton V., Jr. *Joseph Smith's First Vision: Confirming Evidences and Contemporary Accounts.* 2d ed., rev. and enl.

Salt Lake City: Bookcraft, 1980.

_____. *The Heavens Resound: A History of the Latter-day Saints in Ohio, 1830-1838*. Salt Lake City: Deseret Book Co., 1983.

Baker, Mary. "Capuchin Monkeys (*Cebus capucinus*) and the Ancient Maya." *Ancient Mesoamerica* 3 (Fall 1992): 219-28.

Baudez, Claude François. *Jean-Frédéric Waldeck, peintre: le premier explorateur des ruines mayas*. [Paris]: Fernand Hazan Editions, 1993.

Blanton, Richard E., et alia. *Ancient Mesoamerica: A Comparison of Change in Three Regions*. New Studies in Archaeology. 2d ed. Cambridge, England: Cambridge University Press, 1993.

Bloom, Harold. *The American Religion: The Emergence of the Post-Christian Nation*. New York: Simon and Schuster, 1993.

Brown, Robert L., and Rosemary Brown. *They Lie in Wait to Deceive: "A Study of Anti-Mormon Deception."* 4 vols. Mesa, AZ: Brownsworth Publishing Co., 1981-1995.

Bruhns, Karen O. "The Crucible: Sociological and Technological Factors in the Delayed Diffusion of Metallurgy to Mesoamerica." In *New Frontiers in the Archaeology of the Pacific Coast of Southern Mesoamerica*, ed. Frederick Bove and Lynette Heller, 221-27. Anthropological Research Papers, no. 39. Tempe, AZ: Arizona State University, 1989.

Brundage, Burr Cartwright. *The Phoenix of the Western World: Quetzalcóatl and the Sky Religion*. Norman, OK: University of Oklahoma Press, 1982.

Burton, D. Jeff. "The Phenomenon of the Closet Doubter: A Description and Analysis of One Approach to Activity in the Church." *Sunstone* 7 (September-October 1982): 35-38.

_____. *For Those Who Wonder: Managing Religious Questions and Doubts*. 3d ed. rev. Bountiful, UT: IVE, 1994.

Bush, Alfred L. "A Historical Witness." Letter to the editor. *Dialogue: A Journal of Mormon Thought* 23 (Fall 1990): 10.

Carlson, John B. "America's Ancient Skywatchers." *National Geographic* 177 (March 1990): 76-107.

Carmack, Robert M. "New Quichean Chronicles from High-
    land Guatemala." *Estudios de Cultura Maya* 13 (1981): 83-
    103.
Carrasco, Davíd. *Quetzalcóatl and the Irony of Empire: Myths and
    Prophecies in the Aztec Tradition.* Chicago and London:
    University of Chicago Press, 1982.
_____. *Religions of Mesoamerica: Cosmovision and Ceremonial
    Centers.* Religious Traditions of the World. San Francisco:
    Harper and Row, 1990.
Carter, George F. "Before Columbus." In *The Book of Mormon:
    The Keystone Scripture*, ed. Paul R. Cheesman, 164-86. Book
    of Mormon Symposium Series, no. 1. Provo, UT: Religious
    Studies Center, Brigham Young University, 1988.
Cheesman, Paul R. *The World of the Book of Mormon.* Bountiful,
    UT: Horizon Publishers, 1984.
_____. *Ancient Writing on Metal Plates: Archaeological Findings
    Support Mormon Claims.* Bountiful, UT: Horizon Publish-
    ers, 1985.
_____. *The Keystone of Mormonism: Early Visions of the Prophet
    Joseph Smith.* Provo, UT: Eagle Systems International,
    1988.
_____. "External Evidences of the Book of Mormon." In *By
    Study and Also by Faith*, 2 vols., ed. John M. Lundquist and
    Stephen D. Ricks, 2:73-90. Salt Lake City: Deseret Book
    Co., 1990; Provo, UT: Foundation for Ancient Research and
    Mormon Studies, 1990.
Cheesman, Paul R., and Millie F. Cheesman. *Ancient American
    Indians: Their Origins, Civilizations and Old World Connec-
    tions.* Bountiful, UT: Horizon Publishers, 1991.
Clark, John E. "A Key for Evaluating Nephite Geographies."
    Review of *Deciphering the Geography of the Book of Mormon*,
    by F. Richard Hauck. In *Review of Books on the Book of
    Mormon* 1 (1989): 20-70.
_____. "Book of Mormon Geography." In *Encyclopedia of Mor-
    monism*, ed. Daniel H. Ludlow, 1:176-79. New York: Mac-
    millan Publishing Co., 1992.

Clutton-Brock, Juliet. *Domesticated Animals from Early Times.* Austin, TX: University of Texas Press, 1981; London: British Museum, 1981.

_____. *A Natural History of Domesticated Animals.* Austin, TX: University of Texas Press, 1989. Reprint of *Domesticated Animals from Early Times.*

Coe, Michael D. *Breaking the Maya Code.* New York: Thames and Hudson, 1992.

_____. "Pre-Conquest America." In *Swords and Hilt Weapons,* ed. Anne Cope, 218-25. London: Multimedia Books, 1993.

_____. *The Maya.* 5th ed., fully rev. and exp. Ancient Peoples and Places. London: Thames and Hudson, 1993.

Coe, Michael D., Dean Snow, and Elizabeth Benson. *Atlas of Ancient America.* New York: Facts On File Publications, 1986.

Coutts, Alison V. P. "Earnestly Seeking." Review of *Recent Book of Mormon Developments: Articles from the Zarahemla Record,* by Raymond C. Treat. In *Review of Books on the Book of Mormon 7,* no. 2 (1995): 253-55.

Curtis, Delbert W. *Christ in North America: Christ Visited the Nephites in the Land of Promise in North America.* Tigard, OR: Resource Communications, 1993.

Daniel, Glyn, and Christopher Chippindale, eds. *The Past-masters: Eleven Modern Pioneers of Archaeology.* New York: Thames and Hudson, 1989.

Davies, Nigel. *Voyagers to the New World.* Albuquerque, NM: University of New Mexico Press, 1986.

Earhart, H. Byron, ed. *Religious Traditions of the World: A Journey through Africa, Mesoamerica, North America, Judaism, Christianity, Islam, Hinduism, Buddhism, China, and Japan.* San Francisco: HarperSanFrancisco, 1993.

Edmonson, Munro S. *The Book of the Year: Middle American Calendrical Systems.* Salt Lake City: University of Utah Press, 1988.

Eisenberg, John F., Colin P. Groves, and Kathy MacKinnon. "Tapirs." In *Grzimek's Encyclopedia of Mammals,* ed. Sybil

P. Parker, 4:598-608. New York: McGraw-Hill Publishing Co., 1990.

Escalante, Roberto. "El vocabulario cultural de las lenguas de Mesoamérica." In *La validez teórica del concepto Mesoamérica*, 155-65. XIX Mesa Redonda. Mexico City: Instituto Nacional de Antropología e Historia and Sociedad Mexicana de Antropología, 1990.

Fash, William L. *Scribes, Warriors, and Kings: The City of Copán and the Ancient Maya*. New York: Thames and Hudson, 1991.

Faulring, Scott H., ed. *An American Prophet's Record: The Diaries and Journals of Joseph Smith*. Salt Lake City: Signature Books, 1987.

Ferguson, Larry S. "The Most Powerful Book." Letter to the editor. *Dialogue: A Journal of Mormon Thought* 23 (Fall 1990), 9-10.

Ferguson, Thomas Stuart. "Some Important Book of Mormon Questions." *The Improvement Era* 44 (September 1941): 528, 569-71.

_____. "The Wheel in Ancient America." *The Improvement Era* 49 (December 1946): 785, 818-19.

_____. *Cumorah--Where?* Independence, MO: Zion's Printing and Publishing Co., 1947.

_____. "Do You Know How to Read?" *The Improvement Era* 51 (January 1948): 20, 59-61.

_____. *Great Message of Peace and Happiness*. Orinda, CA: [Sun Lithographing, 1952].

_____. Letter to [addressee unknown], May or June 1952. Partially printed in *University Archaeological Society Newsletter*, no. 7 (1 July 1952): [1-2].

_____. "Joseph Smith and American Archaeology." *Bulletin of the University Archaeological Society*, no. 4 (March 1953): 19-25.

_____. "Book of Mormon News and Views." *The Messenger of Northern California*, monthly articles on various archaeological topics from 1952 to 1954.

_____. "The World's Strangest Book: The Book of Mormon." *The Millennial Star* 118 (February 1956): 36-46.

_____. "Introduction concerning the New World Archaeological Foundation." In *New World Archaeological Foundation*, publication no. 1, 3-6. Orinda, CA: New World Archaeological Foundation, 1956.

_____. *One Fold and One Shepherd.* San Francisco: Books of California, 1958; Salt Lake City: Olympus Publishing Co., 1962.

_____. Letter to the editor. *Christianity Today* 5 (27 March 1961): 551.

_____. "Gold Plates and the Book of Mormon." *The Improvement Era* 65 (April 1962): 233-34, 270-71.

_____. Letter to [addressee unknown], 28 December 1967. Partially printed in *Newsletter and Proceedings of the Society for Early Historic Archaeology*, no. 105 (1 March 1968): 9.

Ferguson, William M., and Arthur H. Rohn. *Mesoamerica's Ancient Cities: Aerial Views of Precolumbian Ruins in Mexico, Guatemala, Belize, and Honduras.* Niwot, CO: University Press of Colorado, 1990.

Ferguson, William M., and John Q. Royce. *Maya Ruins in Central America in Color: Tikal, Copán, and Quiriguá.* Albuquerque, NM: University of New Mexico Press, 1984.

Fingerhut, Eugene R. *Explorers of Pre-Columbian America? The Diffusionist-Inventionist Controversy.* Guides to Historical Issues, no. 5. Claremont, CA: Regina Books, 1994.

Freidel, David, Linda Schele, and Joy Parker. *Maya Cosmos: Three Thousand Years on the Shaman's Path.* New York: William Morrow and Co., 1993.

Gallenkamp, Charles. *Maya: The Riddle and Rediscovery of a Lost Civilization.* 3d rev. ed. New York: Viking, 1985.

Gardner, Brant. "The Christianization of Quetzalcóatl: A History of the Metamorphosis." *Sunstone* 10, no. 11 (1986): 6-10.

Garza, Mercedes de la. *Palenque.* Chiapas Eterno. Tuxtla Gutiérrez, Chiapas: Gobierno del Estado de Chiapas, 1992.

[Gee, John]. "References to Abraham Found in Two Egyptian Texts." *Insights: An Ancient Window*, no. 5 (September 1991): 1, 3. "Based on research by John Gee."

_____. *Notes on the Sons of Horus*. Provo, UT: Foundation for Ancient Research and Mormon Studies, 1991.

_____. "Abraham in Ancient Egyptian Texts." *The Ensign* 22 (July 1992): 60-62.

_____. "A Tragedy of Errors." Review of *By His Own Hand upon Papyrus: A New Look at the Joseph Smith Papyri*, by Charles M. Larson. In *Review of Books on the Book of Mormon* 4 (1992): 93-119.

Geist, Valerius. "White-tailed or Mule Deer (Genus *Odocoileus*)." In *Grzimek's Encyclopedia of Mammals*, ed. Sybil P. Parker, 5:212-18. New York: McGraw-Hill Publishing Company, 1990.

Grayson, Donald K. "The Chronology of North American Late Pleistocene Extinctions." *Journal of Archaeological Science* 16 (March 1989): 153-65.

Greenberg, Joseph H. *Language in the Americas*. Stanford, CA: Stanford University Press, 1987.

Griffith, Michael T. *Refuting the Critics: Evidences of the Book of Mormon's Authenticity*. Bountiful, UT: Horizon Publishers, 1993.

Groat, Joel B. "B. H. Roberts' Doubts." Review of *B. H. Roberts: Studies of the Book of Mormon*, ed. Brigham D. Madsen. In *Heart and Mind: The Newsletter of Gospel Truths Ministries* (January-March 1995): 5-6.

Hamblin, William J. "Sharper Than a Two-edged Sword." *Sunstone* 15 (December 1991): 54-55.

_____. Review of *Archaeology and the Book of Mormon*, by Jerald Tanner and Sandra Tanner. In *Review of Books on the Book of Mormon* 5 (1993): 250-72.

_____. "Basic Methodological Problems with the Anti-Mormon Approach to the Geography and Archaeology of the Book of Mormon." *Journal of Book of Mormon Studies* 2 (Spring 1993): 161-97.

_____. "An Apologist for the Critics: Brent Lee Metcalfe's Assumptions and Methodologies." Review of "Apologetic and Critical Assumptions about Book of Mormon Historicity," by Brent Lee Metcalfe. In *Review of Books on the Book of Mormon* 6, no. 1 (1994): 434-523.

Hamblin, William J., and A. Brent Merrill. "Swords in the Book of Mormon." In *Warfare in the Book of Mormon*, ed. Stephen D. Ricks and William J. Hamblin, 329-51. Salt Lake City: Deseret Book Co., 1990; Provo, UT: Foundation for Ancient Research and Mormon Studies, 1990.

Hammond, Norman. *Ancient Maya Civilization*. New Brunswick, NJ: Rutgers University Press, 1994.

_____. "Preclassic Maya Civilization." In *New Theories on the Ancient Maya*, ed. Elin C. Danien and Robert J. Sharer, 137-44. University Museum Monograph, no. 77. Philadelphia: University Museum, University of Pennsylvania, 1992.

Haroldsen, Edwin O. "'Good and Evil Spoken of.'" *The Ensign* 25 (August 1995): 8-11.

Harris, James R. *The Facsimiles of the Book of Abraham: A Study of the Joseph Smith Egyptian Papyri*. Payson, UT: Harris House Publication, 1990.

Harris, John M., and George J. Jefferson. *Rancho La Brea: Treasures of the Tar Pits*. Science Series, no. 31. Los Angeles: Natural History Museum of Los Angeles County, 1985.

Harris, John M., and Shelley M. Cox. "Rancho La Brea Mammoths." *Current Research in the Pleistocene* 10 (1993): 96-98.

Harwell, William S., ed. *Joseph Smith's Grammar and Alphabet of the Egyptian Language*. Doctrine of the Priesthood, vol. 5, no. 10. Salt Lake City: Collier's Publishing Co., 1992.

Hassig, Ross. *War and Society in Ancient Mesoamerica*. Berkeley and Los Angeles and Oxford: University of California Press, 1992.

_____. *Mexico and the Spanish Conquest*. Modern Wars in Perspective. London and New York: Longman, 1994.

Hauck, F. Richard. *Deciphering the Geography of the Book of Mormon: Settlements and Routes in Ancient America*. Salt

Lake City: Deseret Book Co., 1988.

_____. "Archaeology and the Setting of the Book of Mormon." *This People* 15 (Spring 1994): 70-72, 75-78, 80, 83.

_____. "Ancient Fortifications and the Land of Manti." *This People* 15 (Summer 1994): 46-47, 49-52, 54-55.

_____. "In Search of the Land of Nephi." *This People* 15 (Fall 1994): 52-56, 58-60, 63.

Haynes, Gary. *Mammoths, Mastodonts, and Elephants: Biology, Behavior, and the Fossil Record.* Cambridge, England: Cambridge University Press, 1991.

Hedengren, Paul. *In Defense of Faith: Assessing Arguments against Latter-day Saint Belief.* Provo, UT: Bradford and Wilson, Ltd., 1985.

Hosler, Dorothy. "Archaeometallurgy: The Development of Ancient Mesoamerican Metallurgy." *JOM [Journal of Minerals, Metals, and Materials Society]* 42 (May 1990): 44-46.

_____. *The Sounds and Colors of Power: The Sacred Metallurgical Technology of Ancient West Mexico.* Cambridge, MA: The Massachusetts Institute of Technology, 1994.

Howard, Richard P. *Restoration Scriptures: A Study of Their Textual Development.* 2d ed., rev. and enl. Independence, MO: Herald Publishing House, 1995.

Hullinger, Robert N. *Joseph Smith's Response to Skepticism.* Salt Lake City: Signature Books, 1992.

Hunter, C. Bruce. *A Guide to Ancient Maya Ruins.* 2d ed., rev. and enl. Norman, OK: University of Oklahoma Press, 1986.

Hunter, Milton R., and Thomas Stuart Ferguson. *Ancient America and the Book of Mormon.* Oakland, CA: Kolob Book Co., 1950.

Ixtlilxóchitl, Fernando de Alva. *Obras Históricas.* Edited by Edmundo O'Gorman. 2 vols. 4th ed. Serie de historiadores y cronistas de Indias, no. 4. Mexico City: Universidad Nacional Autónoma de México, 1985.

Jessee, Dean C., comp. and ed. *The Personal Writings of Joseph*

Smith. Salt Lake City: Deseret Book Co., 1984.

_____, ed. *The Papers of Joseph Smith.* 2 vols. Salt Lake City: Deseret Book Co., 1989-1992.

Jett, Stephen C. "Precolumbian Transoceanic Contacts." In *Ancient South Americans,* ed. Jesse D. Jennings, 337-93. San Francisco: W. H. Freeman and Co., 1983.

_____. "Before Columbus: The Question of Early Transoceanic Interinfluences." *Brigham Young University Studies* 33, no. 2 (1993): 245-71.

Justeson, John S. "The Origin of Writing Systems: Preclassic Mesoamerica." *World Archaeology* 17 (February 1986): 437-58.

King, David S. "'Proving' the Book of Mormon: Archaeology vs. Faith." *Dialogue: A Journal of Mormon Thought* 24 (Spring 1991): 143-46.

Kocherhans, Arthur J. *Lehi's Isle of Promise: A Scriptural Account with Word Definitions and a Commentary.* Fullerton, CA: Et Cetera Et Cetera Graphics and Printing, 1989.

Kurtén, Björn. *Before the Indians.* New York: Columbia University Press, 1988.

Kurtén, Björn, and Elaine Anderson. *Pleistocene Mammals of North America.* New York: Columbia University Press, 1980.

Larson, Charles M. *By His Own Hand upon Papyrus: A New Look at the Joseph Smith Papyri.* Rev. ed. Grand Rapids, MI: Institute for Religious Research, 1992.

Larson, John A. "Joseph Smith and Egyptology: An Early Episode in the History of American Speculation about Ancient Egypt, 1835-1844." In *For His Ka: Essays Offered in Memory of Klaus Baer,* ed. David P. Silverman, 159-78. Studies in Ancient Oriental Civilization, no. 55. Chicago: The Oriental Institute of the University of Chicago, 1994.

Larson, Stan. "The Odyssey of Thomas Stuart Ferguson." *Dialogue: A Journal of Mormon Thought* 23 (Spring 1990): 55-93.

Lechtman, Heather. "Pre-Columbian Surface Metallurgy." *Scientific American* 250 (June 1984): 56-63.

Lee, Thomas A., Jr. *New World Archaeological Foundation Obra, 1952-1980.* Provo, UT, and San Cristóbal de las Casas, Chiapas: New World Archaeological Foundation, 1981.

_____. *Los Códices Mayas: Introducción y Bibliografía.* Tuxtla Gutiérrez, Chiapas: Universidad Autónoma de Chiapas, 1985.

Lister, Adrian, and Paul Bahn. *Mammoths.* New York: Macmillan, 1994.

Love, Bruce. *The Paris Codex: Handbook for a Maya Priest.* Austin, TX: University of Texas Press, 1994.

Lowe, Gareth W. "Izapa Religion, Cosmology, and Ritual." In *Izapa: An Introduction to the Ruins and Monuments,* ed. Gareth W. Lowe, Thomas A. Lee, Jr., and Eduardo Martinez Espinosa, 269-305. Papers of the New World Archaeological Foundation, no. 31. Provo, UT: New World Archaeological Foundation, Brigham Young University, 1982.

MacFadden, Bruce J. *Fossil Horses: Systematics, Paleobiology, and Evolution of the Family Equidae.* Cambridge, England: Cambridge University Press, 1992.

Madsen, Brigham D., ed. *B. H. Roberts: Studies of the Book of Mormon.* Urbana and Chicago: University of Illinois Press, 1985; reprint, Salt Lake City: Signature Books, 1992.

Madsen, Gordon A. "Joseph Smith's 1826 Trial: The Legal Setting." *Brigham Young University Studies* 30 (Spring 1990): 91-108.

Madsen, Truman G., and John W. Welch. *Did B. H. Roberts Lose Faith in the Book of Mormon?* Provo, UT: Foundation for Ancient Research and Mormon Studies, 1985.

Magleby, Kirk A. *A Survey of Mesoamerican Bearded Figures.* Provo, UT: Foundation for Ancient Research and Mormon Studies, 1983.

Marcus, Joyce. *Mesoamerican Writing Systems: Propaganda, Myth, and History in Four Ancient Civilizations.* Princeton, NJ: Princeton University Press, 1992.

Markman, Roberta H., and Peter T. Markman. *The Flayed God, The Mesoamerican Mythological Tradition: Sacred Texts and*

Images from Pre-Columbian Mexico and Central America. San Francisco: HarperSanFrancisco, 1992.

Marquardt, H. Michael. *The Book of Abraham Papyrus Found: An Answer to Dr. Hugh Nibley's Book "The Message of the Joseph Smith Papyri: An Egyptian Endowment" As It Relates to the Source of the Book of Abraham.* 2d ed., rev. and enl. Salt Lake City: Modern Microfilm Co., 1981.

_____, comp. *The Joseph Smith Egyptian Papers.* Cullman, AL: Printing Service, 1981.

Marquardt, H. Michael, and Wesley P. Walters. *Inventing Mormonism: Tradition and the Historical Record.* [San Francisco]: Smith Research Associates, 1994.

Matheny, Deanne G. "Does the Shoe Fit? A Critique of the Limited Tehuántepec Geography." In *New Approaches to the Book of Mormon: Explorations in Critical Methodology,* ed. Brent Lee Metcalfe, 269-328. Salt Lake City: Signature Books, 1993.

Matheny, Raymond T. "Investigations at El Mirador, Petén, Guatemala." *National Geographic Research* 2 (1986): 332-53.

_____. "El Mirador: An Early Maya Metropolis Uncovered." *National Geographic Magazine* 172 (September 1987): 317-39.

Mathews, Peter. *The Proceedings of the Maya Hieroglyphic Weekend, October 27-28, 1990, Cleveland State University.* Edited by Phil Wanyerka. Austin, TX: Maya Hieroglyphic Weekend, 1991.

McAnany, Patricia A. *Living with the Ancestors: Kinship and Kingship in Ancient Maya Society.* Austin, TX: University of Texas Press, 1995.

McCarter, P. Kyle, Jr. "Let's Be Serious about the Bat Creek Stone." *Biblical Archaeology Review* 19 (July-August 1993): 54-55, 83.

McCulloch, J. Huston. "The Bat Creek Inscription: Did Judean Refugees Escape to Tennessee?" *Biblical Archaeology Review* 19 (July-August 1993): 46-53, 82-83.

McKeever, William. "Yale anthropologist's views remain unchanged." *Mormonism Researched: An Outreach Publication of Mormonism Research Ministry*, no. 15 (Winter 1993): 6.

Mead, Jim I., and David J. Meltzer. "North American Late Quaternary Extinctions and the Radiocarbon Record." In *Quaternary Extinctions: A Prehistoric Revolution*, ed. Paul S. Martin and Richard G. Klein, 440-50. Tucson, AZ: University of Arizona Press, 1984.

Metcalfe, Brent Lee. "Apologetic and Critical Assumptions about Book of Mormon Historicity." *Dialogue: A Journal of Mormon Thought* 26 (Fall 1993): 153-84.

Miller, Mary Ellen, and Karl Taube. *The Gods and Symbols of Ancient Mexico and the Maya: An Illustrated Dictionary of Mesoamerican Religion*. London: Thames and Hudson, 1993.

Millet, Robert L. "The Book of Mormon, Historicity, and Faith." *Journal of Book of Mormon Studies* 2 (Fall 1993): 1-13.

_____. *The Power of the Word: Saving Doctrines from the Book of Mormon*. Salt Lake City: Deseret Book Co., 1994.

National Geographic Book Service. *Wild Animals of North America*. Rev. ed. Natural Science Library. Washington, D.C.: National Geographic Society, 1995.

Nelson, Fred W., Jr. "In Honor of Thomas Stuart Ferguson, 1915-1983." *Newsletter and Proceedings of the S.E.H.A.*, no. 161 (May 1987): 1-6.

Nibley, Hugh. *Abraham in Egypt*. Salt Lake City: Deseret Book Co., 1981.

_____. *Lehi in the Desert and the World of the Jaredites*. Salt Lake City: Bookcraft, 1952. Reprinted in *Lehi in the Desert, The World of the Jaredites, There Were Jaredites*. The Collected Works of Hugh Nibley: Volume 5, ed. John W. Welch. Salt Lake City: Deseret Book Co., 1988; Provo, UT: Foundation for Ancient Research and Mormon Studies, 1988.

_____. *An Approach to the Book of Mormon*. 3d ed. The Collected Works of Hugh Nibley: Volume 6, ed. John W. Welch. Salt Lake City: Deseret Book Co., 1988; Provo, UT: Foundation for Ancient Research and Mormon Studies,

1988.

_____. *Since Cumorah: The Book of Mormon in the Modern World.* 2d ed. The Collected Works of Hugh Nibley: Volume 7, ed. John W. Welch. Salt Lake City: Deseret Book Co., 1988; Provo, UT: Foundation for Ancient Research and Mormon Studies, 1988.

_____. "New Approaches to Book of Mormon Study: Part I, Some Standard Tests." *The Improvement Era* 56 (November 1953): 830-31, 859-62. Reprinted in *The Prophetic Book of Mormon*, The Collected Works of Hugh Nibley: Volume 8, ed. John W. Welch, 54-60. Salt Lake City: Deseret Book Co., 1989; Provo, UT: Foundation for Ancient Research and Mormon Studies, 1989.

_____. *Myth Makers.* Salt Lake City: Bookcraft, 1961. Reprinted in *Tinkling Cymbals and Sounding Brass: The Art of Telling Tales about Joseph Smith and Brigham Young.* The Collected Works of Hugh Nibley: Volume 11, ed. David J. Whittaker. Salt Lake City: Deseret Book Co., 1991; Provo, UT: Foundation for Ancient Research and Mormon Studies, 1991.

_____. *Teachings of the Book of Mormon.* 4 vols. Provo, UT: Foundation for Ancient Research and Mormon Studies, 1993.

Norman, V. Garth. *Izapa Stela 5 and the Lehi Tree-of-Life Vision Hypothesis: A Reanalysis.* Mesoamerican Research Papers. American Fork, UT: Archaeological Research Consultants, 1985.

_____. "What is the current status of research concerning the 'Tree of Life' carving from Chiapas, Mexico?" *The Ensign* 15 (June 1985): 54-55.

Novak, Gary F. "Naturalistic Assumptions and the Book of Mormon." *Brigham Young University Studies* 30 (Summer 1990): 23-40.

_____. "Examining the Environmental Explanation of the Book of Mormon." Review of *Joseph Smith's Response to Skepticism*, by Robert N. Hullinger. In *Review of Books on the*

Book of Mormon 7, no. 1 (1995): 139-54.

Ostler, Blake T. "The Book of Mormon as a Modern Expansion of an Ancient Source." *Dialogue: A Journal of Mormon Thought* 20 (Spring 1987): 66-123.

Palmer, David A. *In Search of Cumorah: New Evidences for the Book of Mormon from Ancient Mexico.* Bountiful, UT: Horizon Publishers, 1981.

Pang, Hildegard Delgado. *Pre-Columbian Art: Investigations and Insights.* Norman, OK: University of Oklahoma, 1992.

Peay, Eugene L. *The Lands of Zarahemla: A Book of Mormon Commentary.* Salt Lake City: Northwest Publishing, 1993.

Persuitte, David. *Joseph Smith and the Origins of the Book of Mormon.* Jefferson, NC: McFarland and Co., 1985.

Peterson, Daniel C. "Book of Mormon Economy and Technology." In *Encyclopedia of Mormonism*, ed. Daniel H. Ludlow, 1:172-75. New York: Macmillan Publishing Co., 1992.

_____. "News from Antiquity." *The Ensign* 24 (January 1994): 16-21.

_____. "LDS Scholars Refute Attacks on the Book of Mormon." *This People* 15 (Summer 1994): 28-33.

Peterson, H. Donl. *The Story of the Book of Abraham: Mummies, Manuscripts, and Mormonism.* Salt Lake City: Deseret Book Co., 1995.

Peterson, Jeanette Favrot. *Precolumbian Flora and Fauna: Continuity of Plant and Animal Themes in Mesoamerican Art.* San Diego: Mingei International Museum of World Folk Art, 1990.

Piña Chan, Román. *The Olmec: Mother Culture of Mesoamerica.* Edited by Laura Laurencich Minelli. Translated from the Italian by Warren McManus. New York: Rizzoli International Publications, 1989.

Poll, Richard D. "Liahona and Iron Rod Revisited." *Dialogue: A Journal of Mormon Thought* 16 (Summer 1983): 69-78.

_____. "Dealing with Dissonance: Myths, Documents, and Faith." *Sunstone* 12 (May 1988): 17-21.

Price, T. Douglas. "The View from Europe: Concepts and Questions about Terminal Pleistocene Societies." In *The First Americans: Search and Research*, ed. T. D. Dillehay and D. J. Meltzer, 185-208. Boca Raton, FL: CRC Press, 1991.

Proskouriakoff, Tatiana. *Maya History*. Edited by Rosemary A. Joyce. Austin, TX: University of Texas Press, 1993.

Raish, Martin H. "All That Glitters: Uncovering Fool's Gold in Book of Mormon Archaeology." *Sunstone* 6 (January-February 1981): 10-15.

_____. "Tree of Life." In *Encyclopedia of Mormonism*, ed. Daniel H. Ludlow, 4:1486-88. New York: Macmillan Publishing Co., 1992.

Raymond, Robert. *Out of the Fiery Furnace: The Impact of Metals on the History of Mankind*. University Park, PA: Pennsylvania State University Press, 1986.

Reader's Digest. *Mysteries of the Ancient Americas: The New World before Columbus*. Pleasantville, NY: Reader's Digest Association, 1986.

Rhodes, Michael D. "Why doesn't the translation of the Egyptian papyri found in 1967 match the text of the Book of Abraham in the Pearl of Great Price?" *The Ensign* 18 (July 1988): 51-53.

_____. "The Book of Abraham: Divinely Inspired Scripture." Review of *By His Own Hand upon Papyrus: A New Look at the Joseph Smith Papyri*, by Charles M. Larson. In *Review of Books on the Book of Mormon* 4 (1992): 120-26.

_____. "Facsimiles from the Book of Abraham." In *Encyclopedia of Mormonism*, ed. Daniel H. Ludlow, 1:135-37. New York: Macmillan Publishing Co., 1992.

Robicsek, Francis. "The Weapons of the Ancient Maya." In *Circumpacifica*, ed. Bruno Illius and Matthias Laubscher, 1:369-96. Frankfurt am Main: Peter Lang, 1990.

Robinson, Stephen E. "The 'Expanded' Book of Mormon?" In *The Book of Mormon: Second Nephi, the Doctrinal Structure*, ed. Monte S. Nyman and Charles D. Tate, Jr., 391-414. Provo, UT: Religious Studies Center, Brigham Young University, 1989.

Russell, William D. "A Further Inquiry into the Historicity of the Book of Mormon." *Sunstone* 7 (September-October 1982): 20-27.

Sabloff, Jeremy A. *The New Archaeology and the Ancient Maya.* Scientific American Library Series, no. 30. New York: Scientific American Library, 1990.

Sampson, Joe. *Written by the Finger of God: Decoding Ancient Languages, A Testimony of Joseph Smith's Translations.* Sandy, UT: Wellspring Publishing, 1993.

Schele, Linda, and David Freidel. *A Forest of Kings: The Untold Story of the Ancient Maya.* New York: William Morrow and Co., 1990.

Schele, Linda, and Mary Ellen Miller. *The Blood of Kings: Dynasty and Ritual in Maya Art.* New York: George Braziller, in association with the Kimbell Art Museum of Fort Worth, 1986.

Schele, Linda, and Nikolai Grube. *The Proceedings of the Maya Hieroglyphic Workshop [on] Late Classic and Terminal Classic Warfare, March 11-12, 1995.* Edited by Phil Wanyerka. Austin, TX: Maya Hieroglyphic Workshop, 1995.

Sharer, Robert J. "The Preclassic Origins of Maya Writing: A Highland Perspective." In *Word and Image in Maya Culture: Explorations in Language, Writing, and Representation,* ed. William F. Hanks and Don S. Rice, 165-75. Salt Lake City: University of Utah Press, 1989.

_____. *Quiriguá: A Classic Maya Center and Its Sculptures.* Centers of Civilization Series. Durham, NC: Carolina Academic Press, 1990.

_____. *The Ancient Maya.* 5th ed. Stanford, CA: Stanford University Press, 1994.

Sheets, Millard. *The Horse in Folk Art.* La Jolla, CA: Mingei International Museum of World Folk Art, 1984.

Smith, George D. "Defending the Keystone: Book of Mormon Difficulties." *Sunstone* 6 (May-June 1981): 45-50.

_____. "Orthodoxy and Encyclopedia." *Sunstone* 16 (November

1993): 48-53.

Smith, T. Michael. *Generic Book of Mormon Geographies: A Baseline Evaluation of Current Research.* S.E.H.A. paper, no. 3. Orem, UT: The Society for Early Historic Archaeology, a Division of the Ancient America Foundation, 1993.

_____. "A New Discovery and Caution." *Ancient America Foundation Newsletter*, no. 3 (December 1994): 3-4.

Snow, Edgar C., Jr. "One Face of the Hero: In Search of the Mythological Joseph Smith." *Dialogue: A Journal of Mormon Thought* 27 (Fall 1994): 233-47.

Sorenson, John L. "Digging into the Book of Mormon: Our Changing Understanding of Ancient America and its Scripture." *The Ensign* 14 (September 1984): 26-37, and 14 (October 1984): 12-23.

_____. *An Ancient American Setting for the Book of Mormon.* Salt Lake City: Deseret Book Co., 1985; Provo, UT: Foundation for Ancient Research and Mormon Studies, 1985.

_____. *The Significance of the Chronological Discrepancy between Alma 53:22 and Alma 56:9.* Provo, UT: Foundation for Ancient Research and Mormon Studies, 1990.

_____. *The Geography of Book of Mormon Events: A Source Book.* Rev. ed. Provo, UT: Foundation for Ancient Research and Mormon Studies, 1992.

_____. *Animals in the Book of Mormon: An Annotated Bibliography.* Provo, UT: Foundation for Ancient Research and Mormon Studies, 1992.

_____. *Metals and Metallurgy relating to the Book of Mormon Text.* Provo, UT: Foundation for Ancient Research and Mormon Studies, 1992.

_____. "Addendum." To John Gee's review of *By His Own Hand upon Papyrus: A New Look at the Joseph Smith Papyri*, by Charles M. Larson, in *Review of Books on the Book of Mormon* 4 (1992): 117-19.

_____. "Once More: The Horse." In *Reexploring the Book of Mormon: The F.A.R.M.S. Updates*, ed. John W. Welch, 98-100. Salt Lake City: Deseret Book Co., 1992; Provo, UT:

Foundation for Ancient Research and Mormon Studies, 1992. "Based on research by John L. Sorenson, June 1984."

_____. "Viva Zapato! Hurray for the Shoe!" Review of "Does the Shoe Fit? A Critique of the Limited Tehuántepec Geography," by Deanne G. Matheny. In *Review of Books on the Book of Mormon* 6, no. 1 (1994): 297-361.

Sorenson, John L., and Martin H. Raish. *Pre-Columbian Contact with the Americas across the Oceans: An Annotated Bibliography.* 2 vols. Provo, UT: Research Press, 1990.

Sowell, Madison U. "Defending the Keystone: The Comparative Method Reexamined." *Sunstone* 6 (May-June 1981): 44, 50-54.

Spackman, Randall P. *Introduction to Book of Mormon Chronology: The Principal Prophecies, Calendars, and Dates.* Provo, UT: Foundation for Ancient Research and Mormon Studies, 1993.

Stock, Chester. *Rancho La Brea: A Record of Pleistocene Life in California.* 7th ed. Revised by John M. Harris. Science Series, no. 37. Los Angeles: Natural History Museum of Los Angeles County, 1992.

Strouhal, Eugen. *Life of the Ancient Egyptians.* Norman, OK: University of Oklahoma Press, 1992.

Stuart, David. *The Yaxhá Emblem Glyph as Yax-ha.* Research Reports on Ancient Maya Writing, no. 1. Washington, D.C.: Center for Maya Research, 1985.

Stuart, David, and Stephen D. Houston. *Classic Maya Place Names.* Studies in Pre-Columbian Art and Archaeology, no. 33. Washington, D.C.: Dumbarton Oaks Research Library, 1994.

Stuart, Gene S., and George E. Stuart. *Lost Kingdoms of the Maya.* Washington, D.C.: National Geographic Society, 1993.

Stubbs, Brian. *Elements of Hebrew in Uto-Aztecan: A Summary of the Data.* Provo, UT: Foundation for Ancient Research and Mormon Studies, 1988.

Szink, Terrence L. Review of *The Messiah in Ancient America*, by Bruce W. Warren and Thomas Stuart Ferguson. In *Review of Books on the Book of Mormon* 1 (1989): 132-34.

Tanner, Jerald, and Sandra Tanner, eds. *Roberts' Manuscripts Revealed: A Photographic Reproduction of Mormon Historian B. H. Roberts' Secret Studies on the Book of Mormon.* Salt Lake City: Modern Microfilm Co., 1980. [Missing part II of "Book of Mormon Difficulties: A Study."]

_____. *Mormonism: Shadow or Reality.* 5th ed. Salt Lake City: Utah Lighthouse Ministry, 1987.

_____, eds. *Ferguson's Manuscript Unveiled.* Salt Lake City: Utah Lighthouse Ministry, 1988.

_____. "Ferguson's Two Faces: Mormon Scholar's 'Spoof' Lives on after His Death." *Salt Lake City Messenger,* no. 69 (September 1988): 1-10.

Tedlock, Barbara. *Time and the Highland Maya.* Rev. ed. Albuquerque, NM: University of New Mexico Press, 1992.

Tedlock, Dennis, trans. *Popol Vuh: The Definitive Edition of the Mayan Book of the Dawn of Life and the Glories of Gods and Kings.* New York: Simon and Schuster, 1985.

Thomas, Mark D. "Swords Cankered with Rust." Review of *Warfare in the Book of Mormon,* ed. Stephen D. Ricks and William J. Hamblin. *Sunstone* 15 (September 1991): 62.

Thompson, Stephen E. "'Critical' Book of Mormon Scholarship." Review of *New Approaches to the Book of Mormon: Explorations in Critical Methodology,* ed. Brent Lee Metcalfe, and *Review of Books on the Book of Mormon,* ed. Daniel C. Peterson. In *Dialogue: A Journal of Mormon Thought* 27 (Winter 1994): 197-206.

_____. "Egyptology and the Book of Abraham." *Dialogue: A Journal of Mormon Thought* 28 (Spring 1995): 143-60.

Tickell, James, and Oliver Tickell. *Tikal, City of the Maya.* Travel to Landmarks. London: Tauris Parke Books, 1991.

Time-Life Books. *The Magnificent Maya.* Lost Civilizations. Alexandria, VA: Time-Life Books, 1993.

Treat, Raymond C. *Recent Book of Mormon Developments: Articles from the Zarahemla Record.* 2 vols. Independence, MO: Zarahemla Research Foundation, 1984-1992.

Tvedtnes, John A. "Significant Contribution." Review of *In Search of Cumorah: New Evidences for the Book of Mormon from Ancient Mexico*, by David A. Palmer. In *Newsletter and Proceedings of the S.E.H.A.*, no. 149 (June 1982): 9-10.

Van Wagoner, Richard S. *Sidney Rigdon: A Portrait of Religious Excess*. Salt Lake City: Signature Books, 1994.

Van Wagoner, Richard S., and Steven Walker. "Joseph Smith: The Gift of Seeing." *Dialogue: A Journal of Mormon Thought* 15 (Summer 1982): 48-68.

Vartanyan, S. L., V. E. Garutt, and A. V. Sher. "Holocene Dwarf Mammoths from Wrangel Island in the Siberian Arctic." *Nature* 362 (25 March 1993): 337-40.

Vogel, Dan. *Indian Origins and the Book of Mormon: Religious Solutions from Columbus to Joseph Smith*. Salt Lake City: Signature Books, 1986.

Warren, Bruce W., and Thomas Stuart Ferguson [*sic*]. *The Messiah in Ancient America*. Provo, UT: Book of Mormon Research Foundation, 1987.

Weaver, Muriel Porter. *The Aztecs, Maya, and Their Predecessors: Archaeology of Mesoamerica*. 3d ed. Studies in Archaeology. San Diego: Academic Press, 1993.

Welch, John W. "New B. H. Roberts Book Lacks Insight of His Testimony." Review of *B. H. Roberts: Studies of the Book of Mormon*, ed. Brigham D. Madsen. In *Deseret News, LDS Church News*, 15 December 1985, 11.

_____. *Finding Answers to B. H. Roberts' Questions and "An Unparallel."* Provo, UT: Foundation for Ancient Research and Mormon Studies, 1985.

[West, Michael, ed.] "Knorosov in Mexico." *Institute of Maya Studies Newsletter* 24 (October 1995): 6-7.

Wilson, Luke P. "The Scientific Search for Nephite Remains." *Heart and Mind: The Newsletter of Gospel Truths Ministries* (Fall 1992): 2-3, 5.

Wirth, Diane E. *A Challenge to the Critics: Scholarly Evidences of the Book of Mormon*. Bountiful, UT: Horizon Publishers, 1988.

Index